To
Lionel

With my best wishes

John J. Gallaher

NAPOLEON'S
IRISH LEGION

L'INDEPENDANCE
D'IRLANDE

NAPOLEON I
L'EMPEREUR
DES FRANÇAIS
A LA LEGION
IRLANDAIS

John G. Gallaher

Southern Illinois University Press
Carbondale and Edwardsville

Library of Congress Cataloging-in-Publication Data

Gallaher, John G.
Napoleon's Irish Legion / John G. Gallaher.
p. cm.
Includes bibliographical references and index.
1. Napoleonic Wars, 1800–1815—Participation, Irish. 2. France,
Armée—Irish regiments. 3. France—History, Military—1789–1815.
4. Ireland—History, Military. I. Title.
DC226.6.P362G35 1993
940.2′7—dc20   92-18518
ISBN 0-8093-1825-3   CIP

The paper used in this publication meets the
minimum requirements of American National
Standard for Information Sciences—Permanence of
Paper for Printed Library Matierals, ANSI Z39.48-1984. ∞

To the men of the Irish Legion
who gave their lives in the service of France

Contents

Maps   *viii*

Preface   *ix*

1. Introduction   *1*

2. The Formation of the Irish Legion   *21*

3. From Irish Patriots to French Soldiers   *53*

4. Walcheren: The Loss of the 1st Battalion   *87*

5. The Peninsular Campaigns   *115*

6. Recruitment and Desertion   *152*

7. The Year of Disaster: 1813   *177*

8. The Restoration and Disbandment of the Legion   *201*

9. Conclusion   *220*

Notes   *225*

Bibliography   *269*

Index   *275*

Maps

1. Ireland   *4*

2. Western Europe   *24*

3. Walcheren   *91*

4. The Iberian Peninsula   *118*

5. The Campaign of 1813   *192*

Preface

The flight of young Irishmen in the eighteenth century from poverty and oppression to military service in foreign countries had become common practice among the urban poor and the peasantry, while it was virtually a tradition in many relatively well-to-do families. There was, of course, no "Irish" army in which they could have served. In the British Isles there was only the king's army and navy, and Catholics were forbidden to hold the rank of commissioned officer. The formation of the Irish Brigade in the French army and of "Irish" regiments in the Spanish army in the early eighteenth century provided an opportunity for a military career where being a Catholic was not an impediment to one's career. Furthermore, anti-English sentiments were high after the Irish support of the Stuart cause was put down in the late seventeenth century and followed by severe oppression. The attitude of many an Irishman in the eighteenth century is summed up in the following verse by Davis taken from the *Memoir of Thomas Addis Emmet and Robert Emmet* (vol. 1, p. 589):

> Too long we fought for Britain's cause,
>   And of our blood were never chary:
> She paid us back with tyrant's laws,
>   And thinned the Homes of Tipperary.
>
> But never more we'll win such thanks,
>   We swear by God and Virgin Mary:
> Never to list in British ranks,
>   And that's the vow of Tipperary.

The tens of thousands of young men who left Ireland in the century following the Treaty of Limerick (1691) came to be known as the "Wild Geese." They took service primarily with the Catholic monarchs of France and Spain. The Irish Brigade at times provided as many as six regiments to the French army of Louis XV and has been the subject of several books. The two best accounts are by John C. O'Callaghan, *History of the Irish*

Brigades in the Service of France, and Maurice N. Hennessy, *The Wild Geese: The Irish Soldier in Exile*. There is also an unpublished book-length manuscript by Thomas J. Mullen, Jr., entitled "The Ranks of Death" in the Trinity College Library (MS 7108) that is a history of the Irish brigades in the services of France and Spain. However, there is no history of the Irish Legion that served in the Napoleonic army. Miles Byrne, who was an officer in the Legion, did write his memoirs, and they are the closest we have to an account of this corps. Although Byrne wrote in the 1850s, forty years after many of the campaigns, I have found few actual errors in his work. The problem with Byrne is that he was writing of his own experiences and recollections with all of his prejudice and biases. Furthermore, as he was in Spain for four years with the 2nd Battalion, he has little to say about the loss of the 1st Battalion at Flushing or the problems of the Regiment back in France. Having said this, I must acknowledge a great debt to Byrne for he helped me to understand the plight of the Irish in the French army and their hopes, their dreams, their aspirations. I hope that I have been able to convey to my readers these feelings half as well as he has in his *Memoirs of Miles Byrne*.

In the process of writing the history of the Irish serving in the Legion, I have tried to trace the evolution of those Irishmen from patriotic republican nationalists to professional soldiers in a foreign army. In the early years they viewed the French army as a temporary necessity that would provide them with the training and support they needed to return to Ireland and liberate it from foreign domination. When the expedition to Ireland did not take place, some of them left the French service, but most remained and began the slow transition to professional soldiers. Throughout the Napoleonic period they clung to the hope, however faded, that Napoleon would return to his plans of an invasion of England and Ireland. They saw France and its emperor as their only means of attaining their goal. By 1814, when Napoleon first abdicated, they were considered to be Bonapartists by the restored Bourbon monarchists. The disbandment of the Irish Regiment was hastened by its enthusiastic support of Napoleon during the Hundred Days. Many of the fine young men who joined the Legion in 1803–4 lost their lives in the service of France. Those who survived sickness and campaigns were retired on army pensions and faded into French provincial life.

There are many individuals and institutions whose contributions to this study were either essential or significant. It was the late Professor Thomas L. Coonan who introduced me to Irish history when I was a graduate student. I regret that he will not see the results of the seed he planted so many years ago. I wish to acknowledge the financial support as well as the moral support I received from the Graduate School and the School of Social Science at Southern Illinois University at Edwardsville. In particular, I wish to extend my gratitude to Dr. Rosemarie Archangel, Dean of the Graduate School, Dr. Stephen L. Hansen, Associate Dean of the Graduate School for research, and Dr. Samuel C. Pearson, Dean of the School of Social Science. Without their support, in the form of financial grants and release time, it would have been extremely difficult to have written this book. A grant from the American Philosophical Society also helped me to do the necessary research in France. I am also thankful for the support and cooperation of the staffs of the Lovejoy Library of Southern Illinois University at Edwardsville, the Bibliothèque Nationale in Paris, the Service historique de l'état-major de l'armée [War Archives] at the château de Vincennes, the Archives nationales in Paris, Trinity College Library, the National Library, Dublin, and archives of Dublin Castle.

I am most grateful to my good friend and colleague Dr. Donald D. Horward of Florida State University for the time-consuming process of reading this manuscript and making corrections and suggestions that greatly improved the final results. Colonel John R. Elting, USA, Retired, also read the manuscript, corrected errors, and made valuable suggestions on how to improve this study. I am deeply indebted to both of these scholars, but I alone am responsible for any errors or mistakes in this study of the Irish Legion.

I would also like to acknowledge my appreciation to several other friends and colleagues who helped to guide me through what were at the time new and unchartered waters: to Dr. Marianne Elliott who pointed the way to various collections in the Dublin archives and libraries; to Dr. Gordon C. Bond for his advice and direction concerning the primary and secondary sources on the English expedition to the Scheldt; to Dr. Benjamin Kennedy for sharing with me his knowledge of the Irish during the Revolutionary years; to Dr. Owen Connelly for reading the manuscript; and to Gary P. Clark who did the excellent maps for this book. Finally, I wish to thank my wife Maia for reading and correcting the manuscript and her patience and understanding during the years I spent writing this book.

Napoleon's Irish Legion

1

Introduction

The tradition of Irishmen serving in the army of the kings of France was one hundred years old when the Revolutionary government abolished foreign regiments in the 1790s. Thus it came as no real surprise in 1803 when Napoleon Bonaparte, then First Consul of France, ordered that an Irish Legion be formed. The war with England had been renewed in the spring of that year after a brief interlude of peace brought about by the Treaty of Amiens. England had been France's most persistent antagonist during the First and Second Coalitions, but had agreed to end hostilities in March 1802 after the Austrians had signed the Treaty of Luneville (February 1801) and she once again stood alone against the French. Both nations desired peace, France to consolidate her gains at home and her conquests on the Continent, England to recuperate from the economic burdens of eight years of seemingly futile warfare. However, the treaty quickly came to be perceived by the English as being more favorable to the French than to themselves. Despite the fact that they had not given up the island of Malta, which had been agreed upon by the terms of the treaty, the English accused the French of violating the treaty by their failure to evacuate Holland, also agreed upon at Amiens. But the violations of the treaty were little more than a pretext, for in the final analysis, the English government believed the Treaty of Amiens was a "French treaty" and that General Bonaparte was continuing to strengthen the position of France on the Continent to the disadvantage of England.[1]

If it is true that Bonaparte did not want a renewal of hostilities with the English in 1803, it is also true that he did little to prevent the rupture of diplomatic relations between the two nations. Faced with war once again, he turned his attention to the development of a grand strategy that would lead to the defeat of the island kingdom. The most direct approach would be the invasion of the British Isles. To this end he began to plan for expeditions not only to England but also to Ireland. The principal French army would land on the coast of England, while a much smaller force would be sent to Ireland. The idea of invading England and/or Ireland did not represent any new or innovative strategic concept on the part of the First Consul. It had been a part of French military thought in virtually every war between France and England from the time of Louis XIV. In fact, French troops had landed in Ireland in the 1690s to support the claim of King James II to the throne of Ireland—and England—in the War of the League of Augsburg.

On 17 March 1690, a French force of 6,000 men sailed from Brest to Ireland at the request of James II. James had been deposed by the English and the Scots in 1688, and his daughter Mary, and her husband, William of Orange, had been invited to ascend the throne. However, just as the English and Scots had freely chosen to replace James II with William and Mary, the Irish chose to keep James as king of Ireland. It is not surprising that the Irish Catholics, and many of the Irish Protestants, remained loyal to King James. In the three years that he had been king of England, Scotland, and Ireland this Catholic monarch had greatly improved the political, social, and economic conditions in Ireland. The Cromwellians were either replaced by the king, or their power and authority were greatly reduced, in most cases in favor of the Anglo-Normans or Irish Catholics. Furthermore, the Irish had every reason to believe that under King James their conditions would continue to improve, whereas under the control of the Protestant English Parliament and its protégés, the Protestants William and Mary, they could expect to lose the benefits of the short reign of the last Stuart monarch.[2] Thus with the exception of a small minority, the Irish recognized James II as king and rose to his defense in 1689 when William sent an army to reimpose the will of England. Under these circumstances the bloodshed that resulted from the "Bloodless Revolution" took place in Ireland.

The arrival of French troops in Ireland was followed by the departure of Irish troops to France. Louis XIV had agreed to send continental veterans to Ireland to bolster the Irish recruits if James would send an equal number of Irishmen to France to assist him in his war against the League of Augsburg. Therefore, on 18 April 1690, five Irish regiments of 5,371 officers and men sailed for France in the same ships that had brought the French to Ireland.[3] They reached Brest early in May and were reorganized into three regiments commanded by Lord Mountcashel (Justin MacCarthy), Colonel Daniel O'Brien and Colonel Arthur Dillon. Collectively, they were known as the Mountcashel Brigade, and they formed the nucleus of the renowned Irish Brigade that served France for the next one hundred years.[4]

The civil war in Ireland did not go well for the forces that supported James II. Late in the year 1691, it came to an end with the signing of the Treaty of Limerick. The loyalist forces of James had held out in the city of Limerick until the forces of William, unable to capture the city, agreed to a treaty that ended the war. In accordance with this treaty, which ended the siege, the Irish army in Limerick, and their families, were to be permitted to sail from Cork and Limerick to France where they would join King James and the Mountcashel Brigade. Other concessions were also made by the English that guaranteed there would not be reprisals taken against the Irish Catholics who had supported James II.[5] That the English did not honor the treaty once the Irish army had sailed to France is a matter of record. The harsh and oppressive Penal Laws imposed on Ireland after the Treaty of Limerick reduced the Catholic population to a state of misery. If the Revolution of 1688 was "Glorious" for England, it was disastrous for Ireland.[6]

The Irish Brigade was under the direct orders of King James, who was the "ally" of Louis XIV, and heavily dependent upon the French King for support. It was stationed at Brest with the intent of returning to Ireland with the French as soon as such an expedition could be undertaken against the English. In point of fact, no such expedition took place, and the Brigade eventually became a part of the French army. The Irish Brigade, as it was known throughout the eighteenth century, maintained its strength over the years by recruiting in Ireland and other parts of western Europe. It fought in the various wars of Louis XV, but it usually was attached to French units in battalion or regimental strength. Its principal claim to fame was its role in the Battle of Fontenoy during the War of the Austrian Succession. At that time, 1745, the Irish Brigade consisted of six regiments plus cavalry. The regiments bore the names of Clare, Dillon, Buckeley, Roth, Berwick, and Lally.

The Battle of Fontenoy opened on the morning of 11 May with cavalry skirmishes. Then a strong English advance against the French center, despite heavy losses, was successful in occupying the high ground in the middle of the French line. At this point in the struggle Marshal Maurice de Saxe, who commanded the French army—under Louis XV, who was present on the field of battle—ordered the Irish Brigade to break the English right flank. With the exception of the Dillon Regiment, the Irish had not seen action during the morning of the battle. They moved forward into position, and then with shouts of "Remember Limerick" they advanced against the English with a vengeance. Supported by French units on their flanks, the Irish drove the English right from its position and sent it in some disorder to the rear. This was the decisive action in the French victory, and it established the reputation of the Irish Brigade.[7]

1. Ireland

During the eighteenth century, the Irish fought in Italy, Spain, Germany, and the Netherlands. The regiments of Walsh and Dillon also fought briefly in North America during the War for Independence. They were a part of a Franco-American force that unsuccessfully laid siege to Savannah in 1779.[8] With the coming of the French Revolution the loyalty of the army shifted from the king to the National Assembly to the nation. In July 1791, the National Assembly passed a decree that dissolved all foreign regiments, except the Swiss, and reassigned many of their officers and men to French units. The army had traditionally owed its allegiance directly to the king, and many of the officers were not sympathetic with the political changes brought about by the Revolution. They did not have a feeling for, or a sense of loyalty to, the French nation or the French people.

At the time the Irish Brigade was dissolved, the Clare Regiment was serving in India, and the Dillon and Walsh regiments were stationed in the West Indies.[9] The last commander of the Irish Brigade was General Daniel O'Connell, uncle of the "Emancipator." Like many of the officers of the Brigade, he resigned his commission and left the service of France. O'Connell took service with the English and helped to form an Irish regiment in the English army. Interestingly enough, he returned to France in 1814, where he lived the rest of his years (d. 1833) on pensions from both the English and the French.[10] There were no Irish regiments during the wars of the Revolution, although Irishmen did serve in the French army during those years. Even so, when England joined the First Coalition in 1793 and the Republican armies gained control of France's frontiers, the Directory began to think seriously about an invasion of Ireland as a means of striking a crippling blow against its enemy.

The grand strategy for attacking England by way of Ireland had not changed for over a hundred years. The French would send a relatively small army to Ireland with large quantities of arms and supplies. The Irish would provide the manpower, and in cooperation with the French, they would drive out the English. What did change between 1690 and 1796 was the form of government to be established in Ireland once the English had been forced to withdraw. In the late seventeenth and throughout most of the eighteenth century the aim was to replace the existing English monarch with the Stuart pretender. Thus Ireland would continue to have a monarchical form of government, but with greater, or total, independence from England. By the end of September 1792, France was a republic and the political minded in Ireland had begun to think of an independent nation with a republican form of government. However, the Irish became less impressed with the French model of republicanism then they were with the American experiment. As had been the case in Ireland over the past centuries, the Irish were not of one mind about either independence from England or about the form of government under which they wished to live. To be sure, there were Irishmen who desired less control from England, but who did not want either an independent nation or a republic. The Catholic majority was as divided as the Protestant minority. The former was in agreement upon their desire to have the Penal Code,[11] which made second class subjects of them, repealed. Yet most of the peasantry was not politically motivated, while the rest of the population was divided on the questions of independence and a new form of government. The Protestants for their part were also divided on the crucial issues of Catholic emancipation, independence, and political structure.

The numerous problems and issues that divided the people of Ireland in 1790 seemed to preclude any possibility of united action on their part to change the existing political, religious, or social structure. Then in 1791, a movement was begun in Belfast that was to have both immediate and long-range effects upon the people of Ireland. A society was formed that called itself the United Irishmen. As the name implied, the founders of the society were determined to include the broadest cross section of the Irish people. In particular, they wanted to bridge the religious gap that had divided the Irish for several hundred years. The principal founders, and the early leaders, were Protestants. Of the eleven[12] founders of the Society of United Irishmen, seven are identified by R. R. Madden as being Presbyterian, and almost two-thirds of the important members through the 1790s were Protestants.[13] Religion was not to be a divisive issue. The society advocated Catholic emancipation, even though some of its supporters were concerned about the social and economic implications. Many Catholics, particularly in the south and west, believed that emancipation meant not only religious and political freedom, but also the reclamation of lands that the Catholics had lost to the Protestants over the past two hundred years. The United Irishmen did not support land reform; their main interest was political reform.

In October 1791, the Society of United Irishmen actually came into existence in Belfast. The following month witnessed the establishment of the United Club in Dublin.[14] The dominant figures in the formative years were Theobald Wolfe Tone in Belfast and James Napper Tandy in Dublin. The society was politically oriented in the eighteenth-century traditon of the Enlightenment. It reflected the American revolt against English domination and was the direct Irish response to the French Revolution. Between 1791 and 1795, it was devoted to political reform within the monarchy and Catholic emancipation. In an address before the Belfast club, Wolfe Tone declared that English influence in Ireland was so great "as to require a cordial union among all the people of Ireland, to maintain that balance which is essential to the preservation of our liberties. . . . That no reform is practicable, efficacious, or just, which does not include Irishmen of every religious persuasion."[15] A few months later, the principal statement of policy of the United Irishmen was issued from the Dublin branch of the society, which rapidly came to be more important than the Belfast branch.

> The object of this institution [the document printed in the *Northern Star* declared] is to make an United Society of the Irish nation. . . . We gladly look forward to brighter prospects; to a people united in the fellowship of freedom; to a parliament the express image of the people; to a prosperity established on civil, political, and religious liberty; to a peace . . . [that provides a] stable tranquility which rests on the rights of human nature. . . . We agree, therefore, in the necessity of giving political value and station to the great majority of the people.[16]

In the first half of the 1790s, the United Irishmen were in agreement that Ireland should remain associated with England under the king, but that reform was necessary for the well-being of the Irish people. However, little by little the society moved to the left, that is in the direction of independence from England, as exemplified by the recently established United States of America, and republicanism as had been recently established in the United States and France. By 1794, the government in Ireland considered the society to be an undesirable and dangerous organization. On 4 May, government troops and police broke into a meeting of the society in Dublin and arrested those leaders who were present. The society, as it had been constituted since 1791, ceased to function. The fainthearted withdrew, but "the more determined and indignant, and especially the republican portion of the body, remained, and in 1795 gave a new character to the association, still called the 'Society of United Irishmen.' "[17] The new, or "reorganized," society championed both republicanism and independence from England. It became a secret society and its aims were both seditious and treasonable. The structure of the society was reorganized so that its members formed small cells of no more than twelve men in order to make the task of informers more difficult.

The new organization of the society was originally civil, but in the last months of 1796, it was given a military character as well.[18] The civil structure called for each cell to have a secretary and a treasurer. Secretaries of five cells were combined to form a lower baronial committee. An upper baronial committee was then formed of one member of each lower baronial. The upper baronial committee was responsible for the activities within a county. Each of the four provinces of Ireland (Ulster, Leinster, Munster, and

Connacht) had a provincial committee or directory of two or three members who were appointed by the upper baronial committees. Finally, late in 1796, there was a central executive directory formed in Dublin. This executive directory was at first composed of four members, however, its membership varied when members were arrested or forced into exile. The original four members were Lord Edward Fitzgerald, Arthur O'Connor, Robert Simms, and Richard McCormick. Shortly thereafter, five additional members were added: William James MacNeven, Thomas Addis Emmet, Joseph Orr, Bartholomew Teeling, and Alexander Lowry.[19] Secrecy was imperative for the safety of the members. Only the secretaries of the lower baronial committees had contact with one another, and each of them knew only one member of the upper baronial committee. Thus an informer, and the society did suffer at the hands of government-paid informers, could gain only limited knowledge of the society unless he was highly placed in the organization.

As the United Irishmen came to accept the necessity of armed action in order to gain their objectives, a military structure was superimposed upon the civil framework. The secretary of each of the twelve-man cells was given the rank of noncommissioned officer, while the delegates to the lower baronial committees held the rank of captain with sixty men in their companies. Ten lower baronials were clustered to form a six-hundred-man battalion with a colonel who was appointed by the captains he commanded. Each county had an adjutant-general who was appointed from above, that is by the central or national executive directory in Dublin. The question of the strength and effectiveness of this military organization is less certain than its organization.[20] The total membership of the United Irishmen was placed at 500,000 men who had taken the oath. Of this number, the Leinster directory estimated that between 280,000 and 300,000 men would be available to fight should the call be sounded.[21] However, more conservative, and undoubtedly more realistic, estimates put the number of men who might be expected to answer a call to arms at about 100,000 men.[22] At the head of this army, the Dublin executive directory appointed Lord Edward Fitzgerald, an aristocrat from one of the oldest and wealthiest families of Ireland. This military force had virtually no equipment or training. Its officers knew nothing of military tactics or strategy. Few of its officers or men had ever been under fire. It had no artillery, no cavalry, and a totally inadequate system of supply and communication. In order to overcome at least some of these shortcomings, the United Irishmen turned to France for assistance.

The first official contact with the French government on the part of the United Irishmen was made in May 1796. Not all of the members of the central directory believed that dependence upon French aid was a wise course of action. It is true that on 19 November 1792, just two months after the establishment of the French Republic, that the Constituent Assembly offered "fraternity and assistance to all people wishing to recover their liberty,"[23] but such a vague statement from a government that was no longer in power in 1796 needed investigation on the part of the Irish. Therefore, the National Directory made contact with the French Directory for the purpose of coordinating a French landing in Ireland and an uprising by the Irish people.

In 1796, France was still experimenting with representative government. Since the Revolution had begun, she had passed through a constitutional monarchy, a republic, which was characterized by the years of the Terror, the Thermidorian Reaction, and finally the Directory. The foreign war was dragging on with no real prospect of a favorable conclusion. It had begun in 1792 with Austria and Prussia, but England and most of the Continent had taken up arms against the French by the end of 1793. France's fortunes had fluctuated under the various governments for four years. But in the summer of 1796, conditions seemed favorable for a military expedition to Ireland. The government in Paris was stronger and more stable than it had been since the outbreak of hostilities. Prussia had signed a separate peace with France, Austria and England were weary, and the insurrection in the Vendée, although not suppressed, was relatively inactive. The military situation on the Rhine and in the Po Valley was either favorable, or at least neutral. Thus, the French could indulge in a military expedition to Ireland as a means of striking at England. Furthermore, the English had been giving aid and comfort to the rebels in the Vendée for more than three years. This aid had been in the form of money, supplies, and naval protection and escort. The French saw an expedition to Ireland as repaying their enemy in kind. They would give aid and comfort to the Irish rebels.

Communication between the National Directory of the United Irishmen and the French government was poor and inadequate. Theobald Wolf Tone had been the first "official" Irish contact with the French. Then in the summer of 1796, Lord Edward Fitzgerald, the United Irish military commander, and Arthur O'Connor, a member of the National Directory, met with General Louis Lazare Hoche in Switzerland. Hoche was the designated commander of the proposed French expedition to Ireland. The three men reassured one another and made promises of mutual support, but no date was set for the military operation.[24] In November of the same year, General Hoche sent Bernard MacSheehy, the future organizer of the Irish Legion, to Ireland. However, this young Irishman, in the service of

France, was instructed to gain information on conditions in Ireland while telling the Irish nothing.[25] The Irish recommended that the French landing should take place in the north because the United Irishmen were strongest and best organized in Ulster. But when the French sailed from Brest late in 1796, their destination was Bantry Bay, which is in southwest Munster, on the opposite side of the island.

The expedition was plagued with difficulties from the outset. The Irish did not know when the French were coming, or where they would land. In fact, they believed that Hoche would come to Ulster. Thus one can imagine their astonishment when word reached Dublin and Belfast that the French fleet was anchored in Bantry Bay. Hoche had sailed from Brest on 16 December with 14,750 men[26] and supplies for the Irish that included 41,644 stand of arms, 5,000 uniforms taken from the royalists at Quiberon, and a supply of Irish national cockades. Wolf Tone sailed with the expedition and would have taken command of the Irish if a landing had been made. But in the fog and rough sea, the French ships were scattered and General Hoche was separated from the main part of the fleet. The French reached Bantry Bay on 21 December, but without Hoche and without orders to land. Tone tried in vain to persuade General Emmanuel Grouchy who, in Hoche's absence, assumed command of the 6,400 troops[27] aboard ship in Bantry Bay, to land the men. After waiting five days, as per his instructions, Admiral François Joseph Bouvet, the naval commander, sailed back to Brest with Grouchy, Tone, and the troops. Hoche, driven to the west by unfavorable winds, did not reach the coast of Ireland until 30 December, four days after the departure of Bouvet and Grouchy. The expedition was a fiasco and an embarrassment.[28]

The United Irishmen were greatly disappointed. There was a general feeling that a golden opportunity had passed them by. If only the French had landed, even in County Kerry, the Irish would have risen. The government in Dublin was completely surprised, and quite unprepared to deal with a French landing and an Irish uprising. But the French did not land, and the Irish did not rise. The episode only served to alert the English to the real danger posed by the United Irishmen. Throughout 1797, repressive measures were taken to destroy the military capabilities of the United Irishmen and to break the spirit of the Irish people. The number of arrests and imprisonments without trial increased greatly. Arms were seized and houses burned. The already bad conditions throughout the country seemed to worsen with each passing month until the United Irishmen felt that they had but two choices; total submission or rebellion.[29] It is, of course, a matter of record that the United Irishmen chose rebellion.

The principal divisive issue among the leadership of the United

Irishmen was not whether they should rise and throw off English domination, rather, it was over the question of French assistance and cooperation,
and when the insurrection would take place. After the disappointment of
the Bantry Bay affair, a number of Irishmen came to believe that they would
have to depend entirely upon Irish resources and Irishmen to drive out the
English and establish an independent republic. They believed that French
assistance would make the task easier, but that Ireland had the means
of achieving independence even without outside assistance.[30] Thus they
advocated preparation for an insurrection, coupled with efforts to gain
French support, with the understanding that the United Irishmen would
rise whether the French arrived or not. As a matter of fact, there were even
some influential United men who were suspect of French intentions. They
feared that once the French army landed in Ireland, it might exert French
influence, or even perhaps domination, once the English had been driven
out.[31] On the other hand, there were members of the National Directory,
notably Thomas Addis Emmet and William MacNeven, who believed that
a successful insurrection could only be achieved with direct French aid.
They supported a rising of the United Irishmen, but only with, and preferably after, a French landing on the island. Thus both the militants, led by
Arthur O'Connor and Lord Edward Fitzgerald, and the moderates, Emmet
and MacNeven as their principal spokesmen, supported efforts to convince
the French government that another expedition should be sent to Ireland
as quickly as possible.

To this end, the National Directory sent representatives to Paris. But
as the factionalism within the United movement continued to grow, the
French government found it increasingly difficult to know with whom to
deal on the continent. Edward Lewins was the "official" representative of
the Directory throughout 1797. He was supported by Tone, who still had
significant influence and friends in Paris. However, Napper Tandy increasingly "came to be regarded as the Irish generalissimo who would lead
French forces in Ireland"[32] when the invasion took place. Despite this
conflict, which was to a large extent a clash of personalities between Tone
and Tandy, and to a lesser extent at this time, O'Connor, who also aspired
to military leadership, the French government dealt with all parties in their
preparations for a return to Ireland. The French Directory had decided
upon another expedition to Ireland, but its members did not share the
urgency felt by the Irish. Consequently, when General Napoleon Bonaparte
and Charles Maurice de Talleyrand-Périgord, minister of foreign affairs,
decided upon a military expedition to Egypt, preparations for the Irish
expedition were delayed. Men and matériel, as well as energy, interest,
and enthusiasm, were diverted from Brest to Toulon. However, a series of

arrests early in 1798 accelerated the deterioration of the United Irishmen in Ireland.

Ever since the Bantry Bay affair, the government in Dublin had been taking repressive action against the United Irish. During the winter of 1797–98, it was reasonably successful in a program to disarm the country. In late February 1798, the English arrested Arthur O'Connor and his small party, which included John Allen, a future distinguished officer in the Irish Legion, as they were attempting to cross over to the Continent. This was followed on 12 March by a raid on the home of Oliver Bond in Bridge Street, Dublin. At the time of the raid, the United Irishmen were holding a high-level meeting, and a number of its most influential members were arrested and imprisoned. With the exception of Lord Edward Fitzgerald, Charles Teeling, and Richard McCormick (the last named having gone into exile) the members of the National Directory were in the hands of the government. A new executive directory was formed with Fitzgerald the dominant figure.[33] With the moderate leadership in prison, in particular Emmet and MacNeven, Fitzgerald and his supporters proceeded with preparations for an Irish uprising with or without French support.

In the last week of May 1798, the ill-fated rebellion took place, despite the fact that Fitzgerald had been arrested on 19 May and the Sheares brothers on the following day. With its most influential leaders in the hands of the government, with many other highly placed members on the run, without French assistance or adequate weapons, poor communications, and in fact lacking almost everything needed for a successful revolution except the will to fight, the southeast counties (Wexford and Carlow) and the east took up arms in a futile attempt to overthrow the government in Dublin. Despite these inadequacies, the rebels made significant gains in the early weeks. Their victories, such as New Ross, were won with zeal and heavy losses. But as the fighting went on, the government forces, with reinforcements from England, suppressed the uncoordinated pockets of Irish resistance. Once order had been restored a white terror swept over the unfortunate land. The repression, which was highlighted by massive arrests and selective hangings, the Sheares brothers, John and Henry, being the most notable, were carried out not merely in the eastern and southeastern counties where the fighting had taken place, but also in the west, which had hardly raised a finger to support the rebellion.

In a desperate effort to stop the executions and the military repression, the state prisoners in Dublin, notably Emmet, MacNeven, and O'Connor, agreed to make full confessions of the activities of the United Irishmen from the conception of the society until their arrests. It is true that O'Connor and several of his close friends did not at first agree to talk to the government, but the execution of Pat Byrne on 26 July convinced them all that cooperation was the only means of putting an end to the useless bloodshed. The "Kilmainham Treaty," as the agreement came to be known, served both parties well. The executions were halted and the government's forces eased up on the population. The Irish government in Dublin, as well as the English government in London, made good political and propaganda use of the confessions of the United Irish leaders.[34] The confessions had somewhat of a tarnishing effect upon the reputations of the state prisoners, particularly as there were many in Ireland who did not understand their motives. But, in fact, the rebellion had already been crushed and the United Society was in shambles, with virtually all of its leaders either dead, imprisoned, or in exile. Crippled as the United Irishmen were by the end of the summer of 1798, the organization survived and would attempt one last insurrection in 1803 under Robert Emmet, the younger brother of Thomas Addis.

The rebellion had a profound effect upon the French. There were two schools of thought in Paris in 1798 with respect to the Irish question. On the one hand there were those who had always advocated a military expedition to Ireland which, after the French had landed, would signal a general rising of the population. This was also the position taken by the moderate leaders in Ireland. The French must land an army *before* the insurrection would begin. However, what was perhaps the predominate view in Paris was that the Irish should *first* raise the standard of rebellion, and then the French would come to their aid with a military expedition. In this manner, they argued, France would be assured that her troops would have the necessary support to prevent a disaster, and to increase the likelihood of a successful undertaking. Paris was leery of the promises being made by the representatives of the United Irishmen and feared that a landing would not be supported by a general uprising, thus leaving the small French army to fight their battle for them. The rebellion in the summer of 1798 united the French in their willingness to send the promised military aid.[35]

When news of the insurrection reached Paris, efforts to ready the expeditionary force at Brest were accelerated. General Jean Joseph Amable Humbert had been given command of the expedition. General Napoleon Bonaparte, who had been given command of the Army of England, that is all of the French troops along the English Channel, could have led an army to Ireland in 1798, but he had given up his command in the spring after informing the Directory that French naval power was insufficient to invade the British Isle, and decided upon an expedition to the eastern Mediterranean. In exile on St. Helena many years later Emmanuel Las Cases quotes Napoleon, reflecting on his decision to go east rather than west: " 'On what', he said, 'do the destinies of empires hang! . . . If, instead of the expedition of Egypt, I had made that of Ireland, if slight deranging circumstances had not thrown obstacles in the way of my Boulogne enterprise—what would England have been to-day? and the Continent? and the political world?' "[36] Despite these words, there can be little doubt but that General Bonaparte had no interest in, and even less knowledge of, affairs of Ireland in 1798. With his departure for Egypt just weeks before the Irish insurrection, taking with him the Mediterranean fleet and 36,000 veterans, there was no real possibility of a major expedition to support the rebellion.

In the absence of a major expedition to England and Ireland, the Directory approved the dispatching of several small ones to support the rebellion of the summer of 1798. The first of these was commanded by General Humbert. It sailed from France on 6 August after hurried last-minute preparations. The small force of 1,036 officers and men could hardly be considered an invasion force, but the personnel were seasoned veterans from Italy and the Rhine. Humbert landed his little army at Killala, in northern Mayo, on the 22nd, and marched south to Castlebar. He was extremely disappointed with the reception that he received. He had been led to believe that the Irish were only waiting for a French landing to rise as one and drive out the English. Instead, he found apathy. The rebellion had already been crushed. Furthermore, it had been primarily an eastern rebellion, and the west of Ireland was not nearly so politically aroused. It is true that Irish peasants did join the French, but in the hundreds, not in the thousands as the Irish in Paris had promised. W. E. H. Lecky, in his *A History of Ireland in the Eighteenth Century*, a very English version of Irish history, says that the uneducated peasants only joined the French to get the uniforms and muskets that Humbert had brought with him.[37] But for whatever reason the Irish joined the French, they proved to be of little benefit in combat. Undisciplined, lacking in the knowledge or use of their arms, and totally unfamiliar with tactics, maneuvers or military life, they contributed little to the expedition.

After winning a victory over General Gerard Lake at Castlebar, in which his inexperienced Irish militia fled from the battlefield before the English troops, Humbert marched east brushing aside a feeble detachment south of Sligo. Then at Ballinamuck, on 8 September, he found himself surrounded by Generals Charles Cornwallis, of Yorktown fame, and Lake, who had been reinforced after his disaster at Castlebar. Eight hundred and forty-four Frenchmen and several hundred Irishmen lay down their arms, and the expedition came to an inglorious end. The French were eventually exchanged and lived to fight another day. But the Irish prisoners were either executed or sent to penal colonies in Australia.[38] While the cliché "Too little, too late" has clearly been overused, it most appropriately describes Humbert's expediton.

Humbert's was the first of three expeditions that the French sent to Ireland in 1798. The second one might be called Tandy's for James Napper Tandy, who had been given the rank of adjutant General in the French army and dispatched to northern Ireland. It was not a military expedition in the sense of Humbert's. Tandy had with him only a handful of French soldiers and sailors, and several United Irishmen. He counted on the men of Ulster to rise upon his arrival, which would then be followed by reinforcements from France. The small party reached Rutland, in Donegal, in mid-September and the Irish went ashore. But hearing of Humbert's surrender, and believing their numbers too small for any serious accom- plishment, they returned to their ship, the *Anacreon*. Then with a great deal of luck Tandy and his United Irish companions reached the coast of Norway and made their way to Hamburg. Hamburg was a neutral city and United Irishmen had been using it as a door to the Continent for a number of years. But when the English learned that Napper Tandy was in the city, they demanded that he be turned over to them as he was a subject of the King's and an insurgent. The French protested that Tandy was an officer in the French army and should thus be returned to France. Unfortunately for the Irish, the town fathers of Hamburg feared English reprisal more than French at that time. Thus Tandy, along with William Corbet, Thomas Blackwell, and Hervey Montmorency Morres, were handed over to the English authorities who immediately imprisoned all four men. Corbet and Blackwell had been with Tandy on board the *Anacreon*, while Morres had fled from Ireland to Hamburg after the collapse of Humbert's expedition.[39] Tandy was tried in Dublin, convicted, but then exchanged for one General Don, and returned to France where he died in 1803.[40] Blackwell and Morres remained in prison until the Peace of Amiens, at which time they were released. Corbet escaped from prison, made his way to France, and when the Irish Legion was formed in the fall of 1803, he was one of the first to enlist.

The third and final expedition was that of Theobald Wolfe Tone. It sailed from Brest on 14 September and arrived at Lough Swilly, Donegal, the second week of October. The flotilla was made up of eight frigates and a ship of the line, and carried three thousand French troops under the command of General Harty.[41] This time, the English navy was on hand, and the *Hoche*, an eighty-four-gun ship of the line, was captured along with three of the frigates. Tone, who was on board the *Hoche*, was taken prisoner. He was tried by a court-martial in Dublin on 10 November and condemned to death by hanging. On the night before his execution was to take place, Wolfe Tone inflicted upon himself a mortal wound from which he died on 19 November.[42]

The year 1798 was a crucial one for the Irish. It probably presented the best conditions and the greatest probability for establishing an independent nation that they had had in the past one hundred years. Those conditions in Ireland were favorable for an insurrection, and there was a very real possibility of receiving military assistance from France. There is every reason to believe that if the United Irish rising had been coordinated with a French expedition of fifteen thousand men, or perhaps even as few as ten thousand, the government at Dublin could have been overthrown and the English driven from the island. It is quite another matter to argue that the Irish could have maintained their independence once the French had withdrawn, or once the English navy had severed supply lines and communication between Ireland and France. Nevertheless, in 1798, the time was right. Unfortunately, the French were not prepared in the summer of that year to make the commitment that would have been necessary, and the United Irish organization was inadequate. Only a small portion of the country rose that fateful summer, and it did so without French assistance. When the French did sent aid, it was equally unorganized and totally inadequate. The result was that the opportunity passed, and conditions would not again be so favorable for another hundred years. The Society of United Irishmen was a broken movement after 1798, and although the French army would become the strongest and best in the world, the French navy steadily declined. So long as the English dominated the seas about the British Isles there was little hope for a serious French expedition to Ireland.

The United Irishmen did not cease to exist as the result of the devastating setbacks of 1798. In Ireland, they were driven further underground as they set about reorganizing and licking their wounds. In France, with the ascent of Napoleon Bonaparte as First Consul late in 1799 and the defeat of the Austrians at Marengo in the summer of 1800, peace became the central theme in everyone's mind. It was of little concern to the First Consul that the Directory had assured the United Irishmen that France would not make peace with England unless it would guarantee the independence of Ireland.[43] The result was that after the fall of 1798 there was little talk of insurrection in Ireland and virtually no talk of an Irish expedition in France. The imprisoned leaders of the United Irishmen remained incarcerated. It is true that most of the state prisoners were released in 1799 in accordance with the "Kilmainham Treaty," but the government declared that the principal figures associated with the '98 rebellion would have to remain in prison until peace had been concluded with France. Naturally, those who were not freed, notably O'Connor, Emmet, MacNeven, and Lawless, accused the government of refusing to honor their word after the prisoners had fulfilled their part of the "Treaty."

The state prisoners posed a problem for the Dublin government and the English Parliament. They had not been brought to trial, and thus not convicted of any crime. Yet they were considered too dangerous to be released on the Continent as they would surely go to France and renew their rebellious activities. At one point in time, the government hoped to deport the prisoners to the United States, but "Rufus King, the American Minister in London, officially announced that the President, under the powers given him by a recent Act, would not suffer any of the traitors from Ireland to land in America, and that if they set foot on shore, he would instantly have them sent back to Europe."[44] This may have expressed the views of the American government under President John Adams in 1799, however, by 1804 the Thomas Jefferson administration made no move against Thomas A. Emmet when he arrived in New York with his family and was publicly received and welcomed by the Irish community. The Dublin government then decided to disperse the less prominent state prisoners. Some were sent to Australia while others were pressed into British regiments overseas. Still others were sent to Prussia to serve in the army or work in the coal mines of Silesia.[45] The remaining state prisoners, those deemed too dangerous to be released, were taken under the jurisdiction of the London government, which was not pleased with the manner in which Dublin had been handling the matter. In mid-March 1799, nineteen prisoners from Dublin and another group from Belfast, were transported to Fort St. George, in Inverness shire, Scotland, where they remained until the Treaty of Amiens was signed.[46]

At Fort St. George the prisoners were fortunate in having a lieutenant governor of the prison, Colonel John Stuart, who was a highland Scot and probably sympathetic to the Irish cause. They were thus treated as well as could be expected under the circumstances. It was during their confinement in Scotland that a deep, serious, and lasting division took place within the ranks of the leadership of the United Irishmen. There had existed factions within the United organization before the 1798 uprising. The moderate faction, led by Emmet, did not agree with the militaristic attitudes and aims of the faction headed by O'Connor and Lord Edward Fitzgerald. At Fort St. George these differences became personal and permanent. The two principal antagonists were Arthur O'Connor and Thomas Addis Emmet. Their respective friends, although not as bitter as they were, tended to divide themselves into two camps. The issue had moved from the realm of strategic differences as how best to achieve the goals of the Society of United Irishmen to one of personal mistrust. Although there is no historical proof, Emmet and MacNeven came to believe that O'Connor had made his peace with the government.[47] They came to this conclusion while at Fort St. George on the basis of circumstantial evidence. Perhaps the main reason for their suspicion was that O'Connor received preferential treatment. His wife and children were allowed to be with him while the wives of the other prisoners were not allowed even to reside in the vicinity of the prison. He was allowed to leave the prison in the day and to return at night. No other prisoner was permitted outside the walls, and indeed Emmet was even confined to his cell for some months. That this treatment of O'Connor bothered his fellow prisoners may be seen in a letter written by Sammuel Neilson, one of the state prisoners at Fort St. George, to his wife on 30 March, 1800: "Mrs. O'Connor and her children remain with Mr. O'Connor, and they have all the liberty of *ranging the Fort and neighborhood*; the other nineteen of us are closely confined as usual." And on 18 May of the same year, he continued on the same subject to his wife: "Mrs. O'Connor and her family are still here, but Mrs. Emmet has hitherto failed in all her applications; there appears to be a MARKED difference."[48] Clearly the perception of the majority of the prisoners was that O'Connor was receiving special treatment, and from that point it was but a short step for them to believe that this privileged treatment was the result of having "made his peace with the government." Neilson declared that of the twenty prisoners "Hudson, Chambers, Tennent, and Dowling alone are on speaking terms with him."[49]

There were other issues that separated O'Connor from Emmet and MacNeven. While they were still in prison in Dublin, O'Connor had refused to cooperate with Emmet and MacNeven when the three had been elected to form a quasi-executive committee to treat with the Dublin government on behalf of all of the prisoners. Finally, it should be remembered that O'Connor had resented the preeminent position of Emmet in the Executive Directory of the United Irishmen in 1797 when both men had been members of that body. O'Connor and Fitzgerald had always opted for a military solution to Ireland's problems, whereas Emmet would support military action only if France was actively involved. Such legitimate differences in strategy led to personal dislike and even hatred. Relative peace prevailed among the prisoners during their confinement at Fort St. George as the result of an agreement among themselves that they would put aside their quarrels so long as they were confined. But upon their release in 1802, Emmet and O'Connor declared that they would fight a duel as soon as they landed on the Continent. However, during the ocean voyage from Scotland their fellow prisoners convinced them that it would only further damage the cause of the United Irishmen and give great comfort to their enemies if either were to kill the other. The duel was called off, but the men remained on the worst possible terms.[50]

With the signing of the Treaty of Amiens in February 1802, the conclusion of hostilities between France and England was formalized. Three and one-half years had passed since the United Irish rebellion had been crushed, and these years had not shown any serious rebuilding of the society. It did still exist underground, but it did not seem to pose a threat to the tranquility of Ireland. Furthermore, with peace between France and England, the possibility of foreign assistance for the Irish was eliminated. The English government thus deemed it safe to release the state prisoners. A warrant was issued for their release, but it did not include the name of Thomas Addis Emmet. His later biographer believed that it was the intention of the government in London to keep Emmet in prison.[51] But Colonel Stuart took it upon his own authority to release him with the others. They sailed aboard the frigate *Ariadne* to Holland where they arrived on 4 July 1802.[52]

Upon their arrival on the Continent the liberated Irishmen, who were prohibited from ever returning to Ireland, fanned out over northwest Europe. O'Connor went first to Calais where he met, quite by chance, some of his English friends on their way from Paris to London. He then traveled to Italy while awaiting permission to reside in Paris. Emmet, who was accompanied by his wife and children, went directly to Hamburg where he visited with friends. The Emmets then settled in Brussels, but their stay was meant to be temporary, as their plan was to emigrate to the United States. Emmet wanted to settle in Ohio and there to practice law. Other former prisoners settled in Hamburg, Brussels, Paris, and in some of the provincial cities of France. However, before the Emmets had made their final preparations to leave Europe forever, Thomas Addis received a special messenger from the Executive Directory of the Society of United Irishmen. The directors asked him to proceed to Paris and to act there as the society's "official" representative. Emmet was reluctant to postpone his departure for America. He had become disillusioned with the idea of French aid to Ireland, and he was suspicious of General Bonaparte. Nevertheless, he accepted the assignment, and in the spring of 1803, he arrived in the French capital and took up residence just outside of the city at Saint Germain-en-Laye.[53]

In 1802 the possibilities of creating an independent Irish nation were at a low point. The fact that the English had released the state prisoners is an indication that they believed the Irish "cause" had been dealt a fatal blow by the suppression of the 1798 rebellion and the Peace of Amiens. The failure of the rebellion, with the arrest or flight of its leaders and most staunch supporters, had removed the threat of insurrection at home, while peace with France removed any hope of outside assistance. However, there were two factors that continued to give comfort to those Irishmen who clung to the dream "of a nation free again." The vast majority of the Irish people desired a change in the political, social, and economic conditions in Ireland, and France and England were traditional enemies. If little could be done at home, then the focus of attention on the part of what was left of the United Irishmen would have to be Paris.

2

The Formation of the Irish Legion

The Irish community of Paris, and indeed all of France, was heterogeneous in its make-up. The men differed in their social origin, educations, religions, financial situations, and occupations. Yet, a great majority of them had in common the desire for change in the conditions in Ireland. However, even on that matter, there was not complete agreement on what changes were necessary. The United Irishmen had come to champion independence from England, but they were not all republicans. Most of the Irish in exile favored Catholic emancipation, but few supported the type of land reform that many of the peasants at home considered to be an intricate part of emancipation. Many of them were of the commercial or professional bourgeoisie, while others had been "petit" bourgeois or artisans. Most were educated, even if they were not fluent in French at the time of their arrival. Some of the Protestants had attended Trinity College or studied in England. On the other hand, the Catholics, who were not allowed to attend Trinity, were likely to have studied at the Irish College in Paris.

Most of the Irish in Paris were there because they could not return to Ireland without fear of being arrested. They had either been sent into exile by the English government, or had had to flee Ireland to avoid apprehension by the authorities. The majority had been involved in the insurrections, rebellions, and antigovernment activities that revolved about the United Irishmen between 1795 and 1803. However, there were Irishmen in Paris and other French cities—notably Bordeaux—with whom the home government had no quarrel. They could have returned to their native land at any time they wished. Most of these men were engaged in business or the professions. There were also the Irish professional soldiers and their sons. These men had served in the Irish Brigade and had remained in France, many of them in the army, after the brigade had been integrated into the republican army. It was from this diverse pool of Irishmen that the ranks of the Legion were recruited.

In the months preceding the formation of the Legion, there were diplomatic maneuvers and intrigues both on the part of the French government and within the Irish community in Paris. Arthur O'Connor had arrived in the capital in the early spring of 1803. He had informed the government in advance of his arrival, and he took the position that he represented the Irish. This claim was based upon the fact that the Central Directory of the United Irishmen had "commissioned" him to go to Paris in 1798, before the rebellion of that year, for the purpose of negotiating with the French Directory military assistance for the anticipated uprising. O'Connor had made his way to England, but he had been arrested and imprisoned as he was preparing to cross over to the Continent. He was first confined in Kilmainham prison and then at St. George. Five years had elapsed from the time the Irish directory had sent him and his arrival in Paris.[1] O'Connor had lost contact with the resistance movement in Ireland. Of the nine members of the directory who had asked him to negotiate with the French, two were dead, six were in exile and one was living in Belfast.[2] But his name was still known in Ireland and he did have friends in Paris. Thus the French government was not unwilling to deal with him when the war with England was resumed in the spring of 1803. However, O'Connor was not the only one in Paris who claimed to speak for the Irish. Thomas Addis Emmet also laid claim to this privilege.

Emmet arrived in the French capital at about the same time as did O'Connor. In 1802, he had reached the conclusion that there was little that could be done for Ireland at that particular time, and he planned to emigrate to the United States with his wife and children just as soon as he could put his affairs in order. He had settled temporarily in Brussels, but then a messenger arrived from Dublin and his plans were altered. The Directory of the United Irishmen asked him to proceed to Paris and to open negotiations with the French government to provide arms, munitions, and money for the projected rebellion that was being planned. Reluctantly, but without hesitation, he postponed his departure for America and traveled south. Thus, by May 1803, there were two men in the French capital, each of whom considered himself the "official" or true representative of the Irish people.

The presence of two popular and influential Irishmen in Paris, both claiming to speak for their people and both with supporters in the capital, presented a problem for the French. Fighting was renewed between England and France in the late spring of 1803, and General Bonaparte, First Consul of the Republic, was already thinking in terms of an invasion of

England.[3] One aspect of this grand strategy was an expedition to Ireland. To be sure, the principal effort of the French would be the landing of a major army on English soil, but Bonaparte believed that a diversionary invasion of Ireland would have great impact on the success of the English campaign. He spoke of a French force of 25,000 men landing in Ireland, which would be a rallying point for a general Irish uprising. The separation of Ireland from England was desirable for the negative impact that it would have on the enemy. But even if Ireland was unable to gain its independence, such an expedition would tie down English troops that could otherwise be used to confront the main French assault across the Channel. Furthermore, the very threat of a French expedition to Ireland would cause the English to maintain a relatively strong presence on that island, reducing the number of men available to defend the channel coast. Thus, the projected expedition to Ireland assumed an important role in the grand strategy for the war with England.

In pursuit of this strategy, General Alexandre Berthier, minister of war, instructed Colonel Alexander Dalton to establish communications with the Irish exiles for the purpose of securing their cooperation with respect to the proposed expedition to Ireland. The son of William, an Irishman who had served in the Irish Brigade, Dalton had been born in France. Having joined the French army at the age of sixteen (in 1791), he served as an aide-de-camp to General Hoche and took part in the expedition to Ireland with Wolfe Tone in 1796. In 1803 he was on Berthier's staff, and because of his Irish ancestry and connections was deemed the proper officer to work with the exiles. Emmet had been unable to secure an interview with the minister of war, but late in May, Dalton called upon him as the "official" representative of General Berthier. He informed Emmet that the French were determined to send an expedition of 25,000 men to Ireland with General André Masséna in command. The expedition, which could not be ready to sail for at least six months, would assist the Irish in establishing their independence from England. Emmet expressed his displeasure at the poor treatment of the Irish exiles since the Peace of Amiens, and hoped that this would change now that England and France were again at war. Then Dalton asked Emmet if he thought there were enough Irish in France to form a legion, and the Irishman replied that he would inquire of his friends in Paris, but that he did not think there were at that time.[4] Dalton also paid a visit to O'Connor and gave him the same information and asked the same questions. The French did not know who spoke for Ireland, and thus were determined to deal with both men until it became clear which of them would be the most valuable in carrying out their plans with respect to Ireland.

The arrival of Patrick Gallagher from Dublin on 31 May lent some

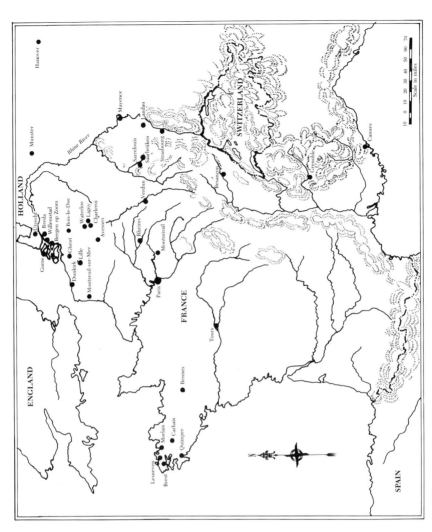

2. Western Europe

urgency to Emmet's mission, and introduced a new dimension to the requests being made by the Irish. Gallagher, who had been active in the United Irishmen in 1797–98 and a close associate of Lord Edward Fitzgerald,[5] not only pressed the Irish Directory's requests for money, arms, and ammunition, he also stated that its members were asking for *officers* to be landed on the coast of Ireland.[6] This latter request reflected their recognition that there were few, if any, military leaders in Ireland, and when the insurrection should take place, for which they were preparing, the trained officers who would lead the Irish masses would have to come from France. It would seem that what the Irish had in mind at this time was French officers to train and lead Irishmen in Ireland. There is no indication that they were contemplating the training of Irish officers in France to serve in Ireland. Nevertheless, the seeds were being sown both in France and in Ireland for the formation of an Irish officer corps.

Negotiations between the French and Irish in Paris continued throughout the summer of 1803, with little apparent progress. When Dalton was sent on a mission by the minister of war, General Oliver Harty assumed his role as intermediary between Berthier and the Irish. Born in Ireland in 1746, he had emigrated to France at the age of sixteen and entered the Irish Brigade in which three of his uncles were already serving. He rose to the rank of general in the revolutionary army, having served under General Hoche on the ill-fated expedition to Bantry Bay in 1796. On Berthier's staff in 1803, and despite his commitment to France, he was sincerely interested in Irish affairs and planned to accompany the projected expedition to his native land.[7] It was in a meeting with Harty on 30 June that Emmet first suggested that the French government employ the Irish emigrants in a military capacity. "Some of our countrymen are already in great distress,"[8] he told the general, and pointed out that France could employ them in the same manner that the English were employing the French emigrants in the English army. Perhaps, he went on, the reestablishment of a corps similar to the old Irish Brigade, which had served the Bourbon monarchy so well for a hundred years, would be appropriate. Harty did not reply in the affirmative, but the wheels soon began to turn that led to the formation of the Irish Legion.

In the second week of July, Harty wrote to John McGuire, one of the more prominent Irish exiles in Paris, who had had to flee Ireland because of his participation in the rebellion of 1798, requesting that he gather information on the Irish exiles. He was specifically asked to draw up a list of names of Irishmen in France, their position in the United Irishmen movement, and the sufferings they had endured at the hands of the English. More important, and the primary purpose of McGuire's task, was to inquire which of them would be willing to serve, either in a military or civil capacity, in the event of an expedition to Ireland.[9] McGuire began at once to collect the requested information, and a lively enthusiasm spread through the Irish community in Paris. The exiles expressed great interest in serving as a part of an expedition against the common enemy. However, if the inquiry was joyfully received by the Irish, both O'Connor, with whom Harty had been communicating on a regular basis, and Emmet were a bit vexed that they had been bypassed in favor of McGuire.[10]

The French had bypassed O'Connor and Emmet in favor of McGuire because the latter was considered neutral in the growing conflict between the two Irish leaders. Indeed, relations between O'Connor and Emmet were worsening, if that were possible, in light of the fact that they had prepared to fight a duel in 1802. O'Connor denied that there was an active directory of the United Irishmen in Dublin and thus that Emmet had any legitimate claim to speak for the Irish. Therefore, even if his own claim as official spokesman was weak, when it was coupled with his influence in Paris among the exiles and his friends in Ireland, he believed that the French government should treat with him exclusively. Emmet considered himself the only agent for the "Provisional Government of Ireland." O'Connor's denial of the existence of the Directory in Dublin proved, he said, that the Irish at home chose not to communicate with Mr. O'Connor because they did not trust him. O'Connor, through his close friend and ardent supporter, Thomas Corbet, made overtures to Emmet for cooperation for the good of their unfortunate homeland.[11] But Emmet, who distrusted and personally disliked O'Connor, refused to have anything to do with him. He believed that O'Connor was too ambitious; that he wanted to command the expedition to Ireland; and that he wanted to become the "First Consul of Ireland."[12] Although O'Connor believed that Emmet was forming a faction opposed to him, he was willing, and by mid-September even anguished, for some form of cooperation.[13]

Within the Irish community in Paris there was already taking shape a factionalism that would flow over into the ranks of the Legion. The "Friends" of O'Connor and the "Friends" of Emmet formed a split in the ranks of the United Irishmen in France that only hurt the cause to which they were all devoted. Miles Byrne, a United Irishman who arrived in Paris in mid-September 1803, wrote in his *Memoirs:*

> When I arrived at Paris, I should immediately have waited on Mr. Arthur O'Connor, had I not heard that he and Mr. Thomas Addis Emmet were on the worst terms; circumstanced as I was with the latter [Emmet], I could not think of becoming acquainted with his enemy. No one, however,

regretted more than I did to learn that two such men should not be on speaking terms with each other; they, whom my countrymen at home looked upon as their most strenuous agents with the French Government, and as consulting with one another at every moment to see what was best to be done. . . . Their misunderstanding must indeed have been of a very serious nature. . . .[14]

The French Government found this internal strife annoying, petty, and inconvenient. Yet Bonaparte had already set the machinery in motion for the invasion of the British Isles,[15] and he did not intend to allow a feud between two Irishmen to have negative effects on his plans. The French were not really sure who spoke for Ireland, but in fact O'Connor and Emmet were the only acknowledged leaders with whom they had contact. As they had no direct communications with Ireland, they had little choice with respect to whom they would negotiate. They, therefore, adopted what might loosely be called a policy. They recognized O'Connor as the man to deal with on military matters and Emmet on most other matters.[16] This was not a happy state of affairs for either the French or the Irish, yet it continued into the late fall at which time Bonaparte let it be known through General Harty that he wanted the Irish to form a committee that would include both Emmet and O'Connor.[17]

By the end of August 1803, Bonaparte had decided upon the formation of a battalion that would be composed entirely of Irishmen or sons of Irishmen. The decree was dated 31 August, but it remained a closely guarded secret within the ministry of war until early December. During the interval, a number of matters relating to personnel needed attention. As it was anticipated that the officer corps of this new unit would be recruited from the ranks of the United Irishmen already in France, it was necessary to determine exactly who they were, what were their qualifications, and what rank they should be given. General Harty set up what he called a "committee" to screen the Irish who had indicated to McGuire that they were willing to serve in a military capacity. Colonel Dalton was also on the committee, and Emmet believed, although he could not be certain, that the third member was Arthur O'Connor. Whatever the make-up of the committee, it would appear that Harty and Dalton made the final decisions, most likely, with some input on the part of O'Connor.[18] Emmet complained bitterly in his "Diary" that O'Connor was securing commissions for men who either had never been United Irishmen, or whose activities in the movement and loyalties to the cause were questionable.[19] It is difficult to determine just how much influence O'Connor had on Harty in the early selection of officers. It would seem that he had greater influence in securing promotions for his supporters after the Legion had been formed.[20] It is interesting to note at this point that O'Connor himself turned down the rank of *Chef d'Escadron* in the French army. Emmet suggested that he did so because he believed that he had as much right to the rank of general as had Napper Tandy.[21] Tandy had been given the rank of general by the Directory on the eve of the 1796 expedition to Bantry Bay. Like O'Connor, he had had no previous military experience.

The last insurrection associated with the United Irishmen took place in Dublin in mid-August of 1803.[22] The principal figure was Robert Emmet, brother of Thomas Addis. The insurrection, which was limited to Dublin, was crushed before it could pick up momentum in the surrounding counties, and Robert Emmet was tried and executed. News that their kinsmen were on the march again caused much excitement in Paris among the exiles. The full extent of the disaster was not known until Miles Byrne arrived in the capital on 17 September. The message that he brought was the necessity of a French expedition "with the utmost speed."[23] Only Dublin had risen. The rest of Ireland was still awaiting the French. But the French government continued to argue that a small expedition was the mistake of 1798, and that neither the ships nor the soldiers nor supplies were ready for a large one. Thus, to the frustration of Emmet and many of his compatriots, the French gave assurances that the preparations for the expedition to Ireland were being accelerated, but no move was made to support the Dublin rising.

In the fall of 1803, the division between Emmet and O'Connor was, if possible, even greater, while the creation of an Irish legion was about to become a reality. At the same time, Dalton was speaking of the Irish being "united into a corps" when the expedition was ready to sail.[24] He already had a list of Irishmen who were to receive commissions, and the rank for which they were recommended. But he made it clear to Emmet that those Irish who did not show a willingness to cooperate, that is, enter the service of France, would be treated as English subjects and sent to the prisoner of war camp at Verdun.[25] This scarcely veiled threat to intern Irishmen who would not take service with the French reflected a growing concern on the part of the French Government with respect to English spies. On 17 November, Dalton told Emmet "that some United Irishmen, whom he could not name, had let suspicion fall on their conduct by being too intimate with Englishmen. Perhaps, said he, their circumstances may have forced them but, he continued, they would soon be cared for when they received their marching orders."[26] It was almost as if the Legion was being created to rid Paris of a troublesome, or even suspicious, foreign element. In early July, at the time McGuire was soliciting information about those who were willing to serve in an expedition to Ireland, General Harty was complaining that the Irish were holding meetings, and the conduct of some was such as to offend the French government.

In a serious effort to establish a credible body that could speak for the Irish, both in exile and at home, the First Consul made it known through Colonel Dalton that he desired the establishment of a committee that would include both Arthur O'Connor and Thomas Addis Emmet. O'Connor, who had been striving to get Emmet to work with him ever since the latter had arrived in Paris, willingly agreed to be a member of the proposed committee. In point of fact, Emmet believed that O'Connor had for some months been encouraging the French to create such an instrument. It would be extremely difficult for Emmet to reject such a committee and thus O'Connor would gain the cooperation of Emmet, which the latter had previously, and consistently, refused. Whether this is true or not, it came very close to being the fact. Emmet, who did not wish to associate his name in any way with that of O'Connor, felt obliged to accept the creation of a committee, but with conditions. The first of these was that it should not be a committee of two, but rather that the committee should "be composed of such a number as that our passions and prejudices and differences would be lost in the cooler feelings of others,"[27] Emmet also received an assurance from Dalton that the French Government would communicate only with the committee once it was established. Finally, both O'Connor and Emmet would submit names of men whom they believed to be qualified to serve on such a committee. Although Emmet saw no need for such a committee and was pessimistic about the good it could do for Ireland, he was fearful that his refusal to cooperate in this endeavor, coming from the First Consul as it did, might be used at some future time to enable the French to renege on promises that had already been made to him and to the Irish.[28]

Much to the disappointment and frustration of the French, the committee was never formed. Emmet recommended for membership on the committee Hampden Evans, John Sweetman, MacNeven, James Joseph McDonnell and William Lawless. O'Connor offered the names of John Chambers, Richard McCormick, Hampden Evans, and John Sweetman. But when Dalton came up with the final list of names to form the committee, in mid-January 1804, it read as follows: Emmet, O'Connor, Sweetman, Chambers, Sampson, Arthur McMahon, and a "friend" of Dalton's. Evans had refused to serve. At this point Emmet declared that the make-up of the committee was unacceptable to him as Chambers, Sampson, and McMahon were O'Connor's nominees and he, Emmet, did not consider them to be neutral in the conflict between himself and O'Connor. Emmet also raised the question of allowing the men of the Irish Legion, which by this time was taking shape at Morlaix, in Brittany, to vote their approval of his membership and, by implication, that of the other names being put forward. But Dalton would have no part of such a democratic process. The talking continued, but the committee never materialized. At one point the French even dropped the idea of a committee and suggested that Emmet and O'Connor "should act together without any committee."[29]

The final chapter of the personal conflict between O'Connor and Emmet was marked by the French government's throwing its support behind O'Connor. On 24 February 1804, O'Connor was appointed a general of division in the French army and assigned to the army at Brest, which was under the command of General Pierre François Charles Augereau. Emmet believed that it was because he and his friends were republicans that Bonaparte supported O'Connor, whom he believed was not.[30] The fact is that Emmet had never liked Bonaparte and had always been mistrustful of his intentions with respect to Ireland. He thought the Irish in France were being used to further the ends and the ambitions of the First Consul rather than for the independence and freedom of the Irish people. During the spring of 1804, he gradually withdrew from active negotiations with the French and remained just outside of Paris in the country house he had rented. He maintained an active correspondence with his friends in the Legion but had little contact with the French government. In October of the same year, he sailed with his family to New York where he became a moderately successful lawyer. Emmet's departure, first from the political scene and then from France, did not bring to an end the division within the ranks of the United Irishmen in exile. The factionalism, which began before the Irish Legion had even been created, scarred the first year of its existence, caused good officers to resign their commissions, and took the life of a fine man (Thomas Corbet) in a hideous duel.

The French government had decided to create the Irish Legion by the end of the summer of 1803, but it was not until 7 December that it became known publicly. The official roster of officers of the 1st Battalion of the Irish Legion indicated that twenty-nine commissions were signed on 6 December, followed eight days later by an additional nine. By the end of January there were forty-three officers and between ten and twelve noncommissioned officers.[31] Adjutant Commander Bernard MacSheehy was named by the First Consul as commander of the Legion and the one responsible for its organization, training, and general well-being. He reported directly to General François-Xavier Donzelot, who was Augereau's chief of staff. MacSheehy had been born in Dublin and educated at the Irish College in Paris. He had not yet finished his studies in 1793, when he joined the French army to avoid being arrested as a British subject. He served on the staff of General Hoche, and in 1796 he traveled to Ireland to assess the conditions in that land prior to the military expedition. Two years later, he sailed with General Bonaparte to Egypt. He was twenty-nine years of age when he received command of the Legion.

His immediate subordinate was *Chef de Bataillon* James Bartholomew Blackwell. Like MacSheehy, he too had been born in Ireland (Ennis, County Clare) and studied at the Irish College in Paris. He studied medicine at the University of Paris, but joined the army before completing his studies. He embraced the Revolution and took part in the expeditions to Ireland in 1796 and 1798. Following the latter, he was turned over to the British by the senate of Hamburg and spent several years in Kilmainham gaol. Shortly after his return to France, he was named battalion commander for the Legion. Despite his title and rank, it was not Blackwell, but MacSheehy, who ran the Irish Legion. MacSheehy issued the orders of the day, secured promotions for the men, communicated with army headquarters, and made all serious decisions affecting the battalion.[32]

Many of the men who joined the Legion when it was formed late in 1803 had been living in Paris. Their lifestyles varied greatly depending upon their ability to acquire money from Ireland once they had arrived in France and the amount of money they had been able to bring with them when they left their native land. Some of them lived comfortably like John Tennent who had the good fortune to be able to bring with him enough money, which he wisely invested, to live from the interest.[33] O'Connor, Emmet, and MacNeven, also lived comfortably on incomes from Ireland. Others, like the Corbet brothers Thomas and William, who were teaching English at French schools, supported themselves by employment as best they could. Still others, such as William Lawless, were able to make arrangements through friends or relatives in Ireland to receive funds on somewhat of a regular basis, which enabled them to live without want and even to lend money to their less fortunate comrades.[34] But some of these men, particularly the newer arrivals, like Miles Byrne, had very limited resources and lived quite frugally in very modest, if not poor, conditions, receiving assistance from time to time from their more affluent countrymen.[35] In October 1803, William Lawless offered to lend money to Miles Byrne to help him live until he would be in a better financial situation. However, the greatest number of these Irish found themselves in France with meager resources. These were men who had already made great sacrifices. Some had spent years in prison, others had lost their lands or other forms of wealth, while still others had suffered physical abuse at the hands of the Anglo-Irish government. As a result of these sufferings and misfortunes, these men were fiercely nationalistic and lived for the day when they could return to Ireland and renew the struggle.

Miles Byrne, described his lifestyle during the fall of 1803 and declared: "Mr. (Valentin William) Derry told me the Irish refugees, with few exceptions, were living in this frugal way, endeavouring to make their money last, as I was doing. . . ."[36] After referring to the room in which he was lodged as "my miserable closet," in the rue du Bac, he described his typical dinner at M. Moreau's in the rue de la Harpe: "Our dinner consisted of two dishes 'mouton au navet' six sous; a 'small beefsteak' seven sous; a quarter of a bottle of wine, two sous and a half; plenty of bread, two sous; water at discretion. The meat was tolerably good, and as M. Moreau was a capital cook, everything was well prepared, and the dinner varied each day."[37] He then moved from the rue du Bac into a room rented by M. Moreau for which he paid twelve franks a month. "Every morning at nine o'clock," he continued with his description of his life in those difficult days, "two sous worth of boiled milk was brought to my room, with a three sous loaf of bread. This loaf sufficed for breakfast and dinner; so my two meals cost about eleven pence per day, or twenty-two sous; I dined between four and five o'clock, the student's hour.—I only paid my bill at the end of the week. . . . As I dined often with friends in town, this note seldom amounted to more than six francs."[38]

Some of the exiles obtained positions as teachers of English in French schools and in this manner were able to support themselves. In 1803 Thomas Corbet was teaching at the Prytanée in Paris and his brother William, who had attended Trinity College before his expulsion in 1798 for political activities, was teaching at the military college at Saint Cyr.[39] Valentine Derry, another of the refugees of 1798, was teaching English at the military college of La Flèche before he joined the Legion in 1803. Another, Patrick Gallagher, who had a wife and children, was employed in the shipping business in Bordeaux.

Those Irishmen who were unemployed in Paris began their day by going to the London Coffee House in the rue Jacob on the Left Bank where most of them lived. They would meet their comrades, read the *Argus,* the newspaper published in English by Lewis Goldsmith, and learn the latest news of Ireland. It became a ritual for many of the exiles, and the day was not complete until they had seen Madame Lecomte, the proprietress of the Coffee House. In the evenings, having little money to frequent the cafes they took long walks about Paris, which usually included a stroll beneath the arches in the garden of the Palais Royal. Hampden Evens and his wife frequently invited their friends, and friends of their friends, to their home after the dinner hour. Their home functioned very much like the "salon" of late eighteenth century Paris and was a great source of joy for many of the Irish who were living alone and many miles from their families and friends.[40]

During the fall of 1803, there was a constant flow of rumors to the effect that the expedition to Ireland was ready to sail, and the Irish in Paris would be employed by the French to rid their homeland of English domination. When the first letters of commission arrived on 7 December, many of the newly created officers were ready to set out for Morlaix at once. They were not as homogeneous a group as might be believed at first glance. It is true that they were all Irish born or sons of Irishmen, and they all desired to be a part of the expedition to Ireland. But here the similarity ended. In the summer of 1804, after he had had eight months to become acquainted with these men, Adjutant Commander MacSheehy described them and their reasons for joining the French army in a letter to the minister of war. On 24 July 1804, he wrote:

This will, without doubt, provide you with some observations on the officer personnel that is here [with the Legion]. It may also direct your action with respect to the Irish who will arrive in the future.

It is necessary to divide them into four classes.

1. The men of talent, of property or of influence in their own country who, having taken an active part in the revolutions in Ireland, were forcibly obliged to leave or who feared they would be victimized as a result of their conduct or their principles.

2. Irishmen born in France; former officers of the Irish Brigade, etc., etc.

3. Those who came to France out of curiosity, etc., etc., and were then arrested as prisoners of war after the rupture of the peace of Amiens.

4. Those who have left England or Ireland for speculation, for bad conduct, bankruptcy and even because of theft, assassination, etc., etc., etc.

1. This first group must be considered as members of the United Irishmen and were sought by the government [of Ireland]. It is unnecessary to give the details of the service that they would be able to render to a French army in attracting [Irish] partisans as well as procuring the resources necessary to wage war [in Ireland]. They exercise a genuine influence among their countrymen, and will bring to us all of the moral and physical force of Ireland.

2. Those with Irish origins will be of no less use. French by education and birth they will reestablish the bonds that unite us to the Irish. Moreover, these officers, for the most part, having previously served in the Irish Brigade, will be very necessary for the instruction of the troops who must be raised in Ireland.

3. The men who came to France out of curiosity and for other reasons; and those arrested at the time [the war was renewed] as prisoners of war, etc., should inspire in us a true mistrust. Just one of these dangerous men could cause the greatest damage, and unless one is absolutely sure of these

individuals, I am convinced of the necessity to remove them [from the Legion].

4. It is the same with the Irish of this group, and with even better reason. Furthermore, these will be ready to make all sorts of the most vile trouble. They will compromise the reputation of the Legion and instead of being helpful to us, these individuals of the last two groups will not hesitate to throw the most hateful suspicions on the Irish [of the Legion] once we are in their country and these same suspicions will be reflected on the French army. . . .[41]

Adjutant Commander MacSheehy was quite correct in defining the first three groups of men who joined the Legion, and his evaluation of the first and second is good. However, his fourth category does not seem to be found in the ranks of the officer corps, and he gave no indication of who might fall into that despicable group. Furthermore, his evaluation of those who might fit his third group was extremely harsh. By late July 1804, when he wrote his evaluation of the men of the Legion, MacSheehy had become disillusioned with the Irish Legion. Factionalism and the internal bickering of the men, who were themselves becoming frustrated over the endless delays of the expedition to Ireland, as well as the interference and pressures from army headquarters, where General O'Connor's influence was still a factor to be reckoned with, were taking their toll on the adjutant commander. He must have sensed the dissatisfaction of his immediate superiors, who successfully had him removed from command of the Legion just weeks after he had bypassed them in the chain of command and had written the above letter directly to the minister of war.

Of the forty-six men who had been given commissions in the French army by the end of January, thirteen were named captain, sixteen were named lieutenant, and seventeen second lieutenant. There were also a few noncommissioned officers and men but their numbers were small and remained so throughout the first two years of the Legion's existence. On 11 October 1804, ten months after the Legion had been formed and when there were sixty-six officers on the roster, there were only twenty-two noncommissioned officers and soldiers.[42] No officer received a rank above that of captain. The Irish were given to understand that upon their landing in Ireland there would be mass promotions as new regiments would be formed with the volunteers who were expected to flock to the support of the small French army. Captains would receive the brevets of colonel or lieutenant colonel; lieutenants would be promoted to the rank of major or captain, etc.[43] Thus while many of the men accepted rank that they believed was beneath that which they deserved, they all expected promotions once the expedition sailed. Needless to say, few of them had the qualifications for the rank of captain or even lieutenant in the French army. What command they may have exercised in Ireland was over untrained and undisciplined militia or guerrilla bands in the hills. As MacSheehy wrote the minister of war, and as was confirmed by General Donzelot after his inspection on 11 October 1804, the officers of the Legion had little knowledge of military tactics or strategy, the use of artillery, or the ability even to drill troops.[44]

In 1804 the Legion was composed of men whose average age was thirty-two years. The youngest, William A. O'Maraud, was only nineteen, while the oldest, John Gibbons, was sixty-three. However, fifty-five percent of the officers were between thirty and thirty-nine.[45] They were, on the whole, an educated group of men, but only a small number of them had had any previous military service. William J. MacNeven and Patrick St. Leger had been educated as medical doctors, while Patrick MacMahon was a Protestant minister. Not only had Thomas and William Corbet taught English at French colleges, but Arthur MacMahon, John Burgess, and Valentine Derry had also been employed as professors of English at St. Cyr, the Prytanée, and the college of La Flèche. Others had been educated at Trinity College, Dublin, or the Irish College in Paris. Their numbers further included men in commerce, like Patrick Gallagher, and artisans, like the tailor John MacGuire. There were also professional soldiers who joined the Legion. Louis Lacy and Patrick Paul O'Kelly (O'Kelley) had served in the Irish regiments of the Spanish army, while William O'Meara and William Barker had served in the Irish Brigade before joining the Legion.[46]

The social and economic status of these men in their native Ireland was clearly upper class. Their lifestyle on the Continent may have been that of the French students or petite bourgeoisie, but they were, as a group, either men of influence and wealth, or the sons of families that possessed those attributes. They had been accustomed to a much better life than either the one they had been living in Paris in 1803 or the one they were living in the Legion in 1804.

The men began to arrive at Morlaix (in Brittany) shortly after the first of the year, in accordance with the date stipulated in their orders. They received an allowance for their transportation, but few, if any, found it adequate to make the journey. Those who did not have additional funds of their own were able to get assistance from T. A. Emmet, who had been given a sum of money by an anonymous donor to aid Irish emigrants.[47] Most of them settled their affairs and traveled by post stage, although some, like Miles Byrne and Hugh Ware, made the journey on foot. Byrne and Ware decided that they would walk from Paris to Brest, not because they lacked the money for the stagecoach, which Byrne would have had to borrow, but because they felt they needed the conditioning to prepare them for the rugged campaign that they expected to undertake in Ireland shortly after their arrival in the west.[48]

The selection of Morlaix as the mustering point for the Legion was dictated because of its location thirty-seven miles east of Brest, which was designated as the port of departure for the projected expedition to Ireland. An army of 15,000 to 20,000 men was being formed in the vicinity of that fine seaport under the command of General Augereau. However, there seems to have been a political, as well as a military, consideration in choosing Morlaix rather than any one of a number of towns in western Brittany for the quartering and training of troops for the coming campaign. Morlaix was the depot for British prisoners of war who were to be either repatriated or sent east to prisoner of war camps. By organizing the Irish Legion at Morlaix, the First Consul could be sure that the English government would hear of it and believe that an expedition to Ireland was imminent. This could serve one of two purposes. It might encourage the English to negotiate a settlement with France, on French terms, which Bonaparte would have welcomed; or it could force the English to send additional troops from England to Ireland to oppose such an invasion. In the latter case, the main French army that was being assembled along the Channel would meet less resistance when it landed in England. There was yet one other consideration. Bonaparte had been extremely displeased with the English government's continual support of the French *émigrés* after the Peace of Amiens. He would now let it be known that he was making good use of the Irish "émigrés." Thus the Irish were, in fact, being used as leverage in seeking a political solution and, at the same time, as a decoy for the principal military operation being planned. In return they were promised assistance in gaining the independence of their native Ireland.

Upon their arrival at Morlaix, the new officers made their own living arrangements. They took rooms and their meals at the local inns, hotels or with families. By mid-January the tailors were making their new green uniforms and Adjutant Commander MacSheehy was seeing that they were issued their swords and other necessary military equipment. New men arrived almost daily during January and were immediately introduced to the military routine. They were instructed in marching, the use of firearms and artillery, and in infantry and cavalry tactics. There was a great deal of enthusiasm and energy expended in these first weeks as everyone believed that the expedition to Ireland would sail in the immediate future, and the men wished everything to be ready for that eagerly awaited day when they would once again set foot on Irish soil.[49]

Adjutant Commander MacSheehy was not entirely pleased with the newly arriving Irish officers, and he was not at all hesitant to express himself to General Berthier. He believed it was unwise to give so many commissions in the French army to men who had virtually no military experience. Such political appointments, in his opinion, would give the Irish a "feeble impression of the rank of officer," and at the same time, it would not leave room for better qualified and more deserving men who would rally to the French—and Irish—cause in the near future. There were places in the Irish battalions for only so many officers. He felt that some of the men who received commissions should have been given the lesser rank of noncommissioned officer.[50] Despite these general views, MacSheehy had no real influence on who was given a commission, or what rank they received until February when he was able to make his own recommendations. He was then invited to submit to the minister of war the names of junior officers to be promoted. The adjutant commander took full advantage of this charge to recommend promotions for men whom he felt had been slighted and, with the concurrence of General Berthier, eighteen Irish officers benefited from MacSheehy's favorable opinion. Promoted from the rank of lieutenant to captain were Valentin Derry, William Dowdall, Pat Gallagher, Thomas MacKey, Eugene O'Herne, Austin O'Meally, John Sweeny, Eugene Therne and Hugh Ware; from second lieutenant to lieutenant were John Allen, John Burgess, Miles Byrne, John Cummins, Jerome Fitzhenry, Christophe Martin, Paul Murray, and Edmond St. Leger.[51] Whereas the original rank given to the Irish officers by General Berthier was heavily influenced by political considerations, based on the recommendations of Thomas A. Emmet, Arthur O'Connor, General Harty and Colonel Dalton, MacSheehy's were, in the great majority of cases, directly related to military aptitude and talent. It should be noted, however, that MacSheehy later secured the promotion of his cousin Patrick MacSheehy, who possessed few, if any, of the qualities necessary to command.[52]

The British prisoners of war at Morlaix were interrogated by MacSheehy and his English-speaking Irish. The information that they acquired on Ireland from the Irish who were in the service of the English was forwarded to the Minister of War.[53] These Irish prisoners of war were viewed by MacSheehy as prospective recruits for the Legion he was organizing. He suggested to General Berthier that those who were deemed suitable for service in the French army be allowed to enlist.[54] Many of the Irish in the British navy had either been pressed into service or had reluctantly taken service with the English to escape the miserable conditions at home. These Irish, although by no means all of them, would prefer serving in an Irish Legion of the French army to spending the rest of the war in a French prisoner of war camp. Some even welcomed the opportunity to return to

Ireland with the French and fight against the English to win independence for their homeland. To this end, MacSheehy proposed to the minister of war that he be permitted to send Irish officers to the various camps where British prisoners of war were detained for the purpose of recruiting Irishmen to join the Legion.[55] By 31 March, MacSheehy had convinced Augereau and his chief of staff, General Donzelot, of the desirability of recruiting Irish prisoners of war to serve in the Legion. On that date Donzelot wrote to the Minister of War:

> At the present time the Irish Legion is made-up only of officers; in order to facilitate their instruction [training] and to give to the corps stability, it would be useful for it to have a certain number of soldiers. I propose that they could be found among the English prisoners of war, of whom it will be found many Irishmen who would, with pleasure, take service with the Legion.
>
> We are able, in this case, to send intelligent Irish officers to the depots with precise instructions. It is desirable that this recruitment would be carried out promptly.
>
> Perhaps it would also be possible [he added, at the end of this letter] to recruit Irishmen in Hanover.[56]

Paris picked up on those recommendations by MacSheehy and Donzelot, and in the summer of 1804 Irish officers were sent to Verdun, Valenciennes, and other prisoner of war camps to interview and recruit men for the Legion. An early example of this type of recruiting was Edward Masterson. He was confined at the prisoner of war camp at Valenciennes at the time he was recruited (14 December 1803) and given the rank of captain in the Legion.[57]

The early months of 1804 were critical to the development of the Legion. The relationship between the officers and their commander, as well as with one another, set the tone for at least the first year. Generally speaking, all went well during January and February. It was true that many of the men believed that they deserved higher rank than the one that they had received upon entering the army, but the promotions of 22 March did much to remove the earlier disappointments. Furthermore, the anticipation that they would very soon be on the high seas returning to Ireland (where additional promotions would take place) and where war against the English would override the quarrels, jealousies, and petty bickering that was so common among soldiers far from danger and engaged in dull and boring garrison life.

The first significant problem, which had devastating effects upon the men of the Legion, was the antagonism that developed between Adjutant Commander MacSheehy and Arthur O'Connor. The origin of this animosity was the First Consul's naming of O'Connor to be general of division in the French army in February 1804. When news of O'Connor's rank reached Morlaix early in March, MacSheehy was shocked and angered. O'Connor had not come up through the ranks. He owed his generalship to political intrigue for he had little knowledge of military affairs and no experience. The expectation that he would be given command of the Irish Legion, and thus the Irish army once it would be formed in Ireland, infuriated MacSheehy. There is no documentary evidence to show that he, Mac-Sheehy, expected to command the Irish on the expedition to Ireland, but he may well have considered himself to be the logical choice. He was, after all, a native born-Irishman, a veteran soldier who had risen through the ranks in the service of France and General Bonaparte, and was presiding over the organization and training of the Irish in the service of France. But with O'Connor holding the rank of general of division and assigned to Augereau's staff at Brest, it became apparent to MacSheehy that it was O'Connor, not himself, who was being groomed for command of the Legion.[58]

One of General O'Connor's first acts upon receiving his commission was to write to Adjutant Commander MacSheehy to inform the latter of his new rank and to order him to send a detailed account of everything that had taken place at Morlaix relating to the Irish Legion.[59] The adjutant commander refused to transmit any information to the general relating to the organization or training of the Legion on the grounds that he had instructions from the minister of war to correspond directly with him. He also wrote to Berthier explaining his action, asking that it be approved, and enclosed a copy of O'Connor's letter.[60] O'Connor had not been given any command at the time he was named lieutenant general. Rather, Berthier wrote to Augereau on 6 March that two days earlier he had ordered General O'Connor to join the Army of Brest, and that he, Augereau, should make use of him as he saw fit.[61] Thus, O'Connor was not given command of the Legion, or any other unit. Augereau, saddled with a political general, simply attached him to his staff, with no actual authority over MacSheehy or the Legion. The adjutant commander continued to report directly to Berthier and to correspond with Augereau through his chief of staff, General Donzelot.

Despite the fact that MacSheehy was able to establish his independence from General O'Connor, Miles Byrne, a lieutenant in the Legion at the time, wrote in his *Memoirs* that this was a turning point for the adjutant commander:

Everything seemed to be going on well, whether from envy and jealousy at seeing Arthur O'Connor raised to the rank of general of division, then the highest in the French army, without having passed through any of the inferior ranks, or for other motives, we could not learn, but all at once, adjutant general MacSheehy became anything but an impartial chief.[62]

MacSheehy was not the only officer of the Legion who resented the rank of general given to Arthur O'Connor. The friends of Thomas Addis Emmet, who had had nothing to do with O'Connor is Paris in 1803, were quite disappointed at what was interpreted as the victory of O'Connor over Emmet. At the same time, the "friends" of O'Connor serving in the Legion rejoiced. The factionalism within the ranks of the Legion can thus be dated from March 1804, when the news of the general's appointment reached Brittany. Still, all of the dissatisfaction in the Legion was not caused by, nor did it center around, O'Connor's high rank. Officers who had not received promotion on 22 March, and who felt that they should hold higher rank, expressed disappointment. A case in point was that of Lieutenant Thomas Markey. He wrote to MacSheehy in rather curt terms asking for an explanation of why he had not been named captain.[63]

During the spring of 1804, the Legion moved from Morlaix because of increasingly crowded conditions. The influx of some fifty Irish officers into a small town that was already housing the officers of an infantry division and its supporting services led to this relocation of the Legion some forty-five miles south at Quimper. Although it was a larger town, on the south coast of Brittany, Quimper proved to be unsuitable for the Legion. In a 31 March letter, General Donzelot pointed out to the minister of war that it already had the officers of the *état-major* of the 2nd Division and those of the 1st Battalion of the 37th Regiment of the line.[64] Therefore, in late April, the Legion was once again on the march. This time it settled in the small town of Carhaix, about fifty-five miles east of Brest in the center of the peninsula. The Irish would remain at Carhaix until the fall of the same year.

The men of the Legion were not particularly happy at Carhaix. They felt exiled so far from Brest and from the sea. It raised doubts in their minds about the seriousness of the French to send them with an expedition to Ireland. From Morlaix, they had gone to Brest and had seen the ships in the harbor being prepared for the expedition and had received news of the preparations on a regular basis. Even at Quimper they saw ships at anchor in the bay that could transport them to Ireland. But at Carhaix, they were isolated from other French units as well as from the sea.[65] MacSheehy was even more displeased with the new location. He complained to the minister of war and to General Augereau that Carhaix was unsuited for preparing the Legion to enter upon a campaign. Everything was lacking, he said, from adequate living quarters to training facilities and material.[66] Berthier tried to console him by assuring him that everything needed would be provided. The minister wrote to Augereau, ordering him to send Generals O'Connor and Donzelot to Carhaix with instructions to provide the Irish with whatever it was that they needed.[67] Thus the Legion remained at Carhaix and continued its training. However, the summer of 1804 was not a pleasant one for the men of the Legion, and it ended in the death of one officer and the resignation and removal of others.

General Augereau was becoming increasingly dissatisfied with the adjutant commander of the Irish. He resented MacSheehy's special privilege of being allowed to correspond directly with the minister of war. All other battalion, regimental, and division commanders in the Army of Brest were required to communicate upward through military channels to Augereau, the commander of the army. On 24 April 1804, the general wrote to the minister of war in order to counter the complaints of MacSheehy. In this letter, he also took the opportunity to point out to Berthier that the adjutant commander and the Irish Legion were a part of the army that he commanded, and that it was inconsistent with military procedures for MacSheehy to communicate directly with the minister of war.[68] To counter MacSheehy's complaints, he assured Berthier, on 25 May, that he would care for all of the needs of the Irish at Carhaix.[69] MacSheehy had not only been given the unique privilege of direct access to the Minister of War at the time he was given command of the Irish Legion, he was also quite well known to General Berthier. He had served on the General's staff on the Egyptian Campaign when Berthier was General Bonaparte's chief of staff. Friction between MacSheehy and army headquarters at Brest was increasing. First it was between MacSheehy and General O'Connor, then between the adjutant commander and General Augereau. Fortunately, he still had the support of the minister of war back in Paris.

There was at least one bright spot in the gray sky of Brittany. The Irish Legion received its own flag shortly after the creation of the empire. On 18 May 1804, the French Empire was proclaimed and General Bonaparte, First Consul of the Republic, became the Emperor Napoleon I. All of the regiments of the army received new imperial flags. The Irish Legion, which had no flag at the time, received a very handsome banner. On one side of the green banner was written "Napoleon I, Empereur des Francais, à la legion irlandaise." The other side had a harp with the words "l'independance d'Irlande." The Irish were extremely pleased with the color and the wording, and they thanked the new emperor in glowing terms.[70]

The establishment of the empire was also the catalyst of a major disaster within the Legion. All military personnel were required to take an oath to support the new imperial constitution and of fidelity to the new emperor. Therefore, on 2 June, MacSheehy issued an order of the day summoning the officers, noncommissioned officers, and men[71] to the parade ground at 12:30 P.M. the next day. The purpose of the assembly was for every man in the Legion to swear the oath that had been prescribed by the Senate on 18 May of that year.[72] At the designated hour on that Sunday afternoon, the men of the Legion were forming their ranks when Captain John Sweeny, passing in front of the formation, made comments to MacSheehy questioning the nature of the oath to be taken and how it might pertain to him as an Irishman and to his relationship with Ireland. He further declared that it would be the first time in his life that he had ever taken such an oath. MacSheehy at once reminded him that France had taken him in as a refugee, that the Emperor Napoleon had given him employment as an officer in the French army, and that Napoleon was the only hope that the Irish people had for the liberation of their country. Without further words, Sweeny took his place in the ranks of the Legion. Then the adjutant commander announced that any man who felt that he could not, or did not wish to, take the oath to support the new constitution and the emperor was free to leave the parade ground. No man left the ranks. The oath was then administrated by MacSheehy, and the formation was dismissed.[73]

The following morning, 4 June, the adjutant commander assembled the Council of Administration of the Legion in his quarters in order that its members might sign the report (*Procès Verbal*) that declared that all of the officers and men of the Legion had taken the oath. MacSheehy was the first to sign the document, followed by Battalion Commander Blackwell. However, when it was presented to Captain Thomas Corbet, he declared that he could not sign a document that he knew to be false. When questioned by MacSheehy and asked to name the men who had not taken the oath, Corbet declared that Captain Sweeny had not taken the oath and that "several other officers had followed his example."[74] He refused to name any other officers, but Blackwell then named Lieutenant Patrick Powell.[75] Blackwell further declared that he agreed with Corbet, but at that time he made no attempt to remove his name from the *Procès Verbal*. Lieutenant Edmond St. Leger then sided with Corbet and Blackwell. Thus the document that was forwarded to General Donzelot, which declared that the swearing of the oath of allegiance was unanimous, was signed by Adjutant Commander MacSheehy, Battalion Commander Blackwell, Captains William MacNeven, Joseph Perret, and Patrick MacSheehy. The signatures of Corbet and St. Leger also appear on the document, but under the following statement: "Not believing that the taking of the oath demanded by the Senate of the Consulate, ordered 18 May, 1804, was unanimous, I can not, as a member of the Council of Administration, sign the present *Procès Verbal.*"[76]

Officers of the Legion came to the support of both Sweeny and Powell. Captains William O'Meara, Patrick Gallagher and William Dowdal declared in a written statement, dated 16 June, that they were standing at Sweeny's right and left on the 4th, and that he did take the oath, as did all of the other officers and men on the parade ground.[77] In yet another document, five officers, Lieutenants John Gibbons, Thomas Read, Louis Dupouget, Thomas MacKey, and Second Lieutenant Edward Gibbons, declared that Powell had taken the oath.[78] The only officers who accused Sweeny and Powell of having failed to take the oath were Corbet, St. Leger, and Blackwell.

Blackwell, who had signed the *Procès Verbal* of 4 June declaring that all members of the Legion had taken the oath, wrote to MacSheehy on the 6th saying that he "was of the same opinion as the other two members [Corbet and St. Leger] of the Council of Administration,"[79] and that he wished to retract his signature from the document. His decision to reverse his position was, according to MacSheehy, the result of pressure put on him by Corbet and St. Leger, who were furious when they became aware that the battalion chief's signature remained on the *Procès Verbal* that had been forwarded to army headquarters.[80]

In the evening of 4 June, the day on which the three officers had accused Sweeny and Powell of not taking the oath, the officers and men of the Legion were drilling on the parade ground. At approximately 6:30 P.M., Captain Sweeny walked up to Captain Thomas Corbet and struck him in the face with his fist. Corbet was knocked to the ground by the force of the blow. In the struggle that followed, Corbet was struck several more times. All of the accounts of this affair agree that Sweeny started the fight.[81] Blackwell, who was present on the field, ordered Sweeny to stop his attack upon Corbet, but Sweeny verbally insulted the battalion commander and continued his assault.[82] Captain Patrick MacSheehy, a relative of the adjutant commander, ran to the latter's quarters and announced that there was a fight in progress on the parade ground. The adjutant commander, and Captain John Tennent, who was with him at the time, rushed to the scene of the disturbance and placed all of those whom he believed involved under arrest. His report of the affair only mentioned Sweeny, Thomas Corbet, and Thomas' younger brother William Corbet as having been arrested.[83]

The men under arrest started off the parade ground, but William Corbet returned to the place where MacSheehy and several officers were still standing. In a loud voice he declared, in English, to the adjutant commander: " 'They are a pack of assassins, or we are among a pack of assassins, or words to that effect,' to which Captain Patrick Gallagher responded [also in English] 'You lie you rascal.' "[84] This remark so angered the younger Corbet that he immediately attacked Gallagher with the butt of the musket that he was carrying. At the same moment, Adjutant Commander Mac-Sheehy stepped in front of Gallagher to prevent the attack and was struck on the left arm by the blow that Corbet had meant for Gallagher. The latter grabbed the musket and wrenched it away from the assailant. As he threw it to the ground, he declared: "It would be beneath my dignity to use this musket against you!"[85] Infuriated by the actions of William Corbet, MacSheehy dressed him down with: "How dare you strike an officer! and especially when you are under arrest! I could have you shot for such an act!"[86]

When the men who had been placed under arrest had left the parade ground, the very frustrated MacSheehy turned to Blackwell and declared that he had not fulfilled his duty in that he had not stopped the disorder. Blackwell simply replied: "What would you have me do?"[87] With these words, the unpleasant episode on the parade ground at Carhaix came to an end.[88]

In the days immediately following these events, both Thomas Corbet and Sweeny wrote interesting letters to MacSheehy. On 5 June, Corbet demanded swift justice for the injuries he had suffered at the hands of Sweeny.[89] This was followed the next day by a second letter to MacSheehy in which he said that he understood the events of 4 June were to be submitted to a *Conseil de Guerre,* and that he wished not only to bring charges against Sweeny but also against Captain Gallagher "for the menacing language he used against me."[90] He further stated that his brother William wished to bring charges against Captains Gallagher and MacNeven "for their insolent remarks and lack of military behavior."[91] Then on 8 June, Corbet offered to drop all charges against Sweeny and Gallagher if the two officers would be removed from the Irish Legion.[92] This ploy was undoubtedly a "political" move on the part of Corbet. As both Sweeny and Gallagher were open enemies of General O'Connor[93] and his "friends," their removal would greatly strengthen the position of the Corbets and their supporters who backed O'Connor in the Legion.

When John Sweeny wrote to MacSheehy the day after his attack upon Corbet, he declared that the latter had offended him on the drill field in front of many officers by his "regards, his words and his gestures." He further considered Corbet's denunciation of him to the Council of Administration as an attack upon his honor, the honor of the men of the Legion, and on Ireland itself. With respect to his assault upon Corbet, he wrote: "I only did that which is the custom in my country towards one who does not conform to the ways of an honorable man."[94] Sweeny concluded this three-page letter by accusing Thomas Corbet of being a leader of the "vile intrigues" that had disrupted the tranquility of the Legion since its formation.[95] He made no attempt to apologize. Rather, he said that he acted as one should act when dealing with a man who had no honor and who had called into question his honor and loyalty and that of his native Ireland. The "vile intrigues" to which he referred further underlies the factionalism that had formed along the lines of the pre-Legion division within the ranks of the United Irishmen.[96] The two Corbets, St. Leger, and Blackwell were "friends" of O'Connor, while Sweeny, Gallagher, MacNeven, and Tennent had all been close to Thomas Addis Emmet.

The *Procès Verbal* of 4 June reached army headquarters at Brest by the 7th, and was brought to the attention of Marshal[97] Augereau.[98] In order to determine precisely what the situation was at Carhaix, the marshal ordered General Donzelot to make an on the spot inspection as soon as possible.[99] But before the general arrived at Carhaix, MacSheehy sent to Augereau the letters signed by the fellow officers of Sweeny and Powell attesting to the fact that they had taken the oath of allegiance on the parade ground on 3 June. In a lengthy letter that accompanied the documents the adjutant commander assured the marshal that he should have "no doubts about the loyalty of the Irish Legion. The whole affair was motivated by the personal hatred of some individuals."[100] Just three days earlier he had written a bitter denunciation of Blackwell to Donzelot in which he concluded that the battalion chief had shown himself unfit to command the Irish by his vacillating position with respect to his signature on the *Procès Verbal* and his poor conduct on the parade ground at the time of the fight between Corbet and Sweeny. He further suggested that Blackwell should be removed from his command.[101]

News of the controversial *Procès Verbal* and the fight on the parade ground had reached Paris by the last week of June.[102] On the 27th of that month, the minister of war wrote to Augereau in rather vague terms that he understood that four or five officers of the Irish Legion were involved in some kind of intrigue. "I therefore invite you," he wrote, "to give the necessary orders to send those four or five officers to Rennes where they will have no duties and will be placed under the surveillance of the civil and military authorities."[103] The minister of war also wrote MacSheehy and informed him that he had "invited" Marshal Augereau to take the affair under consideration and, that if he, Augereau, deemed it wise or necessary, he should send the men in question to Rennes. He then instructed Mac-Sheehy to send all pertinent information on the men and the events in question to Marshal Augereau and to communicate directly with the army commander.[104] Berthier clearly did not wish to become involved directly with what he considered to be an "in-house" affair, and he seemed to be a little perturbed that MacSheehy was bringing this matter directly to him. Needless to say, Augereau was quite satisfied that Berthier had ordered MacSheehy to deal directly with him, that is, through "proper" military channels. The adjutant commander, with no other options open to him, cooperated fully with the army commander through General Donzelot.

In accordance with his new instructions MacSheehy wrote to Donzelot and made specific recommendations with respect to the men who were involved in the events of 3–4 June. He recommended the removal from the Legion of Blackwell "for his feeble debauchery," and of Thomas Corbet for his "wretched spirit of intrigue."[105] With respect to Sweeny and William Corbet he was less harsh. He believed that each of them had the qualities of a good soldier, and that they were both influential in the south of Ireland and thus, in the event of an expedition to that country, they would render very valuable service. Nevertheless, they were both guilty of violent actions and should be disciplined. He thought that they might spend a short time in prison at the Chateau de Brest, and then be placed in a French regiment to complete their training and to learn some discipline, and finally be returned to the Legion prior to the expedition to Ireland. Gallagher was considered innocent of any wrong doing. St. Leger had simply been misled by Thomas Corbet and should remain in the Legion without disciplinary action.[106]

The final report on this embarrassing affair was written by Donzelot and sent to Augereau, who in turn sent a copy on to the minister of war. After Donzelot had gathered all of the relevant correspondence and documents, he went to Carhaix and made an on the spot inspection. In what might be called the "official" report, which he entitled "Report on that which took place at Carhaix on 3–4 June, 1804, between Mm. Blackwell, Thomas Corbet, William Corbet, Sweeny, Gallagher, and St. Leger, Officers of the Irish Legion," he first detailed the events of those two days, and then expressed his opinion on each of the men involved and made his recommendations. He criticized Blackwell for his weakness, as exemplified by his first signing the *Procès Verbal* and then retracting his signature, and for his poor handling of the fight between Corbet and Sweeny. He then declared that Blackwell was unfit to command the Irish Legion and recommended that he be relieved of his command and transferred to another regiment. Thomas Corbet's refusal to sign the *Procès Verbal* was seen by the general as political intrigue. He "is young," Donzelot concluded, and "he has talent and a good [military] disposition; but in this circumstance, he had displayed a spirit of intrigue. . . . His departure is necessary for the tranquility of this corps [Legion]."[107] As for Captain Sweeny, he "has too violent of a temperament to remain in this corps. He is capable and has a good military disposition, but he has a turbulent character."[108] William Corbet, he continued, "has made statements, too indiscrete in the presence of other officers to remain in the battalion. He has a pleasant and honest character. He is knowledgeable of military affairs, intelligent, and has a good military disposition."[109] As for Gallagher and St. Leger, he declared that the former "had taken no active part in this affair, [thus] should remain in the battalion";[110] and that the latter "had only followed the example of Thomas Corbet. He should also remain"[111] in the Legion. Thus he recommended that four officers of the Legion should be removed, but he did not ask for, or even suggest, that any further action be taken against them.

Donzelot included in his report statements by General O'Connor and Adjutant Commander MacSheehy on each of the men involved. Their attitudes with respect to each officer is almost predictable when one considers the political alignment that had developed in the Legion. O'Connor had only praise for Blackwell, the Corbets, and St. Leger, all of whom could be considered as "friends" of the general. He particularly chastised Sweeny, and he put down Gallagher as a "political suspect."[112] MacSheehy was a little more objective in his evaluation of these men. Yet in the final analysis his comments were negative on Blackwell and the two Corbets, while more understanding in his criticism of Sweeny. He found no fault with either Gallagher or St. Leger.[113]

By the second half of July, the winds of change began to blow with some intensity and new leadership was given to the Irish Legion. In "Notes Confidentielles" to Marshal Augereau, Donzelot wrote:

> If justice is to be equal [in the Irish Legion] and to avoid all prejudices, it is important that a superior French officer be named to command the Legion. It is necessary that he be a total stranger to all parties and all opinions that divide them. He must see to the well-being and the instruction of everyone without being affected by individual passions.[114]

When the marshal agreed with his assessment of the situation at Carhaix, Donzelot, on 23 July, recommended *Chef de Bataillon* Antoine Petrezzoli to replace Blackwell as commander of the Legion.[115] The latter had become completely frustrated and discouraged as the result of his loss of respect on the part of the Irish officers under his command and the poor opinion of him held by MacSheehy under whose direct orders he served. He, therefore, asked the minister of war for, and received, sick leave and withdrew from Carhaix. Donzelot, in his recommendation of Petrezzoli, said that he was "firm, intelligent, and foreign to the factions that divided" the Irish. "He will reestablish harmony and will pass judgment on each officer on the basis of talent and morality."[116] Although this original appointment of Petrezzoli was, on paper, temporary, there was never any serious consideration of bringing Blackwell back to the Legion. Born in Parma, Italy, Petrezzoli was thirty-eight years of age when he took command of the Irish. He had entered the French army as an enlisted man and rose through the ranks during the revolutionary wars. His military record was sound— lieutenant in 1793, captain in 1794. He made the Italian Campaign with General Bonaparte in 1796–97, and in 1799 he received the rank of *chef de bataillon* on the field of battle.[117] Before being attached to Augereau's staff late in the spring of 1804 he had commanded the 1st Battalion of the 16th Light Infantry Regiment. His commanding officer, Colonel J. I. Harispe, characterized him as being firm, intelligent, loving his work, and of good character.[118] Petrezzoli possessed not only the military qualifications to command the Legion, but more important, he was not Irish. He had no Irish political affiliations and, as Donzelot had put it in his recommendation to Augereau, he could "see to the well-being and the instruction of everyone without being affected by individual passions."[119] This then was the man who took over the Irish Legion in September 1804 and for the next several years guided and supervised its training, and prepared it to enter upon campaign.

The fate of Adjutant Commander MacSheehy proved to be similar to that of Blackwell. As early as 8 July, Marshal Augereau wrote to the minister of war: "Everything that I have seen relating to Adjutant Commander MacSheehy proves to me that he is incapable of commanding the Irish corps. It is necessary to replace him with an officer who is discreet, firm and completely military."[120] MacSheehy was also attacked by General O'Connor, who stood to gain influence over the Legion if the adjutant commander were removed. The relationship between the two men had not been good since O'Connor's promotion to the rank of general and his subsequent interference in the organization of the Legion. He now took the opportunity of the Sweeny/Corbet affair to write to Augereau to explain to him that it was MacSheehy who was the principal cause of the disunity within the ranks of the Irish at Carhaix. He also cleverly emphasized MacSheehy's authority to communicate directly with the minister of war as a source of the Legion's problems because he knew it to be the one aspect relative to MacSheehy's command that most annoyed Augereau.[121] Donzelot's "Notes Confidentielles," in which he wrote that "it is important that a superior French officer be named to command the Legion,"[122] was as much a call for MacSheehy's removal as it was for that of Blackwell's. He believed that a clean sweep at the top was necessary if the Legion was to emerge as a functioning military unit in the French army. Thus Marshal Augereau, and Generals Donzelot and O'Connor were all three in agreement that the adjutant commander had to be removed.

MacSheehy clearly cannot be blamed for the internal dissent in the Irish Legion. Before assuming the task of organizing and training the Irish in France, he had not been a party to the O'Connor-Emmet schism in the ranks of the United Irishmen. It was the combination of the power struggle and personal conflicts that had developed within the ranks of the United Irishmen which must be blamed for the sad state of affairs that existed in the summer of 1804. These problems had their origins in Ireland, had grown among the exiles in Paris, and had then carried over into the Legion. Nevertheless, MacSheehy had become a part of the problem. He was no longer able to function as a viable mediator to heal the wounds of the Irish in France, and his removal from the Legion was the only prudent measure open to the French authorities.

Rumors that the adjutant commander was to be relieved of his command were rampant by the end of July. On the 29th of the month, a handful of Irish officers, who had come to dislike MacSheehy, prematurely celebrated the news that he was to be removed and that General O'Connor was to be given command of the Legion. So disruptive were they that the town authorities were called out to restore order. All of the officers, except Captain John MacGuire, managed to avoid apprehension. However, the affair caused the mayor of Carhaix to ask MacSheehy to take action against these men, and he used the terms "drunken state," "scandalous scene," and "nocturnal orgies" in his description of their conduct.[123] In his letter to the minister of war describing this event, MacSheehy called it "a victory orgy." He said that when it had become known that the Corbet brothers, whom he called "their leaders," would not be sent to Rennes[124] to be disciplined, and rumors of his replacement became widespread, the troublemakers began to celebrate, and were even openly insulting to him.[125]

By August of 1804, army headquarters at Brest had decided that Adjutant Commander MacSheehy must be removed from his command. However, as he had been appointed by the minister of war himself, it was he who must be convinced that MacSheehy could no longer function effectively, and that, in fact, he was a liability to the Irish Legion. General O'Connor once again took the opportunity to lay full blame upon the man whom he had come to view as his rival for the internal control of the Legion. This political figure, now in a military uniform, denounced MacSheehy as having "sacrificed the tranquility and the honor" of the Legion because of his petty jealousy over his, O'Connor's, promotion to the rank of general of division.

Furthermore, he had misused his authority over the Irish to form an anti-O'Connor party among the officers of the Legion and had turned against the general's supporters, with whom he had previously been on very good terms.[126]

On 24 July, MacSheehy had sent an evaluation of the men of the Legion to the minister of war (see pages 33–34 of this chapter) in which he divided the men who had joined the Legion into four categories. Although he believed that the greater part of the Irish officers fell into the good or acceptable categories, he classified some of them as having left Ireland because of "bad conduct," and others as being "thieves, assassins, etc."[127] In mid-August Berthier forwarded a copy of MacSheehy's report to Augereau and indicated that he agreed with, or accepted, the former's evaluation of the make-up of the Legion. He then very pointedly asked Augereau what he was going to do about the situation.[128] Needless to say, the marshal was not pleased with what could only be considered as a reprimand from the minister of war. He was being told, politely to be sure, that his house was not in order, and that he should take measures to "shape-up" the Irish Legion. MacSheehy's authority to communicate directly with the minister of war had been resented by Augereau and his staff since the formation of the Legion. Now that the internal conditions of the Legion had reached a seemingly intolerably low point, and with criticism coming from his superior, Augereau decided to act. MacSheehy was ordered to report to army headquarters at Brest and, pending approval from the minister of war, was relieved of his command.[129] Battalion Commander Blackwell was already at Brest.[130] With the only two senior officers removed from the Irish Legion, it stood in need of a new commander. The man appointed to this post was *Chef de Bataillon*, Antoine Petrezzoli.[131]

Official approval for the removal of MacSheehy came from the minister of war on 18 September,[132] and for the removal of Blackwell and the appointment of Petrezzoli on 27 September.[133] Furthermore, the new commander of the Legion was ordered to report directly to General O'Connor, who was still serving on Marshal Augereau's staff.[134] This meant that the Legion commander no longer had the authority to communicate directly with the minister of war. It might also be pointed out that Petrezzoli owed his command to Donzelot and Augereau, whereas MacSheehy and Blackwell had been appointed by General Harty and the minister of war. Thus the privileged position that the Irish Legion had enjoyed since its formation was lost, and in many respects it began its evolution into simply another foreign regiment in the service of France.

The final episode of the turbulent summer of 1804 was the tragic duel between Captains Thomas Corbet and John Sweeny. In the third week of

September, the Corbet brothers and Sweeny were released from arrest pending further action as the result of their conduct in June. Augereau had already decided to send the three officers to Rennes, a course of action that had been approved by the minister of war. However, immediately upon their release from custody, and before any action was taken against any of the three, Thomas Corbet challenged Sweeny to a duel. The following account was written and signed by Captain William MacNeven. It was also signed by Captain Hugh Ware and the new commanding officer of the Legion, Petrezzoli.

> This third complementary day [20 September 1804] at 4:30 in the afternoon, Captain Sweeny was challenged to a duel by Captain Ware, acting on behalf of Captain Thomas Corbet. Captain Ware proposed to Captain MacNeven, who acted as second to Captain Sweeny, to fix the distance at which they would fire. It was fixed at ten paces. They also decided that Captain MacNeven would give the signal [to fire], which would be: *one, two, three*. The first would be a warning, the second would be to arm [the pistols], and the third to fire. On the first discharge Captain Corbet was wounded slightly. The second had no effect. At that point, Sweeny proposed to switch to épées; but this was refused by Corbet. Captain Ware insisted that the combat be continued with pistols. Captain MacNeven then declared that he felt reluctant to continue to give the command to fire; and that if they decided to continue, he proposed to give to each of the combatants their loaded pistols and let them bring the affair to an end themselves, and not fight to the death. Captain Ware refused, and the fight continued with each receiving a loaded pistol, and with the rules to fire remaining the same. At the word *two*, the signal to arm, Captain Corbet fired, which was contrary to the agreed upon rules. To correct this wrong, Captain Ware insisted that Captain Sweeny fire. This gesture was refused by the latter because he believed that Captain Corbet had been given his pistol already charged [armed], and thus it fired on the signal to arm. The next time, Captain Corbet violated the agreed upon conditions in the same manner, and again he gave the same explanation. At this moment, Captain Ware proposed to reduce the distance from ten paces to six, and to change the command from *one, two, three,* to *arm, fire*. This was granted, and seeing that there was no opposition, he measured off the [new] distance. Under these modifications, the combat continued, and Captain Sweeny was wounded in the arm. This did not satisfy Captain Corbet, who continually wanted the fight to go on. On the next exchange, Captain Corbet was wounded a second time, but still he persisted, saying that as he was not yet *hors de combat*, he wished to continue the fight. The combat continued and on the next exchange, he was so seriously wounded that he could not continue. It was thus that this unhappy affair came to an end, in which Captain Sweeny did no more than to obey.[135]

At the end of MacNeven's account of the duel, Captain Ware added the following:

I approve of all of the content of this report, except the paragraph [sentence] that says a second time Captain Corbet violated the agreed upon conditions. I further declare that Captain Corbet conducted himself as he did inadvertently. . . .[136]

The signature of Petrezzoli was a simple acknowledgment that he had read MacNeven's account before it was sent on to General Donzelot. He had had no knowledge of the duel until after Corbet had died of his wounds the night of the duel.

The entire Sweeny/Corbet affair was a tragic and embarrassing series of events that could have brought an end to the Irish Legion. It certainly left deep scars and raised troubling questions as to the benefits that might be derived from this type of political corps. Yet it did survive, and it did so because the conditions which had been responsible for its creation, both French and Irish, had not changed. Napoleon still planned to invade England with an Irish diversion, and the Irish still looked forward to returning to their native land with a French army at their backs.

3

From Irish Patriots to French Soldiers

The appointment of Antoine Petrezzoli as commander of the Irish Legion was a prudent and necessary step in the proper direction. If the Legion was not to be disbanded, and there were rumors to that effect that were being taken seriously by the Irish officers,[1] drastic changes were necessary. By the end of the summer of 1804 there was no question of MacSheehy or Blackwell remaining at their posts. An experienced battalion commander, with the full confidence of Marshal Augereau and General Donzelot, who had absolutely no Irish affiliations, was needed. Petrezzoli met these qualifications. He was an Italian who had come up through the ranks of the Revolutionary army, and had served under General Bonaparte in the First Italian Campaign (1796–97). It is unlikely that he was pleased with his new appointment. He must have been fully aware of the turbulent conditions that existed in the Legion, and he surely also knew that there were no quick or easy solutions at hand. Nevertheless, good soldier that he was, he accepted the challenge and assumed his new command.

The Legion was not, indeed, in the best of condition in the fall of 1804. Its principal weaknesses were its internal personal rivalries, poor discipline, and chaotic administration. The "O'Connor" and "Emmet" factions continued to exist despite the departure of T. A. Emmet from the political scene.[2] The men who had supported Emmet when he had actively sought the leadership of the Irish in exile continued to oppose O'Connor and became increasingly hostile towards the general's supporters. The two factions combined may well have been a minority within the Legion, but they were the most influential, active, and outspoken members of the corps. Thus the disruptions they caused were out of proportion to their numbers. The Sweeny/Corbet duel in mid-September marked the apex of the internal problems. Not only had their brother officers been offended and embarrassed by what they had come to perceive as petty and personal rivalries, but the principal antagonists were either removed from the Legion or voluntarily removed themselves. Thomas Corbet was dead, and John Sweeny resigned his commission and was allowed to quit the army, marry, and settle in France.[3] MacSheehy and Blackwell were both relieved of their commands. William Corbet was shattered by his brother's death and seriously considered quitting the army and joining his family in New York. Although he remained with the Legion in 1804, within two years he did resign and resume his teaching position at St. Cyr.[4] MacNeven declared in his letter of resignation that he could not, indeed would not, serve under General O'Connor. He asked for, and received permission to emigrate to the United States.[5] Gallagher, without waiting to be formally discharged, simply left the Legion in late July, with the knowledge and the unauthorized approval of MacSheehy.[6] He was eventually given permission to live in Bordeaux, where he resumed his previous occupation in the shipping trade until his untimely death in 1813.[7] General O'Connor emerged as only the nominal leader of the Irish. He was still consulted on matters of Ireland, but the everyday operations of the Legion were in the hands of Petrezzoli, who bypassed O'Connor, and corresponded directly with General Donzelot. O'Connor remained on Augereau's staff, and was recognized by the Irish officers as the most influential of their number, but there remained in the Legion men like Byrne, Lawless, and Allen, who distrusted and disliked him. Nevertheless, with the principal antagonists gone, and with good and strong leadership from the new battalion commander, the internal political conditions began to improve.

The breakdown of discipline was another serious problem in the summer of 1804. General Donzelot, in his report to Marshal Augereau on 11 October of the same year, following his inspection of the Legion, reported that "Harmony had been troubled for a while in the Corps."[8] *Troubled* was certainly an understatement for the breakdown of discipline that marked the last four months of MacSheehy's command. The Sweeny/Corbet affair was only the most glaring example. Lieutenant Miles Byrne described in his *Memoirs* the turbulence that prevailed. Adjutant Major Flixis Couasnon, a French officer who was involved in the instruction of the Irish officers, "made use of some expression which displeased captain [Austin] O'Meally."[9] When the instruction was completed, O'Meally then "told him he was a coward, and unworthy to be admitted amongst gentleman, etc."[10] When Couasnon took the matter to his superior, MacSheehy, the Adjutant General, "told him at once he should challenge him [O'Meally], and he sent for Captain William O'Mara [sic] and bid him be second to Caugnan [sic]."[11] The two men fought with pistols, Captain Hugh Ware acting as O'Meally's second, and Couasnon was wounded. MacSheehy then at once ordered O'Meally arrested and had him thrown into prison at Brest for fifteen days.[12] Such an affair only further undermined discipline in the Legion.

Furthermore, evidence of disciplinary problems was reflected in a memo signed by MacSheehy that indicated dissatisfaction with five officers: Second Lieutenants Patrick P. Kelly, Landy[13] and Michael Sheridan; Lieutenants Terence O'Reilly and Thomas Read. Although it is not dated, it was written in the late summer 1804. In this document, the adjutant commander complained of the poor character and conduct of these officers. He described Lieutenant Read as "mischievous." He complained that Lieutenant Kelly had been driven from an Irish regiment in the service of the Spanish king for having broken and stolen religious articles; and that Lieutenant Sheridan, a convicted forger in Ireland, had no aptitude for the military, and that he should serve in some other capacity.[14] In this same vein, the minister of war wrote to Marshal Augereau in August that it had come to his attention "that the conduct of many individuals in the Legion was reprehensible,"[15] and he asked the army commander what it was that he intended to do in order to correct the situation. Moreover, awareness of these problems in the Legion had spread beyond the military. M. MacMahon, a professor of English at St. Cyr, wrote to Captain Valentin W. Derry of the Legion that he understood "there is neither subordination nor discipline in the Corps."[16]

The French, from Napoleon and Berthier down to Augereau and Donzelot, perhaps could not have been expected to foresee such problems. They possessed, after all, little knowledge of the Irish or Irish affairs, and men like Harty and Dillon, upon whom they relied, had lived their entire adult lives in France, and were of only limited assistance. The Irish exiles of the Rebellion of 1798 were civilians with political, not military, backgrounds and aspirations. Many of them were already in their thirties and forties. They had accepted commissions in the French army so that they could return to Ireland and, with French troops at their back, establish an Irish government in Dublin. They did not intend, in 1803, to become officers in the service of Napoleon or France. They were fiercely independent men who had defied the English-controlled government in Ireland, and indeed the entire British Empire, and taken up arms against that government. Such men could hardly be expected to readily submit to the discipline of the Napoleonic army. But if discipline was weak and lacking, the administration of the Legion was in a shambles.

"It is not surprising," wrote Donzelot in his report of 11 October, "that the Inspector [himself] found the administration of the Corps in a state of disorder."[17] The financial registers were in disarray, personnel could not be accounted for, and the minutes of the council meetings were either missing or inadequate for an understanding of the affairs of the Legion.[18] Donzelot was meticulous in his exoneration of Petrezzoli and placed full responsibility upon the shoulders of MacSheehy. Many of the problems of the Legion may have had extenuating circumstances surrounding them, or had deeply rooted origins that went back to Ireland, but the administrative breakdown reflected the poor management of Petrezzoli's predecessor.

There were other problems of a lesser nature that plagued the Irish Legion in this formative period. Some of the officers did not speak or read the French language, and others had only a marginal command, which was limited to a military vocabulary. Of the fifty-five Irish officers for whom data is available with respect to their French language skills, only forty-five percent of them could read and write the language. Eleven percent were "passable" in the language, fifteen percent could speak or write little French and sixteen percent still knew no French ten months after the Legion had been formed.[19] Furthermore, the Legion had sixty-six officers, but only twenty-two noncommissioned officers and soldiers.[20] This proved to be a hindrance in training the officers as they had no one to command. It is true that the purpose of the Legion was to train officers who would command Irish troops after they had landed in Ireland. But its training was hampered under such conditions.

To paint an entirely negative picture of the Legion at the time Petrezzoli assumed command would be quite incorrect. When General Donzelot inspected the Irish, less then a month after MacSheehy's departure, he reported that he "was satisfied with the general condition" of the corps.[21] He also expressed a guarded, or qualified, "praise" for the military instruction of the officers. They were well instructed in the basics of the military profession, but were weak in strategy, the ability to command, and self-assurance. In particular, their voice commands were inadequate, and he made rather exacting recommendations for improvement.[22] The number of officers who caused most of the disruption in the Legion was perhaps twenty-five percent—or less. The majority of them went about their daily routine without incident. They were looking forward to the expedition to Ireland, and were striving to prepare themselves for positions of command in the Irish regiments that were to be formed after the landing in their native land. Many of these officers were not, and never had been, United Irishmen. Thus they were less likely but not immune from becoming involved in internal conflicts. Donzelot also pronounced the administration of the Legion to be greatly improved. The books were in order for the 11 October inspection and the commander was trying to make sense out of the garbled reports, records, and ledgers of the previous administration.[23] It is true that he felt instruction on specific aspects of their training was weak, but the general tone of his report was that the Legion, under Petrezzoli, was getting back on track.

Within a month of his arrival, Petrezzoli was making strides towards pulling the Legion back together. Discipline was improving according to Donzelot's report, although he mentions, not by name, that there still were two troublemakers.[24] The new commanding officer was above partisan politics and had no favorites. There were those who believed that everyone in the Legion should be Irish, but under the existing circumstances, virtually all were willing to give Petrezzoli a chance to restore order and the credibility of the Legion, which had declined to a recognizably dangerous point.

The months following Petrezzoli's appointment as commander of the Legion went generally well. Internal tensions having been reduced, the men continued to rally about the one most unifying factor of the Legion: the projected expedition to Ireland. There were continuous rumors to the effect that the invasion of England and Ireland would take place in the immediate future, and based on information that found its way to Lesneven, the Irish had every reason to believe that they would soon be on their way "home." The great majority of them seriously desired to learn the military arts so that they would be able to employ their knowledge once in Ireland, and to instruct the Irish who would join their ranks. Their desire for a tranquil environment in which to continue their training may be seen in their mass demonstration against the intrigues and indiscipline of Second Lieutenant Patrick P. O'Kelly. Born in Waterford, Ireland, O'Kelly had served in the Spanish army before presenting himself at Carhaix. Mac-Sheehy, with little knowledge of the man, gave him a commission in the Legion. He had never been an United Irishman, and thus was not a part of their bickering in the summer of 1804. Nevertheless, Donzelot's report of 11 October, described him in such terms as: "Bad conduct, little instruction, given to wine, a spirit of intrigue, quick-tempered."[25]

O'Kelly had been a general troublemaker since he had joined the Legion on 22 March 1804. But, in early December, he penned two brief documents in which he stated that Adjutant Major Couasnon was "a liar and a *lâche*.[26] This prompted Petrezzoli to take action, and to write the following to Donzelot on the afternoon of 5 December:

> I am sending you Second Lieutenant O'Kelly who is being escorted by Captain [Louis] Lacy, who will have the honor of giving to you this letter. The conduct of this officer [O'Kelly] is most shameful. His statements and his slanderous writings are such an outrage that honor no longer will permit

him to remain in this corps if there is to be general tranquillity, obedience and subordination.[27]

Then, at 7 P.M. that same day, he added the following postscript: "After having placed this officer [O'Kelly] under house arrest and a guard at his door, he went out and actively provoked a duel."[28] Curiously enough, the duel O'Kelly fought was not with Couasnon, whom he had antagonized, but with another French officer in the Legion, Second Lieutenant Denis Thyroux.[29]

On the morning after the O'Kelly-Thyroux duel, more than thirty officers of the Legion presented themselves at Petrezzoli's quarters in order to testify to their indignation over the dishonorable conduct of those few, particularly O'Kelly, who were giving a bad name to the Legion and their native Ireland.[30] O'Kelly was removed, and the men continued with their training. But the problems of the Legion were being met and handled in a piecemeal manner. There was a need to raise the more significant and fundamental questions concerning the corps.

In the late summer of 1804, MacSheehy had raised the question of the basic organization of the Legion. He actually proposed a plan that would have provided for a regimental structure that would include two infantry battalions supported by cavalry and artillery. But it was sharply criticized by General O'Connor, and with MacSheehy's dismissal as commander in September, nothing more was heard of his plan.[31] Then in December 1804 Donzelot, in a five-page letter to the minister of war, raised questions of true substance, and in some instances dared to pose possible solutions. Some of his statements in December seem to contradict the report he sent to Marshal Augereau just seven weeks earlier. It may be either that he had changed his views, or that the 11 October report was an attempt to show the Legion at its best in difficult times. Which ever the case, his December epistle is so revealing that substantial portions of it must be quoted.

> At present, the Legion has not received a definitive organization.
> If the invasion of Ireland should take place at this time, the Legion could only be considered as a political vehicle. The men of the Legion would all be employed in forming battalions [with Irish soldiers] or in administration. In this case there is little need now for it to be occupied in forming a regular military organization, and it should be less strict on choosing the individuals who make up the Corps.
> If on the other hand this Corps does not fulfill the function for which it was established, will the French government form of it a national regi-ment . . . similar to those that had existed before the Revolution? If this is the government's intention, then there should be fixed guidelines, and admission to the Legion should be strictly in accordance with that goal.

Now you know, M. Marshal, that many of the officers now in the Legion are not fit for military service, and their rank can only be explained in terms of an expedition [to Ireland].

The ignorance and bad conduct of certain members of the Legion would seem to require that they be removed.

But there are two measures that can be taken, which are of the greatest urgency for the destiny of this Corps. The first of these is to isolate all of those officers whose conduct is reprehensible and incorrigible. The second is to freeze the rank of all of the other officers, and not permit any changes or promotion of any kind without your express authorization. This would be a means of reducing the growth of division that feeds itself on pretentions that are founded on the partiality of commanders.

I have endeavored to put a sufficient amount of detail into my reports on personnel so that you would be able to make the necessary decisions. . . .

[Adjutant Commander MacSheehy] promoted many officers too quickly. This abuse is perhaps understandable in the formation of a new Corps. . . .

The decree of 13 Fructidor, an 11 [31 August 1803], that created the Irish Battalion, prescribed in article 2, that there would not be formed a second battalion until the first [battalion] was at double strength.

Did the government mean by that article that a second battalion would not be formed until the first had a double complement of officers, NCOs, and soldiers, or simply of officers?

In the first case, M. Marshal, nothing can be presented to you until there is proposal for organization. Furthermore, there exist no soldiers in the Corps.

In the second [case], one can put before you the structure for two battalions, because there exist enough officers to fill them. Upon adopting this formation, it will be necessary to provide only an *Etat-major* [head-quarters] for one battalion, and to determine how many soldiers will be needed.

If the government intends to keep this Corps, for some political reasons, it is desirable that it should have the means of recruiting United Irishmen, as well as [Irish] from among the English prisoners of war and those living in other continental states and any other convenient means. This would result in their [the officers] gaining instruction and discipline, and if they were kept occupied, they would not have time for intrigue, and it would enable them to develop a liking and custom for the service.

Some officers have already obtained from you their discharge and permission to emigrate to the United States. It is probable that if, by the coming springtime, the expedition [to Ireland] has not taken place, a large number of the most capable officers will ask for the same authority. There would remain in the Corps only the less desirable officers.

I would also like to speak, M. Marshal, of several officers of French origins, who, contrary to the instructions of article 3 of the order of 13 Fructidor, an 11, have been admitted into this Corps. There names are: Mm Lieutenant [Henri] Mougenot, Second Lieutenant Thyroux and Second Lieutenant [Augustin] Osmond. It would have been difficult for this illegel admission of these officers not to have caused complaints. Furthermore, there have been demands for their removal based upon that precise order. However, as their conduct is irreproachable and their presence in the Corps a benefit to the commander, I had not wanted to make a statement with regards to them. If you decide to remove them [from the Legion], I recommend that they be transferred to a French regiment with the rank of second lieutenant. . . .[32]

The lack of organization was a problem for the Irish, but as Donzelot's letter indicated, it was only one of a number of problems. Nevertheless, there was not a true battalion structure. Petrezzoli was a "battalion" commander, but he presided over 67 officers[33] and a handful of noncommissioned officers and soldiers. There were no companies for the captains nor platoons for the lieutenants to command. Thus there was no sense of, or feel for, a battalion. There existed simply a large group of junior officers going through what might be called "officer training school." Even the terminology was confused. Neither the high command nor the Irish themselves were quite sure what to call this group. Throughout the correspondence of 1804, both official and unofficial, the terms "Legion," "Corps," and "Battalion" were used seemingly at random. Donzelot generally referred to the Irish as a "Corps," although he occasionally spoke of a "Legion." Petrezzoli used the term "Battalion," perhaps because he was a *chef de bataillion*, and it seemed to him to lend a bit more prestige. The minister of war and the Irish themselves used "Legion," and, in fact, it was an "Irish Legion" that had been created by the decree of 1803.

Donzelot was, of course, quite correct in pointing out that the Legion was "political" in the winter of 1804–5. One need only recall that it was created for political reasons, and that the men who were given commissions in it were political refugees. There were a handful of men who had had previous military experience. For example, Captain Edward Masterson had served in the British army; Captain William O'Meara had served in the Irish Brigade in the French army until it was disbanded, and then in the British army until 1801; Patrick O'Kelly had served in the Spanish army as had Captain Louis Lacy; and Captain Eugene O'Herne "had served in many armies before the Revolution."[34] But even these men joined the Legion basically for political reasons. The French uniform that the Irish wore simply provided a military means to achieve political aims in Ireland that they had been unable to achieve in the 1790s by other tactics. However, Donzelot was probably wrong when he implied that it would be "only" of political value if the expedition to Ireland had taken place at the time he wrote. The Irish officers had had ten months of training, however imperfect it might have been. If they had been landed in Ireland with the proposed 18,000 French regulars,[35] the Irish people would have rallied to their green flag with its inspiring inscription "L'Independance d'Irlande," and they would surely have been a *military* factor in Napoleon's overall equation for England and Ireland. The Irish would have had not only that national zeal and inspiration that had been a part of French victories during the Revolutionary period, but they would also have had at their side the French army itself.

The question that Donzelot raised in his letter of the government's intentions with respect to the Legion is perhaps the most profound. At the time of his writing, Napoleon fully[36] intended to send expeditions to England and Ireland. On 4 October 1804, the minister of war wrote to Marshal Augereau rather specific instruction.

I am informing you Monsieur Marshal, that the Emperor has resolved to carry out the expedition to Ireland.

There is at Brest the means to transport 18,000 men under the orders of Admiral H. J. A. Ganteaume.

I will inform you of the organization of this corps of 18,000 men,[37] and when the troops must be at Brest.

General Marmont is ready with 25,000 men to embark at Texel.

General Marmont will receive orders to land in Ireland, and he will be under your orders.

If the information that His Majesty has received from the Irish refugees and from the agents he has sent to Ireland is correct, large numbers of Irish will join you as soon as you land; thus you must march directly on Dublin. If on the other hand this national movement is slow in materialzing, you should take up a [defensive] position and wait for the arrival of General Marmont's army corps, and for the landing of the Grand Army [in England].[38]

With the expedition to Ireland in an advanced state of preparation, and Napoleon seemingly prepared to invest 43,000 men in the undertaking, what was needed was a "political" legion, not merely a battalion or two of Irish troops. There is no documentary proof that Napoleon wished to replace English control of Ireland with French control, although there were Irishmen, in particular T. A. Emmet, who either believed this to be his intention or who were suspicious of his motives. What is more probable is that he hoped to exert French influence in Ireland by virture of the French support and through men like O'Connor who would owe their political position in Ireland to him and his army. But in the final analysis, Napoleon was primarily concerned with England not Ireland. Aid to the Irish, whether in the form of an Irish Legion, or an expedition, or the establishment of an independent Irish government, all was simply peripheral to the central goal, which was the defeat of England. Thus a purely military organization, similar to that of all of the units in the French army was not considered to be necessary for the Irish at that time. When the expeditions to England and Ireland were "postponed" in September of 1805, and the Grand Army marched east to the Danube, it gradually became evident that the Legion would not be going to Ireland, and that if it was to be of any use to France, it would have to become a regular military unit in the French army. But in the winter of 1804–5, this was not yet the attitude in Paris.

When Donzelot moved to the question of rank in the Legion, he touched a sensitive nerve. At the time of the formation of the Legion, the Irish exiles in France were enthusiastic about the prospects of returning to Ireland with French military assistance to overthrow the English government in Dublin. They were not particularly concerned about the rank that they received, because they had no intentions of remaining in the French army any longer than it would take to reach Ireland and drive out the English. Moreover, the French had made enlistment in the army a prerequisite for taking part in the expedition, and there did not seem to be any other choice. The First Consul did not want Irish civilians involved in the military operation. Dissatisfaction with the rank they had received began as soon as the Irish reached Morlaix, when men who had accepted the rank of lieutenant or second lieutenant met captains whom they believed to be less meritorious than themselves. Rank had been assigned in three grades (captain, lieutenant, and second lieutenant), by and large on the basis of recommendations from General Harty and Adjutant Commander Mac-Sheehy. Then in late January 1804, MacSheehy secured the promotion of a number of officers whom he believed had been admitted to the Legion at too low a rank.[39] After O'Connor was named general in February of the same year, he became increasingly involved in recruiting new men and securing promotions for his friends and supporters. Rank had become political, not military in the Legion. United Irishmen believed that rank should have been based on previous service to the cause of Irish independence; a reward, if you will, for past hardships and suffering on behalf of the "cause." Newly enlisted officers, who had no connections with the United Irish movement or the rebellions of 1798 and 1803, quite naturally, wanted some other criteria to serve as the basis for rank. Thus there was friction, and even hostility, on the part of men who had lost all of their possessions in Ireland, served time in prison and had been driven into exile, towards those whom they came to consider as opportunists. Donzelot's recommendations to deal with this diversity were sound, and in general were accepted by Marshal Berthier. However, much of the damage had already taken place, and men like Lieutenant Byrne remained dissatisfied for years[40] because he, Byrne, believed that politics, not ability, had prevented his promotion in the summer of 1804.

The question of forming a second battalion was a relatively moot one in view of the fact that there was not yet the organization of a first battalion. But the question of non-Irish holding commissions in the Legion posed a rather serious problem. The Legion was still destined for Ireland. The basic concept was to prepare Irish officers to lead Irishmen. It made no sense at all to train Frenchmen in the Legion. Would they make the expedition to Ireland? If so, would they be called upon to lead Irishmen once they had arrived? If French officers were to lead Irish troops, they could be drawn from any regiment in the army, with the only qualification being that they spoke English. There was not, in fact, any good reason for the three men in question to be in the Irish Legion. Donzelot was absolutely correct in suggesting that they be transferred to a regular French regiment. It is true that there were a number of officers in the Legion who had been born and raised in France, but whose parents were Irish. Patrick St. Leger was typical of those who fell into this category. He was a surgeon attached to the staff and was popular in the Legion.[41]

Finally, the question of resignations from the Legion was addressed by Donzelot. An increasing number of Irish were dissatisfied, disenchanted, and disappointed. They were also bored with the peacetime routine in the small provincial villages and towns of western Brittany. As winter came on, it seemed unlikely that a major military operation, which involved crossing the English Channel, would be undertaken before late spring. After the initial resignations of the men who were involved in the Sweeny/Corbet affair, there was a lull until spring of 1805. It is true that the paperwork for the removal of O'Kelly was begun in December, but it was not until May that there was a new exodus from the Legion. The correspondence from the disenchanted Irish to the minister of war varied only slightly in its expression of frustration. The letters began by pointing out that the authors had joined the Irish Legion after considerable sacrifice in the cause of Ireland, and that they believed their service would benefit the interests of both Ireland and France. But they had come to the conclusion that nothing had been accomplished, nor would anything be accomplished, to benefit Ireland by their presence in the Legion. That is to say, they no longer believed that there would be an expedition that would land them in their native country. In conclusion, they all expressed their devotion to France, and asked for permission to reside in France or in some friendly country.

Captain Valintine Derry, a thirty-eight-year-old United Irishman, expressed these sentiments quite well in his letter of 3 May 1805 to the minister of war:

Since 15 Thermidor an 7, I have been in France and have made myself available to serve my second *patrie*. I have lost everything in my native land and had despaired of ever returning. Then I received your orders to go to Morlaix. I abandoned my close friends [in Paris] and the independent life I had made for myself in France in order to make one last sacrifice for Ireland. I have been a sad and silent spectator of the events that have taken place in our corps since its formation. I have waited for a complete change in the organization that would reflect the views of the French government and those of the people of Ireland that would have been useful to Ireland and respectable for France. After a long wait in vain, I see that I cannot render any service to my country by remaining a part of the Irish Legion. I, therefore, ask your Excellence to grant me a discharge and to grant me permission to settle in France.

Upon once again becoming a simple citizen, I will be no less useful to my country and to the government which has befriended me and for which I will always render sentiments of fidelity, respect and gratitude.[42]

Petrezzoli, in an undated memorandum written in the spring of the same year, gave the names of eight Irish officers who had been relieved of their duties and who were in various stages of being discharged. These officers had been denounced by Marshal Augereau to the minister of war as insubordinate, poorly trained, and of poor *Tenue* (i.e., military bearing, appearance, and attitude). Several were said to be incapable of commanding, and they were collectively described as intriguers and a cause of the trouble in the Legion since its formation.[43] The officers named, and the city in which they requested permission to reside are: Second Lieutenant Denice Thyroux: Paris; Lieutenant Fecorbert Morisson: Lamballe; Côtes du Nord; Lieutenant Thomas Read: Brussels; Lieutenant John Coummins: Bayonne; Second Lieutenant Patrick O'Kelly: Madrid; Second Lieutenant Mathieu Reynoldt: Madrid; Second Lieutenant Richard Landy: Brussels; Second Lieutenant Michael Landy: Bordeaux.[44] However, Lieutenant Morisson was allowed to rejoin the Legion six months later because of his previous military service. During the twenty-four years he spent in the French army, he had risen from private to lieutenant, and had suffered "numerous" wounds, one of which he had received at the Battle of Marengo.[45] Nevertheless, he was disciplined by being sent to Lamballe and placed under surveillance before resuming his duties with the Legion.[46] The unfortunate Morisson, who was fifty-four years of age at the time, died just three years later at Flushing of malaria.[47] Captain Nicolar Tyrrel, on the other hand, poses somewhat of an enigma. Miles Brynes, who served in the Legion in these years as an officer, wrote of Tyrrel in his *Memoirs*: "Never joined the Legion from the bad state of his health. He was one of the Irish exiles much considered by all his acquaintants."[48] By "Never joined the Legion" Byrne most likely meant that Tyrrel had not gone to Morlaix and actively taken up his commission. However, he is carried on the rosters of the Legion in 1804, and the report to the minister of war dated 25 June 1805 certainly indicates that he was a member of that corps, and that he had been a source of trouble in the preceeding year.[49] As his name does not appear on later rosters of the Legion, it must be assumed that his discharge from the French army took place in the summer of 1805. The remaining six officers were also removed from the Legion at that time.

The movement of personnnel in the Irish Legion was by no means exclusively that of exit. In fact, there was a continuous increase in the total strength of the corps throughout its first eighteen months. So liberal were the requirements for joining the Legion, and at least in the eyes of some members, so ineffective was the screening of new candidates, that, in light of the problems of the summer of 1804, expressions of criticism reached as high as Marshal Augereau. In two letters written to the marshal by Captain Thomas Markey,[50] these views are clearly articulated. On 25 July 1804, he wrote to Augereau:

> You will permit me, my General [sic], to remind you that I had the honor to tell you at Bayonne that it was essential to have regard for the political character as well as the moral character of the individuals of those who offered their services as officers in the Irish Battalion. Unfortunately, as the present circumstances show, this advice was not sufficiently taken. I implore you once again, my General [sic], to permit me to again tell you how essential it is that such measures be adopted.[51]

Then seven weeks later, on 15 September, he again wrote to the marshal. If care is not taken with respect to those who are allowed to join the Legion, he declared, "It will prove, despite what one may think, that this Corps is destined to become a refuge for those who have fled their country because of crimes deserving of the utmost punishment. . . ."[52]

Markey's sentiments were undoubtedly motivated by his United Irish orientation and his displeasure at seeing men given commissions equal to his own who had neither suffered for the Irish cause nor had strong feelings for the creation of an independent Irish republic. Nevertheless, his views were shared by others in the Legion. On the other hand, there were men who were petitioning for admission into the Irish Legion. They were a curious lot, ranging from Colonel Henry Dillon, ex-commander of the Dillon Regiment of the old Irish Brigade and brother of the late General Arthur Dillon,[53] to Luke Masterson, who had just arrived in Hamburg from Ireland.[54]

Some men had a rather exalted opinion of the role they would play in the Legion, while others simply wished to serve the Irish cause. Colonel Dillon, by virtue of the rank he had held in 1792, was willing to join the Legion as a regimental commander, but not as a captain, the highest commission given to any member of the Irish corps.[55] It is not surprising that Dillon did not serve in the Legion. Thomas James, who described himself in a letter to the minister of war as being "English by nationality, but whose father and mother are Irish,"[56] asked to be commissioned as a captain in the Legion. His name does not appear on the rosters. Nor does the name of M. Kearney, a United Irishman who had helped General Humbert in 1798, and who petitioned in the summer of 1804 for admission into the Legion.[57] But if some were rejected or declined the rank they were offered, MacGueken is another case in point,[58] most applicants seem to have been accepted in 1804 and 1805.

Sixty-three-year-old John Gibbons was given the rank of second lieutenant upon the strong recommendation of General O'Connor. The general assured Donzelot that Gibbons "had the reputation of being a very brave man and a true Irish patriot; and that he had the qualities required to perform well the functions of a second-lieutenant."[59] On the basis of O'Connor's recommendation, Donzelot requested, and received, a commission for Gibbons in late August 1804. But when Donzelot inspected the Irish Legion in mid-October and actually met Second Lieutenant Gibbons, he wrote the following notes in his report: "An old man who is respectable and recommendable because of his age, his conduct and his past suffering; he is not fit for military service. . . ."[60] He is perhaps the best example of a "political" appointee; one who would have influence in Ireland after the Legion had landed. Three years later his battalion commander, Petrezzoli, wrote of him: "He is incapable of being an officer, . . . inept, . . . inclined towards drunkenness."[61] He died at Antwerp in the same year (1807) that Petrezzoli wrote his report.[62]

Another recruit of the summer of 1804 was William Auguste O'Morand, who provides a striking contrast to John Gibbons. In the spring of that year, MacSheehy requested that the eighteen-year-old O'Morand, who was a student at the military school at Fontainebleau, be commissioned as a second lieutenant in the Irish Legion.[63] He joined the Legion that same summer, and Donzelot wrote quite favorably of him in the fall.[64]

A more unusual type of request came from James MacCarthy of the 24th Infantry Regiment. An Irishman by birth, he had joined the French army as a private shortly after being forced into exile as the result of his activities in 1798. His transfer to the Irish Legion was approved by Marshal Augereau and the minister of war, and he was commissioned a second Lieutenant.[65] And then there was the case of C. Komabacio, who was apparently admitted to the Legion by MacSheehy in the very early days of its formation. However, as he was not Irish, the minister of war rebuked the adjutant commander and Komabacio was quickly removed.[66]

The recruiting of men into the Legion became entwined in the internal struggle, as did almost every aspect of the Legion in the summer of 1804. John Richard Burgh, a friend of General O'Connor's, requested a commission in the recently formed battalion. The general recommended to the minister of war that Mr. Burgh be given the rank of captain as he was not only a United Irishman and a friend, but he was also a protestant minister. However, when Burgh arrived at MacSheehy's headquarters, he was inducted into the army as a simple soldier. The adjutant commander justified his action on the grounds that he already had sufficient officers. Some weeks later, when O'Connor arrived at Lesneven where the Legion was quartered, the general, with the consent of Petrezzoli, who had replaced MacSheehy, promoted Burgh to the rank of second lieutenant.[67]

The British army provided yet another source of recruits in 1804. In the spring of that year, eight British soldiers landed on the coast of Normandy. These Irishmen, in the service of His Majesty, King George III, had deserted from their regiment, which was stationed on the Isle of Jersey, when they had heard of the formation of the Legion. They reportedly told General Harty that there were other Irishmen in their regiment who would do as they had done if they had the opportunity.[68] Indeed, they were quite correct, for on 4 June, five more Irishmen who were serving in the 48th Regiment of the British army stationed on the Isle of Jersey, sailed a small boat to the mainland of France. As those who had come before them, they wished to join the Irish Legion. General Antoine Laroche, commander of the 14th Military District, sent the men to Carhaix, from whence they were conveyed to the Legion and taken into the French army.[69]

This arrival and departure of Irishmen had only one serious effect upon the Legion, and that was to reduce the internal tension and friction that had been so troublesome in the summer and fall of 1804. Most of the men who left the service in this period had been United Irishmen, with strong political and personal feelings. On the other hand, the men who joined the Legion in this period were not so politically oriented, nor were they part of the personal conflicts that had been rampant among the Irish. Thus the men of the Legion continued, in a more peaceful setting, their preparations for the expedition to Ireland.

In the fall of 1804, expectations of the pending expedition were still very high. In Paris, as well as in Brittany, serious plans were being made to transport Marshall Augereau's army to Ireland. The bulk of the Legion spent the winter at Lesneven, but some of its officers were sent to Landernau where they served directly under the command of General Harty. They remained at Landernau until the spring of 1805, at which time they rejoined their comrades at Lesneven.[70]

It was while the Legion was divided that the coronation of the Emperor Napoleon I took place in Paris. General Bonaparte had become First Consul of the French Republic in 1799 following the *coup d'état* of 18 Brumaire. He had then been given the title of First Consul for life in 1802, with the right to name his successor. The Constitution of the Year VIII (1799) had given him extraordinary powers, and in fact, it was not so much his powers that were increased by the creation of the empire, as it was his prestige. The proclamation of the empire was dated 18 May 1804, but the coronation did not take place until 2 December. Each regiment in the army sent two representatives to Paris for the ceremonies and celebrations. However, General Donzelot did not think that the Irish Legion should be allowed to send representatives. It was only the strong intervention of General O'Connor on behalf of the Irish that persuaded Marshal Augereau and the minister of war to allow two Irish officers to make the journey.[71] Captains William Corbet and John Tennent, who were recognized as the two senior captains in the Legion by virtue of service with the French army prior to the formation of the Legion, were chosen for the honor of representing the Irish on this auspicious occasion.[72] Not only did Corbet and Tennent attend the coronation and the festivities that accompanied it, but they both remained for months afterwards in Paris. Prodding eventually brought Tennent back to Lesneven by the end of February 1805, but late in March Corbet had still not returned. It was necessary, on 25 March, for the minister of war to request that Marshal Joachim Murat, the governor of Paris, order Captain Corbet to rejoin his Legion. Only then did the reluctant Corbet, who wished to be transferred out of the Legion, leave Paris for Lesneven.[73]

Life in Lesneven during the spring of 1805 was a mixture of preparation for the coming expedition and entertainment. Miles Byrne described the social life in the following manner:

> Concerts were organized by the officers, who played on different instruments, with the young men of the town, who were musicians. Captain Lawless and the two Saint-Legers arranged those musical meetings.—At a ball given by the officers of the Legion, I was appointed one of the stewards, and I had the mission of being bearer of the invitations to the society of Landernau, . . . indeed our time passed cheerfully enough at Lesneven. We used sometimes to hire horses and ride to Brest. . . . We always returned in high spirits and full of hope, to our garrison.[74]

There was general tranquillity within the Irish Legion as the summer of 1805 approached. The usual grumbling and restlessness of garrison life was present, but the bitter divisions that had marked the previous summer were absent. Then an unfortunate incident took place that caused the immediate removal of the Legion from Lesneven. A relatively minor dispute occurred between Captain Patrick MacSheehy, a relative of the former commander of the Legion, and the son of the mayor of the town of Lesneven, Monsieur Carrandra. They fought a duel just outside of the town with pistols. After both men had fired one shot their seconds were able to persuade them that the matter was settled. Young Carrandra had wished to continue the duel with swords, however, his second prevailed and both men returned to town. Once among his friends, the young Frenchman related the events that had taken place and added "Those Irish officers won't fight but with pistols." Lieutenant Augustin Osmond who happened to be present said to him: "I am one of those Irish officers, and I am ready to prove to you the contrary."[75] Carrandra and Osmond then returned to the field and fought with swords. The mayor's son was seriously wounded, and was carried to his father's home in what was believed to be a dying state. The news of these events quickly reached army headquarters at Brest, and that very night the Legion was ordered to leave Lesneven and to march to Quimper on the southern coast of Brittany.[76]

The general boredom of garrison life may help to explain the foolishness of the duels involving the two Irish officers and Carrandra, but it is no justification for the near loss of life. The confrontation that arose between Captains William Corbet and John Tennent was also due, at least in part, to the prolonged inactivity on the part of the Irish. The lack of meaningful duties and obligations, which were the direct result of having a battalion organization with a surplus of officers and less than thirty noncommissioned officers and soldiers, left those energetic men to occupy themselves, as best they could, while awaiting the expedition to Ireland. It is hardly surprising that in these months the men spent a portion of that time trying to determine who were the senior officers in each rank. Both Corbet and Tennent claimed to be the senior captain by virtue of service in the French army before they were commissioned as captains in the Irish Legion. The confrontation became serious in the summer of 1805 as the time seemed to be at hand for the invasion of Ireland. Once the Legion would land on Irish soil, regiments would be formed using Irish volunteers, and promotions would be made. The senior captains would become regimental and battalion commanders. Lieutenants would become company commanders. Thus, to establish oneself as the senior captain in the Legion could mean becoming second in command, after General

O'Connor, (excluding the Italian Petrezzoli) and would not merely assure that individual the rank of colonel, but very likely he would become a general of brigade, as the Legion would expand.

John Tennent had been named *chef de bataillon* in the year VI (1797–98) by General Jean Baptiste Jules Bernadotte, who at that time was minister of war. The French were preparing to send expeditionary forces to Ireland and Tennent was to be a part of one such miniarmy. However, his commission was only provisional, and when the scheme proved to be a failure in 1798, Tennent did not sail with either of the ill-fated expeditions, but rather returned to civilian life. It was not until 7 December that he was again commissioned in the French army as a captain in the Irish Legion. William Corbet actually saw active service with the rank of captain in 1798. He had sailed with Napper Tandy to northern Ireland. However, what was more important was that on 18 December 1802 his commission as captain in the French army was officially approved.[77] The controversy was resolved by recognizing Corbet's official appointment on 18 December 1802 and rejecting Tennent's "provisional" (1798) appointment. Thus Corbet was one year senior to Tennent. However, it all became somewhat academic when the expedition did not sail to Ireland, and Captain Corbet was transferred, not against his wishes, out of the Legion. It was General Harty who put forward the compromise formula. Tennent, although his request for the rank of *chef de bataillon* was rejected, became the senior captain, and Corbet was transferred to the divisional staff with the title adjutant captain, that is captain on staff duty. Harty had pointed out that Corbet, who was fluent in both the English and French languages, would be of much greater service as a staff officer than he would be in the Legion.[78] Thus a situation that was potentially divisive was settled with Corbet leaving the Legion, but receiving an additional title, which could be interpreted as additional prestige, and Tennent, without additonal rank, left as the senior Irish officer in the Legion. Harty was very concerned in the summer of 1805 that this confrontation over seniority in the Legion might develop into a serious schism such as the Thomas Corbet/John Sweeny affair of the previous year.[79] Fortunately for the Legion, it did not!

The invasion of England and Ireland was actually scheduled to take place in the summer of 1805. The French fleet in the Mediterranean, after a diversionary movement to the West Indies, was to arrive off of Brittany and Normandy, and provide the naval superiority deemed necessary for the Channel crossing. The French army, encamped from Brittany to the mouth of the Elbe, was poised for the final assault on the British Isles. Six army corps were designated for the invasion of England, while Marshal Augereau's corps was to sail to Ireland. The Irish at Quimper knew little of the grand strategy, and since the entire operation depended upon Admiral Pierre Charles de Villeneuve's arrival with the Mediterranean fleet, there was no date for the army's departure. The Irish passed the summer in a high state of anxiety. The ships to transport them to their native Ireland could be seen in the harbor at Brest, and they expected to depart at any time. Rumors abounded as to when they would sail, and where in Ireland they would land. But the planning and preparations, as well as the hopes and the dreams, where all in vain. The timidity of Villeneuve led him to abandon the plan when he reached the English Channel and sighted ships, which he believed, incorrectly, to be Admiral Horatio Nelson's squadron in support of the Home Fleet.[80]

While the men of the Irish Legion were looking westward in anticipation, in the summer of 1805, the real war clouds were developing in the east. Encouraged by the English, Austria and Russia were preparing to renew the struggle for control of central Europe. The formation of the Third Coalition was a great success for English diplomacy. Never again would Napoleon have such a free hand on the continent of Europe that he could mount so serious a threat to England and Ireland as he had in 1805. By mid-August, the news from central Europe was critical. The Austrians were advancing to the west, and Napoleon could no longer ignore the threat to his domination of Germany and Italy. On 26 August, he signed the orders that turned the Grand Army away from the British Isles and began its triumphal march to the Danube which culminated in the victory over the Russians and Austrians at Austerlitz (2 December 1805).

As Marshal Augereau's VII Corps left Brittany early in September, the fate of Ireland seemed to be sealed. The expeditions to England and Ireland were not totally abandoned; according to the emperor they were merely postponed until he could reestablish the security of his rear. Austria, and to a lesser extent Russia, would have to be dealt with first, and then he would again turn his attention, and his resources, to the invasion of Britain. But if there was serious doubt about an expedition to Ireland after the departure of the army from its Channel camps, the destruction of the combined Franco-Spanish fleet off Cape Trafalgar by Admiral Nelson on 21 October 1805, was the decisive blow. The army could have returned to the English Channel after a successful campaign and have been again ready in the summer of 1806 to sail for England and Ireland. But the loss of twenty ships was a blow that would require years from which to recover. It is sufficient to say that the French navy never did recover from its losses at Trafalgar, and although there was, from time to time, talk of sending expeditions to Britain, there was never again a serious effort, nor a comprehensive plan with any hope of success, made to send the Irish Legion to Ireland.

The Legion remained at Quimper when the VII Corps followed the Grand Army into Germany. It was still made up almost exclusively of officers, with only a few NCOs and soldiers. As its purpose was to train officers to serve exclusively in Ireland, there was never any question of it accompanying Augereau's corps. It would have been totally useless to Napoleon in central Europe. Nevertheless, there was great sadness among the Irish when they were forced to admit to themselves that there would not be an expedition to their native Ireland. For nearly two years, they had lived and worked with but one goal, and now it was *postponed*, perhaps forever! This great disappointment at first stunned the men of the Legion. Some reacted by resigning their commissions, others requested to be transferred from the Legion into a French regiment so that they would see active service. The majority of the Irish, although saddened at the turn of events, took a wait and see approach. They told themselves that the expedition had not been canceled, only postponed. There was still hope that when French hegemony was confirmed on the Continent that Napoleon would return to his plan for an expediton to Ireland. Furthermore, many of the Irish officers had no place to go should they quit the French army. They had been living in Paris as exiles without a future before joining the Legion. Many of them realized that they would have to start life anew in a foreign land if they resigned. On the other hand, if they remained in the Legion, they would be ready for the day when they might return to Ireland with the French and drive out the English.

Second Lieutenant Joseph Parrott expressed the attitude of one group of officers in his letter to the minister of war when he wrote in the early fall of 1805:

> When I entered the Irish Legion, I was motivated only by the desire to establish the independence of Ireland. To achieve that end, I have sacrificed a lucrative profession. The hope of again seeing my native country has enabled me to support the two years of injustice that I have suffered since the formation of this Corps.
>
> Today, that hope no longer exists. The project for the expedition to Ireland has been abandoned. There remains only the consolation of being employed in the service of France. I am languishing here; my youth is being lost in idleness. . . .
>
> I, therefore, request that Your Excellence accept my resignation and grant me at the same time permission to establish myself in Paris.[81]

Second Lieutenant Robert Lambert, who also requested to be discharged, explained his feelings to the minister of war in the following manner:

I have the honor of telling you that I have sacrificed the best years of my life and all that was dear to me for my country's cause. Furthermore, when I received your orders to go to Morlaix [to join the Legion] I used that occasion to show my devotion to the common cause. In the time that I have spent with the Legion, I have been mortified over the organization [of the Legion] which renders it incapable of serving either the French government or the people of Ireland.

Because of this, I am no longer able to remain [in the Legion], and I request that Your Excellence grant me a discharge . . . and permission to reside in France. . . . [82]

Three other Irish officers wrote to the minister of war at that time, but not to ask to be discharged, rather they wanted to be transferred out of the Irish Legion and into an active French regiment. They were weary of inactivity, and when the Grand Army marched off to meet the Austrians, they wanted to be a part of the campaign. These were men who were ready to become professional soldiers, and advancement in rank was to be found in battle, not encamped in western Brittany. Captain Louis Lacy had already been a professional soldier in the service of the king of Spain when the Treaty of Amiens was renounced and war between France and England was renewed. He received permission from the Spanish government to leave its service, and was named captain in the 6th Infantry Regiment of the Army of Boulogne. When the Irish Legion was formed in December 1803, he was transferred into that unit. But when the Campaign of 1805 began, he also lost faith in the Irish project and requested active duty in a French regiment. Lacy, who had been born in Spain of Irish parents, did not have the same nationalistic feelings as most of the men in the Legion. He was much more of a soldier of fortune than an Irish patriot. Because of his previous military experience and his ability, he had been named adjutant major in the Legion on 24 July 1805. Battalian Commander Petrezzoli wrote a lengthy comment in the margin of Lacy's letter to the minister of war in which he spoke very highly of the new adjutant major, but approved his request for a transfer in rather reserved terms. [83] It is thus not surprising that Lacy was not given permission to leave the Legion. In view of his future defection while serving in Spain, it is probably unfortunate that he was not allowed to join a French unit. [84]

Second Lieutenant Joseph Gillmer was another officer of the Legion who asked that his training and talents be put to better use. In his letter to the minister of war, he lamented that for two years he had languished in Britany in inactivity. With the army marching off to war, he wanted very much to be a part of the combat that would surely take place. [85]

Of the men requesting to be transferred from the Legion to the Grand

Army, Captain William Dowdall's letter to the minister of war is perhaps the most revealing. Neither Lacy, who was born in Spain, nor Gillmer, who was born in Liverpool, England, were typical of the native-born Irish. But Dowdall, a native of Dublin, who had lost all that he had in Ireland and had been driven into exile, typified the majority of the men in the Legion. He complained that while the Irish Legion was organized like a military unit, it had become in fact a place for pensioners. Without wishing to seem ungrateful, he said that he wanted to be useful, to put his military training and knowledge to the test, and to perfect them for the day when they would be used in his native Ireland. For these reasons, he was requesting to be transferred to a French regiment that would take part in the campaign shaping up in central Europe.[86]

These requests put Petrezzoli in an uneasy situation. He understood the frustrations of the men under his command, and could not oppose their motives.

> Many officers of the Corps that I command [he wrote to the minister of war] have requested my permission to write to Your Excellence to implore you to reassign them to French regiments that will take part in the continental war. I believe that it is my duty not to oppose their demands because I am convinced that their motives are to be of service to His Majesty and to the army. But on the other hand, even if this trend is not general [among the men of the Legion] the Corps will be considerably weakened and will lose its best officers.[87]

Marshal Berthier, who had joined the Grand Army as Napoleon's chief of staff, was not only preoccupied with the army marching into Germany, he fully understood what Petrezzoli was telling him. If he were to approve the three transfers he had received, there would be many times that number in the next dispatch. The Legion would have to be dissolved and Napoleon would have to admit that the expedition to Ireland was not merely postponed, but abandoned. The emperor was not ready to take such a step in the fall of 1805, therefore, the Irish Legion would have to remain intact. Discharging officers who no longer wished to serve was one matter, but transferring good officers out of the Legion into other regiments was quite another. Consequently, no transfers were approved, and the Legion, in a state of dejection, remained unchanged at Quimper.

The only event of interest, and one that broke the monotony of the fall of 1805 for some of the officers, was the conducting of recruits from Brittany to Strasbourg and then on to Venice. A handful of men, including William Corbet, who had not yet been transferred from the Legion, Terence O'Reilly, John Allen, and John Burgess made the journey, which lasted several months.[88] It was also at this time that General O'Connor went into voluntary semiretirement. When the VII Corps left Brittany the general went to Paris where he married the daughter of the late Marie Jean Amboine Caritat, marquis de Condorcet. Following his marriage, O'Connor purchased the Chateau de Bignon and its estate in the Loiret. Although he received his full pay as a general of division, he held no command in the remaining years of the empire.[89]

The spring of 1806 found the Irish Legion still languishing at Quimper with no hope of an expedition to Ireland. The Grand Army had not returned to its Channel camps after the victories of 1805 as many Irish had hoped that it would. Rather Napoleon had sent his triumphant soldiers into winter quarters in southern Germany with no indication at all that they would return even to France. It became increasingly difficult to generate any enthusiasm or interest for training and preparation for an expedition that everyone knew had been postponed indefinitely, if not canceled altogether. The social calender was also dull, with the exception of the marriages of Captains Edward Masterson and Louis Lacy.[90] These events provided the highlights of the social season.

There was also the departure of more men as the disappointment over the postponement of the expedition intensified. Second Lieutenant Robert Lambert, who had been talking about leaving the Legion for months, was discharged on 1 March 1806. He cited as reasons for his departure the "dissolution of the Army of Brest," and the "disarming of the fleet" at Brest. He concluded that as there would not be an expedition to Ireland, he was no longer of any use to the French Government. He requested permission to reside in France, and expressed his attachment to the emperor.[91] Second Lieutenant Charles Gaillot, a French quartermaster officer serving in the Legion, was also discharged on 1 March.[92]

Two other officers of the Legion requested in June that they be discharged. Second Lieutenant Robert Swanton asked that he be granted a discharge and permission to sail to New York in order to join his father and his brother who were refugees in that city. He made no mention of the aborted expedition or the Irish cause, only that he had desired to go to America.[93] He had been in trouble in the spring of 1806, and had been imprisoned at the Chateau de Brest for bad conduct. A report to the minister of war recommended that he be discharged as quickly as possible because he was an embarrassment to the army. However, the report also said that his loyalty to France was questionable, and suggested that if he were allowed to go to the United States, that he might very well not remain there. That, in fact, he might go on to England and win favor there by giving the enemy whatever information he had that would be of interest to them. It was, therefore, recommended that after his discharge, he be sent to a provincial town and there placed under police surveillance.[94]

Lieutenant Augustin Gibbons was yet another Irish officer who resigned his commission in June of 1806. Gibbons was devoted to the Irish cause. He had served with General Humbert in 1798 and had joined the Legion at the time of its formation. But he complained that he could not support his wife, children, and himself on the pay of a lieutenant in the French army. That in fact he had spent 2,000 francs of his own money since he had joined the Legion, and he could no longer supplement his army pay. With the expedition to Ireland postponed, he wished to leave the army for the welfare of his family.[95] Petrezzoli supported his request, [96] and Gibbons rejoined his family and remained in France.

In the summer of 1806, Captain William Corbet requested and received his discharge from the army. The recommendation that he be transferred from the Legion to the staff of his division had not been implemented. Even if it had been, there is no indication that he would have remained in the service at this time. He was disappointed that there would not be an expediton to Ireland. Inasmuch as he had joined the army solely for the purpose of returning to Ireland, he was determined to quit the army until such time as an expedition might again be reasonably expected to take place. Should events take a favorable turn, he wanted to be able to reenter the army at the rank of captain. He had contacted the military school at Saint-Cyr where he had been teaching English before joining the Legion, and the school wanted him to return to his former position. In addition, he had not felt comfortable in the Irish Legion since his brother Thomas had been killed in the duel with John Sweeny in September 1804.[97] Corbet was allowed to return to his teaching position, but when his former comrades marched off to Spain in 1808, to fight the English, he realized that he could not find self-fulfillment in the classroom in time of war. He reenlisted in the army with his former rank, but he did not rejoin the Irish regiment, according to Miles Byrne, because of his brother's tragic death. He was placed in the 70th Regiment, the former Berwick regiment of the Irish Brigade, and saw service in the Iberian Peninsula. He rose to the rank of colonel in the Napoleonic army. After thirteen years on half pay, he was again employed in the French army (1828) and made the campaign in Greece against the Turks. In April 1831, under the July Monarchy, he was given the rank of general of brigade. He retired at the mandatory age of sixty-two, and resided in Paris until his death on 12 August 1842.[98]

Morale in the Legion reached its lowest point in the spring of 1806. There seemed to be no direction or purpose for the Irish in this special unit of the French army. Without an expediton to Ireland, of what use was a battalion of Irish officers and no soldiers? This frustration was put into writing by Captain Thomas Markey in mid-April when he wrote to the minister of war:

> My greatest amibition is to be able to serve my unhappy country as well as to show my gratitude to the [French] government. The reason that I am writing to you is to try to open the eyes of His Excellence, the Minister of War, to the unhappy state in which the Irish refugees find themselves; and also to the fact that the generous intentions of His Majesty, the Emperor, on their behalf are not being served. They remain in an unfortunate situation . . . , but in the right circumstance they will prove their fidelity to a government that protects them and they will never lend their name to deceive that government.
> Our Corps is understood to be composed of Irish expatriates—or individuals who had been obliged to leave Ireland for political reasons, but of the forty-seven officers who make up the Corps, there are only eighteen who fit that description. The Irish patriots want to be, and they are, despite all reports, attached to the august person of His Majesty the Emperor and King. They understand that the humiliation of Great Britain is the only thing that will renew their hopes. They were exiled forever from their native country and have no hope of ever returning except through the aid of the power of the Emperor and the direction of his genius. All of the goals that they hold so dear are closely bound up with the glory and prosperity of France.
> The frequent discharge of officers and the desertion of our noncommissioned officers and soldiers must show how our organization is corrupt; and the events that have taken place with respect to the bookkeeping of the Corps must cause His Excellence to decide to change our system or to dissolve the Legion.[99]

The state of "The bookkeeping of the Corps" referred to a bit of confusion and misunderstanding that occurred in the late spring of 1806. It was a minor affair that generated much correspondence.[100] However, the thrust and general tone of Markey's letter reflected the sentiments of the men of the Legion, and in particular, the refugees. If it had not been for the fact that changes were already in progress, the Irish Legion would undoubtedly have had serious internal problems. But the decision had already been made to put the talents of the Irish officers to use, if not in the cause of Ireland, at least in the service of France.

In June 1806, the Legion at long last received marching orders. With war clouds once again gathering over central Europe, the Irish believed that they would join the Grand Army. To be sure, they had mixed feelings. On the one hand, they were turning their backs on Ireland and the sea. On the other hand, with the expediton to Ireland postponed, temporarily they hoped, the years of boring inactivity seemed to be at an end. There were neither promotions, nor glory, nor excitement to be had at Quimper. Whereas all of the advantages, and disadvantages, of an active campaign seemed to await them in Germany. Those men who had been solely intent on returning to Ireland, and who had families, professions, and/or businesses to return to, had already left the army. Those who remained were prepared to make the necessary adjustments to become professional French soldiers. Many still hoped that France would eventually aid Ireland to achieve independence, and that by remaining in the army, they would be ready and prepared to render the maximum assistance to their native country. The very fact that Napoleon did not dissolve the Legion was viewed by these men as a positive factor. So long as the Irish officers remained together, it seemed to imply that there would be an expedition to Ireland.

The Irish first marched to Rennes, by way of Pontivy. After resting several days, they moved on to Alençon. Their spirits, which had picked up on the march with the expectation of joining the Grand Army in Germany, sank when they reached Alençon and were told to find permanent quarters. Much to their chagrin, they sat, bored and disappointed, in eastern Brittany, while the armies of Napoleon destroyed the Prussians at Jena-Auerstadt on 14 October 1806. It was not until mid-November, after Napoleon had occupied Berlin, that the Legion again received instructions. This time it was ordered into Germany. The march took it south of Paris on the way to Verdun. Many of the officers were able to obtain permission to spend some days in the capital visiting old friends. At Verdun, there occurred an interesting episode. Miles Byrne recounts it as follows:

> The town of Verdun, where we should have halted one night, being the depot of the english prisoners of war, the governor took upon himself to lodge the irish legion in a suburb, lest its presence might be disagreeable to those prisoners; at day-break he had the draw bridge let down and the gates opened to let the legion march through, before the english prisoners could have light to see and contemplate our green flag, and its beautiful inscription, so obnoxious to them, "The independence of Ireland!"—Our march however through the town at that early hour attracted great notice; as our band played up our national air of "Patrick's day in the morning," we could see many windows opened and gentlemen in their shirts enquiring across the street, in good english, what was meant by this music at such an early hour. "Why damn it Burke, you ought to know that air" was answered from one window to another.[101]

The Irish marched on to Sarrebrouk and finally Mayence. Mayence was as far east as the Legion was to go. The city was the principal base of supplies for the Grand Army, and it was at this point that prisoners of war who had been captured after the battles of Jena and Auerstadt crossed the Rhine on their way to prison camps in France. When the Irish arrived at Mayence in early December, they were ordered to take up temporary quarters. As they settled down on the banks of the Rhine, their Legion at long last became a true military unit. Twelve hundred Polish and Irish prisoners of war volunteered to join the French army.[102] The vast majority of this number were Poles who had been pressed into the Prussian army. They were given to believe that Napoleon was favorably disposed to the reestablishment of a Polish state after the defeat of the Russian army. In fact, the emperor was, at that very time, marching east from Berlin into Poland to engage the Russians and to "liberate" the Polish people. It is then not surprising that the Polish prisoners of war were willing, even enthusiastic, to join the French army. That they were placed under Irish officers may have at first been somewhat of a surprise. But they had just been under Prussians, and the alternative would have been to be under French officers as there were not Polish officers available.

No figure is given for the number of Irish-born soldiers who were taken into the Legion at that time. These Irishmen had taken an active part in the rebellion of 1798, and had been confined in Irish prisons or aboard English prison ships awaiting exile to Australia. The English sold the able-bodied Irish prisoners to the Prussian king who put them to work in the coal mines of Silesia. When Prussia prepared for war with France, many of these Irishmen were pressed into the army, and were taken prisoner by the French after the Prussian forces were defeated at Jena and Auerstadt and scattered over central Germany. These Irish were delighted with the opportunity to join the French army as a part of the Irish Legion. They would serve under Irish officers, some of whom they had fought side by side with in the rebellion of 1798. They would no longer be prisoners of war, and they would not be returned to Prussia and the near state of slavery they had lived under for the past seven years. There was even held out to them the possibility of returning to Ireland with the "expedition," and of fighting once again for the independence of their native land. Indeed, if the Polish prisoners gladly joined the French, the Irish were overjoyed at the opportunity to be free of their Prussian masters and to have the hope of returning home. Byrne mentions by name (last names only) some of the Irish whom he, or his comrades, had known and fought with in 1798: Foster, Gunning, Dalton, Cane, Doyle, O'Brien. Then he wrote that there were "many others from the counties of Wexford and Wicklow, who knew me from my childhood."[103]

The Poles and Irish who filled out the ranks of the Legion were quite pleased with the conditions they found in the French army. The pay, rations, and living conditions of the French soldiers was much better than that of the Prussians. The discipline was less severe, and punishment for minor offenses was more reasonable. The result was a general atmosphere of tranquility and cooperation in the Legion. The new recruits were issued clothing, shoes, and equipment from the well-stocked warehouses of Mayence, and by the end of December, the Legion was ready to march. It was ordered south of Landau, in the Palatinate, to do garrison duty. There was some additional recruitment of Polish prisoners in the early months of 1807, and a seven-foot-tall Prussian prisoner who became the Legion's drum major and its pride and joy.[104]

As the Legion settled into the routine of garrison duty, a serious problem arose which disrupted the tranquility of the officer corps. Marshal François Etienne Christophe Kellermann, who commanded the army of reserve on the Rhine, of which the Legion was then a part, decided to incorporate the Irish into the 2nd Legion of the North as its 5th Battalion.[105] When the Irish at Landau learned of the marshal's intention there was much agitation and, according to General Jean François Dejean's report to the minister of war, the resignation of three Irish officers. The three officers in question, Lieutenants Paul Murray and John Burgess, and Second Lieutenant Joseph Parrott, wrote to the minister of war in the second week of January and asked to be returned to civilian life.[106] They did not make any mention of the inclusion of the Irish battalion into one of the Legions of the North, however, they stressed the point that the expediton to Ireland had been called off and that they had joined the French army to fight the English in Ireland, not to serve in a continental war. The letter of John Burgess reflected the sentiments of Parrott and Murray. He wrote:

> When I received from Your Excellence a commission in the Irish Legion, that Corps seemed to be particularly destined to serve against English, and I only took up arms to contribute to the crushing of that tyrant of my country. Unfortunately, events have postponed that expedition. I had continued until now to hope that the expedition [to Ireland] would take place. But now that it is the intention of His Majesty the Emperor to employ the Irish Corps in the continental war, I request that Your Excellence grant me permission to retire from a service that is foreign to me, and to permit me to reside in Paris where I will resume my first occupation, that of working for the liberation of Ireland.[107]

Even though Burgess did not openly say so, Petrezzoli declared that the reason for the resignations was because the Irish Legion was ordered to join the 2nd Legion of the North.[108] He further charged that Captains William Lawless and Thomas Markey had been the principal agitators in the Legion who had stirred up resentment, and were responsible for the resignation of their three brother officers. Petrezzoli also said that "Lawless and Markey had frequently been the chief intriguers who have caused agitation within the Battalion.[109] Markey did not follow the example of Burgess, Parrott, and Murray, but Lawless did offer to resign his commission.[110]

The report from the Bureau of the Infantry (2nd Division) which informed the minister of war of these problems in the Legion also contained a fundamental criticism of the Irish officers and a far-reaching recommendation. After pointing out that Captain Markey had been criticizing his battalion commander, the report reminded Marshal Berthier that the Irish officers had not supported Adjutant Commander MacSheehy or General O'Connor. Furthermore, they have always been divided among themselves over the future system of government for their own country. "Perhaps, rather than keeping them all in one battalion [it concluded], it would be better to disperse them throughout the different foreign corps, and only reunite them in the event of an expedition to Ireland. If they should refuse this measure, they should be entirely separated from the army."[111]

Exactly why the Irish Legion did not become the 5th Battalion of the 2nd Legion of the North is not certain. The most likely explanation is that it was not ready for combat, and the Legions of the North were preparing to join the Grand Army in Poland for the campaign against the Russians that would take place as soon as the weather would permit. The language barrier between officers and men was a serious problem. The Polish soldiers who made up the vast majority of the Legion did not speak French or English. Besides their native language, they understood German military commands and had been trained in Prussian maneuvers. It would take time for them to learn the minimum amount of French to understand their Irish officers, and they also had to be schooled in French tactical movements. These were by no means insurmountable problems, but they would require time and effort. The Poles had already been trained as soldiers by the Prussians; it was not like working with green recruits. But the legion to which they would have been attached was needed in Poland at once. Thus the Irish and Poles were left behind.

Another problem of the Irish Legion was that its commander was writing to the minister of war that there were officers who were unfit for campaign. Some because of their age, others because of their attitude, but the bottom line was that Petrezzoli clearly did not want to lead them into battle. Every petty problem seemed to lead to resignations, or the threat of resignations. There were far too many prima donnas, agitators, and old men who, when they were not quarrelling with one another, were complaining over his head directly to the minister of war.[112]

Poor Petrezzoli had to be much more of a diplomat than a battalion commander. "I do not know how to put into words" he wrote to the minister of war in April 1807, "the methods of firmness and of prudence that I must employ to maintain good order and discipline."[113] There had been a period of relative quiet and harmony, a honeymoon, if you will, following the Sweeny/Corbet duel and the removal of Battalion Commander Blackwell and Adjutant Commander MacSheehy. But many of the Irish officers were fiercely independent men who had not entered the French army to become professional soldiers, and if they remained in the army after the expedition had been postponed, it was either because they believed France was Ireland's only hope of gaining independence, or because they had little waiting for them in civilian life. They were slowly becoming professional soldiers in a foreign army, and many of them grudgingly so. There had not been promotions in the Legion for three years, that is, since its formation, because it had not taken part in the campaigns and battles of central Europe in 1805 and 1806. And even in 1807, with a campaign against the Russians shaping up for the summer, the Legion was doing garrison duty west of the Rhine. The few honors and titles that were granted only created problems.

Shortly after the rank and file of the Legion was filled with Polish soldiers, Marshal Kellermann sent Lieutenant Joseph Kosloski to the Irish Legion and Petrezzoli requested that this ten-year veteran be employed as the adjutant major of the battalion with the rank of captain. Kosloski had an impressive military record that included service on the staff of Marshal André Masséna during the Italian campaign of 1805. Captain Louis Lacy was performing the duties of adjutant major at the time Kosloski arrived in January, 1807. Although the minister of war approved Kosloski as adjutant major, Petrezzoli found it necessary, in April, to reverse his decision and to reinstate Lacy. His hand had been forced by the Irish officers who would neither take orders from, nor cooperate with Kosloski.

> As for Lieutenant Kosloski, [Petrezzoli wrote to the minister of war] the majority of officers of the Legion would not want to see him as Adjutant Major because he was not Irish. Knowing well the character of the [Irish] officers, I felt that this officer [Kosloski] should not be exposed to their mistreatment. For the good of the service, I believe that Your Altesse should appoint a Frenchman as Adjutant Major. . . . I believe that this would contribute very much to abate the spirit of independence that reigns among the officers under my orders. This is a dangerous spirit that they are unwilling to relinquish.[114]

The battalion commander also recommended that Kosloski be promoted to the rank of captain, and concluded this lengthy letter on almost a pathetic

note: "I am the only one who is able to understand the unpleasant occur-
ences that a Chief feels in commanding such a corps."[115]

Petrezzoli's unhappy position did not improve. One week later, he
again was complaining about his officers and recommending that some of
them be removed. This time the problem centered around a Prussian
officer. Marshal Kellermann had taken an interest in Captain Smalian Delhora, and he sent him to the Irish Legion in April 1807 to command a
company. Delhora arrived just prior to a general inspection, and he wished
to take part in the final review. Seeing Lieutenant Patrick Powell at the head
of a company, in the absence of his sick captain, Delhora, who outranked the
lieutenant, demanded that he pass in review at the head of the company in
place of Powell. As the captain had no orders giving him command, the
lieutenant refused to give way, and actually pushed the superior officer out
of the way. Delhora reported the incident to the battalion commander, and
Petrezzoli had Lieutenant Powell arrested and imprisoned him to await
trial. The Irish officers were furious. They drew lots, and Lieutenant John
Allen won the "honor" of challenging the Prussian to a duel. However,
when he did so, instead of fighting, Delhora again went to Petrezzoli and
Allen was also imprisoned. Next, it was the turn of Lieutenant Terence
O'Reilly. This officer confronted Delhora on the parade ground and demanded that he fight on the spot or give him his word of honor to do so as
soon as formal arrangements could be made. The captain agreed to find a
second and duel with swords. The duel took place, and Delhora was forced
to agree to ask for a transfer out of the Legion.[116]

It was precisely this kind of affair that was so frustrating to Petrezzoli.
On 13 April 1807, he wrote disparagingly that Captain Delhora had all of
the qualities of a good officer who would be an asset to his command. But
alas, he "had already written to Marshal Kelerman [sic] to inform him that
it was impossible for him to remain in this Corps."[117] Furthermore, he went
on, there were many intrigues against him on the part of the Irish, and it
was only with great difficulty that he was able to thwart them. "It is with
the greatest pain [he wrote] that I see these same troublesome and indolent
men with a surprising incapability for everything that concerns the military
profession."[118] He then implored the minister to accept the resignation of
Captain Lawless, which the captain had written at the time the battalion
had been ordered to join the 2nd Legion of the North. The other officer
whom Petrezzoli could no longer tolerate was Captain Markey. This man,
he wrote, "had declared . . . that if an Angel were to descend from the
heavens, and if that Angel were not Irish, he would take no orders from
him."[119] He also pointed out that Markey had been one of the main men
who had denounced Adjutant Commander MacSheehy when he had com-

manded the Legion, and that he (MacSheehy) had even been born in Ireland! Finally, Petrezzoli concluded by declaring that "In removing . . . from the Corps the infirmed and the aged, who are as discontented as the others, and several inept officers . . . it would make possible the appointment of several other officers, in particular Captain Delhora and three Polish officers."[120]

Berthier did not take the battalion commander's advice. Lawless and Markey remained in the Legion as did those unnamed "infirmed and aged" and "inept officers" to whom he had referred. Thus, it comes as no surprise that in midsummer 1807 Petrezzoli was still complaining of the Irish officers, although he was satisfied with the progress of the rank and file. "The corps has already a reputation for 'Tenue' as well as for good discipline," he wrote, but "It would have been easier if the officers would have paid more attention to the housing and equipment of their men, but whether through thoughtlessness or negligence, I still do not know which, those details remain unattended.[121]

The problems facing Petrezzoli in 1807 may not have been as serious as those that had confronted MacSheehy in 1804, nevertheless, the lack of discipline, the fierce clanish and nationalistic characteristics displayed by the Irish made it extremely difficult, if not impossible, for the Legion to function as a military organization. In many respects, it was still a "political corps." However, now it was a political corps that seemingly had lost its political base. It was not going to Ireland to establish an independent government in which its officers would play a significant role. It was becoming a foreign legion in the French army, and if it were to go into battle, it would be fighting and dying for France and the Emperor Napoleon, not for Ireland and the oppressed Irish people. The undisciplined conduct and the general discontent on the part of the Irish was, to a large extent, the result of their frustrations. They had nowhere else to turn. If Napoleon and France did not support them, then the movement, which had begun in Ireland in the 1790s, would be dead. Indeed, it had already died in Ireland.[122] The officers of the Irish Legion, and a handful of civilians living in Paris and throughout France, were all that was left of the movement that had shed so much blood and led to such suffering in 1798. Clearly, the Legion in 1807 was not fulfilling the desires and aspirations of either the Irish or the French.

It is very likely that the Legion was saved in 1807 by the appointment of General Henri James Clarke, the future duc de Feltre, as minister of war. Clarke had been born in France of Irish parents. His father, Colonel Thomas Clarke, had commanded the Dillon regiment in the old Irish Brigade, while his maternal grandfather, William Shee (O'Shee) had also served in the Brigade. In 1782, Clarke completed his studies at the Ecole Militaire at Paris and was commissioned in the Berwick regiment of the Irish Brigade. His father having died when Henri was young, he came under the care of his uncle Colonel Henry Shee, who was secretary to the duc d'Orleans. He was quickly promoted to the rank of captain in a hussar regiment, but in 1789, he quit the army and served for two years as a diplomat at the Court of Saint James. During these years, he spent some time in Ireland where he became acquainted with his relatives and nurtured his pro-Irish sentiments. He returned to the army in 1791, and supported the principles of the Revolution. Serving with the armies of the Rhine, he rose to the rank of general. Under the Directory, he served in the Typographical Bureau, as did General Bonaparte, and in 1797, he worked with the commander of the Army of Italy to bring about the Peace of Campo Formio. He attached himself to Bonaparte, and in 1804, became the emperor's private secretary for military affairs. He was with the Grand Army for the campaigns of 1805 and 1806. When Berthier's functions as both minister of war and chief of staff of the Grand Army became more than one man could handle, Napoleon named Clarke to head the war ministry.[123]

Clarke took a special interest in the Irish Legion at a time when it was more of a nuisance than an asset to Napoleon. He increased it from one battalion to three within two years, and when the foreign legions in the army were reorganized in 1811, and it became the 3rd Foreign Regiment, he saw to it that it retained its national identity by adding to its title "Irish." There seems to be little doubt but that the new minister of war looked favorably upon the Irish. E. Fieffé, the noted French historian on foreign troops in the French army, wrote of him: "The Duc de Feltre, remembering that he was of an Irish family, had a fondness for this [Irish] regiment, which he wanted to maintain at all cost. He wanted it to be composed only of Irish subjects, and this desire flattered his national origin."[124] However, Byrne is critical of Clarke for not supporting the Irish during the years of the empire, and for being openly hostile towards them under the Bourbon Restoration.[125]

The Legion spent only a short time at Landau. By mid-February, it marched to the English Channel and took up quarters at Boulogne-sur-Mer. Many of the Irish officers took this move as a sign that Napoleon still intended an expedition to England or Ireland. However, their joy was short-lived. In June, the Legion was moved to Antwerp where it again performed garrison duties. The Irish officers, although disappointed at leaving the coast, were pleased to come under the command of General Harty, who commanded the brigade in which they were placed. But again, they were only a few months in that large city. In September, they were

ordered to the island of Walcheren. There was no joy over this new assignment. The island was a remote outpost at the mouth of the Scheldt River
that formed the first line of defense for the great naval base at Antwerp.

By the time the Legion had settled down on Walcheren in the fall of
1807, it had taken on the characteristics of a foreign battalion in the service
of France. From the point of view of the French, it was really no different
from the Prussian or Polish regiments, or the Italian units serving under the
imperial eagle. The army itself was losing the revolutionary characteristics of
a national, or peoples, army and becoming a Napoleonic, or Imperial, army.
Nationality was becoming less important, and loyalty to the Emperor was
the dominant factor that held it together. Being Irish had been the principal
ingredient, indeed, a required one, at the time the Legion had been formed
in 1803; and its *raison d'être* was the expedition to Ireland. But by the end
of 1807, all of this had changed. There was to be no Irish expedition in the
foreseeable future. The imperial army was in central Europe, which had
dominated events, and Napoleon's full attention, for the past two years.
Everything had changed, including the Irish Legion. It is true that there
remained Irish officers in the Legion who still looked toward Ireland. They
still hoped that one day they would return to their native land, and with
French support, drive out the English. But their numbers had been thinned
by the resignation of many of their cohorts who had despaired of the dream
of 1803. Those who remained in the Legion had gradually accepted the
reality of the situation. They were Irishmen in the French army. They
would fight the battles of France and the emperor. However, as England
was still at war with France, they could reason that the battles of France
were not too estranged from those of Ireland, particularly if they involved
the English. Even the make-up of the rank and file of the Legion was not
what had originally been designed. Instead of Irish volunteers raised in
Ireland after the landing, the majority were Poles who had little interest in
the Irish cause. The *Irish Legion* was fading rapidly, and the *3rd Foreign
Regiment (Irish)* was gradually coming into existence.

4

Walcheren: The Loss of the 1st Battalion

The island of Walcheren, which had recently been separated from Holland and annexed to France, was no more than twelve miles across at any point. It had but two towns of any consequence, Middelburg and Flushing. The latter was by far the more important as it had an adequate harbor and was well fortified. The batteries of Flushing dominated the entrance of the Scheldt, so that an enemy, the English, would first have to silence its guns before any serious attack could be made on Antwerp, the most important French naval facility facing Britain. The island was scarcely above sea level and virtually flat. The northern and western portions were marshy and poorly drained. Severe storms and high tides caused flooding, which on occasion resulted in the loss of life.

The Legion was first quartered at West Capelle, but this extreme western section of the island proved to be so devastating to the health of the men that in November it was moved inland to Ter Verre and Middelburg and the following month to Flushing. Throughout the fall of 1807, the Legion suffered the drastic effects of malaria. Referred to alternatively as the "Walcheren Fever" or simply "the Fever," it tended to be more disabling than deadly, although deaths were not uncommon. Early in December 1807, Commanding General Lows-Claude Monnet de Lorbeau wrote of the Irish Legion:

> This Corps, just as the 1st Prussian Regiment, has had an epidemic [of fever] with ravaging effects ever since its arrival here. Nearly all of the officers are sick. Commander Petrozolli [sic] has been on his deathbed since his arrival and a large number of the troops are in the hospitals.[1]

Even after moving to Flushing the fever continued to reduce the effectiveness of the Legion. "Having only a feeble constitution," wrote Lieutenant

John Burgess shortly after his arrival at Flushing, "I suffered for two months from a fever."[2]

Byrne, writing of the medical problems of the Irish Legion said that "Captain Ware never could have recovered had he remained at Flushing, he was so reduced by the fever."[3] Fortunately for the captain, he was ordered to join the Battalion of the Legion that had recently been sent to Spain. Byrne himself came down with the fever. Although he consumed large quantities of Jesuit bark (quinine), which was believed to be the only cure, his condition only worsened. In his *Memoirs* he wrote the following of his illness:

> Our surgeon major [Patrick] Saint-Leger being in a dying state, I had to call on doctor Moke [Mokey], one of the first physicians in Flushing. He, seeing the worst symptoms, my feet greatly swelled, and that the great quantity of bark that I had taken did not stop the fever, he advised me of all things to change the air.—I obtained, in consequence of his certificate, a leave of absence for a month.[4]

Byrne took his leave in Brussels and gradually recovered his health, but shortly after his return to Walcheren, the hated, and dreaded, fever returned. And so it was with the majority of the Irish officers as well as the Polish and Irish rank and file of the Legion. It was only with their departure from the unhealthy climate of the lower Scheldt that they were able to leave behind them the Walcheren fever.

If the fever was a major concern to the officers and men, it was by no means the Legion's only problem. In the first week of December 1807, almost immediately after their arrival at Flushing, General Monnet held a general inspection. His report to the minister of war reveals the shambles in which he found the Legion.

> I have the honor of addressing you [he wrote on 9 December, 1807] on my inspection of the Irish Battalion.
>
> I wish that I was able to send you a more satisfactory report on the various aspects of this Corps, and that this inspection which I have just completed could have offered a clearer and more precise result. For twenty days, I have been studying the registers of the Council [of the Legion], which were three meetings in arrears, and which can only be described as—irregular.
>
> The most complete disorder reigns in the use of the Legion's money. Everything is worn out, and the designated purpose [for these funds] has not been observed. It is only necessary to offer one case. The administration of this corps is totally corrupt. The Council has proven by its bad management that it never considered its duties, and that it absolutely ignored the laws and regulations that lay out and establish its responsibilities. It left to

chance the operations of the clothing officer, and there are no records of his transactions. . . . Most of the soldiers do not have their [pay] books, and their bad condition shows that they have not received all of the equipment and clothing to which they are entitled. This absolute disorder may be attributed to the situation of this Corps. The officers, noncommissioned officers and soldiers who make it up are foreigners and speak very little French. Consequently nothing is accomplished on the company level. . . .

I believe, Monseigneur, that it is indispensable that you send to this Corps several noncomissioned officers to reestablish order, and in doing so this measure will do no more than prevent the total disorganization of this Corps.

It is also indispensable that the accountability of this Corps in materiél and money be again verified by the review of a subinspector because of the confusing results of my inspection. . . .

I was satisfied with the instruction of the soldiers. It was good and of a high quality. But the "tenue," the company records and the bookkeeping cause me to believe that there is a great deal of laxity on the part of the officers towards their duties. . . .[5]

General Monnet also explained that the Fever was of epidemic proportions in the Legion, and implied that this contributed to the problems of the Legion.

On 30 December 1807, the chief of the Bureau of Inspection forwarded a three-page summery of General Monnet's inspection of the Legion to the minister of war. He had available to him all of the documents related to the inspection.[6] In addition to summarizing Monnet's report, he wrote:

The Battalion Commander [Petrezzoli] wrote a note on each one [of the officers] for the Inspector. There are among these officers individuals without education, unfit for military service, who will never become good officers. Furthermore, they have a bad *Tenue* and are careless, and . . . some of them foment intrigue and are undisciplined.[7]

There seems to be little doubt but that the overall condition of the Irish Legion in 1807 was poor. Nor was the Fever the cause of its problems, although the sickness of so many officers and men most likely exacerbated the already deteriorated situation. Yet when one remembers that many of these officers were given their commissions on the basis of their political influence in Ireland, or because of the amount of suffering they had undergone at the hands of the English, it becomes quite understandable that there would be poor or even incompetent army officers among them. First MacSheehy, and then Petrezzoli, had complained to their superiors, and even to the minister of war, that there were officers in the Legion who were unfit to command. But neither man had the authority on his own to remove those whom he deemed unqualified, and as the Legion was destined for Ireland and political influence was equally, if not more, important than military talent, Napoleon would not allow its ranks to be depleted.

As one aspect of General Monnet's inspection, Petrezzoli wrote a brief evaluation of each officer in the Legion. Although this document has built into it the prejudicial feelings of the battalion commander, when his biases are discounted, it does present a general profile of the Legion at this point in time. Forty officers are listed, but as Captain Bernard MacSheehy had been absent for several years, there were thirty-nine on active duty. The bright spot of this document is its reference to four men as being "excellent" officers (Captains Louis Lacy, Jerome Fitzhenry, and Smalian Delhora, and Second Lieutenant Augustin Osmont) and four others as being "very good" (Captain Joseph Kosloski, and Lieutenants Terence O'Reilly, Edmond Saint Leger, and John Allen). On the other hand, he deemed nine of his subordinates incompetent (Captains Patrick MacSheehy, William Barker, and Patrick Brangan, Lieutenants Christopher Marlin, Paul Murray, and Patrick MacMahon, Second Lieutenants Bernard MacDermotte, John Gibbon, and Jerome Dowling). His description of these officers knew no limits. For example, he said of Marlin, Gibbons, and Dowling that they have no understanding of military affairs and "were incapable of ever being officers." Of P. MacSheehy, Barker, and MacMahon he wrote: "He has never been of any use to the Corps," while Brangan, Murray, and MacDermotte had "no education or understanding of the military [and were] incapable of ever being a good officer." In addition to the nine men whom he considered imcompetent, he described eight others as "poor" (Captains John MacGuire, William Dowdall, and Thomas Markey, Lieutenant John Burgess, and Second Lieutenants Joseph Parrotte, John Campbell, John Reilly, and Alexander Devreux). Thus in the opinion of the battalion commander fully 44 percent of his officers were poor or incompetent. The remaining men were either referred to as "good" officers (Captains Victor Gregoire, Patrick St. Leger, John Tennent, Edward Masterson, and Auguste O'Maley, Lieutenant Miles Byrne, and Second Lieutenants Joseph Gillmer, François Eagar, and Denis Thyroux), or they simply met with general approval (Captains William Lawless, Hugh Ware, and Patrick MacCann, and Second Lieutenants Michael Sheridan and August O'Morand.)[8]

In Petrezzoli's comments the word "undisciplined" was used frequently to describe his subordinates, even when he felt they were good officers. Four were singled out as having a drinking problem (Dowling, O'Morand, Campbell, and Marlin), while the expression "bad attitude" was commonly attributed to those whom he considered to be poor officers. He wrote off Patrick MacMahon as being too old "more than 50 years old." Actually, the

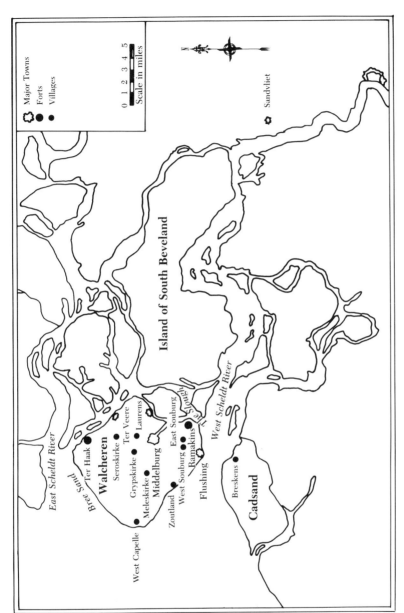

East Scheldt River

Bree Sand

Ter Haak

Walcheren

Seroskirke

Ter Veere

Grypskirke

Laurens

Meleskirke

Middelburg

West Capelle

Zoutland

West Souburg

East Souburg

Ramakins

Souly

Flushing

West Scheldt River

Breskens

Cadsand

Island of South Beveland

Sandvliet

3. Walcheren

lieutenant was only forty-three, but his commander said that "he has never been of any service or use to the Corps."[9]

General Monnet's evaluation of the rank and file of the Legion was much more favorable. He found them to be good soldiers and well instructed, although their uniforms and equipment were not in good condition. When one considers that the vast majority of them had been trained originallly in the Prussian army or the English army or navy, it is impossible to determine to what extent the Irish officers were responsible. The Irish did instruct them in French maneuvers and tactics, but they did not begin with raw recruits. Nevertheless, the training and ability of the soldiers under their command did reflect favorably upon the officers of the Legion. In conclusion, it should be said that while the reports, based upon this inspection, cast a shadow upon the officers as a whole, the Irish battalions, would account well for themselves when in 1808 and 1809 they went for the first time into combat.

By the end of 1807, the Legion had been in existence for four years, although for three of those years it was little more than a battalion on paper. It's strength stood at 1,551 officers and men.[10] In November of that year, it was reorganized into two battalions. The 2nd Battalion was sent to Spain[11] in November to join the army commanded by Marshal Joachim Murat that marched to Madrid in 1808. Because so many of the officers were sick with the Fever, it was necessary to select those who were healthy for the battalion destined for Spain. Captain Louis Lacy was given command of the battalion, as he was the senior officer who was not on the sick role. The departure of some 800 men left behind a battalion of which the majority of the officers and men were in the hospitals of Flushing and Middelburg. Battalion Commander Petrezzoli continued to command the Legion, and recruitment efforts were intensified so as to make possible the formation of a third battalion.

While the 2nd Battalion marched to Madrid in the winter of 1808, the 1st continued to do garrison duty on the island of Walcheren. The social life at Flushing provided little distraction for the officers who eagerly looked forward to any duty that would take them from the island. The cold weather reduced substantially the number of cases of the Fever, but many of the officers and men were slow in regaining their strength. Furthermore, many of the men had relapses from time to time, so that it was not until they left the unhealthy climate of Zealand that they were finally freed of the hated Fever. If the positive side of winter was an improvement of the health of the men on Walcheren, it also introduced the stormy season. In January 1808, Flushing suffered a great disaster when a fierce storm caused the dikes to give way and the low-lying section of the city and the surrounding districts were inundated. The water reached a depth fifteen feet in some parts of the city. There was no loss of military lives, although large quantities of supplies and gunpowder were lost. The civilian damage to property was appalling, and the loss of life caused much suffering.[12]

The remainder of the winter and the spring of 1808 was uneventful on Walcheren. The general condition of the 1st Battalion gradually improved according to a report to the minister of war.[13] There were personnel changes and the usual problems which the Irish officers seemed unwittingly to generate. In February, Captain Hugh Ware was sent to join the 2nd Battalion in Spain, and Lieutenant John Burgess was discharged. Then on 12 May, Second Lieutenants John Campbell and Jerome Dowling were ordered to Spain. It was also in May that a replacement arrived for Captain Patrick St. Leger, the Legion's surgeon since 1804, who had died of the Fever on 14 December 1807. The new medical officer was Adjutant-Major Louis Prevose. It might be noted at this point that in addition to St. Leger, two other officers of the Legion had died in the second half of 1807: Lieutenant Louis Dupouget (8 July) and Lieutenant John Gibbons (3 October).[14] Finally, on 25 July, 1808, a second large detachment was ordered to Spain. This detachment is sometimes referred to as the 3rd Battalion of the Irish Legion, but only five officers can be identified and 600 men. Captain Jerome Fitzhenry, as the senior officer, was in command. This detachment joined the French army at Pampeluma where it was merged with the much depleted 2nd Battalion.[15] The Fever continued to reduce the number of officers and men who were fit for duty at Flushing. Captain Edward Masterson was given prolonged leave to recover his health, as he had been quite ill ever since his arrival on Walcheren.[16] Captain Patrick MacSheehy had seen no active service since the summer of 1807. He had been given permission to retire to Aix-la-Chapelle to reestablish his health. His battalion had actually lost track of him for more than a year, but had carried him on its roster. In October of 1808, Petrezzoli learned indirectly that he had been living in Paris since August of that year. MacSheehy had apparently asked the War Office to be retired on a military pension, for Petrezzoli, in a letter to the minister of war, after stating that he had been of no use to the battalion says, "However, on the grounds that he is an Irish refugee [in France], and furthermore because of his infirmity [malaria] it seems that he deserves the good will of the government, and it is on these grounds that I recommend him to you [for a pension]."[17]

Captain Patrick MacCann posed yet another problem for Battalion Commander Petrezzoli. The captain had been considered a troublemaker and Petrezzoli had tried, unsuccessfully, to have him removed from the Legion. Then in January 1808, the battalion commander accused MacCann of desertion in the face of the enemy, and asked that he be court-martialed. The case had little merit. Rather it reflected the strained relations between the two men. MacCann had been placed in charge of a detachment of troops at a small camp at Dishoch [Dishoek] about four miles west of Flushing on the coast. Each evening the Captain returned to Flushing where he spent the night and returned to his command in the morning. Petrezzoli, when he learned of these unauthorized departures—"desertions" he called it—placed MacCann under arrest for one month and sought his court-martial. What is interesting about this affair is that it did not remain an internal matter handled by the battalion commander. Instead, we find the commanding general, Monnet, taking it to the minister of war! Although the captain was not court-martialed and his reputation was saved, his career ended the following year when he died of wounds received in battle.[18]

MacCann had further problems in the spring of 1809. As one of the senior captains of the recently constituted 1st Battalion of the 3rd Foreign Regiment, he became a member of the battalion's administrative council. However, Petrezzoli removed him from the council and replaced him with Captain Joseph L. Koslowski. The reason given for MacCann's removal was that he did not speak or understand the French language well enough to take part in the proceedings of that body. This action on the part of the battalion commander led to a formal protest by two other members of the council, Captains William Dowdall and William Barker. These two senior captains of the battalion declared that MacCann did in fact have sufficient command of French to take part in the deliberations, that he was senior in time of rank to Koslowski, and they demanded that he be reinstated on the council. General Monnet was drawn into the conflict and by the end of May it had reached the ministry of war in Paris. Captain Koslowski continued to sit on the council, under protest, through the summer, until the matter was settled in mid-August when the garrison of Flushing surrendered to the English and MacCann died of his wounds.[19]

The whole affair was clearly a continuation of the friction and bad feelings that existed between some of the Irish officers and their Italian battalion commander. It also reflected resentment at a Polish officer replacing an Irish officer on the important Administrative Council. Koslowski was an excellent officer with a good record[20] but he was not Irish! Had MacCann, whose French was extremely poor,[21] been replaced by a junior Irish officer the affair would undoubtedly have ended at that point. However, the Irish officers were still clinging to the concept of an *Irish* regiment, which would be made up at least of Irish officers. They wanted Irish noncommissioned officers to be promoted to fill vacancies in the officer corps rather than Poles or Germans filling such openings.

Another problem that plagued the Legion at this time was the detachment of six officers to Brest. Captains William Lawless, Thomas Markey, Patrick Brangan, Lieutenant Paul Murray, and Second Lieutenants Alexander Devreax and John Reilly had been "lent" to the navy on 1 March 1807. At the time of their departure, the Legion was overstaffed with officers and their absence caused little inconvenience. However, with the departure of the 2nd Battalion to Spain late in 1807, followed by a second battalion in the summer of 1808, coupled with the number of officers sick at Flushing, the absence of the six came to be a hardship. By the end of 1808, both Petrezzoli and General Monnet were pleading with the minister of war for their return.[22] The officers themselves also requested that they be allowed to return to Flushing or, if that was not in the best interest of the service, that they be sent to join the Irish battalion fighting in Spain.[23] Finally, on 11 May 1809, the minister of war wrote to the commanding officer at Brest to send the Irish officers, not to Flushing or to Spain, but to Landau to become the core of a new 3rd Battalion of the Legion.[24] Despite these orders all six officers were listed on the June report of the 1st Battalion, and Murray, Devreux, and Markey were shown as present at Flushing. Lawless, Reilly and Brangan were indicated as still being at Brest, although when the siege of Flushing began early in August, they were in the city with their battalion.[25]

There was yet one other problem that continually troubled the Irish Legion. Between 1806 and 1809, there were four Polish officers in the Legion. It is true that more than half of the soldiers in the Irish battalions were Poles, and in the absence of sufficient Irishmen this was acceptable to the Irish officer corps. But they wanted the officers to be Irish. Moreover, the Polish officers did not wish to be in an Irish Legion. Second Lieutenants Michael Lipinski and Dribinski found themselves in the Legion in 1806 when it was formed into a combat strength battalion. They maintained that a mistake had been made and immediately requested to be transferred. In 1807, when Polish battalions were being formed in the French army, they asked to be sent to join one of the new units. But, more than two years passed before their names were dropped from the lists of officers in the Irish Legion.[26]

The other two Polish officers, Captain Joseph L. Koslowski and Second Lieutenant Jean Zelenski, remained in the 1st Battalion. Koslowski came to be somewhat acceptable to the Irish officers, and served on Petrezzoli's staff as adjutant major for some months in 1808 and 1809. At the siege of Flushing, he was the company commander of the carabiniers, one of the two elite companies of the battalion.[27] Zelenski seems to have joined the 1st Battalion at Flushing in the winter of 1808–9, as he first appears on the list of officers in March 1809. The documents tell us only that he was the second lieutenant in Captain William Barker's 3rd Company of the 1st Battalion.[28]

In the spring of 1809, the Irish Legion was given a new name and organization. By a decree dated 13 April, the emperor established the 3rd Foreign Regiment.[29] Through the intercession of the minister of war, Henri-Jacques Clarke, a second-generation Irishman, the regiment was allowed to add "Irish" to its title. Some references to it are simply "3rd Foreign Regiment," but the officers themselves always added the "Irish," and in fact most references are to the "Irish Battalion" or the "Irish Regiment." The Regiment was originally composed of the two existing battalions, with the 1st at Flushing and the 2nd serving as part of the Army of Spain. There would be added a 3rd, 4th, and 5th battalion at such time as the emperor would designate. The Regiment would have the same organization and make-up as a French light infantry regiment, that is chasseurs. It would be commanded by a colonel who would have his own staff, and each battalion would have companies of *carabiniers*, *voltigeurs*, and *fusiliers*. The first four battalions would each be commanded by a *chef de bataillon*.[30]

The 1st Battalion of the newly formed Irish Regiment was nothing more than the old 1st Battalion of the Irish Legion. The term "Legion" had been used less and less in 1807 and 1808. In its place, one finds the "1st Irish Battalion" and the "2nd Irish Battalion," and in Spain that terminology continued to be used even after the formation of the regiment. The 1st Battalion was headquartered at Flushing and Petrezzoli remained its commanding officer. Napoleon did not name a colonel for the regiment until the summer of 1809, and then, under the influence of his minister of war, Clarke, Colonel Daniel O'Meara received the command. The battalion at Flushing did not have a full complement of officers in the spring and the first half of the summer. In March, more than half of its officers were reported either "on mission" (at Brest or on recruiting assignments) or on leave (as Tennent and MacSheehy) for reasons of health.[31] By the first of July, the situation had improved. There were only four vacancies in the officer's ranks, and of the twenty listed, only three were still absent on mission at Brest.[32] The complement of noncommissioned officers and soldiers was less impressive. This figure is given at just over 450 at the time of the siege.[33] Considering that the battalion was composed of four companies of *fusiliers*, one of *carabiniers* and one of *voltigeurs* its strength should have been closer to 800 men. Irish officers were recruiting among the British prisoners of war, but by midsummer, the new recruits were being sent not to Flushing, but to Landau where a new Irish battalion, the third, was being formed.[34]

The Irish battalion formed only a small portion of the garrison on the Island of Walcheren when the English landed on 30 July 1809. General Monnet had under his command two battalions of the Prussian Regiment (1,709 men), a battalion of returned French deserters, referred to as "the Flushing Chasseurs," (1,089 men), the 1ˢᵗ Colonial Battalion (869 men), the 1ˢᵗ Irish Battalion (480 men), and from several different units 349 artillerymen.[35] This little army, cut off from the rest of Europe by water and weakened by the Walcheren Fever, was far from the pride of the French army. Indeed, only a small minority were even Frenchmen. The battalions that made up the garrison were not considered to be first line fighting units. In the event of an English invasion the Walcheren garrison was to slow down the enemy's advance, to hold out as long as possible at Flushing, so as to buy time to gather an army in the vicinity of Antwerp to repel the foe.

The English expedition to the Scheldt had several goals. Its principle one was the destruction of the French fleet in the Scheldt and of the naval facilities at Antwerp and Flushing. The success of the expedition would have been a crippling blow to French naval power and reduce still further the possibility of a future invasion of England or Ireland. The second aim of the "Grand Expedition" was to aid their hard pressed Austrian ally who was in the immediate danger of losing the war in East-Central Europe. After an initial success at Eckmuhl (19–23, April) on the upper Danube, Napoleon had been fought to a standstill at Aspern-Essling, just below Vienna (21–22, May). He had regrouped his forces, and on 6 July defeated the Archduke Charles at Wagram. The Austrian army had retreated to the North, but on 10 July, Charles asked for an armistice. The British expedition, which had been planned months earlier as a means to divert French troops, and attention, from Austria, arrived in Zeeland too late to be of any real help to its ally. But whether or not it assisted Austria, it still could serve the primary purpose of delivering a severe blow to French naval power.[36]

The grand strategy of the English was to enter the west branch of the Scheldt and sail up the river to the vicinity of Sandvliet, about ten miles from Antwerp, and there to land the army on the east (right) bank. Then a combined land and naval attack would be launched against Antwerp and its naval facilities. In order to carry out this plan, there were certain secondary objectives that would have to be taken first. Before the ships of the line or the troopships could enter the West Scheldt either Cadsand on the south (left) bank or Flushing, on the north (right) bank, or preferably both, would have to be in English hands in order to silence the French guns. The original plan to land troops on Cadsand was canceled due to bad weather and confusion, or at least misunderstandings, at the highest levels in the English command.[37] It was then decided to land on the north side of the island of Walcheren, as the fleet would be sheltered from the adverse winds at Veere Gat. The island would be occupied and Flushing attacked and captured. Then the main fleet would be able to enter the West Scheldt and move up the river.

The English, who always patrolled the mouth of the Scheldt to challenge the departure of French ships, began to appear in strength between 23 and 26 July. By nightfall on the twenty-eighth, the first troopships had arrived off of Walcheren. General Monnet, who had been concerned about the size of the English build-up since the twenty-sixth, sent his second in command, General Pierre-Jacques Osten, to West Capelle in order that he might personally observe the enemy and keep him better informed. On the morning of the twenty-ninth, as Osten later described it, he viewed an English fleet that consisted of men of war, frigates, brigs, and troopships the numbers of which were increasing rapidly by the hour. At noon, he was convinced that the English intended to land on Wacheren.[38] He sounded the general alarm and ordered the 1st Irish Battalion and the 1st Battalion of Colonials, which were with him at West Capelle, to the point where he believed that the enemy might land.[39]

General Osten, with the Irish and Colonial battalions, arrived at Bree Sand in the early afternoon of the twenty-ninth. From that point on the north coast of the island, he could observe the movements of the English fleet. The English sailed along the north coast of Walcheren into the mouth of the East Scheldt and took up a position that extended from a point north of Fort Ter Haak westward along Bree Sand.[40] In the afternoon, Osten was reinforced by the 2nd Battalion of the Prussian Regiment. As night fell, he left the Prussian battalion just west of Fort Ter Haak to observe the enemy, and with the Irish and Colonial battalions, he returned to West Capelle to watch a second portion of the English fleet, which was west of the island and numbered about 113 ships. Osten could not be sure on the night of 29 July whether the enemy would land on the north coast of Walcheren, or attack Flushing on the south coast. But on the morning of the thirtieth, the English squadron off West Capelle sailed into the East Scheldt and joined the divisions that had spent the night off Bree Sand. There could no longer be any doubt as to the intentions of the enemy. Osten marched the Irish and Colonial battalions back to Bree Sand. He informed General Monnet back at Flushing that there were 300 ships off of the north coast of the island, and that they would soon begin disembarkment.[41]

General Stewart Bruce commanded a small Dutch force on the island that had garrisons at Ter Haak, Ter Veere, Middelburg, and several smaller villages. Osten sent his aide-de-camp, M. Leniennier to General Bruce to inform him of his movements and to arrange a coordinated defence of the island.

> The General [Bruce] answered that I [Osten] may do as I please, but that I should not at all count on him. That the English were in too great a strength to oppose their landing; that in consequence he would limit himself, if he was attacked, to destroying his batteries at the fort [Ter Haak], and he would retreat to Ter Veere. After that letter, I judged that it was useless to talk to that General.[42]

Thus forced to rely solely upon his own resources, Osten deployed his force in order to hamper (he could not hope to prevent) the English landing. At the same time, he wisely made plans for a fighting retreat southward across the island by way of Seroskerke and Middelburg. General Monnet was asked to send 300 men of the Battalion Flushing Chasseurs to take up a defensive position on the road between Middelburg and Flushing to cover and/or support his retreat.[43]

Osten deployed his three battalions with the Prussians on his right. They maintained contact with Fort Ter Haak on their right, which was still garrisoned by the Dutch. In the center, on Bree Sand, was the Irish battalion with two six-pounders in the gap between it and the Prussians. The Colonials make up the left flank with two three-pounders. In his report, written more than a year after the events had taken place, Osten wrote: "The three battalions under my orders totaled about 1,200 men."[44] However, General Monnet, in his report dated 30 July 1809, gave the strength of the three battalions as: Colonials, 869 men of whom 144 were hospitalized; Irish, 480, including 39 in the hospital; and the 2nd Prussian Battalion, 829, 27 of whom were hospitalized.[45] This would imply that Osten should have had more than 1,900 men under his orders. The explanation would seem to lie in the fact that detachments up to company strength were scattered over the western and central portions of the island, and that what was left to him under his direct orders at Bree Sand to oppose the English landing was 1,200 men.[46]

The English began their ship to shore operation at 4 P.M. on 30 July. Lieutenant General Fraser's division was first over the sides and into the boats. At the same time the gunboats moved in close to the beach and delivered so deadly a fire on the Irish and Colonials that they were forced to seek protection behind the dikes. The English came ashore in strength. By nightfall, they had debarked three divisions and had consolidated their beachhead. The Irish and Colonials fell back in disorder on Seraskirke after a stout resistance and heavy casualties. On the French right, they lost both pieces of artillery when the civilians hired to transport the guns cut the harnesses and saved their horses. On the left Osten himself had to intervene in order to save one of the three-pounders. The other gun fell to the advancing enemy.[47] General Bruce was as good as his word. When the English advanced on Fort Ter Haak, the Dutch fired a few rounds, spiked their guns, and withdrew before the enemy was even prepared to attack.[48]

On this first day of combat, the Irish battalion fought well. When the Prussian battalion broke and fled to the rear in disorder, *Chef de Bataillon* Petrezzoli and a handful of men blocked the road and forced the Prussians to turn about and face the enemy. This action, according to Osten's aide-de-camp, M. Le Meunier, who was with the 2nd Battalion of the Prussian Regiment, prevented the destruction of the battalion.[49] After displaying much courage in opposing the English landing at Bree Sand, the Irish, and the Colonials, attacked by overwhelming numbers, were driven back in disorder. The task of covering the retreat was given to the Irish company of voltigeurs. Their "remarkable *sang-froid*" enabled the small detachment to reach Seroskirke and regroup.[50]

On the morning of 31 July, Osten found his position at Seroskirke untenable. The Dutch withdrawal from Fort Ter Haak had exposed his right flank, and the English advance on Ter Veere threatened to turn that flank. On his left, the enemy advance down the west side of the island further compromised his position. And if his strategic situation was not bad enough, some of his troops had already fled to Middelburg during the night. There was nothing else to do but to rally and reorganize his little force and retreat south to Middelburg.[51]

"The town of Middelburg had no fortifications," wrote General Osten, "and was absolutely defenseless. The Dutch troops had been withdrawn by General Bruce. Middelburg thus remained only with its national guard, and everyone knows what the bourgeois will do."[52] Fortunately, the retreating French were not vigorously pursued. The earl of Chatham, John Pitt, who commanded the English army, spent more than half of the day regrouping his forces. It was not until the early afternoon that his army of 13,893 men[53] advanced southward in three columns. By nightfall, the English had reached St. Laurens, Grypskirke, and Meleskirke, with patrols reaching to the outskirts of Zoutland. With the enemy thus poised for an attack on Middelburg, it is hardly surprising that Osten continued his retreat.[54]

When Osten reached the unfortified town of Middelburg, he learned that the mayor and the city fathers had already sent a delegation to the English for the purpose of negotiating the peaceful occupation of the town by the enemy. The general made immediate plans to evacuate the town and fall back to the heavily fortified city of Flushing. He ordered the Irish battalion to West Souburg, and the Colonials to East Souburg. Both villages lay about two miles north of Flushing and would serve as outposts to slow down the enemy's advance. However, as the Irish battalion was "very exhausted" from rearguard actions during the retreat, Osten asked Monnet to relieve it as soon as possible. The 3ʳᵈ Battalion of the Prussian Regiment was ordered to West Souburg and the weary Irish retired to Flushing.[55]

The following day (1 August), after the surrender of Ter Veere in the morning, the English attacked the forward position at East and West Souburg and drove the defenders back under the protection of the guns of Flushing. Monnet rounded up the fugitives in Flushing from Osten's battalions and sent them back to their units. By the end of the day, the English were in possession of all of Walcheren except Flushing on the south side of the island. General Bruce had evacuated his Dutch troops to the island of South Beveland after having contributed virtually nothing to the resistance. He was later court-martialed for failing to use his troops to support Osten's resistance to the invasion and for giving up the strongly fortified position of Batz without firing a shot. He was stripped of his command, dismissed from the army, and imprisoned for a short period of time.[56]

By an order of the day, on 1 August, Monnet reorganized his command into one brigade, and placed it under the direct orders of General Osten. At this time, it was Osten who actually assumed command of the defending army in the field. This proved to be a wise move on the part of Monnet, for Osten was a good field commander, while he himself was at best an adequate peacetime garrison commander. It was also on the first that reinforcements began to arrive in Flushing from Breskens, which was situated directly south (about two miles by water) of the besieged city on the left bank of the Scheldt. The English were not able to successfully blockade Flushing by water until 6 August, at which time their gunboats had passed from the East Scheldt, by way of the Slough which separated Walcheren from South Beveland, to the West Scheldt east of Flushing. The following reinforcements (totaling 3,123 men)[57] reached the beleaguered city between 1 August and 6 August:

1 August	65ᵗʰ Regiment, 3ʳᵈ Battalion	660 men
2 August	8ᵗʰ Provisional Demibrigade, 4ᵗʰ Battalion	
	22ⁿᵈ Regiment, 2 companies of the 5ᵗʰ Battalion	608 men
	54ᵗʰ Regiment, 2 companies of the 5ᵗʰ Battalion	
	45ᵗʰ Regiment, 2 companies of the 5ᵗʰ Battalion	
	72ⁿᵈ and 108ᵗʰ Regiments, detachments (Cannoneers)	375 men
4 August	48ᵗʰ Regiment, 3 companies of the 4ᵗʰ Battalion	320 men
6 August	8ᵗʰ Provisional Demibrigade, 3ʳᵈ Battalion	
	13ᵗʰ Light Infantry, 3 Companies of the 5ᵗʰ Battalion	550 men
	27ᵗʰ Light Infantry, 3 Companies of the 5ᵗʰ Battalion	

| 48th Regiment, 3 Companies | 420 men |
| Prussian detachment | 190 men |

When the Irish battalion reached Flushing, or sometime very shortly thereafter, it received a new commanding officer. *Chef de Bataillon* Petrezzoli became General Monnet's chief of staff, and John Lawless took command of the battalion. The documentation for this change of command is sparse. General Osten makes no mention of Lawless in his twenty-eight-page account of these events, but then he mentions only a few of the battalion commanders by name. The pertinent cartons of documents of the siege of Flushing provide only one account of Lawless assuming command and that is Lawless' own report to the minister of war. In this nine-page document, he wrote: "I left Landau on 22 July to take command of the 1st Battalion of the Irish Regiment."[58] He further stated: "Having arrived at Flushing, M. Petrezzoli informed me, when handing over command, that the Battalion was about 450 men strong."[59] Lawless did not mention the date of his arrival in Flushing, nor the date he assumed command of the Irish battalion, but he began his narrative of the fighting at Flushing with 1 August. Furthermore, he states that he was in Antwerp when the news of the English landing on Walcheren reached that city, and that he left that very night for Flushing to join his comrades.[60] From this information, it might be assumed that he reached the besieged army, most likely by way of Breskens, as there was still communication across the Scheldt, on 1 August.

It was also on 1 August that the Irish suffered heavy casualties when the English attacked all along the French perimeter. Lawless stated that the battalion "lost one-third of its numbers killed or wounded"[61] on that day. He mentioned by name Captains William Dowdall and Patrick Mac-Cann and Lieutenants Chistophe Martin and John Zelinski as having been wounded, and added that two of them, whom he did not name, died of their wounds. Lieutenant Terence O'Reilly and Second Lieutenant Joseph Gillmer distinguished themselves in the fighting and received the praise of all of the officers at Flushing. O'Reilly commanded the company of voltigeurs, 100 men strong, who occupied a farmhouse as an advance post. The company was attacked by "infinitely superior forces" supported by two pieces of field artillery. The Irish held their ground for two hours under this heavy fire during which time many were killed or wounded. Lawless' report also mentions a number of noncommissioned officers, most of whom were wounded in the fighting, for their distinguished service on that bloody day.[62]

"From the 3rd to the 13th [of August] nothing remarkable happened to the [Irish] Battalion except that it was always in an advance position."[63]

There were skirmishes almost daily which resulted in casualties, but the English spent that time bringing up siege guns and preparing positions for them. The guns had been unloaded at Ter Veere along with entrenching tools, ordnance, and other essentials for a siege. They had to be transported over roads that were in very bad condition and which were already crowded with the movement of supplies and troops. Moreover, to complete the isolation of Flushing, it was necessary to capture the fortified position of Ramakins, about four miles east of the city. In the first days of August, guns and siege equipment were sent to Ramakins. Only after it surrendered on the third and the siege equipment was moved to Flushing did serious work begin in preparation for the bombardment of the last French position on Walcheren. The besieging army, which numbered over 20,000 men,[64] took up a position that extended from the dike west of Flushing northeastward to Souburg, and then southeast back to the dike on the side of Flushing. The principal gun positions were to the west of the city because of the high ground. The work on the gun positions went forward steadily, if slowly. The French posed no serious threat, although the guns of Flushing opened fire from time to time just to harass the workers.

On 4 August, the French forces under General Monnet were reorganized into two demibrigades. *Chef de Bataillon* Gauthier commanded the eastern half of the defensive perimeter, and *Chef de Bataillon* Serier, the western half. The Irish battalion was assigned to Serier's demibrigade, and it held a position on the right of his sector. This put the Battalion approximately in the center of the perimeter, due north of the city. The Irish were not involved in the only French offensive action of the fighting. On 7 August, Serier commanded three columns that marched out against the English to probe their position and gain intelligence on their strength. This action accomplished little except to confirm the fact that the enemy was in strength within 2,000 yards of the walls of Flushing. Casualties were high, 7 officers and 333 men killed, wounded, or taken prisoner, for such predictable information.[65]

General Monnet made the very serious decision to open the sea dike on 6 August. He had orders directly from Napoleon to open the dikes and inundate the island should it be necessary for the defence of Flushing.[66] The opening was made East of the city, but Monnet was perhaps too cautious and did not cut the dike early enough or deep and wide enough. It was not until the twelfth or thirteenth that the rising waters became a real problem for the English. They had to evacuate some trenches and gun positions, and a few roads were covered by water, although they were still passable, but it did not force a withdrawal from their siege positions or prevent the bombardment that brought about the surrender of the city.[67]

The anticipated bombardment began at noon on 13 August. "Fifty-eight pieces of large calibre [artillery], ten frigates, which had forced the passage [up the West Scheldt] on the 11th, and a great number of gunboats, . . . fired on the town a terrible fire that continued until the evening of the following day. The fire of the land batteries was directed primarily against the demi-brigade of the left."[68] The 1ˢᵗ Colonial Battalion, which together with the Irish Battalion and the Flushing Chasseurs made up the demi-brigade of the left, immediately abandoned its position when the enemy guns opened fire. Except for one officer and a handful of men, the Colonials attempted to enter the town, but *Chef de Bataillon* Serier had the west gate closed and the Colonials eventually regrouped outside of the walls. Serier at once placed himself at the head of a company of the Irish battalion and led it forward to retake the position abandoned by the Colonials. This operation was successful, thanks to the discipline and *élan* of the Irish. Having stabilized the line at one point, Serier had to rush to another critical section. A portion of the Battalion of Returned French Deserters had also retired without orders at the commencement of the bombardment. Once again, the *chef de bataillon* was able to reoccupy the original position. Thus the French held all of their initial positions throughout the afternoon.[69]

"At 5 P.M., the enemy infantry attacked all of the advance posts of the demi-brigade of the left."[70] The Irish and the Colonials held on the two extreme flanks, but the Flushing Chasseurs, who held a critical section of the line on the left center, were driven from their position. This in turn forced the pickets of the center to retreat as their flank became exposed. However, the line did not break, and Serier was able to direct heavy fire on the English infantry and limit its advance. The Irish held firm on Serier's right. They occupied their original position at the end of the day.[71]

The Irish did not suffer heavy casualties on the thirteenth. They had hastily dug trenches during the day which protected them from the enemy artillery and infantry attack. But their battalion commander, William Lawless, was seriously wounded and had to retire into the town. In the fighting of the evening of the thirteenth, he was struck below the right eye by a musket ball that lodged below his ear.[72]

At 9 A.M. on the morning of the 14th seven ships of the line which were anchored near the Nolle, approached to within half a cannon shot of the town and gave the signal for the general bombardment to the ten frigates, gunboats, and all the land batteries and incendiary rockets. All of these forces fired a most terrible fire without example. More than 1100 cannon rained death and desolation on the town. In the beginning, our batteries responded rather vigorously although we did not have nearly enough gunners to service all the pieces. . . .

In a very short time, many of our pieces were dismounted; a number of the gun carriages were very old and shattered after one report from their pieces. . . . In less than an hour, we lost half of our artillerymen. Finally, our batteries were reduced almost to silence by the extraordinary fire of the enemy. The principal powder magazine was the prey of the flames and threatened the town with total and immediate destruction. It was only with the greatest difficulty that we succeeded in saving it. The building used to store provisions was consumed.[73]

With the guns of Flushing all but silenced by the evening of 14 August,[74] and several quarters of the city on fire, General Monnet asked the English for terms of surrender. Negotiations were completed on the fifteenth and the commander announced to his troops that the struggle had ended. Monnet surrendered without terms, and he and his men were made prisoners of war. The entire garrison of Flushing was transported to England where the men remained until the end of the war. However, following the capitulation, a small number of men did avoid the English and made their way back to France.

Chef de Bataillon William Lawless and Lieutenant Terence O'Reilly successfully eluded the English army and the Royal Navy and reached Antwerp safely. Lawless, who had been seriously wounded in the last days of the siege, had made his way to the home of Doctor Mokey. The doctor, who was a friend of Lawless, cared for his wound and hid him when the English occupied the city. Despite the seriousness of Lawless' wound, he and O'Reilly, who had joined him after the surrender, decided to attempt an escape from Flushing by boat. Their plan was to cross the West Scheldt to French-held territory. However, the vigilance of the English blockade forced them to turn back before they were halfway across, and they again went into hiding. First at Doctor Mokey's, then in a farmhouse outside Flushing, and finally back in the city, the two Irish officers evaded the enemy for more than six weeks. Finally they were able to hire an open boat that was used for transporting vegetables and other foodstuffs, and make good their escape.[75]

Lawless carried with him the eagle from the top of the flag that Napoleon had given the Irish Legion in the summer of 1804. He had guarded it dearly since the surrender of Flushing, being determined that it would not fall into the hands of the English. After a hearty welcome by Marshal Jean Baptiste Bessières at Antwerp, he was sent to Paris where he was received by the emperor himself. Not only was he the highest ranking officer to escape from Flushing, but he had saved the regiment's eagle, a feat greatly appreciated by the symbol-minded soldier-emperor. Lawless was given the Legion of Honor and command of the 1st Battalion of the Irish regiment, which was being reformed at Lindau.[76] Lieutenant O'Reilly was also well received upon his return. He was promoted to the rank of captain and received the Legion of Honor.[77]

The Irish battalion had suffered heavy casualties by the time Flushing had surrendered. Captains William Dowdall and Patrick MacCann, who had been seriously wounded in the fighting that preceeded the siege of Flushing, died of their wounds in the hospital at Ghent. MacCann had been seriously wounded in the arm, and died following the amputation of the arm.[78] Lieutenant Christophe Martin also died as the result of his wounds. Captain William Barker and Lieutenant John Zelinski were wounded in the fighting, and made their way back to France. It is not clear precisely how these four wounded officers reached French positions. It is most likely that they were evacuated from Flushing to Breskens before 6 August when the English completed the blockade of the besieged city. Lieutenants Martin and Zelinski had been wounded on 1 August, five days before the blockade was totally effective.[79]

The remaining officers of the Irish battalion were made prisoners of war. However, as the surrender signed by General Monnet made no special provisions for the Irish officers, and as they feared some form of mistreatment at the hands of the English, having been once British subjects, they changed their names and took refuge in French units. For example, Second Lieutenant Joseph Gillmer, who was born in Liverpool, joined the 3rd Battalion of the 65th Regiment of the Line. Lieutenant Arthur MacMahon, who was later killed at the Battle of Waterloo, Second Lieutenants François Eagar, born in County Kerry, and Charles Ryan, born in Dublin, also faded into French battalions. Captain Joseph L. Koslowski, born at Lemberg, Poland, was left in command of the remaining 114 noncommissioned officers and soldiers of the Irish battalion.[80]

Koslowski, who had commanded the company of grenadiers in the Irish Battalion, was the only captain of the battalion who had not been wounded in the fighting on Walcheren. When Lawless was wounded and forced to retire from the battle on 13 August, Captain Koslowski was given command, and was provisionally named *chef de bataillon* by General Monnet. Thus he was the ranking officer when, as prisoners of war, the Battalion sailed for England on 19 August.[81] In October 1809, he escaped from England and made his way to Antwerp. Upon his return from captivity, he requested that he be confirmed in the rank of *chef de bataillon*, which Monnet had provisionally bestowed upon him at Flushing. But as he had too little time in rank, having been recently promoted to captain on 15 March 1809, his request was denied.[82]

Lieutenant Charles Ryan also escaped from England and returned to

France. Upon his arrival in England from Flushing, he had been sent to a prison camp at Norwich with the Irish battalion. He was recognized as being Irish and an officer, and was given the privileges due to his rank. One of these privileges was limited freedom. In 1812, Ryan took passage with a band of smugglers who were intercepted at sea by the English while trying to reach the French coast. Ryan convinced the English that he was not a smuggler but had simply booked passage on the ship to London. He was released and made his way to Deal. Within fifteen days, he was able to make arrangements with another ship and again put to sea. This time, he reached Calais, on 21 May, and rejoined the Irish regiment.[83]

Lieutenant Patrick MacMahon is yet another Irish officer who escaped from England. Although no elaborate account of his return to France is found in the archives, his name appears on a list of officers of the 2nd Battalion of the Irish regiment as of 1 January 1811. A footnote on the document indicates that he had been taken prisoner at Flushing, but had returned to France.[84]

There is no record of what became of Second Lieutenants Joseph Gillmer and François Eagar after they were made prisoners of war. It is presumed that they were taken to England under assumed names. Byrne wrote of them the following in his *Memoirs*:

> Nor did the council of administration of the Irish regiment in France, ever hear what had become of two very distinguished officers, Lieutenants Gilmor [sic] and Eagar. They were with Colonel [sic] Lawless when he was wounded, and if they escaped, they could have returned to France after the restoration, and have received their pay up to 1814, for five years, which was due to them, and which was paid to Captain MacMahon and others who were taken at Flushing. They were then at liberty to quit, if it suited them.[85]

The roster of officers dated 1 July 1809 bears the names of Captain Thomas Markey, Lieutenant Paul Murray, Second Lieutenants Alexander Devreux, Patrick Brangann, and John Reilly. It further states that these five officers, as well as Lawless, were "en mission à Brest." With the exception of Lawless, these officers were not with the battalion in August 1809. They had been at Brest but in July were ordered to Landau, along with Lawless, where a new battalion of the Irish regiment was being formed. One final officer, Second Lieutenant John Gibbons, was listed as being present with the 1st Battalion on 1 July. However, there is no mention whatsoever of this young man as having taken part in the fighting, or as having been made a prisoner of war. He is the only officer of the battalion for whom there is no documentation as to where he was, or what he was doing between 29 July and 15 August 1809.[86]

1ˢᵗ BATTALION, IRISH REGIMENT[87]
1 July 1809

Companies	Names	Rank	Status
	Petrezzoli, Antoine	Chef de Bat.	P.O.W.
Etat Major	Vacant	Aide Maj.	—
	Gregoire, Victor	Quartermaster	P.O.W.
	Vacant	Surgeon, Adj. Maj.	—
	Koslowski, Joseph L.	Capt.	P.O.W. escaped
Carabinier	Vacant	Lt.	—
	Eagar, François	2nd Lt.	P.O.W. escaped
	Lawless, William	Capt.	Wounded escaped
1st	Murray, Paul	Lt.	Absent
	Devreux, Alexander	2nd Lt.	Absent
	Markey, Thomas	Capt.	Absent
2nd	Martin, Christophe	Lt.	Wounded
	Reilly, John	2nd Lt.	Absent
	Barker, William	Capt.	Wounded
3rd	MacMahon, Arthur	Lt.	P.O.W. escaped
	Zelinski, John	2nd Lt.	Wounded
	MacCann, Patrick	Capt.	Died of Wounds
4th	Vacant	Lt.	
	Ryan, Charles	2nd Lt.	P.O.W. escaped
	Dowdall, William	Capt.	Died of wounds
Voltigeur	O'Reilly, Terence	Lt.	Escaped
	Gillmer, Joseph	2nd Lt.	P.O.W.
Others	Brangan, Patrick	Capt.	Absent
	Gibbons, John	2nd Lt.	P.O.W. (presumed)

The reorganization of the Irish Legion into a regiment required the appointment of a commander with the rank of colonel. The man who was named to be the first commander of the Irish Regiment was Colonel Daniel O'Meara. O'Meara was one of five sons of Captain John O'Meara, a native of Tipperary and an officer in the Clare Regiment of the Irish Brigade. All five of the sons were officers in the same regiment prior to the French Revolution. His twin brother William rose to the rank of general in the Napoleonic army and was created a baron. William had joined the Irish Legion in 1804 when it was formed, but within two years he had become aide-de-camp to General Clarke, the future minister of war, and rose rapidly in the ranks. Born at Dunkirk, Daniel joined the Brigade and rose to the rank of captain. During the Revolution, he emigrated to England and took service in the army of King George III. After the Treaty of Amiens, O'Meara returned to France, and with the renewal of hostilities, rejoined the French army. In 1809, with the rank of colonel, he was the commander of Brugus in Spain when the minister of war, who was married to his brother William's sister-in-law, appointed him colonel of the Irish Regiment. According to then-Captain Byrne, who knew O'Meara in Spain, the appointment was not popular with the Irish officers of the Regiment.[88] O'Meara was not seen as an Irish patriot, never having lived in Ireland, and his appointment was viewed as political favoritism based on the marriage ties of his twin brother. Byrne wrote of him:

> Colonel Daniel O'Meara . . . was sent to Landau to take command of the Irish regiment, a most injudicious appointment, as will be seen. General [Paul Charles François] Thiebaud [*sic*: Thiébault] could not help saying how unfit O'Meara was, for many reasons. First he was then advanced in years [45 years of age], and knew nothing about commanding, having only served on the staff; besides he was prone to the glass.[89]

Nevertheless, O'Meara arrived at Landau by August of 1809, and took command of the Regiment.

An even less popular appointment on the part of Clarke was that of *Chef de Bataillon* John F. Mahony to command the 3rd Battalion of the Regiment. Mahony had held a commission in the Irish Brigade, but emigrated to England when the Brigade was disbanded. He took service in the English army and fought against the French in Egypt. When the Treaty of Amiens brought an end to the fighting, Captain Mahony sold his commission and returned to France. He made a considerable sum of money gambling and lived well over the next years. But by 1809, his luck had changed, and he had lost everything. He, therefore, decided to return to a career in the military. Clarke gave him a commission with the rank of *chef de bataillon* and sent him to Landau to organize the newly authorized 3rd Battalion of the Irish Regiment. The Irish officers who had been serving in the Legion for more than five years, while Mahony was living a comfortable life in Paris off of his dubiously acquired winnings, were extremely angered by this appointment. As Byrne so mildly put it: "It was too bad indeed, to see such Irish patriots as William Lawless, Thomas Markey, John Tennent, K. Paul Murray, P. Brangan, etc., serving as captains in the battalion commanded by this adventurer."[90] Mahony was so unpopular with the officers under his command and so incompetent as a battalion commander that he was relieved of his command shortly after the battalion arrived on active duty in Spain.

The 3rd Battalion began to take form in May 1809. In that month, five of the six Irish officers at Brest were ordered to Landau to form the nucleus of the Battalion. By the end of the summer, it had more than 400 officers and men. Although the officers were Irish, with some exceptions, the noncommissioned officers were mostly French, while the soldiers had been recruited from the prisoner of war camps in eastern France and western Germany. The general procedure was to send officers of the Battalion to the various prisoner of war camps to interview and sign up men. Landau was strategically located just west of the Rhine, about midway between Strasbourg and Mainz, in the old Palatinate. This gave the Irish officers easy access to the prisoner of war camps at Verdun, Strasbourg, Mainz, Sarralbe, Bitche, and Mézières. These were the principal camps from which recruits were engaged and sent to Landau. Captain Markey enrolled 312 men at Mézières in July. In the same month, recruits arrived from Strasbourg and Mainz. Lieutenant Rielly had some difficulties recruiting at Sarralbe, and was able to send only 58 men. At Bitche, Lieutenant Devreux enrolled 53 men.[91] The greater part of these recruits were placed in the 3rd Battalion. Recruiting continued after the departure of that battalion for Spain (October) with the new men placed into the Regiment's 4th Battalion. Through the months of August and September, recruits continued to arrive in "large" numbers. However, once again there was a problem of the shortage of officers and, in particular, noncommissioned officers.[92]

The officers of the Irish Regiment generally had little difficulty recruiting in the prisoner of war camps. The Poles who were taken prisoners in the war with Austria in 1809, while preferring to serve in Polish battalions, were not averse to joining the 3rd Foreign Regiment, even if its officers were predominantly Irish. The primary targets of the recruiting officers were the Irish who had become prisoners while in the service of King George. These men were actually sought out by the Irish officers. They were offered a dual incentive: escape from the life of a war prisoner, and the opportunity to fight against the English. By 1809, the theme of fighting to liberate Ireland, which in the early years of the Legion was dominant, had grown tired and worn. There seemed little real hope of an expedition to the homeland, but should France be victorious over England, was it not likely that Ireland would become independent? In any event, hopes were raised, promises made, and Irishmen were recruited. Finally, there were even some Scots and a few Englishmen recruited.[93]

Recruiting prisoners of war had built-in problems and uncertainties. Were the men joining the French army simply to escape the rigorous and unpleasant life in the prison camps when there seemed to be no peace in sight? England and France had been at war for thirteen years (with a brief interlude brought about by the Treaty of Amiens), and there was no reason to doubt but that the war would last another five or ten years. Many an Irishmen believed that it was better to live as a soldier in a French uniform than to rot as a prisoner in an English uniform. Other Irishmen in the service of England, particularly the Catholics, had little or no allegiance to the English king. They were virtually mercenaries fighting for their pay, and French pay was as good as English pay. Furthermore, the discipline in the French army was less severe than that in the Royal Navy, and the quality and quanity of the food was much better. The motivation of these new Irish recruits was frequently quite different from the officers and men who joined the Legion between 1804 and 1806. There was less patriotic and anti-English sentiment among the recruits of 1809, and more self-interest. These recruits would be less reliable and more prone to desertion. The French armies of the Revolution and the early Napoleonic years were nationalistic. They marched, camped, and fought with little concern for desertion. The men might forage, or stray, or lag behind, but they would rejoin their ranks, rally about their eagles, and fight with determination when called upon to do so. The recruits taken into the 3rd and 4th Battalions of the Irish Regiment were of a dubious character. Many would desert before the units even reached Spain, and others would go over to the English in the course of the Peninsula Campaign of 1810–11.

Finally there was the problem of converting the Irish sailors of the English navy into French infantrymen. Virtually all of the Irish prisoners of war in the French camps had been taken from English ships. They had never served in an army, were unaccustomed to marching, and knew nothing of infantry tactics or maneuvers.[94] The long march from the Rhine to northern Spain would contribute to the high rate of desertion.

The officer corps of the two new battalions was in somewhat better condition and much more reliable. The 3rd Battalion may have had a poor, and in the opinion of some, incompetent, commander, but the officers who served under him were capable and experienced men. Captains Tennent, Markey, Magrath, and Brangan, Lieutenants Rielly, Devreux, and Jackson were officers upon whom Mahony could count to handle the day-to-day functions of their units. Yet, to fill the officer ranks of an expanding regiment required a continuous flow of junior men, particularly lieutenants and second lieutenants. Some came up from the ranks of the non-commissioned officers. In May 1809, General Monnet named four first sergeants whom he believed suitable for the rank of second lieutenant. Two of the men, Sergeant Majors Joseph Menten and Jacques Thuillier, were granted com-missions and posted to Landau.[95]

The bulk of the officers were either reassigned from the 1st Battalion, recruited from prisoner of war camps, or volunteered for service in the Irish Regiment. The first category provided most of the company commanders. The prisoners who joined the battalions were usually Irishmen who had served the English. Thomas Brown, twenty-four years old and of County Cork, and Alexander Hamilton, thirty-four years old and of County Antrim, were at Sarralbe when Lieutenant Rielly proposed to them that they join the Irish Regiment. Both men had been captains of merchant ships flying the flag of England. Rielly had the authority to enlist noncommissioned officers and soldiers, but officers had to be appointed by the minister of war. Therefore, Brown and Hamilton wrote to Clarke requesting commissions in the Regiment.[96] Both men had been at Verdun until 1808, at which time they had been transferred to Sarralbe because of poor conduct. But at Sarralbe, they had been model prisoners.[97] Both men joined the 4th Battalion with the rank of sergeant, but expected commissions as 2nd lieutenants to come from the minister of war. Two other captains of English merchant ships were recruited from Verdun. Patrick MacCarthy and Hinderson Bourke, both Irishmen, were given commissions as lieutenants in the 3rd Battalion.[98] Yet another Irishman, Thomas Canton, was given the rank of captain in the 4th Battalion. He had joined the Hibernian Regiment of the Spanish army in 1797 and risen to the rank of captain when taken prisoner in the fighting in the Peninsula.[99]

Not all of the officers who joined the Regiment in 1809 were Irish. Sergeant Major Daniel Ross, a Scotsman who had served eight years in the Dillon Regiment of the Irish Brigade and then in the 87th Regiment, was commissioned a second lieutenant and joined the 4th Battalion.[100] Jacques Beelart, a Dutchman was also posted to the 4th Battalion in the fall of 1809. His recommendation went to the minister of war with the imprimatur of Marshal François Etienne Christophe Kellermann.[101]

Not everyone who sought a commission in the Irish Regiment was accepted. Auguste St. Leger, the younger brother of Captain St. Leger of the 2nd Battalion of the Regiment, asked to be commissioned a second lieutenant. However, when it was pointed out to the minister of war that Auguste was only sixteen years of age and a student at the Irish College in Paris, he refused the request saying that the young man should remain in school until he was eighteen at which time he would be commissioned.[102] The case of Gustav d'Arbon (Darbon) proved to be more unusual than that of the others who asked for employment. He was a Swede who had, so he claimed, once been an aide-de-camp to M. Cardell, adjutant general of the king of Sweden, with the rank of captain. In the fall of 1809, he was a prisoner of war at Nancy. There is no explanation of how he became a prisoner, only that he had been two and one-half years in the Nancy camp. His request for a commission in the French army and service in a foreign regiment was granted by the minister of war on 8 November, and he was ordered to join the 4th Battalion of the Irish Regiment at Landau with the rank of second lieutenant. On 14 November, d'Arbon reminded the minister that he had held the rank of captain when taken prisoner and asked for that same rank in the French army. When his request was denied, the Swede refused the commission offered to him and remained at Nancy as a prisoner of war.[103]

The 3rd Battalion received its marching orders before the middle of August 1809. Its ultimate destination was Burgos, Spain, where it would join the 2nd Battalion already stationed in that city.[104] In late July the emperor had ordered the preparations for the Battalion's departure to be accelerated, and although it was not up to full strength, 856 men,[105] it left Landau in the second half of August. However, because of unrest among the German population in the Rhineland, the Battalion was first marched north to Bonn. From that city on the Rhine *Chef de Bataillon* Mahony wrote an enthusiastic report on the condition of his battalion, while at the same time admitting to some problems. "The six days of marching we have just made went well and the spirit of the men is good. The two principal ethnic elements of which the Battalion is composed now are getting along well, although this was not the case when we departed."[106] He said that the troublemakers came from among those recruited at the English prisoner of war camps. They were inclined to steal whenever the occasion presented itself. The Battalion was not at full strength, he continued, because it had been ordered to march from Landau on short notice and before it had a full complement. There had also been about thirty deserters, most of whom had already been arrested and returned. He optimistically believed that the rest of the men were reliable. Mahony concluded by saying that "There is little intelligence on the part of the officers present. Our noncommissioned officers do most of the work."[107] What he did not reveal at the time was the serious problems in the Battalion.

On 18 October, the minister of war received a report from the Bureau of Inspection which announced that the nine French noncommissioned officers of the 3rd Battalion, mortified by the bad conduct of their men, requested that they all be transferred out of the Irish Regiment.[108] Clarke was angry that this matter had not been resolved quickly and at a lower level of command. He first ordered that the two first sergeants most involved be broken to the rank of common soldier and transferred to another regiment. But when the officers of the Battalion backed the noncommissioned officers, the minister reconsidered. The affair was concluded by refusing the requests for transfers, reprimanding the noncommissioned officers for their inappropriate conduct, in particular Sergeant Fichaux who had written the letter, and giving them minor punishments.[109] Clearly all was not well with the 3rd Battalion from the very beginning. The quality of the rank and file was not good. Further problems could only be expected.

In mid-October, the minister of war was informed that the adjutant major, Captain Vacher, could no longer fulfill his duties because of his poor health.[110] He was replaced by Captain Joseph Parrot. Desertions continued as the Battalion turned south in October and made its way to Spain. At this same time Clarke ordered 300 men from the depot at Landau, men who were nominally considered to be the nucleus of the 4th Battalion, to join the 3rd Battalion.[111] However, because these men were in no condition to undertake the long march, their departure was delayed until December. On the sixth of that month, a detachment of 500 men, which included 15 sergeants and 33 corporals, marched out of Landau to join the 3rd Battalion at Burgos.[112] This action served to retard greatly the formation of the 4th Battalion. The large number of men sent to bolster the 3rd Battalion was needed in part to replace the men who had deserted during the long and strenuous march to Spain.[113]

The 4th Battalion of the Irish Regiment came into existence in the fall and winter of 1809–10. As early as mid-August, when the 3rd Battalion was about to leave on its indirect march to Spain, officers and men were being designated as part of the new unit, and Captain John Tennent was being proposed as its commanding officer.[114] Yet the 3rd Battalion continued to have a higher priority than the 4th. Recruiting continued, and men arrived almost daily at Landau. By mid-October there were 577 men in the new battalion.[115] Yet there was a shortage of officers and noncommissioned officers.[116] The departure of 500 noncommissioned officers and men to Spain virtually wiped out the 4th Battalion, and required that it start building anew.

On 15 November, Colonel O'Meara wrote to the War Ministry that he needed noncommissioned officers for the 4th Battalion. "The number of Irish recruits [he wrote] is considerable, but they are of poor quality because they were mostly sailors and not accustomed to serving on land."[117] The shortage of noncommissioned officers before, and particularly after, the departure of the large detachment on 6 December, made it impossible for the new recruits to receive the training they needed. As late as 31 December, O'Meara was writing that the Battalion still had few noncommissioned officers and that although recruits continued to arrive, the Battalion could not undertake a campaign. He suggested that the 2nd Battalion, which had been two years in Spain on active duty, send experienced men to Landau to be promoted to corporal or sergeant in the 4th Battalion.[118]

5

The Peninsular Campaigns

The meeting between Napoleon and the Tsar Alexander of Russia in the summer of 1807 at Tilsit is often said to mark the high point of the career of the emperor of the French. He had won brilliant military victories over the Austrians and Russians in 1805, and over the Prussians in 1806. Although Eylau was an incomplete victory, he again defeated Alexander's army at Friedland in June 1807, and was the unquestioned master of the continent of Europe. The Treaty of Tilsit was a French treaty, and although Napoleon had not invaded Russia, and in fact made some concessions to the tsar, he was clearly in control. The groundwork for the Continental System was in place. English ships and English goods would be excluded from the Continent in an effort to bring that "nation of shopkeepers" to its knees by destroying, or at least seriously crippling, its economy. There seemed to be few limits to French power and influence from the Pyrenees to the Niemen, from Naples to the Baltic. Yet there was some unfinished business south of the Pyrenees.

The Berlin (1806) and Milan (1807) decrees were the formal documents that set out the terms of the continental blockade. However, it was up to the local governments, with the French army at their backs, to enforce the decrees. Generally speaking, the success of the blockade was directly related to the amount of influence and pressure that Napoleon could bring to bear upon the local authorities. The Kingdom of Portugal proved to be one of the weakest links in the blockade. By virtue of its distance from Paris, its separation from France by Spanish territory, and its traditional friendship with England, Portugal was perhaps the least inclined to close its ports to the English for the benefit of the French. To achieve the desired ends, Napoleon signed the Treaty of Fontainebleau with Spain, which called for the conquest and division of Portugal. With the approval of the Spanish government, General Jean-Andoche Junot, the future duke of Abrantès, crossed the Pyrenees in the fall of 1807, and on 19 November entered Portugal. Lisbon was occupied and closed to English shipping, but far from settling affairs in the Iberian Peninsula, Junot's campaign only marked the beginning of a disaster.

In 1807, Spain was nominally a French ally, and the government at Madrid had agreed to enforce the Berlin and Milan decrees. But the government was weak, corrupt, and ineffective. English goods entered the country almost at will. Napoleon decided that if the Continental System was to achieve its goal in the Peninsula, his armies would have to control both Portugal and Spain. To this end, in 1808, he ordered his brother-in-law, Marshal Joachim Murat, soon to be King Joachim of Naples, to march to Madrid under the pretext of sending a French army to lay siege to the English fortress at Gibraltar. As a Spanish ally, Murat's army was received with guarded friendship. But once in control of Madrid and the lines of communication back to the Pyrenees, Napoleon undertook the overthrow of the Bourbon monarchy and gave the throne of Spain to his older brother Joseph. In the Bayonne Affair (May and June 1808), Napoleon secured the abdications of both Charles IV and his son Ferdinand VII, and with the support of hand-picked Spanish notables, replaced the Bourbons with Joseph Bonaparte. The emperor believed, or at least hoped, that his problems south of the Pyrenees would be solved. However, even before the events at Bayonne, there had been serious trouble in Madrid that foretold of the difficult years ahead. In the course of the next four years, an Irish battalion was to share the bloodshed and the hardships of the Peninsular War.

The first Irish to serve in Spain were ordered to Bayonne in the fall of 1807. The detachment consisted of 800 men, and was commanded by Louis Lacy, the senior captain who was not sick with malaria at the time. There is little information on this detachment other than it was formed into a battalion and made up a part of the army that Marshal Murat led to Madrid in the spring of 1808. The 2nd Battalion, as this unit came to be known, was camped outside of the city, as was the bulk of Murat's command, when the population rose up against the French on 2 May. It was ordered into Madrid and took part in repressing the uprising. This unsuccessful insurrection was only a prelude to what was to take place. Just eleven days after King Joseph had taken up residence in his new capital, a general rebellion spread throughout Spain in the wake of General Pierre Dupont de l'Etang's capitulation at Baylen (12 July). Joseph deemed it wise to withdraw from Madrid and all of central Spain. The Irish Battalion fell back towards the Pyrenees with the king and the rest of the French army. Fortunately, Napoleon had ordered troops to garrison the towns and cities to protect the lines of communication between Madrid and the French border. Thus, the retreat was carried out in a reasonably orderly manner. Although Napoleon ordered his brother to hold the Douro River line, Joseph did not stop until he had crossed the Ebro.[1]

Captain Lacy had remained the acting battalion commander, but had never been promoted to the rank of *chef de bataillon*. What happened to this Spanish born Irishman is best told in the words of Miles Byrne.

> Before the battalion received orders to march from Madrid, Captain Lacy disappeared. Being a Spaniard by birth, he had numerous acquaintances in Madrid, and it was thought at first that he had fallen a victim to some jealous rival, particularly as his horse, money and effects of every kind were found at his lodgings, and his servant could give no clue where he might be found. It was only at the battle of Ocano the year after, that it was rightly known what had become of him; there he commanded a brigade of spanish cavalry against the french and escaped amongst the last from the field of battle.—He was afterwards named captain general of Catalonia by the Cortes of Cadiz, and was one of their devoted supporters, but after the return of King Ferdinand from imprisonment in France, Lacy being considered too liberal, soon fell into disgrace with his majesty, who suspected him to be at the head of a conspiracy in favor of the constitution of 1812. He was tried by a court martial, condemned to death, and sent to the island of Majorca, where his guards shot him as soon as he landed.[2]

Lacy's defection was both an embarrassment and a loss to the Irish Legion. Born at St. Roch, Spain, in 1776, of an Irish father, he had served in the Irish Brigade of the Spanish army until he resigned his commission and went to France. He was one of the most experienced and capable officers in the Legion, and Adjutant Commander MacSheehy singled him out as the best officer in his command. Being a Spaniard at heart, he undoubtedly was unwilling to serve France in the subjugation of the Spanish people.[3]

More than a year passed before it was realized that Louis Lacy had actually defected to the enemy. On 23 May 1809, the prefect of the Department of Finestère wrote to the minister of war on behalf of his wife. In that letter, it was pointed out that she had received no information from the War Office or from his comrades-in-arms as to the fate of her husband, only that he was no longer with his battalion. Beside the generally accepted theory that he had been assassinated by the insurgents in Madrid, the prefect asked the War Office to check the possibility that he may have died of his wounds, or of an "ordinary" illness, in a hospital. Clearly twelve months after his disappearance the French did not know any more than that he was missing in action.[4]

In July 1808, the Irish Battalion at Flushing sent a second detachment

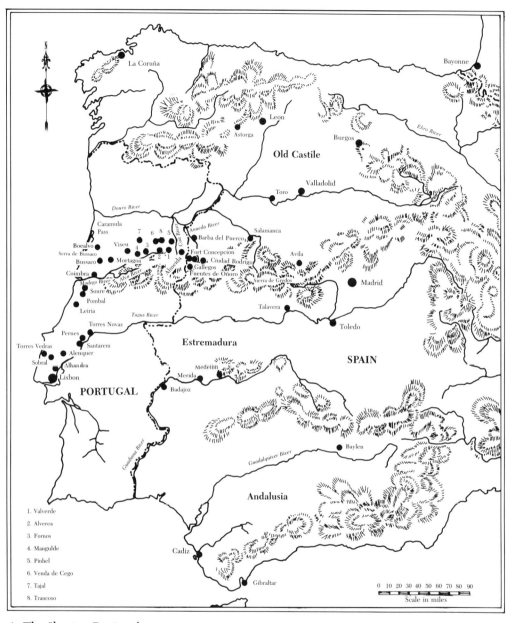

La Coruña

Bayonne

Leon

Astorga

Burgos

Old Castile

Ebro River

Douro River

Valladolid

Toro

Caramula
Pass

Anueda River

Salamanca

7 6 8 5

Boealvo

Viseu

Barba del Puerco

Serra de Bussaco

4 3

Avila

Bussaco

Mortagoa

2 1

Fort Concepcion

Ciudad Rodrigo

Coimbra

Gallegos

Madrid

Modego River

Fuentes de Oñoro

Soure

Mea River

Sierra de Gredos

Pombal

Leiria

Tagus River

Talavera

Torres Novas

Pernes

Toledo

Torres Vedras

Santarem

Estremadura

SPAIN

Alenquer

Sobral

Alhandra

Medellin

Lisbon

Merida

PORTUGAL

Badajoz

Guadiana River

Baylen

Guadalquiver River

Andalusia

1. Valverde

2. Alverea

3. Fornos

4. Mangulde

5. Pinhel

Cadiz

6. Venda de Cego

7. Tajal

8. Trancoso

Gibraltar

0 10 20 30 40 50 60 70 80 90

Scale in miles

4. The Iberian Peninsula

of 600 officers and men to Spain. The 2nd Irish Battalion had been stationed at Pamplona, some thirty-five miles due south of San Sebastián, after the retreat from Madrid. In September, these reinforcements, under the command of Captain J. Fitzhenry, reached Pamplona. The 2nd Battalion had been greatly diminished since its arrival in Spain, thus the two units were reorganized into a single battalion. As Captain Lacy was presumed killed or taken prisoner at that time, Captain Fitzhenry, the senior officer, was given command of the Battalion. Born in County Derry in 1778, he had joined the society of United Irishmen and fought in County Wexford during the Rebellion of 1798. When his brother-in-law, John Colclough, was executed in the White Terror that followed the insurrection, Fitzhenry took his wife and two children to France. In 1803, he sent his wife and, by then, three children back to Ireland before the renewal of hostilities, and in December he joined the Irish Legion, which he believed would sail for Ireland in the immediate future. Having entered the Legion with the rank of captain, he received good reports over the years from his superiors.[5]

Upon his arrival at Pamplona, Fitzhenry found the remnants of the 2nd Battalion in the worst possible condition. The Battalion made up part of Marshal Moncey's army corps, but it seems to have been shifted from one unit to another within that army so that no one had taken a serious interest in its general condition. Fitzhenry took charge and worked hard to pull the six companies together.[6] Even with the arrival of the officers from Flushing there was still a shortage that could only be remedied by the War Office in Paris. From September to December 1808, the officer corps was as follows:

Etat-Major

Chef de Bataillon	vacant
Captain Commander	Fitzhenry, Jerome
Adjutant Major	vacant
Quartermaster officer	vacant
Medical officer	vacant
Adjutant NCOs	Perrey, Jacques, and François Brelivet

Carabinier

Captain	Ware, Hugh
Lieutenant	vacant
Second Lieutenant	Parrott, Joseph

1st Company

Captain	MacGuire, John
Lieutenant	Vacant
Second Lieutenant	Dowling, Jerome

2nd Company

Captain	vacant
Lieutenant	Byrne, Miles
Second Lieutenants	Theridan, and John Zelinsky

3rd Company

Captain	O'Malley, Austin
Lieutenant	vacant
Second Lieutenant	Mullauny, Charles

4th Company

Captain	vacant
Lieutenant	St. Leger, Edmond
Second Lieutenant	Bragiere

Voltigeur

Captain	vacant
Lieutenant	Allen, John
Second Lieutenant	Osmond, Augustin[7]

At the urging of Fitzhenry, Marshal Moncey requested, and the minister of war approved, a number of promotions that became effective 16 December 1808. Fitzhenry was promoted to *chef de bataillon*. Allen was named captain of the voltigeurs; Byrne, captain of the 2nd Company, and St. Leger, captain of the 4th Company. Promoted to lieutenant were Parrott and Osmond. Michael Sheridan, who had recently joined the Battalion was also promoted from second lieutenant to lieutenant. Up from sergeant to second lieutenant were Jacques Perry, James MacEgan, William Keller, and Michael Russell. Shortly after these promotions were made, Lieutenant Osmond left the Battalion to become aide-de-camp to Brigade General the Prince C. F. d'Isembourg.[8]

The delicate position of the French along the Ebro River was spared any serious discomfort by the lack of unity among the Spanish. The Junta, which served as a quasi government in the absence of either Charles IV or Ferdinand VII, could only agree on its rejection of Joseph Bonaparte and French domination. Each of the various Spanish armies had its own commander in chief, and cooperation, as well as communication, was almost totally lacking. Nevertheless, Napoleon decided that if he was to control the Peninsula, he would have to go personally to Spain at the head of a strong French army. To this end, he met with Alexander of Russia at Erfurt in September 1808 to secure his position in central Europe against possible Austrian interference. This accomplished, and with 300,000 men south of the Pyrenees, or on their way, the emperor went himself and took command. The Spanish armies in the north were brushed aside and Madrid retaken.

The English had landed an army in Portugal in the summer of 1808, and forced General Junot to give up his position at Lisbon. To the disappointment of the government in London, Junot was allowed safe conduct back to France with his entire army and its artillery and baggage. In the fall of the same year, the English force, then under the command of Sir John Moore, marched to the northeast into Spain to support the Spanish armies. When Napoleon became aware of his presence in the province of Leon, he at once directed all available troops to the west in an effort to cut Moore's retreat back into Portugal and to force his surrender. However, this most capable Scot was able to extract his little army from the danger and escaped northwestward to the port of La Coruña. There he defended the city until the English navy arrived and evacuated what was left of his weary army. Unfortunately, Sir John Moore was mortally wounded on 16 January 1809 by a French cannonball while directing the defense of La Coruña. On that day, the English army lost one of its finest field commanders. [9]

Fitzhenry's battalion was nearly at full strength in December 1808, when it was ordered from Pamplona to Burgos for the purpose of marching against Moore. But as the general perceived his danger and rapidly marched off to Coruña, the Irish Battalion was never within striking distance of the English force. This proved to be a disappointment to those Irishmen who had fought against General Moore in Wexford in 1798. Moore had commanded one of the English armies that had put down that bloody insurrection, and survivors of that unhappy campaign like Battalion Commander Fitzhenry, Captain Byrne, and others were most anxious to once again test their mettle against General Moore and his English army under much more favorable conditions than those of 1798. [10]

As Moore escaped to the sea, the Irish Battalion took up garrison duties in Burgos. Their disappointment at seeing the English army escape battle was somewhat lessened when the Battalion had the honor of posting guard in Burgos during the emperor's brief stay on 17 January 1809. It was the first time that Napoleon had seen a unit of the Irish Legion, and while there is no record of his feelings with respect to it, Captain Byrne believed that he was favorably impressed. "His [Napoleon's] subsequent decrees to have the first Irish regiment of the Legion organized into four war battalions and a depot is a proof of the good impression made on him by the battalion at Burgos, commanded by Fitzhenry." [11]

When the Irish settled down at Burgos in January 1809, Colonel Daniel O'Meara commanded the city. It was the first encounter between the future colonel of the Irish Regiment and the men who would serve under him. Within a few months, O'Meara was ordered back to France and then to Landau and his new command. The Battalion at Burgos was under the orders of General Darminac when it arrived, but very shortly he was relieved by General Paul Charles Thiebault. The new commander of Old Castile was partial to the Irish as it was an Irishman, General James O'Moran, who, in 1792, had taken young Thiebault from the ranks of the volunteers and made him a captain.[12]

After posting guard for the emperor, the Battalion engaged in the less glamorous task of constructing a fort for the protection of the city of Burgos. But the increased activities of the Spanish guerrillas caused the men to put down their shovels and again take up their muskets. From February to May 1809, the Battalion did escort duties and was sent out on patrols to skirmish with local guerrillas operating in the hills of Old Castile. However, the officers of the Battalion still found the time and the means to celebrate St. Patrick's day. On 17 March, they gave a great dinner for the Irish and the near-Irish at Burgos. They invited Colonel Daniel O'Meara and Captain Charles O'Neil of the 47th Regiment. The 47th had been the Walsh Regiment of the Pre-Revolutionary Irish Brigade, which the captain's father General John O'Neil had commanded. There were still a few other Irish officers in the 47th, and they were also invited. There was even a Prussian officer, of the recently formed Prussian Regiment serving in Spain, and a Mr. Plunkett who were invited. The latter claimed that his grandfather was an Irishman who had been in the service of Austria. Finally, there were sons of Irishmen who had served in Irish regiments in the Spanish army. Miles Byrne said that the Irish exiles celebrated St. Patrick's day with more enthusiasm than if they had been living "in the green Island."[13]

Early in May 1809, news reached Burgos of the reorganization of the Irish Legion into the Irish Regiment. The battalion in Spain was officially designated the second and that at Flushing the first, while a third battalion was to be formed at the depot at Landau. This meant that a regimental commander with the rank of colonel would be appointed, and the officers of the 2nd Battalion not only wanted that commander to be an Irishman, but to be *Chef de Bataillon* J. Fitzhenry. To that end, they wrote a letter to another Irishman, Henri Clarke, who had it within his power, as minister of war, to influence the emperor in the naming of a new colonel. "For five years [they wrote] the Irish Legion has obeyed orders from commanders who were foreign to their country [Petrezzoli] or to its common cause [MacSheehy]," and added that those officers had little zeal or intelligence.[14] But events in Paris had already precluded the denial of their request. The minister of war, who had family ties to Colonel O'Meara, had already forwarded his name to the emperor for his approval. Moreover, a report from the Bureau of Infantry pointed out that Fitzhenry had only been named *chef de bataillon* five months earlier and thus had too little time in rank to be promoted to colonel. The bureau was also critical of the slanderous remarks directed against Petrezzoli, although he was unnamed in the letter of 5 May, and labeled them "unjust."[15] The result was that O'Meara was named to command the Regiment and Fitzhenry remained at the head of the 2nd Battalion.

It was also in May 1809 that the Irish Battalion was ordered to Leon where for a brief period it formed a part of the army of General François Etienne Kellermann, son of Marshal François Etienne Christophe, Duke of Valmy. Kellermann's army was to march against the Spanish army of the Marquis de Romana, which was causing trouble in the north and threatening French communications between Burgos and Bayonne. But as before, the fighting was primarily of a guerrilla nature, and by midsummer the Irish were back at Burgos escorting the mail and chasing small bands of Spanish guerrillas in the hills of Old Castile.

Fighting the guerrillas in Spain was distastful duty for the Irish in the French army. Some of the officers and noncommissioned officers of the Irish Battalion had fought as irregulars in the hills of Wexford and Wicklow in 1798. The term "guerrilla" was coined during the Peninsular War, but the Irish of 1798 had been as much guerrillas as were the Spanish of 1809 whom they were now employed to hunt down. Indeed, the attempted French suppression of Spain in 1808–12 could be compared, in some respects, to the English repression of Ireland at the end of the eighteenth century. One might speculate as to the outcome of the efforts of the Irish in 1798 if they had been given as much help by the French as the Spanish and Portuguese were given by the English less than a decade later. In any event, it is understandable that the Irish disliked fighting Spanish civilians who were defending their country against the French army. Indeed, the French soldiers themselves were not happy with the guerrilla warfare in the Peninsula. The French thought of themselves as liberators, and were demoralized to find that they were treated as oppressors by the Spanish population. They further hated, as did the Irish, the irregular and "uncivilized" tactics employed by the guerrillas, which led to atrocities by both sides. The Irish, as well as the French, longed to march against a regular army, preferably the English in Portugal.[16]

Despite the fact that the Irish tended to sympathize with the plight of the Spanish people, they did not see Spain as being in the same situation as their native Ireland. In a discussion with the parish priest of a small town in northern Spain Captain Byrne responded in the following manner to the priest's statement that there was a great similarity between Ireland and Spain as they were both being oppressed by a foreign power:

> I answered there could be no comparison, as in his country, at that moment the inhabitants were not persecuted and deprived of their civil rights on account of the religion they professed. I allowed however that the Spaniards had suffered in their disastrous wars on account of the monarchs imposed on them: one time from an Austrian branch, another from the house of the Bourbons of France, and then from the Buonaparte family: whilst in poor Ireland the millions of unemancipated catholic serfs were kept in bondage by a protestant ascendency of a few hundred thousand individuals, acting there the part of the cruel task masters of England. That in changing the Spanish dynasties, no religious persecutions took place in Spain. I perfectly agreed with him that the Spaniards had a right to govern themselves and to choose the form of government they wished; whilst on the other hand, I maintained that no matter who the chief of the French government was, he became responsible to the nation to take the best means to secure the friendship of the neighbouring states, and their perfect neutrality in time of war; that it could never be forgotten, that after the revolution of 1789 when hostilities began, protestant Prussia and catholic Spain were the first powers to attack and invade France . . . and again in 1806, had the battle of Iena been lost by France, your king Charles the fourth was prepared to declare war against her.—Now under all those circumstances, a sure guarantee was required by the French government from the Spanish nation: I am far from pretending that the right means were taken to secure it.[17]

Byrne then added the comment:

> I could not help admiring the patriotism of this enthusiastic ecclesiastic; he reminded me of the virtuous clergymen who suffered torture and death, as martyrs, both in the field and on the scaffold, in Ireland in 1798, endeavouring to set their country free from the cruel foreign yoke. Historians writing on the wars of that period seem to disapprove the part some Irish clergymen took in them, whilst they admire the Spaniards fighting against catholic France.[18]

It was this kind of reasoning that enabled the Irish to serve Napoleon and France in the Peninsular War, although they clearly wished to march against the English army in the west rather than engage in the petty, although dangerous and exhausting, tasks of escort duty and counterguerrilla warfare.

News of the surrender of Flushing and the loss of the 1st Battalion of the Irish Regiment reached Burgos by the end of the summer, 1809. This caused great sadness as it was believed that all of the officers and men were either taken prisoner or killed. The news that a number of the officers had escaped, or had been evacuated after having been wounded, filtered south into Spain slowly over the next months. It was not until the end of November that those serving in Spain learned of the return of William Lawless and Terence O'Reilly. Both men were very popular in the Regiment, and their escape from Flushing caused much joy among the men of the 2nd Battalion.

The Battalion remained in Old Castile the entire year of 1809. Before the year had ended, there were four vacancies in the officer corps.[19] One officer lost to the Battalion was Lieutenant Augustin Osmond, who had been serving as aide-de-camp to the prince of Isemberg. He was promoted to captain and later named adjutant major of the 4th Battalion, which was being formed at Landau in the fall of that year. Osmond was a good officer and his departure was a loss to the Battalion. Another loss was that of Second Lieutenant Joseph Parrott. Having been promoted to lieutenant, he was sent to the 3rd Battalion to serve it as adjutant major.[20] To fill the vacancies in the officer corps, Jerome Dowling and Charles Mullauny were promoted to second lieutenant from sergeant. Brelivet received the brevet of second lieutenant effective 6 August 1809.[21] Despite those promotions the Battalion was still short of officers, and Fitzhenry was trying again in November to secure the promotion of three of his first sergeants (Setting, Jacques Perry, and Devamoret) to second lieutenant.[22] On 1 December, the 2nd Battalion had eighteen officers, four short of its full complement.[23]

At the beginning of the new year, the 2nd Battalion was still stationed at Burgos and performing the same dreary, and often dangerous, duties that had occupied it throughout 1809. Marching and countermarching against the guerrillas, which involved occasional skirmishes while escorting supplies and mail, and guard duty kept the officers and men on their feet, or in the saddle, long hours for many days at a time. Commander Fitzhenry complained that the Battalion was overworked,[24] but to no avail. Captain Edmond St. Leger was unable to hold up under the rigorous schedule. By the end of 1809, his health had declined to the point that Fitzhenry asked that he be sent back to France as he was of no use to the Battalion in Spain. At the same time, he requested promotions to fill the vacancies in the officer corps.[25]

Then in the middle of January the 3rd Battalion of the Irish Regiment arrived at Burgos. Its long march, which had taken it first north from Landau to Bonn, and then up the river and across France and the Pyrenees, had extracted a heavy toll. Of the 1,356 men[26] who left the depot, only about half[27] arrived in Spain. Its ranks had been depleted by desertion and physical fatigue. The recruits from the prisoner of war camps had come from the ranks of the British navy, and were quite unaccustomed to long marches. More significant, however, was the high percentage of deserters. Englishmen passing as Irish, and Irishmen who were not anti-English had joined the Irish Regiment in order to be freed from the prisoner of war camps. Many of these men had no wish to serve in the French army, and they took the first opportunity to desert once the Battalion was on the march and discipline and security were relaxed.

Colonel O'Meara had remained at Landau to supervise the organization of the new 4th Battalion. Therefore, when *Chef de Bataillon* Mahony arrived at Burgos with his Battalion, Fitzhenry, as the senior battalion commander, assumed command of the Irish Regiment in Spain.[28] Shortly after the arrival of the 3rd Battalion, the French forces in Spain were reorganized. An Army of Portugal was formed, which was composed of three army corps. The 2nd Corps was commanded by General Jean-Louis Reynier, the 6th Corps by Marshal Michel Ney, and the 8th Corps by General Jean Andoche Junot. Command of this army was given to a reluctant Marshal André Masséna, duke of Rivoli, prince of Essling. Napoleon had decided to put an end to English interference in the Peninsula. He had defeated the Austrians once again in the summer of 1809 (the Battle of Wagram, 5–6 July) and imposed upon the vanquished the Treaty of Schonbrunn (14 October 1809). With central Europe again under control, he could concentrate on affairs south of the Pyrenees. Men and supplies began to flow south for a major offensive against Wellington and his Portuguese ally. The emperor, who had personally conducted the Austrian campaign, decided that he could not leave Paris to campaign in Portugal. He, therefore, chose one of his most capable, and experienced, lieutenants to command this new army. But Masséna, while still quite able, had lost some of the fire and enthusiasm that had propelled him to high rank and fame. Of his three corps commanders, Ney may have been the most capable and his 6th Corps, made up of veterans of the Grand Army of 1805–7, was the most experienced and best prepared to march against the enemy. General Reynier was a good corps commander, but his troops were a mixture of veterans and recruits. The 8th Corps was the least prepared. Junot was a good division commander when serving under a leader such as Napoleon. At the head of a corps, however, he could be considered as little more than adequate. Moreover, the 8th Corps was composed of a large number of conscripts who were about to make their first campaign.[29] Moreover, although Ney was an excellent corps commander, he resented the fact that he had to serve under Masséna. He considered Masséna his equal and was reluctant to take orders from him. The campaign would be marred by the personal conflict between these two great soldiers.

With the formation of the Army of Portugal, the Irish Regiment became a part of Junot's 8th Corps. The Corps was composed of three divisions which were commanded by Generals Bertrand Clausel, Jean Solignac, and Joseph

Lagrange. The Irish were assigned to General Solignac's 2nd Division. Together with the 65th Regiment of the line, they made up the 2nd Brigade of the Division which was commanded by General Jean Guillaume Thomières.[30] Shortly after the middle of July, 1810, the Prussian Regiment joined Solignac's 2nd Brigade.[31]

The Irish were happy to leave Burgos in March 1810 and march to Rio Seco. To be a part of the Army of Portugal and to march against the English was the fulfillment of their hopes and desires ever since they had arrived in Spain. Yet all was not quiet or harmonious within the Regiment. There was internal maneuvering for promotion as a result of the rapid expansion of the Legion from two battalions into a regiment of four, and rumors had it that there would soon be a fifth battalion. Two new battalions had already been formed, and with the loss of the 1st Battalion at Flushing it would have to be reorganized and staffed with officers, presumably from the other battalions. A colonel and three battalion commanders had been named along with the promotion of a number of lieutenants and second lieutenants, and according to Captain James MacGuire, the captains of the 2nd and 3rd Battalions were "moving heaven and earth" to get the brevets of *chef de bataillon*.[32] As the senior captain in the Regiment, MacGuire felt it in his own best interest to write to the minister of war pointing out his seniority and asking that he be kept in mind when the Regiment had an opening for another battalion commander. He was also suspicious that Fitzhenry and Captain Allen were maneuvering behind the scenes to secure Allen's promotion before his.[33] Nor did the arrival of Colonel O'Meara at Rio Seco put an end to the jockeying for promotion. The officers of the 2nd Battalion may have considered him a friend and fellow Irishman when he had been the commander of Burgos in the spring of 1809, but they resented his having been named colonel of the Regiment over men who were more capable militarily and more desirable politically.[34]

The internal problems of the Regiment tended to diminish, except for the near universal disapproval of Colonel O'Meara and Commander Mahony, as the Irish approached the enemy and serious combat became imminent. However, before the French army could march west into Portugal and confront Wellington, Masséna had to gain control of several key fortified cities that were in the hands of the Spanish and the English. The two most important were Ciudad Rodrigo and Almeida. The former was in Spain, the latter in Portugal, with approximately thiry-five miles of rugged terrain separating them. Cuidad Rodrigo was the most important of the two because the French wished to use it for their principal base of supply during the coming campaign. Masséna ordered Marshal Ney to lay siege to the city with his veteran 6th Corps. General Reynier's 2nd Corps was south of

Ciudad Rodrigo with patrols extending as far as the Tagus River. To the north was Junot's 8th Corps. As Ney was making preparations for the siege and moving his divisions towards Cuidad Rodrigo, Junot's 1st Division lay siege to Astorga.

The city, which is situated some fifty miles west of Leon in the province of the same name, was a base for supplies and operations of the Spanish forces in the northwest. Its capture would remove the threat of Spanish forces advancing into Old Castile and give the Army of Portugal a greater sense of security with respect to its right flank and right rear. General Clausel's division had completely surrounded the city by the first days of April 1810, and soon after began to dig the trenches and parallels that were needed to attack a fortified position. Then General Solignac's 2nd Division replaced the 1st and Causel moved west to make contact with the enemy and prevent any attempt to relieve the besieged garrison. The Irish battalions spent the next weeks in the trenches digging under fire. By 19 April the trenches and parallels were completed and the siege guns in place. Junot called upon the Spanish to surrender, but they refused. He then ordered that a breach be made in the wall, and the big guns opened fire. The firing continued for two days by which time a breach had been made in the section of the wall before the trenches. The time had come for the final assault.[35]

For the purpose of mounting the breach an elite battalion was formed of chosen troops from all units of Solignac's division. Its command was given to one of Junot's aides, Captain Legrave. John Allen's company of voltigeurs was the Irish contribution to this assault battalion. Furthermore, the Irish were given the rather dubious honor, in light of the heavy casualties they would suffer, of leading the attack. Allen took his men through the parallels and trenches to within 200 yards of the wall. Then at 5 P.M. on 21 April, he led them over the top of the trenches, across the open ground under heavy enemy fire, and mounted the breach. His men occupied a house just behind the rampart and held their position throughout the night. The remaining companies of Fitzhenry's battalion were also in the thick of the fighting. Every company had men killed and wounded while carrying ladders to the breach in preparation for the full-scale assault at dawn. The Battalion's adjutant major, Lieutenant Jacques Perry was wounded and assistant surgeon Charles A. Gougie lost an arm. Indeed the two Irish battalions brought much honor upon themselves during the siege, and particularly in the final days. Allen's drummer received the cross of the Legion of Honor for continuing to beat the charge after losing both of his legs.[36]

With the first rays of morning light there appeared a flag of truce on the city wall. The Spanish realized that with the breach in the hands of the

French further resistance would be useless and would result only in a great loss of life on both sides as well as the destruction and pillage of the city. Therefore, the commander surrendered at the discretion of General Junot, and the 5,000-man garrison marched out and laid down their arms. Allen's voltigeurs had suffered heavy casualties as did the assault battalion as a whole; 750 men out of the 900 were killed or wounded taking and holding the breach on 21–22 April.[37] The Irish Regiment was assigned the task of escorting the Spanish prisoners of war from Astorga to Valladolid. Allen and the remnants of his company were permitted to remain at the captured city. His heroic part in the siege was rewarded with the cross of the Legion of Honor. Lieutenant Perry, who had been wounded carrying a ladder to the breach, also received the Legion of Honor.[38] When the Regiment returned from Valladolid it was assigned to garrison Astorga, and Colonel O'Meara was named its military governor. The colonel functioned well in this position, as he had the previous year at Burgos. The Irish maintained order in the city and imposed strict discipline on the French soldiers. Because of these measures looting was held to a minimum.[39]

Less than three weeks after the surrender of Astorga Colonel O'Meara reported on the poor condition of the Irish Regiment to undertake the impending campaign into Portugal.

> I have the honor to explain to you [he wrote to the minister of war] that the two Battalions, of approximately equal strength, number only about 1100 men under arms. Even more serious, they no longer resemble a regiment. I implore Your Excellancy to give the necessary orders that the depot [Landau], which had 1100 men in March [1810], send a second battalion in order to complete the two that are here [in Spain]. The 3rd Battalion has need of officers. Despite the fact that its numbers are equal to those of the 2nd [Battalion] there is no resemblance in quality, and [Battalion Commander] Mahony is so badly supported [by the officers of his battalion] that he must do everything himself.[40]

On 1 February 1810, less than a month after the 3rd Battalion had arrived at Burgos, acting Battalion Commander Fitzhenry reported that for its six companies there were only two captains, Brangan and Murray; four lieutenants, Alexander Devreux, Jackson, Reilly, and Bourke; and four second lieutenants, Doxal, Delany, Menten, and Demonlague. Two of these men, Doxal and Reilly, were not even in Spain at the time.[41] Thus, of the eighteen positions, excluding the staff officers, in the Battalion only eight were actually filled. Two other officers should have been with the 3rd Battalion. One of them, Captain Thomas Canton, had reported himself sick at the hospital at Bordeaux after telling his fellow officers that he would not serve in Spain. After O'Meara arrived, he asked the minister of war to take action against him.[42] However, his departure most likely improved the combat readiness of the Battalion. Another misplaced officer was the Scotsman Ferguson. He had become acquainted with General Clarke before the latter had assumed the position of minister of war. He had absolutely no military training or background, but he was a "well-bred gentleman" over fifty years of age when, in 1809, he sought a position with the French government. The minister of war, because of their friendship, gave him a commission in the army and sent him to Landau to serve in the Irish Regiment. He ended up in Spain at the head of a company, even though he could not speak enough French to give basic commands. Marshal Masséna took pity upon him, and rather than taking him on campaign into Portugal, allowed him to retire to the 8th Corps' depot at Valladolid until such time as he could return to Landau.[43]

Colonel O'Meara desperately sought promotions from the minister of war as well as troops from the depot at Landau. But his pleas and his recommendations were received with little sympathy at the War Ministry. Early in August 1810, General Clarke not only refused his requests, but scolded him for even asking. The minister pointed out that even though Captains Canton, St. Leger (who was ill at Landau), and Ferguson were of no use to the Regiment in Spain they were still carried on the roster. Therefore, their places were not vacant and could not be filled by someone else. He had ordered Canton to join his battalion in Spain,[44] but he pointed out that until St. Leger and Ferguson were transferred out of the Regiment or retired from service for poor health they could not be replaced. He also explained that Second Lieutenant Parrott and Lieutenant Perry would not be promoted at that time because there were no vacancies for them in the battalions in Spain. On the other hand, Clarke did recommend to the emperor that Sergeant Major Setting be named second lieutenant, Lieutenant Jean Jacques Demeyere be named captain, and Captain Hugh Ware be promoted to *chef de bataillon*.[45] Ware was then ordered back to Landau where he was given command of a newly organized battalion. Yet when all was said and done, the two battalions of the Irish Regiment in Spain remained undermanned on the eve of the Portuguese campaign.

The summer of 1810 was taken up with the sieges first of Ciudad Rodrigo and then of Almeida.[46] The operations at Ciudad Rodrigo were carried out by Ney's 6th Corps. The Irish Regiment had no part whatsoever in the fall of that fortress. However, it was involved in the operations against Almeida. After spending the month of June between Ciudad Rodrigo and Almeida, a portion of the Regiment saw action when Masséna ordered a probe of the enemy's position west of the rivers Azaba and Agueda. Captain

Hugh Ware, not yet ordered to Landau, was given command of an elite "battalion" to serve as part of a formidable reconnaissance force led by General Charles Marie Eseorches de Saint-Croix. On 4 July, Saint-Croix, who commanded the 8th Corps' cavalry brigade, crossed the Azaba with about 800 cavalrymen and five battalions of infantry. Ware's hastily assembled "battalion," of unknown strength, marched with this force, which Junot himself accompained. Saint-Croix encountered Portuguese cavalry at the small town of Gallegos and drove it back towards Alameda where it was supported by English infantry. Having determined that the English were not in great strength before Almeida and did not seem to be prepared to launch a serious effort to relieve the besieged city of Ciudad Rodrigo, Saint-Croix retired behind the Azada and the Agueda, while leaving a strong presence on their west banks. Ware's "battalion" played an active part in the fighting on 4 July, and brought to himself the attention of his superiors. It was less than two months after this engagement that Captain Ware was recommended for the brevet of *chef de bataillon*.[47]

The Irish Regiment spent the month of July and the first weeks of August at Ledesma. On 10 July, Ciudad Rodrigo surrendered to the French and Masséna was able to concentrate his forces on his next objective, which was the capture of Almeida. This town was perhaps the finest Portuguese fortress on the Spanish frontier. Wellington, as he fell behind the Coa River left Almeida well garrisoned and supplied. The English spoke of it as being capable of holding out against a French attack for ninety days.[48] Such an estimate, if exaggerated, reflected the expectation of a prolonged siege.

Junot had asked for the privilege of besieging Almeida, but Masséna gave the task to Ney and his 6th Corps. The French moved west in the last week of July and in early August, and encircled the fortress. Then, while General Claude François Ferey's division took up a position west of the Coa, General Jean Gabriel Marchand's division prepared to dig. Trenches were opened on the night of 15 August, and the siege began in earnest. Solignac moved his headquarters to St. Feleces de los Gallegos, just east of the Spanish-Portuguese border. He had with him General Thomière's 2nd Brigade, the 65th Line, the Prussian Regiment, and the Irish Regiment. The Brigade's assignment was that of supporting Marchand should Wellington advance and attempt to raise the siege. However, the English commander had no intention of coming to the aid of Almeida. Thus the Irish had no active role in the siege. After ten days of digging trenches, the siege artillery was in place and the parallels were dangerously close to the fortress. At 5 A.M. on the morning of the twenty-sixth, the guns opened fire. The shelling continued all day with seemingly little serious damage to the fortress. Then at 7 P.M., there was a tremendous explosion within Almeida.

The powder magazine with 150,000 pounds of gunpowder, 4,000 charged projectiles, and over a million infantry cartridges exploded destroying a great part of the town. The garrison was left with virtually no powder (only 39 barrels survived the disaster) or cartridges. Continued resistance was no longer possible. The fortress surrendered on the morning of 28 August. No eyewitness survived the explosion. It seems that a charged bomb fired by the French landed in the courtyard in front of the principal magazine. The doors of the building were open because Portuguese soldiers were transferring barrels of powder from that magazine to the ramparts. The bomb rolled down the steps into the open magazine and exploded.[49] With Almeida in French hands the last obstacle was removed that had held up the invasion of Portugal. But before the Irish marched west with Masséna's army, Colonel O'Meara and *Chef de Bataillon* Mahony were relieved of their commands.

The exact date on which Junot removed O'Meara and Mahony is elusive. Byrne, a captain in Fitzhenry's battalion at the time, later wrote that it had been in May 1810. But O'Meara was writing to the minister of war and signing himself "Colonel of the Irish Regiment" as late as 24 August of the same year.[50] Finally, there is a letter from Clarke to the "Prince Vice Connetable" (Marshal Berthier) dated simply "August 1810," in which he writes "Your Serene Highness has already been informed of the order given by General the Duke of Abrantès to remove from the Irish Regiment, which is in Spain, Colonel O'Meara and *Chef de Bataillon* Mahony."[51] Thus it would seem that both officers had been relieved of their duties in the Irish Regiment before the end of August, but the exact date remains uncertain. O'Meara was assigned to Solignac's staff and Fitzhenry was named acting commander of the Regiment in Spain. Mahony was attached to Junot's staff and Captain Allen was given command of the 3rd Battalion. However, when Allen's promotion to *chef de bataillon* was not approved, he was replaced by Captain O'Malley who was the senior captain with the Regiment in Spain.[52]

O'Meara had been given command of the Irish Regiment because his brother was married to Clarke's sister, not because of his military qualifications. The minister of war had recommended him to Napoleon, and the emperor had approved the appointment. It is true that Clarke was not totally pleased with O'Meara's handling of the Regiment. He had refused the colonel's recommendations for promotions and had criticized his handling of vacancies in the summer of 1810. He was also critical of the manner in which recruiting was being carried out by the Irish Regiment in 1810, and complained to O'Meara that too many Englishmen were being recruited from the prisoner of war camps, and that there were too many desertions.

The colonel felt that Clarke was being unduly critical and vigorously tried to defend himself.[53] Yet, despite this friction, the minister of war did not take kindly, or lightly, the removal of his *protégé* by a field commander who had not bothered to consult with him on the matter.

Junot, on his part, was acting in the best interest of his own command. The army was about to march against Wellington's army and he saw O'Meara as totally imcompetent to command the Irish battalions in combat. On 14 September, an obviously frustrated Junot wrote to Masséna that it was time he spoke frankly of the affairs of the Irish Regiment. "Colonel O'Meara is not capable of commanding a squad of ten men,"[54] he began. "His officers have often told me that he is not capable of commanding the Regiment, and furthermore, that he is only capable of commanding in a noncombat situation."[55]

Clarke, who clearly felt slighted by what he considered to be Junot's heavy-handedness, struck back at Fitzhenry and Allen, whom he believed to be the principal intriguers against O'Meara and Mahony. To Marshal Berthier, through whom the affairs of the French armies in Spain were nominally conducted, he wrote the following:

> By certain information [presumably from Captain O'Malley], I have learned that these measures taken against two officers, whose personal qualities convey full confidence, had been provoked by the intrigues of *Chef de Bataillon* Fitzhenry, who has had for some time pretensions to be employed as the Colonel of the Regiment, and who has not obtained in the corps enough consideration to merit such an advancement.[56]

He went on to inform Berthier that the reunion of the two Irish battalions into one gave him the favorable occasion to remove Fitzhenry from the Regiment because he was a troublemaker. He also added that Captain Allen, who was no stranger to the intrigues in Spain, should not be included in the newly reorganized battalion, and that he should be sent back to France with Fitzhenry.[57]

When Junot heard of Clarke's maneuvering back in Paris, he not only defended his own actions, but came to the support of Fitzhenry.

> As for Fitzhenry [he wrote to Masséna], I believe that he desires to be a colonel, but that ambition is no different from that of everyone else. That which I can say for him is that he is . . . filled with energy and zeal, and that without him there would not be 200 men left in the Irish Regiment within eight days. This Regiment has a weak officer corps. There are those who do not know how to command, and Fitzhenry supplies leadership. You now have the truth of this matter. I support neither one nor the other [Fitzhenry nor O'Meara], but I assure you on my honor that if monsieur

O'Meara takes command and monsieur Fitzhenry returns to France, there will no longer be an Irish Regiment.[58]

Acting on Junot's comments and advice, Masséna supported his corps commander and ignored the minister of war. Fitzhenry and Allen remained with the Army of Portugal. However, this affair was a serious blow to Fitzhenry's career. He now had an enemy at the head of the War Office in Paris through which all promotions must pass. So long as Clarke remained minister of war, Fitzhenry had little hope of being promoted. Allen would fare little better. He did not receive the brevets of *chef de bataillon* until the eve of Napoleon's first abdication in 1814.

Mahoney's transfer to Junot's staff also provoked Clarke. The minister had been personally responsible for securing command of the 3rd Battalion for Mahony. That he had been incompetent as a battalion commander did not seem to be of importance to Clarke, but that he had been removed without his consent vexed him greatly. Junot expressed complete satisfaction with Mahony as a staff officer,[59] and the officers of the 3rd Battalion were equally satisfied that he had been removed from the Regiment.

By the end of the summer of 1810, the two Irish battalions in Spain were indeed in poor shape. Both were at about half strength. O'Meara had asked the minister of war to send a battalion of men from Landau to bring the two in Spain up to full strength. But rather than send more men, Napoleon decided upon the reorganization of the 2nd and 3rd Battalions into one single battalion that would be known as the 2nd Battalion of the Irish Regiment. The officers and men who would not be assigned to the new battalion would be sent back to the regimental depot at Landau and they would be employed in new battalions that were being formed.[60] The actual orders were not drawn up until December and merger did not take place until February 1811.

Basic preparations for the invasion of Portugal had been under way since the spring of 1810. But the sieges of Ciudad Rodrigo and Almeida had diverted and used large quantities of food and matériel while occupying the 6th Corps and the attention of Masséna and his staff. With the surrender of those fortified cities, the Army of Portugal could concentrate on its principal mission, the march on Lisbon. The date set for the general westward advance was 16 September. The men of the 2nd and 8th Corps, who had generally been inactive during the sieges, were ready and anxious to move. Not that they were happy about a campaign in Portugal, but rather they wished to put the whole affair behind them as quickly as possible. So anxious was everyone to begin this campaign that Ney's 6th Corps actually started a day early, on the fifteenth, and pushed the enemy's advance patrols to the west.

The French army that advanced into Portugal numbered 62,476 men and 2,471 officers. Its numbers had been diminished by the losses suffered during the two sieges and by 3,368 officers and men left behind to garrison Cuidad Rodrigo and Almeida.[61] The veterans of the 6th Corps led the way with General Louis Henri Loison commanding the advance guard. Reynier's 2nd Corps marched behind the 6th. The 8th Corps took a parallel road to the north and with the army's artillery and heavy supply wagons marched about one day behind Loison. The 6th and 2nd Corps crossed the River Coa and moved west through Valverde, Alverea, Fornos, and Mangulde to the city of Viseu. Junot's corps, with General Clausel's 1st Division leading the way, took a miserable road through Pinhel, Venda de Cego, Tajal, and into Viseu. From the first day of the campaign discipline became a problem. At Pinhel, the troops broke ranks and pillaged the town. The Portuguese had totally evacuated Pinhel so that there was neither local authority nor inhabitants to stop the troops or to complain to the French officers, who might have curbed this bad conduct on the part of their men. Pillaging and looting would increase as the campaign took the French army further from its supply bases and into the heart of Portugal. Food became scarce, and with the towns and villages emptied of their populations, the army took everything of use or value. As the English and Portuguese retreated before Masséna's columns, they tried to destroy anything that might aid the French. They even went so far as to poison the springs and wells in an attempt to make the French advance as difficult as possible.[62]

The two Irish battalions, which were classified as light infantry, marched at the head of Solignac's 2nd Division. As they were following Clausel, they were in the middle of Junot's marching column. In this position, they did not have contact with guerrillas or Portuguese irregulars who harrassed the head and rear of the 8th Corps. When the artillery fell behind Junot's main body on the eighteenth, because the road was in such bad condition, the Portuguese attacked it just west of Trancoso. Only the rapid return of three Prussian battalions, who formed the rearguard of the 8th Corps, saved the artillery and the heavy baggage wagons that were with it. The enemy was driven off, but none too soon. Had the army's artillery and baggage been captured or destroyed, the campaign would very likely have ended within a few days of its having begun.[63]

Loison reached the city of Viseu on the morning of 19 September. It had been abandoned by its population, much to the surprise of the French. As the divisions of the 6th Corps marched into Viseu during the day, Loison and his men marched out to take up an advance position to the southwest on the road to Bussaco. Although the 8th Corps' advance guard reached the outskirts of Viseu late on the nineteenth, it was four days before the rear guard, which accompained the artillery, reached the city. Junot's two divisions remained at Viseu until the morning of 24 September. Loison had driven the enemy out of Mortagoa by the evening of the twenty-third and camped within five miles of the Serra de Bussaco. The 6th and 2nd Corps poured down the road from Viseu, and on the morning of the twenty-sixth, both Ney and Reynier were in the presence of Wellington's entire army.

The Anglo-Portuguese army had been united as it retreated from the Spanish border. Wellington had 61,454 men under his direct command. His army had taken up a strong position along the ridge of the Serra de Bussaco, which ran north and south across the path of the advancing French. He seriously intended to stop the French march on Lisbon at this favorable point. He hoped that success at Bussaco would cause the French to abandon their goal and to withdraw back into Spain. His position was excellent. There were only three roads available to the French over the Serra de Bussaco. The Anglo-Portuguese army blocked the two in the center, while the third, twelve miles north of Bussaco, was not marked on the French maps and was not generally known. Thus if Wellington's army could hold its position, the French would have no acceptable option to a general withdrawal.

On the morning of 27 September, Masséna ordered Reynier and Ney to attack the Anglo-Portuguese positions on the heights of Bussaco. The two attacks were not well coordinated. The 2nd Corps moved up the steep slope, but, although several battalions actually reached the heights, it was thrown back in disorder. Reynier's assault had already failed before Ney's corps was seriously under way. The men of the 6th also reached the heights near the convent of Bussaco, but a vigorous counterattack drove them back down the mountain in disorder. The strong Anglo-Portuguese position, which was defended with *élan*, coupled with the inability of the French to support their attacks with either their artillery or cavalry, because of the steep, wooded, rocky terrain, caused Masséna to hold his army at the bottom of the mountain and to seek some other means of achieving his objective. He sent out cavalry patrols to the north and south to explore the possibility of outflanking Wellington. Sainte-Croix, with units of the 8th Corps' cavalry, found the third road, to the north, over the mountains.[64]

After dark on 28 September, the French army began its movement around Wellington's left flank. The Irish and the entire 8th Corps had not fired a shot, although Masséna had suffered 4,123 casualties and lost an additional 364 men taken prisoner.[65] They had been held in reserve behind the 6ᵗʰ Corps the entire day of the battle. Because of its position in the rear of the army, the 8ᵗʰ Corps now led the withdrawal and the maneuver around the enemy's flank. A cold rain fell all night on the demoralized French army as Clausel's 1ˢᵗ Division led the way through Boialvo, over the Caramula Pass, which Wellington had failed to fortify or defend,[66] and into Sardao. Sardao was set in a great plain that ran north and south behind Wellington's position on the heights of the Serra de Bussaco. Once the French army had reached that point, his position was outflanked. On the twenty--ninth, the English commander realized what had taken place and ordered a general retreat south through Coimbra in the direction of Lisbon.

The 8ᵗʰ Corps met no resistance as it marched through the rain on the narrow road over the Caramula pass and into Sardao. With Clausel's 1ˢᵗ Division still at the head of the army, the French turned sharply to the left and moved south towards Coimbra. They passed behind the abandoned English position at Bussaco and, after Sainte-Croix's cavalry and Clausel's infantry had roughly handled Wellington's rear guard, occupied Cardao. The city, the third largest in Portugal, had been virtually abandoned. The English had left behind only the wounded from the Battle of Bussaco. This included the seriously wounded English and Portuguese as well as the French. To these unfortunate victims of war, Masséna added the sick and wounded who accompanied the army. The French alone numnbered over 4,000 men.[67]

When the 8ᵗʰ Corps arrived at Coimbra, it posted guards at the gates to the city and camped on the banks of the Mondego. However, as the walls of Coimbra were in disrepair and there were numerous places at which the city could be entered, it was impossible to keep out the soldiers. Men from virtually every unit of the corps made their way into the empty city and began to loot and plunder the shops and homes. Some effort was made to prevent the ravaging of Coimbra, but for the most part, the soldiers within the walls had their way. Even officers and the troops responsible for main-taining order were seen actively looting. In due time, Junot was able to clear the city of the marauders, post adequate guards, and patrol the streets. Nevertheless, when Masséna became aware of what had taken place in Coimbra, he reprimanded Junot in strong terms. "I am discontented with the conduct of the 8ᵗʰ Corps," he wrote on 2 October 1810, "and I may be forced to replace it in the battle order. . . . I am commander of the Army of Portugal, and I have the power to send back to France those who fail in their duty."[68]

From Coimbra Masséna's army continued its march south on the main road to Lisbon. The 8ᵗʰ Corps was still leading the advance. There was a general feeling among the French that the English would not now risk a general battle, but would embark from Lisbon, and perhaps other ports, and leave Portugal to the mercy of Napoleon.[69] They could after all always return to the Peninsula at a more favorable time and place. In the first week of October, the French had absolutely no knowledge of the defensive positions that Wellington was preparing for the protection of Lisbon. It appeared at that time the most serious problem Masséna faced was the Portuguese regular, and irregular, army units operating behind his advancing column. On 7 October, only a few days after Reynier's 2nd Corps, which brought up the rear of the army, had crossed the Mondego and left at Coimbra the wounded with an inadequate guard, a Portuguese army commanded by an Englishman, Colonel Nicholas Trant, occupied the city and captured the two convents on its outskirts, which were serving as hospitals. All of the French sick and wounded fell into the hands of the enemy. Napoleon, who recognized the negative effect on morale of losing one's wounded to the enemy, was displeased and critical of Masséna's actions.[70]

The Irish battalions formed the advanced guard of Solignac's division and marched directly behind the 1st Division. They moved through Leiria, Rio Maior, and Alenquer to Sobral. Here, for the first time, the French realized that Wellington intended to give battle in an attempt to prevent the fall of Lisbon. The Anglo-Portuguese army, with a field force of 59,000 men and an additional 28,000 occupying the fortifications,[71] was dug in along a range of hills and mountains that extended from the Tagus river just south of Alhandra to the Atlantic ocean west of Torres Vedras.

Junot's 8th Corps was the first to reach the Torres Vedras line. It took up a position in the center of the line at Sobral. Reynier's 2nd Corps moved on to his left while Ney's 6th Corps formed the French right. Messéna's army thus faced Wellington's position from Alhandra, on the Tagus River, to the Atlantic coast. The French observed, scouted, and probed the enemy's position, but found no weak point that they were willing to attack. In point of fact, Masséna's army was in somewhat of a state of disarray when it reached the Torres Vedras line, and the longer an attack was postponed, the stronger became the Anglo-Portuguese position. Thus the French sat for five weeks before the Line. During that period they consumed what food was available in the immediate vicinity, and decided that no attack could be made on the strong enemy position until they received reinforcements and supplies from Spain. Masséna had been promised both, and he was determined to await their arrival before committing his army to battle.

By the middle of November, the French commander had decided to withdraw from his position before the Torres Vedras Line. The army was finding it increasingly difficult to find food, its position was exposed along a thirty-mile front, and there was no indication that the promised reinforcements would arrive in the immediate future. The army began its withdrawal the night of 14–15 November. Despite the delays and confusion that accompany such an operation, within a few days the army had taken up a new position some thirty miles north of the Torres Vedras Line. Reynier's headquarters were at Santarem, on the right bank of the Tagus. Junot and his 8th Corps were in the vicinity of Pernes, while Ney was behind them in reserve. The French held the country from Santarem north, with its left along the Tagus River. This region, which had not been despoiled by the English or the Portuguese, provided the French with a new source of food and supplies. Wellington advanced his army and probed the new French line, but he was not anxious to engage Masséna's force in battle. "I could lick those fellows any day," Wellington is reported as having said, "but it would cost me 10,000 men and, as this is the last army England has, we must take care of it."[72] He further believed, and quite correctly, that time was on his side. The French could not remain indefinitely deep in Portugal. Masséna would have to receive substantial help within a few months or withdraw. Anglo-Portuguese intelligence, which was better than that of the French, did not indicate that such aid was on its way from Spain.

The French army sat for the next three months. Most of its energy was expended in the increasingly difficult task of feeding itself. The troops lived in poor conditions, and generally on half rations. They were bored and unhappy, and morale was low. There was even quarreling and a lack of single-mindedness at the highest level of command.[73] There was a plan to occupy the left bank of the Tagus, and bridging material was gathered and the engineers made great preparations, but the army could not remain in the vicinity of Lisbon without support from Spain, and that support did not arrive.

The Irish battalions were camped in the vicinity of Pernes after the pullback from the Torres Vedras Line.[74] They had the same difficulties securing food as the rest of Junot's Corps.[75] They lived on half rations and whatever they could find, at the expense of the poor local inhabitants, within foraging range. The health of the officers and men was generally better than that of the army as a whole. In mid-January, for example, the battalions reported only fifteen men who were too sick to perform their duties.[76] When the time arrived for the army to withdraw from the Tagus, the Irish were in reasonably good condition.

Sometime in the second half of February 1811, the 3rd Battalion of the Irish Regiment was merged with the 2nd. Napoleon had decreed on 28 October 1810 that the Irish Regiment should be reduced to two battalions. The 1st and 4th, which were at Landau, would be united and called the 1st Battalion, while the 2nd and 3rd would become the 2nd Battalion.[77] However, as the 2nd and 3rd Battalions were on campaign in Portugal, no action was taken with respect to them until February of the following year. Masséna had reported that "desertions, which have manifested themselves in the 3rd Battalion of the Irish Regiment in the 8th Corps of the army, have reduced that battalion to the strength of a company, and there were only four officers present.[78] He therefore ordered the soldiers of the 3rd Battalion to be incorporated into the 2nd along with enough of the officers and noncommissioned officers to fill the vacancies in that battalion. The result was a battalion of more than 600 officers and men under the command of *Chef de Bataillon* Fitzhenry. There are two conflicting sets of figures for the strength of the 2nd Battalion after the reorganization. The major general of the army, Marshal Berthier, reported to Napoleon on 11 February 1811 that there were 24 officers and 481 men in the two Irish battalions.[79] However, a detailed statistical report of Junot's 8th Corps dated 11 February, gives the field strength of the 2nd Battalion at 29 officers and 530 men plus 1 officer and 102 men "detached," or a total of 662.[80] The higher figure is most likely correct. It corresponds more closely with the 1 January 1811 statistical report, which gives the two Irish battalions at 23 officers and 525 men "present," 2 officers and 7 men detached and 3 officers and 104 men in the hospital. This would put the Irish strength at 664 officers and men at the beginning of 1811.[81] Finally, Miles Byrne, a captain in the 2nd Battalion on the campaign, states that when the Irish reached the Spanish frontier in early April, "We had nearly seven hundred men present under arms."[82] In accordance with instructions from Paris, the officers and noncommissioned officers who were not needed to fill the vacancies in the 2nd Battalion were sent back to the regimental depot at Landau. That detachment was commanded by Captain Joseph Parrott. The men were to form the nucleus of a third battalion for the Regiment.

Masséna decided upon a limited withdrawal to a new position north of the Mondego River with Coimbra as the center of his defensive line. His staff drew up the detailed plans, and the retrograde movement began the night of 5–6 March. General Clausel's 1st Division led Junot's Corps to the north with the rest of the army behind it. The Irish marched through Torres Novas and Pombal to Soure, about ten miles south of the Mondego. They marched at the head of Solignac's division and were not engaged in any combat. Wellington was caught by surprise when the French army withdrew, so that it gained a full day's march before the British reacted.

Coimbra and the right (north) bank of the Mondego River were held by Colonel Nicholas Trant and his six battalions of Portuguese militia, who were supported by four more militia battalions upstream.[83] While the French advance guard was searching for a ford to cross the river, the

Coimbra bridge having been cut, Wellington caughtup with the rear guard and applied pressure. Masséna realized that he could not cross the Mondego with the opposite bank held by the enemy and Wellington pressing him from behind. His only alternative was to turn to the east and march back into Spain. The first phase of the French maneuver in March, from the Tugau to the Mondego, might be referred to as a "strategic withdrawal," but beginning with the second phase on 14 March, the French army was in full retreat.[84]

During the retreat from Portugal Marshal Ney commanded the rear guard. Each regiment of the army took its turn furnishing a battalion to make up the extreme rear. The Irish Battalion thus served under the "Bravest of the Brave" during a portion of the campaign.[85] The retreat was conducted in an orderly manner, except for the affair at the bridge over the River Ceira.[86] On Saint Patrick's Day the army crossed the River Alva. There is no indication as to how the Irish commemorated the feast of their patron saint, but it is unlikely that they had either the time or the inclination for much of a celebration. The task at hand was to save what was left of the Army of Portugal. There were only rearguard skirmishes after the Alva was crossed. Wellington quickly outmarched his own supplies and the French left nothing behind them that could have been of use to the enemy. Thus Masséna's beleaguered force reached Spain with a minimum amount of harassment on the part of the enemy.

Protected by the guns of Almeida and Ciudad Rodrigo, reinforced by their garrisons and fed and supplied by their depots and the Spanish provinces behind them, Masséna stopped his retreat and turned about to again face the enemy. It was at this time that the quarreling and bickering between the army commander and Marshal Ney reached the point of no return when the latter refused to accept orders from his superior. Masséna had no choice but to remove Ney from command of the 6th Corps, which he had led since the formation of the Grand Army in 1805. General Louis Henri Loison, as the senior general officer, was given the Corps, and the marshal left the army to return to Paris.[87] Wellington's forces advanced to the Spanish frontier and even laid siege to the fortress of Almeida. However, as he had no siege guns or equipment, he had no hope of taking the town except by a prolonged siege that would starve its garrison into submission.

There was little fighting between the two armies during the month of April. Wellington was gathering his forces on the Spanish frontier, and Masséna was regrouping, reequipping, and resting his troops after their six-month ordeal in Portugal. Both men knew that the war had not ended, but was merely moving into another phase.

Before the French army reached the Spanish border efforts were being made to resupply the troops. One of the greatest needs of the men was for new shoes. While the army was still in Portugal, General Solignac ordered an officer from each regiment to leave the army and go ahead into Spain to secure the necessary articles that were needed for the men in their respective units. Captain John Allen of the Irish Battalion was one of those officers. Allen and several other officers of the 2nd Division reached Spain late in March, and on the 26th departed Ciudad Rodrigo for the interior. The small band was attacked by Spanish guerrillas commanded by Don Julian Sanchez. In the fighting that took place Allen received four saber wounds before he and his companions were taken prisoner. He was transported to the south of Spain where he was imprisoned in a fortress near Cádiz.[88]

Nothing was heard of Allen for several months, and it was feared that he had been killed by guerrillas who were active everywhere in western Spain. Then his good friend Captain Byrne received a letter from Allen imploring him to do all that was possible to secure his exchange for a Spanish prisoner of war of equal or superior rank. He had heard that he would soon be turned over to the English and shipped back to a British prison. Because of his anti-English activities before he had fled Ireland, Allen was fearful of falling into the hands of the English. Through the intercession of Captain William Corbet, Marshal Auguste Frédéric Louis Viesse de Marmont, who had replaced Masséna in May as commander of the Army of Portugal, took up the cause of Captain Allen. The marshal sent a personal request to Marshal Claude Victor, who commanded the French army before Cádiz, asking him to give Allen preferential consideration in the event of an exchange of officers because he was an Irishman whom the English may not see fit to treat as a French prisoner of war. By the same courier Byrne was able to send the prisoner 1,000 francs which, despite the bitterness of the war in the Peninsula, reached him in an enemy prison. Even with such special efforts made on the part of Allen, it was eighteen months before an exchange could be made and he was able to return to his regiment in France.[89]

The bitter divisions that had torn the Irish Legion apart and led to the death of Captain William Corbet's brother Thomas in 1804 had been healed by time and the fortunes, and misfortunes, of war. John Allen and Miles Byrne had been strong supporters of Thomas A. Emmet in those turbulent years in Brittany, and although neither of them had played an active or prominent role in the death of Thomas Corbet, they were not friends of General Arthur O'Connor or his staunch supporter William Corbet. When William rejoined the French army in 1809 he did not return to the Irish Legion. With his former rank of captain, he entered the 70th Regiment. In June, he became an aide-de-camp to Marshal Marmont, and when the latter was sent to Spain to replace Masséna, Corbet accompanied him. When Byrne went to Corbet to ask for his assistance on behalf of Allen, the marshal's aide immediately took up the cause of a fellow Irish expatriate who had fallen upon difficult times. It might also be mentioned at this point that in 1828 *Chef de Battaillon* Byrne and Colonel Corbet became good friends while serving with the French army in Greece.[90]

The Army of Portugal went into quarters in the vicinity of Salamanca and Toro before the middle of April 1811. The Irish Battalion, marching with Solignac's Division, camped for two nights outside of Ciudad Rodrigo. The troops drew rations from its storehouses and on the 8th of April continued their march on the road to Salamanca. Before the Battalion had gone many miles, a messenger arrived with orders for the Irish to return to Cuidad Rodrigo and to form a portion of the city's garrison. Although much disappointed, the Battalion returned and took up quarters in the city. The governor, General Rheno, was pleased to have them and he treated the officers and men well.

> On entering the town, [Byrne later wrote] every man got a loaf of fine white bread, the first they had tasted for several months, and a ration of meat and wine.—This, with being tolerably well lodged, made both officers and men soon forget the miseries they had suffered in the severe campaign of Portugal.[91]

When the Irish Battalion was ordered back to Ciudad Rodrigo on 8 April, *Chef de Bataillon* Fitzhenry turned over command to his senior captain, Austin O'Mally, to conduct it back to the city. Fitzhenry then rode on towards Salamanca to secure permission for his battalion to rejoin the 8th Corps, which was going into cantonment in the vicinity of Toro. His mission was successful, and after spending several days at Salamanca, during which time he gathered some seventy men of the Battalion who had been convalescing there and who were ready to return to active duty, he prepared to depart. On 19 April, this small band marched out of Salamanca on the high road to Ciudad Rodrigo. On 22 April, on the last leg of its journey, from Ledesma to Ciudad Rodrigo, it was attacked by Don Julian Sanchez's guerrillas, and the survivors, including Fitzhenry, were taken prisoner. The wife of one of the soldiers escaped in the night and brought the sad news to Ciudad Rodrigo.[92]

The men of the Irish Battalion thought, quite naturally, that Fitzhenry would share the same fate as Captain Allen, if indeed the latter was still alive. As prisoners of war, they would be held in captivity with the possibility of being exchanged at some future date for Spanish officers. The loss of their popular battalion commander was felt throughout his corps. One might very well imagine the surprise and the shock of the officers and men when in June it became known that Fitzhenry had been seen at liberty, and wearing his sword, at Wellington's headquarters. In fact, it was reported that he was preparing to leave the Peninsula and return home to his family in Ireland.[93]

When this news reached Marmont's headquarters the marshal ordered that Fitzhenry be charged with desertion and court-martialed *in absentia*. However, as the army was continually engaged with the enemy through the summer and fall of 1811, the court-martial proceedings were delayed. On 2 December, the court convened at Placencia in Estremadura. The presiding officer was Colonel Beuret, the commanding officer of the 17th Regiment of the old 2nd Corps. The other six members of the court were from the 22nd Regiment of General Clauzel's division and the 65th Regiment that made up a part of Thomière's brigade—which included the Irish Battalion. At the conclusion of the hearings, four of the seven officers voted against Fitzhenry and three voted for acquittal. As a guilty verdict required five votes, Fitzhenry escaped condemnation by one vote.[94]

While his fate in the eyes of the French army was being deliberated upon at Placencia, Fitzhenry was living in County Wexford with his family. Furthermore, there were rumors that Fitzhenry had planned with the Reverend Doctor Curtis, the influencial head of the Irish College at the University of Salamanca, to be captured and to be returned to Ireland. Byrne concluded his account of the affair with the following:

> He [Fitzhenry] would not allow that he had been guilty of the foul, cowardly crime of desertion, or that the superior of the Irish seminary at Salamanca, the reverend doctor Curtis, had used his great influence with the English general in chief Lord Wellington to obtain him his pardon and liberty, or that the reverend doctor Curtis had previously arranged with the chief of Spanish guerrillas, Don Julian [Sanchez], to have an ambuscade prepared for Fitzhenry and his detachment of 70 men. These matters could never be rightly ascertained, but one thing is certain, Fitzhenry never could raise his head in consequence, and his last moments were embittered by the recollection, whilst the reverend doctor Curtis was promoted catholic archbishop of Armagh and primate of all Ireland.[95]

Whether or not Fitzhenry was in collusion with the Reverend Doctor Curtis *before* his capture may never be known. It is quite possible that he saw Curtis while he was in Salamanca, although it cannot be documented. That which is most likely is that Curtis, knowing that Fitzhenry was leading a small company of men to Ciudad Rodrigo, communicated that information to the English, or to Don Julian Sanchez. Curtis had been spying on the French for some time and sending intelligence reports to Wellington.[96] When Masséna's army retired to Salamanca, Don Julian Sanchez and his guerrillas were ordered by Wellington to prevent communications, supplies, or reinforcements from reaching Ciudad Rodrigo.[97] The guerrillas attacked every convoy that moved along the main road. Thus, even without information from the Reverend Doctor Curtis they would have surely attacked Fitzhenry and his seventy men. Once Fitzhenry had become a prisoner of war his innocence becomes more questionable. Curtis may very well have intervened on his behalf to secure for him a pardon from the English government and his return to Ireland. "Honor" would have dictated that he remain a prisoner of war and loyal to France. As an Irishman, he may have felt that he had performed his duty to his adopted nation, and that once a prisoner there was nothing more to be done!

Yet there is another consideration that must be taken into account. Fitzhenry, not entirely through his own actions, had made an enemy of the powerful minister of war, Henri Clarke. The removal of Colonel O'Meara in particular, but also that of *Chef de Bataillon* Mahony as well, had angered Clarke. Fitzhenry had been given command of the Irish Regiment in Spain without Masséna or Solignac even consulting the War Office. Furthermore, both Junot and Solignac had supported Fitzhenry at the time, and gave him to believe that he would be named colonel of the Regiment in the course of time. But when it became known how displeased Clarke was over the affair, the two generals in Spain backed off and the full blame and anger of the minister of war seemed to fall upon Fitzhenry. He could hardly feel that he had any future in the French army so long as Clarke remained minister of war. Thus once he was a prisoner of war in the hands of the English, it is perhaps understandable that Fitzhenry would accept the attractive offer made to him by the "enemy" to return to Ireland and live quietly with his wife and three children whom he had not seen since they had left France in 1803.[98]

His fellow countrymen whom he had left behind in Spain and France were not so understanding of Fitzhenry's course of action. He had been very popular with the Irish of the Legion and with the men of his battalion. But they believed that by his actions, that is, accepting the English pardon and the offer to return to Ireland, he brought dishonor upon them in particular and the Regiment in general. Byrne summed up his own feelings, and presumably those of the men who had served with him in Spain:

> Had Fitzhenry been sick, he might have got permission to go to recover his health in France; but the die was cast, and his military career tarnished.

Apparently he cared little about the unmerited stain he brought on the reputation of the Irish serving in France; but fortunately the subsequent brilliant conduct of those brave officers, whom he abandoned, soon did away with the bad impression made at the war office by his desertion.[99]

The news of Fitzhenry's defection was also received as a cruel blow by the Irish back in France. Major William Lawless, the ranking officer in the Regiment since the removal of Colonel O'Meara, felt it necessary to denounce his countryman's actions and to profess, in the strongest terms, the loyalty of the Irish. On 19 June 1811, he wrote from Bois-le-Duc to the minister of war:

> How can I impress to Your Excellence the dishonor, and the state of humiliation into which we have been plunged by the desertion of Fitz-henry and his complicity [with the enemy]!!! How can I express the feelings of indignation, of loathing, and of horror for a betrayal so notorious and an ingratitude so atrocious! Is it necessary that a wretched person put an indelible stain on a nation whose loyality has become proverbial! His compatriots knew him as an intriguer, and impostor, but they did not suspect him of being capable of treason. . . . [100]

Lawless went on to protest the loyalty of the Irish in the Regiment. Four weeks after he had written his condemnation of the "deserter," Lawless received a response from the minister of war. "The defection of the former *chef de bataillon* Fitzhenry" Clarke wrote on 17 July, "will not in any way affect the confidence that you have inspired in His Imperial Majesty. The faults were personal, and under a just government, the faults of a single individual can not fall back upon the corps of which he [Fitzhenry] was a part."[101]

If the letter written by Lawless was more severe, biting, and bitter than the words of Byrne in his *Memoirs*, it may well reflect the timing and the intended audience. Byrne put to paper his feelings and his reactions to the events of the spring of 1811 some forty years after they had taken place. He had had years to talk and to think about his former friend and companion-in-arms and what he had done and why. He had clearly neither forgiven nor forgotten, but he had mellowed. Lawless' situation was quite different, he wrote to the minister of war as soon as he had heard that Fitzhenry had gone over to the enemy. He expressed an immediate reaction, which was based on incomplete information. Furthermore, he was writing to a minister of war whom he knew to be hostile towards Fitzhenry. He felt it imperative to distance the Irish in the French army, and indeed the entire Irish Regiment, from Fitzhenry and the disloyalty that surrounded him in the summer of 1811. His words were harsh, angry and bitter. Finally, it might be pointed out that Lawless had not served under, or with, Fitzhenry for almost four years. He had not shared the misery and hardships of the Portuguese campaign nor the trials and tribulations of service in Spain. Byrne, on the other hand, had been with him through the good times and the bad, from the formation of the Legion in 1803 until his capture in 1811.

The defection of Fitzhenry was felt with greater pain by the Irish, both in Spain and in France, than that of Captain Louis Lacy in 1808. Even though Lacy actually fought against the French after joining, or perhaps it is more correct to say rejoining, the Spanish army he had, after all, been born in Spain, spoke the language, and had even served in the Spanish army—as had his father before him. He had joined the French army, that is, the Irish Legion, in 1803 to make the expedition to Ireland and help liberate it from English domination. He had not joined the Legion to help impose a French monarch and a French government upon the Spanish. The Irish of the Legion were disappointed and embarrassed when it became known, more than a year after the fact, that he had rejoined the Spanish army. Yet the mitigating circumstances made Lacy's actions somewhat understandable, albeit not acceptable. Fitzhenry's actions, however, were an entirely different matter. He had made his pact with the devil himself—King George! Lacy could be associated with the poor and oppressed Spanish people, something with which the Irish could easily relate. But to come to an understanding with the English, at whose hands so many of the men of the Legion and their families had suffered and who prevented many of them from ever returning home, was seen as an act of betrayal, not so much of the French army or the Emperor Napoleon, but of Ireland and the Irish people. It was this feeling of betrayal, for which Byrne could never forgive him, and that motivated William Lawless' unmerciful attack upon Fitzhenry.

By the last week of April 1811, Masséna had decided to gather his army and march to the relief of Almeida, which had been surrounded and cut off from all supplies since the beginning of the month. On 3 May, the Irish Battalion rejoined its brigade at Ciudad Rodrigo, and marched with it the next day to meet the waiting allied army. Wellington had drawn up his 36,000 men along the high ground from Fuentes de Onoro on his right (south) flank to Fort Concepcion on his left. On the 5th, Masséna, with superior numbers (48,000 men), but fewer pieces of artillery, attacked and attempted to turn the allied right. Heavy fighting took place in Fuentes de Oñoro and on the slopes in the vicinity. But the French failed to break Wellington's right, and made only a feeble attempt to maneuver him out of his strong position. Masséna had held Solignac's Division in reserve behind the center of his line to be used in the event of unforeseen trouble, or to throw into the fight once the enemy had been broken or turned. As neither happened, and there was little action in the center or on the French right, the Irish remained idle all day. They did not fire a single shot, nor, of course, did they suffer a single casualty. They simply remained in place for two days and then withdrew with the entire army.[102]

Masséna had failed to lift the siege of Almeida, which was his primary objective. He, therefore, decided to try to save the garrison. He sent word to General Antoine François Brennier, who commanded the fortress, and who would soon command the 6th Division in which the Irish would serve, to destroy the fortifications and artillery and to breakout towards the north so as to cross the River Agueda by the bridge of Barba del Puerco. On the night of 10 May, Brennier led his small garrison of 1,300 men out through the north gate. The French pushed aside the weak enemy blockade and, in a forced march that lasted all night, reached the bridge of Barba del Puerco just as the English and Portuguese were closing on their rear. Under the cover of fire from a regiment of Reynier's 2nd Corps, which had been sent to cover their withdrawal, Brennier's men crossed the Agueda and rejoined Masséna's army. Thus the brief campaign in May came to an end, not with the more desirable result of resupplying Almeida, but at least with the saving of its garrison. The bulk of the French army had pulled back to Ciudad Rodrigo the night of 8–9 May after Brennier had signaled to Masséna that he had received his orders to evacuate.[103]

On the same day that General Brennier evacuated Almeida, Marshal Marmont assumed command of the Army of Portugal. He took his new army back to its depots at Salamanca, Toro, and Valladolid, where it was reorganized, reequiped, and rested. One of the major problems that had faced Masséna during his Portuguese Campaign, and was virtually disabling at times, was that he had to deal with corps commanders who considered themselves his equal, as did Marshal Ney, or near equal, as did Junot. In order to enhance the authority of the new army commander, Napoleon ordered the army corps dissolved and reorganized into six divisions. The two remaining corps commanders, Junot and Reynier—Ney had already departed—and all of the former division commanders except Clausel and Solignac were sent back to France. The Irish Battalion became a part of the 6th Division of the army, which was commanded by General Brennier, who had been promoted to general of division after his daring and successful escape from Almeida. The new division consisted of three regiments, the 22nd, 65th and 17th. However, the army was only to enjoy two weeks of rest before it was again on campaign.

The military situation on the southern portion of the Spanish-Portu-guese frontier grew desperate in the late spring of 1811. The fortified city of Badajoz, which was the key to the valley of the Guadiana River in Estremadura, and the logical invasion route into Andalusia, was being blockaded by the Anglo-Portuguese army. After Masséna's attempt to relieve Almeida had failed and Marmont had taken the Army of Portugal into cantonment, Wellington had taken his army south to Badajoz in order to threaten Andalusia. Marshal Nicolas-Jean de Dieu Soult, who commanded the Army of Andalusia in southern Spain, asked for Marmont's support to raise the blockade of Badajoz before it was starved into submission. Marmont, in a rather unusual act of cooperation without direct orders from Napoleon, gathered his army and marched south.

Breaking camp in the early days of June, Marmont's divisions covered 250 miles over difficult roads and terrain in only fifteen days. They crossed the Sierra de Gredos and then the Tagus to arrive by 18 June at Merida on the banks of the Guadiana River where they linked up with Soult's army. Together they marched west on Badajoz. Wellington fell back into Portugal and took up a strong defensive position. On 20 June, Marmont entered Badajoz. The blockade had been lifted without a battle, and over the next several weeks the city was resupplied and the garrison changed. Neither Soult nor Marmont had any desire to attack Wellington in the strong position he had taken, and the English general did not dare to advance against a French army that was superior in numbers. Soult left an army corps of some 10,000 men in Estremadura south of the Guadiana to watch the enemy and to support Badajoz. He then took the rest of his army back into Andalusia. In mid-July, Marmont crossed to the north bank of the Guadiana and took up a central position astride the Tagus. To the north, he occupied the passes over the Sierra de Gredos, while his southern flank reached almost to Merida on the Guadiana.

Marmont put his army into cantonment in northern Estremadura and western New Castile so that he would be in a position to concentrate his forces either on the Guadiana, should Wellington again attack Badajoz and threaten southern Spain, or in southern Leon north of the Sierra de Gredos should Ciudad Rodrigo be in danger. His divisions were spread widely over a vast portion of west-central Spain so as to enable them to live off of the land. Even so, it was necessary to bring in food from as far east as Toledo.[104]

When Marmont put his army into cantonment, the Irish were ordered to Trujillo and then Avila. "They had pleasant quarters in the mountains during the hot summer of . . . 1811," wrote Byrne in his *Memoirs*, "the soldiers being well fed and well lodged for the months of July and August."[105] Then in mid-September, the grenadier and voltigeur companies of the Irish Battalion, under Captain Byrne, were ordered to General Brennier's headquarters at Bexar. Once the division was concentrated, it marched north with the whole of Marmont's army, less General Maximilien Foy's Division, to relieve Ciudad Rodrigo, which was blockaded by the Anglo-Portuguese army. General Jean-Marie Dorsenne, commander of the Army of the North, moved south from Salamanca and joined Marmont for the final advance on the city. Wellington, who had collected 46,000 men, retired west of Ciudad Rodrigo in the face of the combined French armies of 58,000. Marmont, who commanded the French force, raised the blockade and after probing the enemy in force with his superior cavalry decided not to attack Wellington in his strong position. Thus having achieved his limited objective, of resupplying Ciudad Rodrigo, the marshal retired. The campaign ended much as the joint action with Soult in June had ended, without a major battle and the restoration of the status quo.[106]

Upon the army's return from Ciudad Rodrigo early in October, 1811, General Brennier's 6th Division was ordered into Plasencia to keep a watch on the central Portuguese frontier. It was while the 2nd Irish Battalion was in northern Estremadura that it received a new battalion commander. Auguste Dillon, recently promoted to *chief de bataillon*, assumed command in early November. Dillon was the son of General (Count) Theobald Dillon. Born in Dublin, Theobald Dillon joined the family regiment in the service of France at the age of fifteen. He served with the regiment in the war for American independence, notably at the siege of Savannah. When the French Revolution established a constitutional monarchy, Colonel Dillon, commander of the Dillon Regiment of the Irish Brigade, remained in the service of the king. Shortly after war broke out in 1792, General Dillon was murdered by his own troops after they had panicked in the face of an Austrian army. The new *Chef de Bataillon* had been born in France of a true military family. Veterans of the early years of the Legion might question his devotion to the cause of Irish independence, but not his military abilities. He had served on the staff of General Junot in 1810–11 before his promotion and appointment in the Irish Regiment.[107]

Shortly before Dillon took up his new command, a controversy that had plagued the Irish Battalion ever since the merger of the 2nd and 3rd Battalions had taken place came to a head. The root of the problem centered about the question of seniority in rank. When the 3rd Battalion of the Legion was formed in the summer of 1809, some of its new officers were nominated "provisionally" by the minister of war for ranks that were confirmed by the emperor some months later. In the time span between their nomination and confirmation, officers of the 2nd Battalion serving in Spain were promoted by order of the emperor. There had not been a problem until the two battalions were merged into one. Then the officers of the former 3rd Battalion declared that they held seniority in rank from the date of their nomination by the minister of war, while the officers who had served in the 2nd Battalion before merger maintained that seniority began with imperial confirmation.[108] The matter was finally settled in favor of the date of confirmation by the emperor, but it had strained some relationships within the officer corps before it was all forgotten.

In December 1811, orders arrived in Spain for the return to France of the officers and noncommissioned officers of the Irish Battalion. The privates were to be incorporated into the Prussian Regiment serving with the Army of Portugal. Many of the Irish officers and noncommissioned officers had been campaigning in Spain and Portugal for more than four years and were extremely pleased with this news. Serving south of the Pyrenees was more dangerous, harsh, and undesirable than in any other part of Europe where the French army was active. On 25 December, the 120 officers, sergeants, corporals, and drummers stood inspection for the last time in Spain, and after bidding a sad farewell to their troops, marched north through Toledo to Madrid. They had to wait in the Spanish capital for ten days in early January until a convoy was formed, because it was too dangerous for so small a column to travel the guerrilla-infested hills between Madrid and the French border. Upon reaching Valladolid, by way of Segovia, they had another eighteen-day delay. But in February they reached France, and the rest of the journey was relaxed and almost enjoyable. It was not until 11 April that they arrived at Bois-le-Duc, the new location of the regimental depot.[109]

The Irish Legion had contributed two battalions plus 500 men to the Peninsular campaigns over a period of four years. Its ranks had continually been depleted by combat, sickness, and desertions. Never reaching regimental strength or organization, the Irish battalions remained something of a stepchild with no high-ranking officer taking a serious interest in their well-being. Yet the Irish served with honor and, on occasion, distinction on numerous campaigns. At Astorga they were in the vanguard of the final assault. On the march to Lisbon they frequently led the 8th Corps. During the withdrawal from Portugal they took their turn as the rearguard. They earned the respect and admiration of the officers and men with whom they served because they could be counted upon to do their duty no matter what the conditions or circumstances. The officers and noncommissioned officers who returned to France in 1812 did so with pride in their service south of the Pyrenees.

6

Recruitment and Desertion

The year 1810 was one of comparative peace for Napoleon and Europe. The emperor was still at war with England and there was fighting in the Iberian Peninsula, but he had peace with those nations that could most threaten his empire. Prussia had been crushed in 1806, Austria again defeated in 1809, and if Russia was acting in a more independent manner, it did not pose a direct danger at that time. The agreements made at Tilsit in 1807, which more or less divided Europe between Napoleon and Tsar Alexander I, were already breaking down, but England had no allies and could cause no serious problems except south of the Pyrenees, a theater of operations that Napoleon insisted upon treating as secondary. Under these "peacetime" conditions, which discounted the war in Spain and Portugal, the Irish Regiment was recruiting actively in the prisoner of war camps in France and Germany and forming new battalions.

While the 2nd Battalion of the Regiment was seeing active service in northern Spain during the fall of 1809, and the 3rd Battalion was marching south to join it, the recently created 4th Battalion was experiencing the growing pains of adolescence. On 23 August 1809, orders had been issued for the formation of a fourth battalion, but as the 3rd was being sent to war, it continued to receive top priority in the distribution of matériel and recruits. It was only after the departure of 500 men, on 6 December, that serious efforts were made to create the 4th Battalion of the Regiment. Landau remained the regimental depot, and it was there that the officers and new recruits were quartered, equipped, and trained.

John Tennent, a thirty-two-year-old native of Belfast, was promoted to the rank of *chef de bataillon* (9 November 1809) and named commandant of the new battalion. He was well educated and quite literate in both English and French. The son of a wealthy landowner in northern Ireland, both John and his brother William had been active in the Society of United Irishmen.

In 1797 John had fled to France. However, his brother had been captured and sent to prison in Scotland with Arthur O'Connor and Thomas A. Emmet. In 1799 John Tennent had served in the Army of the North under General Guillaume Marie Ann Brune. With the provisional rank of *chef de bataillon*, he had helped to drive the combined Anglo-Russian army out of Holland. When the Irish Legion was formed, Tennent, who had returned to civilian life and was living comfortably in Paris, reentered the French army with the rank of captain.[1]

Colonel O'Meara's departure from Landau to take command of the "war battalions" in Spain left Major William Lawless the ranking officer at the regimental depot. The rank of *chef de bataillon* is frequently translated into English as "major," but, in fact, by 1809 the French army had a rank of major, which was primarily an administrative title. A regiment had one major who was second in command to the colonel. Lawless had been named *chef de bataillon* in July 1809 and then major in November of the same year. Battalion Commander Tennent was responsible for the training and discipline of the 4th Battalion, while Lawless had the regimental responsibilities for recruiting, supplies, and other such obligations. Throughout the year 1810, the greatest problems for the Regiment in France were recruiting and supplying the recruits with clothing and equipment.

From the creation of the 4th Battalion until 14 February 1810, there were 1,196 men recruited for service in the new unit. However, 500 of those men, including sergeants and corporals, were sent to Spain under the command of Captain Augustin Osmond to be incorporated into the 3rd Battalion. This left the 4th below strength and with a shortage of noncommissioned officers.[2] Recruiting officers were sent out from Landau to the camps where English army and navy prisoners were interned. The recruiters were authorized to enlist Irishmen, Scotsmen, and Germans to serve in the Irish Regiment below the rank of second lieutenant. They were strictly forbidden to recruit Englishmen. The appointment of all officers came through the War Office over the signature of the minister.

One of the most active and successful of those recruiters was Captain Terence O'Reilly. He went to Briançon in the last week of March 1810 and in less than a month enrolled 760 prisoners of war to serve in the French army. By 20 April he had sent 500 recruits from Briançon to Landau in detachments of 120 to 130 men. They marched under the orders of a noncommissioned officer of the Regiment and an escort of *Gendarmerie*. The remaining 260 recruits were unable to leave Briançon because they lacked the clothing and shoes to undertake the long journey from the department of Hautes Alpes to the Rhine. O'Reilly complained to the minister of war that "the difficulty of providing for these men, who find themselves for the most part almost naked, the clothing necessary to make the journey [to Landau] had delayed by some days their departure."[3] The local authorities refused to help him in this matter so that he was forced to buy clothing, on credit, from the local merchants so that the new recruits would be able to undertake the strenuous 450-mile march to join the Regiment.[4] General J. B. Delaroche, under whose command the prisoner of war camp at Grenoble was operated, also sent 176 men who had been recruited from the English prisoners.[5]

The influx of new recruits compounded the supply problems that already existed at Landau. The pleas by Major Lawless for clothing had gone unanswered through the winter and spring of 1810. The men at Landau had passed the rigorous winter "dressed only in their rags."[6] The only relief they received came with the warming weather of spring. Their deprivation caused substantial dissatisfaction, which spread to the new recruits as they arrived through the months of spring. The training of the Battalion had been greatly retarded because, as Lawless put it, of "the impossibility of putting guns in the hands of naked men."[7] The 4th Battalion had received uniforms and equipment for 823 men. But 500 men, fully dressed and equipped, had been sent to the 3rd Battalion. The other 323 uniforms had been distributed among the remaining men and the recruits coming in on the basis of the greatest need. Thus one received a coat, another a shirt, and yet another pants. Virtually no one had a full uniform, and the vast majority of the men were living in the rags they had on at the time they had arrived at Landau.[8]

This lack of clothing was considered by the officers to be the most serious problem facing the 3rd Battalion at Landau. The men who were recruited in the prisoner of war camps expected, and Lawless believed rightly so, that they would receive adequate clothing upon joining the French army. The inability of the Regiment to clothe its men led not merely to dissatisfaction and grumbling in the ranks but also to a breakdown in discipline, a retardation of training, and desertions. At the beginning of May, Lawless was still pleading with Paris to send uniforms without delay. With the continuous arrival of recruits, he said that the Regiment would soon have 2,000 men to outfit.[9] There was also a shortage of officers for the 4th Battalion. Most of the officers who were at Landau in the summer of 1809, or who arrived during the fall, were placed in the 3rd Battalion. When Tennent took command of the 4th, it had fewer than half of the officers needed. To fill the vacancies, officers were ordered to Landau. In some instances, noncommissioned officers were promoted to second lieutenant. There were other cases of prisoners of war who held commissions in the English navy or army who were given their same rank in the French army.

Yet not everyone who wanted a commission received one. In January 1810, three English Royal Marines arrived at Landau: Lieutenants George Cauffield, Andress Russe, and Robert C. Mortine. All three were native-born Irishmen of "good families," and they requested permission to join the Irish Regiment. The Battalion's Council of Administration recommended them to the minister of war for the rank of second lieutenant, but on 12 August 1810 they were still not listed among the officers of the Regiment.[10]

The case of Sergeant Morfie, of the 4th Battalion was more unusual. He was requesting the rank of captain. Morfie had joined General Jean Amable Humbert during his brief campaign in western Ireland in 1798 and was given, by the general, the rank of captain. Taken prisoner by the English, he had been able to pass himself off as a French officer and was exchanged. In December 1803 he was recruited into the Irish Legion with the promise of a commission; but as that promise was never approved by the minister of war, Morfie had remained a sergeant for six years. Moreover, as Colonel O'Meara did not believe that he would make a good officer, no action was ever taken on his request.[11]

In early May 1810 Napoleon ordered that the Irish Regiment recreate its 1st Battalion. Colonel O'Meara had recommended the formation of a fifth battalion as early as 26 January 1810 on the basis of recruitment in the English prisoner of war camps. But General Deschamps, the head of the Bureau of Infantry, advised against such a move at that time, pointing out that there was not, in fact, a 1st Battalion in the Regiment.[12] New orders clearly stated that the 4th Battalion was to be completed first, and that the officers and men left over would form the nucleus of the new 1st Battalion. The noncommissioned officers would be chosen upon the recommendation of the Council of Administration. However, it was required that there be at least one French noncommissioned officer in every company, as was already the case in the other battalions of the foreign regiments, because of linguistic problems.[13]

The formation of yet another battalion, the third within a year, increased problems for Lawless and the Council of Administration, and added to the confusion that already existed between Paris and Landau. By the first week of June, there were conflicting sets of figures on the number of men recruited by the Irish Regiment, the number of men actually present with the Regiment at Landau, the number of uniforms sent to Landau, and the number of men still to be outfitted and equipped. One set of figures came from Paris: "Le Ministre Directeur de l'Administration de la Guerre, Ministre d'Etat,"[14] the other set from Major Lawless at Landau.[15] The Irish Regiment had more men than uniforms, and with the continuation of active recruiting the situation would most likely worsen. A serious strain was being put upon the officers at Landau as a result of the rapid influx of recruits without a corresponding appointment of new officers. On 9 May, and again on 2 June, Lawless sent recommendations for promotions and appointments for the two battalions.[16] However, the wheels moved slowly in Paris, and there remained a shortage of officers throughout the summer and fall of 1810.

On 23 May Lawless wrote a rather curious request to the minister of war. After pointing out that no one had as yet been named to command the 1st Battalion, which carried and guarded the regimental eagle, he asked that *Chef de Battaillon* Tennent be transferred from commandant of the 4th Battalion to that of the 1st Battalion.[17] Tennent and Lawless had been very close friends since their days together in the Society of United Irishmen back in Ireland.[18] Lawless also requested that Captain Osmond, Tennent's adjutant major, be moved from the 4th to the 1st Battalion. The reason for this latter transfer was that Tennent and Osmond worked very well together, and it would make it possible for the new commandant of the 4th Battalion to choose his own adjutant major. What Lawless did not know at the time of his request was that the minister of war had already forwarded the name of Captain Hugh Ware for that position to the emperor for his approval, and that he had no intentions of disrupting the orderly and smooth flow of paperwork that was already in motion. Thus Lawless' request was not acted upon, and Ware, who was serving with the 2nd Battalion in Spain, was promoted to *chef de bataillon* and returned to Landau and took up his new command.[19]

Early in June 1810, the minister of war requested an explanation from Major Lawless for the high rate of desertion from the Irish battalions at Landau. By the major's own figures, there had been 186 desertions from Landau in the preceeding ten months out of 2,363 men recruited from the prisoner of war camps.[20] The desertion rate of eight percent was unacceptably high, even for a foreign regiment, but especially one that was presumably quartered in comfort at its depot. Lawless began his explanation by reiterating his frequent complaint that there had been, and still was, a lack of uniforms. This shortage, in turn, prevented the troops from going about normal training because they could spend only brief periods outdoors until the weather became warm in the late spring. "The necessity of leaving those men in their quarters." Lawless wrote, "and consequently with nothing to occupy them, has produced a deterioration of morale and a decline in discipline, which is contrary to the *esprit de corps* that would have been established by useful activities, good habits and supervision."[21]

Lawless next cited the lack of officers, which led directly to a lax supervision of the troops and a decline in discipline. He further pointed out that of the eighteen officers at Landau for the two battalions, a number of them were too old or too infirm to be of use. "The 4th Battalion has not one officer per company," he declared, "who is capable of undertaking a campaign."[22] In a statistical report dated 12 August 1810, he listed ten line officers and five staff officers, which included himself and Tennent. Six of those officers he deemed unfit for active duty: Captain William Barker had lost his right arm at Flushing in 1809; Captain Achille Magrath was the quartermaster officer and "incapable of undertaking a campaign"; Captain Thomas Wall was "too old to undertake a campaign"; Lieutenant Christopher Martin "had been wounded at Flushing and it was impossible for him to undertake a campaign"; Lieutenant Reiff was "incapable of undertaking a campaign"; and Second Lieutenant George Ross was "old and infirmed."[23] This aspect of the problem could be quickly eliminated, he pointed out, if action were taken on the names he had submitted for commissions.

Another important cause for the high rate of desertion, according to Lawless, was the "humanitarian" manner in which Napoleon approached the problem. The major believed that captured deserters were treated with too much leniency, and that the knowledge of light penalties encouraged some to desert and failed to discourage others. This "humanity," as he put it, was interpreted as weakness by men who had lived under the brutal laws of the English navy or the Prussian army.[24] Lawless also addressed the charge that Englishmen had joined the Irish Regiment with the premeditated intention of deserting at the first opportunity. He explained that this was not the case. It was not the men recruited from the English prisoner of war camps who were leaving, in fact no more than six or seven had deserted, but the continental Europeans, particularly the Germans. Indeed, it was almost impossible for an Englishman to desert from Landau and reach the safety of the British Isles. But the location of the regimental depot at Landau, a German-speaking department of France (in 1810) that was only fifteen miles from the Rhine, made it very easy for German recruits to make their way back to their native districts and comparative safety.[25]

The remedies for desertion from the Irish Regiment were both simple and obvious, according to Lawless. With the manufacture and distribution of uniforms, the first problem would disappear. Action by the War Office on the recommended promotions would solve the second. Harsh discipline for deserters would help to discourage the practice; and finally he suggested that the regimental depot be moved from Landau, and close proximity of the Rhine, into central France. "Our position [in eastern France] offers the greatest opportunity for desertion," he concluded, "not only to the Germans, but to those of all the nationalities who compose our Regiment."[26] Support for Lawless and his recommendations came from General C. F.

Desbureaux, commander of the 5th Military Division, in whose jurisdiction the Irish Regiment's depot at Landau was situated.

Desbureaux went to Landau in mid-July 1810 to inspect personally the battalions of the Irish Regiment. Upon his return to Strasbourg, he wrote a lengthy report to the minister of war in which he described the conditons that he found and made recommendations. He began his report on a positive note. "I was very satisfied with the zeal and conditions of the officers," he wrote, and added that the men were "capable of rendering great service."[27] On the other hand, he pointed out that there was a shortage of officers and suggested that the needed number of officers be sent to the 1st Battalion. He further observed that the men of the Regiment "are in the greatest state of need" from lack of clothing, and recommended that action should be taken to remedy the shortage. He also found thrity-six soldiers incapable of service and ready for retirement because of poor health or old age, and suggested that they be discharged with a pension. Perhaps most surprising in General Desbureaux's report, and not mentioned in any other correspondence from or about the Irish Regiment, was his statement that there were "twenty-eight children" fourteen to seventeen years of age who did not have "the strength necessary for active service." He found this to be an unsatisfactory condition and recommended that the practice of recruiting men under the age of eighteen be discontinued. A note in the margin of Desbureaux's report, made at the War Ministry, says "write to Lawless and tell him not to admit children, but only men fit for service."[28]

The general's final observation was with respect to the nationalities in the Regiment. He suggested that the large number of Germans in the Irish battalions may have been a mistake. They would be of greater service to the emperor if they were in a German regiment, such as the Westphalian. The Irish Regiment should recruit young Irishmen to fill its ranks. In this way the morale and the discipline of the Regiment would be greatly improved.[29] Then on 14 July General Deschamps wrote the minister of war reiterating the same points made by Desbureaux.[30] He received his information on the Irish battalions from Desbureaux and Lawless. There is no indication that he made an inspection at Landau. However, a notation in the margin of his letter initialed by the minister of war says: "Leave the Germans there," that is, in the Irish Regiment.[31] Thus the Germans remained, and indeed the Irish even asked for permission to recruit additional Germans. The Council of Administration of the Regiment requested permission, on 27 June, to recruit at the prisoner of war camp at Mont-Dauphin. The request was made that Captain O'Reilly, who was still recruiting at Briançon, be allowed to go to Mont-Dauphin where Germans were being held who had been in the service of England. According to the

Irish, those Germans at Mont-Dauphin would prefer to serve in the Irish Regiment of the French army rather than languish in the prison camp until the war ended.[32] However, General Deschamps recommended against the continued recruitment of Germans by the Irish. He pointed out that in Spain there had been a high percentage of German desertions from the French army, and as the Irish Regiment had two battalions already serving south of the Pyrenees, it would be a mistake to recruit at Mont-Dauphin.[33] The minister of war did not give the Irish permission to expand their recruiting, but he did forward to Napoleon the names of eight non-commissioned officers recommended by Lawless for the rank of second lieutenant.[34] This latter action, which resulted in the eight men being promoted, was a significant factor in alleviating the shortage of officers in the 1ˢᵗ Battalion. It was also in the first half of July that news of the removal of Colonel O'Meara as commander of the Regiment in Spain reached Landau. It undoubtedly caused some anxiety with the provisional appointment of *Chef de Bataillon* Fitzhenry as commanding officer of the two battalions preparing for the Portuguese campaign. Major Lawless wrote at once to the minister of war asking that he be considered for the vacant position.[35] But if affairs at Landau were somewhat unsettled in the first half of the summer of 1810, the last week of July brought a major shock.

In a letter to Lawless, dated 24 July, the minister of war informed him that the emperor, in an order of the fourteenth of the month, had forbidden recruitment in the prisoner of war camps that housed prisoners of the English army or navy. Moreover, Napoleon decreed that all men of English or Scottish origin serving in the 1ˢᵗ or 4ᵗʰ Battalions of the Irish Regiment at Landau be removed. They would be turned over to General Desbureaux, commanding officer of the 5ᵗʰ Military Division, and escorted to Sarrelouis where they would be interned once again as prisoners of war. He further ordered that the minister send his aide-de-camp, *Chef de Battaillon* Thomas Markey, who had been until recently a captain in the Irish Regiment, to Landau with special authority. Markey was to examine every soldier in the two battalions in question and to remove all whom he deemed to be of English or Scottish origin. This order of the emperor's did not apply to the 2ⁿᵈ or 3ʳᵈ Battalions of the Regiment, which were in Spain, only to those at Landau. Lawless was also told that the new uniforms and equipment, which were in short supply at Landau, should be taken from the English and Scots before their departure.[36]

Markey was dispatched at once to his old regiment to undertake the rather unpleasant task assigned to him. Lawless and the officers of the battalions were ordered to give him their fullest cooperation so that not one Englishman or Scot would remain in the French army at Landau. While

Markey was carrying out his instructions to the letter, the minister of war, who felt personally criticized in this affair, was writing to Napoleon explaining that the emperor had been fully informed of the recruiting in English prisoner of war camps. He also knew that not one undesirable would remain in the Irish Regiment at Landau.[37]

On 2 August, General Desbureaux was able to report that Markey had screened three of the twelve companies at Landau, and that 221 men had been stricken from the rolls and sent on their way to Sarrelouis. The process was continuing, and it was estimated that the number of men removed would reach 1,000.[38] In point of fact, by the time Markey had completed his task, 932 men he had recognized as being either English or Scottish were removed from the rolls of the Irish battalions and sent to Sarrelouis.[39]

Lawless and the officers of the two battalions, while giving Markey their full cooperation, were dismayed and frustrated at the depletion of their ranks. In mid-June, General Desbureaux had reported that there were 1,825 officers and men in the Irish Regiment at Landau. Of that number, 806 were in the 1st Battalion and 825 in the 4th. The remainder made up the staff of the Depot.[40] The two Battalions had been at near full strength except for the lack of officers for the 1st Battalion. Less than three weeks after Markey's arrival, on 12 August, the 1st Battalion had only 329 officers and men and the 4th, 526. Together with 126 officers and men of the Depot, the regiment at Landau stood at 25 officers and 956 men.[41] Virtually one-half of the noncommissioned officers and soldiers of the battalions at Landau had been removed and sent to Sarrelouis. Lawless poured out his frustration in a letter to the minister of war in which he acknowledged that in the enthusiasm to create two new battalions at Landau, Englishmen and Scots had been recruited along with Irishmen and Germans. However, he said that "after a . . . profound examination of their principles and motives, I was sure that if some among them enrolled themselves with the intention of deserting, the great majority of the Scots at least joined with the intention of identifying with us."[42] He based this belief on the fact that the "great majority" of the Scots preferred to remain in the Irish Regiment rather than be exchanged and returned to English service. Having expressed his regrets and stated his opinion, Lawless pledged that he and the officers at Landau would do all within their power to restore order and discipline, which had been shattered by the removal of so large a number of the noncommissioned officers and men of the battalions. He concluded by saying that he could not send the men to Sarrelouis naked, but had to allow them to wear the shoes, pants, shirts, etc., that had been issued to them.[43]

Chef de Battaillon Markey's report to the minister of war confirmed all that Lawless and General Desbureaux had already written. In addition, however, he brought out a few points of which Lawless, at least, must have been aware but never mentioned in his correspondence.

> From the information that I have gathered [he wrote on 14 August], the Irish Regiment has fallen prey for a number of months to intrigue caused by the animosity that existed between the Irish and the English. One expected at any moment to see it flare up in a brawl between the two parties which would have thrown the regiment into the greatest disorder. But the wise measure [the removal of the English] on the part of Your Excellence has put an end to this dissension and I believe assures that one will not hear another word of any trouble.[44]

Markey's is the first and only mention of internal friction between the Irish and English in the Regiment. This may well be because Englishmen had not been recruited into the Irish Legion before 1809; or if they had, their numbers were so few that they dared not express opinions that would conflict with those of the Irish.

Markey also reported that he had found some Irishmen in the Regiment whose "spirit was unsuitable for the corps of which they were a part."[45] He further determined that other Irishmen were not fit for service. He did not give numbers of these individuals, but he did remove them from the Regiment and send them to Sarrelouis. Markey also remarked that a "spirit of desertion" was strong among the Germans in the Regiment and pointed out that the depot's close proximity to the Rhine and Germany facilitated their desertion. He then concluded by saying: "I cannot end without pointing out that the absolute nudity in which the soldiers of the Irish battalions were left last winter at Landau contributed to the high rate of desertion, of whom twenty were Irishmen."[46] Although Lawless gave a figure of 186 desertions from the Regiment over a period of ten months prior to 6 June 1810, he made no mention that any of them had been Irish.[47] In fact, in all references to desertion he gave the impression that it was the "foreigners" in the Regiment, the Germans and other continentals, who were deserting. Markey's report is the only one to point out that some Irishmen, a very small number to be sure, also deserted.

This further underscores the fact that not all Irishmen were anti-English and desirous of serving in the French army, even if it be in an "Irish" regiment. A specific example is that of James Neill, an Irishman who had been a merchant officer under the English flag. He had been taken prisoner in 1805, along with his son Daniel, and sent to Valenciennes. In 1810, he had been transferred to Auxonne with the other merchant officers, but his seventeen-year-old son had remained at Valenciennes. Although Irish recruiters had been active at Auxonne, James Neill chose to remain a prisoner of war. However, Daniel had been recruited by Captain Alexandre Desbureaux to serve in the Irish Regiment. In August 1810, James Neill wrote to the minister of war requesting that his son, being only seventeen years of age, be removed from the Irish Regiment and returned to him at Auxonne.[48] There is no evidence that Daniel left the French army, nor of his feelings in this matter, but clearly his father wanted no part of the French service for himself or his son.

The Irish battalions at Landau had already been purged and the turmoil that had resulted was subsiding when Colonel O'Meara wrote to the minister of war to clear himself of any blame for the recruiting of Englishmen into the Regiment. The news of Napoleon's anger over the enrollment of Englishmen in the Regiment had reached Spain. In his own defense O'Meara explained:

> The officers who were sent to recruit in the various [prisoner of war] camps had copies of the instructions transmitted by Your Excellence dated 21 June, 1809. I am forced to say that they put them aside, and primarily Mr. Markey who seems to have the intention of improving his own situation by the number of men he recruited by taking everyone, without making any distinctions, of whom a great number were interested only in regaining their freedom without any consideration of the consequences. I was not slow to perceive the bad composition of the men who were being re-cruited.[49]

One can only speculate on how this nasty attack upon the minister of war's new aide-de-camp, which was most likely quite correct, was received in Paris. However, having been recently relieved of his command of the Regiment in Spain, O'Meara was still bitter and in no mood to accept responsibility for the dereliction of duty on the part of Markey and the other recruiting officers who were more interested in the quantity of recruits than they were in their quality.

The removal of half of the men from the 1st and 4th Battalions may have solved some problems, but it created another, two undermanned battalions. In addressing this new problem, Lawless proposed two possible solutions. The two could be merged into one battalion, or the Regiment could be allowed to recruit east of the Rhine in prisoner of war camps, such as the one at Frankfurt, where there were no Englishmen.[50] Napoleon was evidently not sympathetic to either of these suggestions. The two battalions were not merged and no authorization was granted to resume recruitment of any kind or at any place.[51]

The battalions languished through the fall of 1810. Then as the new year began, serious changes took place. By an imperial decree dated 1

January 1811, the Regiment was reorganized, and a week later moved from Landau to Bois-le-Duc [Hertogenbosch]. The 1st and 4th Battalions were consolidated into one. The new battalion was designated the 1st.[52] The 2nd and 3rd Battalions in Spain were also ordered to merge by the decree, but it was several months before the order was carried out. *Chef de Bataillon* John Tennent was given command of the new 1st Battalion, with Captain Osmond his adjutant major. The battalion had a full complement of officers. The remaining fourteen officers, including *Chef de Bataillon* Hugh Ware, were assigned to the regimental depot.[53]

At the same time that the Regiment was reorganized, it was moved to a new depot at Bois-le-Duc in southern Holland. The 1st Battalion and the men of the depot arrived at their new headquarters in the middle of January. Despite the fact that Lawless reported the Battalion and men in good condition,[54] morale, which had been declining through the fall of 1810, continued to be a problem in the winter of 1811. By the second week of March, the major reported the situation at Bois-le-Duc to be desperate. There had been no recruiting since August of the previous year when half of the troops of the two battalions had been removed. "We are like all other corps," he lamented to the minister of war, "in which there is no longer an influx of new recruits, becoming corrupt and weary, just waiting to become a shadow of a regiment with no military use and without any political consideration."[55] He went on to plead with Clarke to use his influence to save the Irish Regiment by allowing it to resume recruiting and providing for its needs. After pointing out the political advantages of an Irish corps in France's war against England, he turned to the question of recruiting. So many young men had inquired about the possibility of joining the Regiment, according to Lawless, that an entire battalion could have been recruited since leaving Landau. He proposed a solution to the problem. The English denied Irish Catholics many of the advantages accorded to other classes of citizens. Lawless proposed that the Regiment be allowed to recruit Irish Catholics from "good families." In this manner neither Englishmen nor Scots, the two classes objected to by Napoleon, would be enlisted into the corps.[56] He was sure that in this selective way the regiment could employ men of good quality to fill its ranks.

Lawless' pleas did not fall upon deaf ears in Paris. The Irish minister of war did use his influence, and the bureaucratic wheels in the capital began to move—if ever so slowly. Napoleon, who was already thinking in terms of an enormous army with which he could invade Russia, now considered increasing the Irish Regiment to four or even five battalions. He ordered, and received, a list of the noncommissioned officers with the nationality and length of time in rank for each man.[57] He had already received similar information on the officers of the Regiment.[58] The emperor was insistent that the officers of the Regiment be Irish, or at least a great majority of them, and as many of the noncommissioned officers as possible, with a minimum of fifty percent, also be Irish. The nationality of the rank and file was of less concern. He was reluctant to order the formation of new battalions without some assurance that the Irish Regiment would indeed have Irish leadership. In mid-May, Major Lawless went to Paris to argue the case for the expansion of the Regiment, but still no firm decisions were made.[59]

Just before the major conferred with Clarke, General Deschamps, chief of the Bureau of the Infantry, sent the minister of war a report on the Regiment.

> The Irish Regiment [he wrote] reduced to two battalions, of which one is employed in Spain and the other at Bois-le-Duc, finds itself menaced with disintegration as a result of being forbidden to recruit.
>
> The commander [Lawless], in order to prevent this disintegration, has requested the authority to enroll Germans. The Emperor, to whom a report is being made to show the political importance of this Regiment, had make it known on 11 March, that he would consent to the recruitment of Germans if he was presented with evidence that there were enough officers and non-commissioned officers who were Irish to form the framework of a regiment of five battalions.[60]

He went on to point out that information furnished by the Chief of the 2nd Division [General Tabarie] showed that there were seventy officers in the Regiment, and forty-eight of them were Irish. The remaining twenty-two officers were primarily French.[61] The two existing battalions of the Regiment required only forty-three officers, Deschamps pointed out, leaving twenty-seven, which was more than enough to staff another battalion.

With respect to the noncommissioned officers of the Regiment, the Infantry Bureau chief reported that there were fifty-one in the 1st battalion, of whom half were Irish.[62] In the absence of any exact listing, he estimated that there was an equal number of noncommissioned officers in the 2nd Battalion in Spain, and that they were also divided equally between Irish and non-Irish. In any event, he said that Lawless had assured him that there would be no shortage of noncommissioned officers, because there were "ample good soldiers in the battalion to be promoted to the ranks of the noncommissioned officers."[63]

The bureau chief concluded that if it was not absolutely required that all officers and noncommissioned officers be Irishmen, a full strength regiment, presumably of at least four battalions, could be formed with the authorization for recruiting among the Germans. "If the Minister does not intend to augment the Regiment [by recruiting Germans]," he warned, "it should be pointed out that the result will be the complete disintegration of this corps which is already in a very feeble condition."[64] Deschamps concluded by recommending that the Irish Regiment be permitted to recruit Germans in order to save the corps. Still no definitive action on recruitment was taken in Paris. It is true that the wheels of the bureaucracy continued to turn with the Bureau of Inspection (the 4th Division) collecting information and writing memos,[65] but recruiting was not authorized.

From May to July there was a rather minor problem over nine Irish prisoners of war. They had been sent to Flushing in the late Spring of 1811, but it is not clear from the correspondence from which English prisoner of war camp they had been dispatched. They were sent to Flushing because that city had been the location of the 1st Battalion until its capture by the English in August 1809, a fact of which someone had not been informed. The Irish had first been put in prison when they arrived at Flushing and then transferred to the prison at Bois-le-Duc. Major Lawless secured their release and "received" them at the regimental depot despite the existing ban on recruitment. This matter remained unresolved until the Regiment was at last given permission to resume recruiting in the fall of 1811.[66]

By August 1811 morale at Bois-le-Duc was extremely low, and there did not seem to be any relief in the immediate future. Depressed and frustrated, William Lawless took pen in hand and wrote an eight-page document, which he entitled simply "Notes sur le Régiment Irlandais."[67] After a brief sketch of the history of the Irish Legion, in which he referred to former commander MacSheehy as a "Scatter-Brain" and former commander Petrezzoli as "the most incapable man in the world," he described what he believed to be the basic problems of the Irish Regiment. He considered the principal problem to be that the existence of the Irish corps, whether one called it a Legion or a Regiment, was viewed as temporary. It had been formed, and presumably continued to exist, for the purpose of an invasion of Ireland. In the absence of the projected expeditions against the British Isles, it seemed to be in limbo, with the possibility of simply being disbanded in 1811. The second problem facing the Regiment was its organization. For more than three years it had been virtually two separate corps, one serving in Spain and the other in northern France. There had been practically no communication between the two "heterogeneous elements," to use Lawless' own words. This had resulted in a total lack of "esprit de corps."[68]

To rectify the mistakes of the past and to solve the existing problems, Lawless offered a liberal amount of advice. Above all it was necessary, he began, to stop viewing the Irish Regiment as being different from the other regiments of the army and to give it a number like all of the other regiments. This would make it a permanent part of the Napoleonic army. He then suggested that all Irishmen of good families be welcomed as officers into the Regiment; that noncommissioned officers be promoted who, by their conduct and service, had shown themselves worthy and qualified; that a recruiting system be established which would function in Holland, Hanover, and Hanseatic towns that would enlist good men, and not vagabonds who would desert at the first opportunity; that the regimental commander be given a freer hand in the organization of the corps; that the battalions be reunited and the officers reassigned within the Regiment; and finally, that there be established a true depot that would handle the affairs of the Regiment.[69]

Lawless finally addressed the question of the administration of the Regiment. He believed it to be in much better condition than one might have expected, considering the other problems. The recently reorganized 1st Battalion had been merged with the 4th, and thus he had no comment on its brief existence. He believed the 2nd Battalion to be in good order, but as it was in Spain, and had been there for three years, he pleaded ignorance of its affairs. Because of the administrative organization of the Regiment, he told the minister of war that he would have to communicate directly with its commander. The 3rd Battalion, also in Spain for the previous eighteen months, was in a state of great confusion. In point of fact, the 3rd Battalion had been in confusion ever since it left Landau. The quality of its recruits had been poor and desertions had been many. The removal of Colonel O'Meara and *Chef de Bataillon* Mahony had left it without leadership, and some action was needed. Lawless was apparently not aware that the 2nd and 3rd Battalions had been merged following the Portuguese Campaign. The 4th Battalion, the organization and administration of which he had personally directed and supervised, was in good order and had been since its formation in August 1809. It had recently been renamed the 1st Battalion and the embryo of the 1st had been incorporated into the 4th.[70] Lawless' "Notes," which met with the approval of General Deschamps, chief of the Bureau of Inspection, had a desirable effect at the War Ministry in Paris, and from what may be considered as a low point for the Irish Regiment in the summer of 1811, its affairs began to improve.

In August 1811, the four foreign regiments in the French army were given numbers. By imperial decree, dated 3 August, the Irish Regiment was renamed the 3rd Foreign Regiment.[71] However, the new name of the former Irish Legion did not please Lawless, the Irish, or the other nationalities. They felt that the name *3e Régiment Etranger* still left them something less than equal to the other regiments, which had a number followed only by *Régiment*. Lawless even pointed out to the minister of war that the foreign regiments of the old regime had been given numbers in the early 1790s like the other French regiments. When the Irish Brigade was disbanded after the establishment of the republic, the Dillon Regiment became the 87th Regiment, the Walsh Regiment the 92nd Regiment, etc. Even the old Swiss Regiment received a number. All of these regiments were composed primarily of foreigners, yet the word *foreign* was not in their names. What the men of the Irish Regiment wanted was a number without the designation *foreign*.[72] Nevertheless, its name remained 3rd Foreign Regiment for the duration of the Napoleonic Empire. The decree of 3 August 1811 that changed the name of the Irish Regiment also removed the ban on recruitment and stated that the Regiment would be made up of four battalions. But as late as 23 October the minister of war had not issued the orders or made available the financing for the Regiment to resume recruiting. Its effective strength had dropped to 1,010 noncommissioned officers and men according to General Deschamps.[73] The Regiment's Council of Administration wrote to General Clarke on 11 October, imploring him to issue the necessary orders so that recruiting could again begin. The council said that the time was favorable for recruiting because there were many foreigners of good quality who were actively seeking to join the Regiment, but without authorization they had to be turned away. The council feared that a golden opportunity was being missed and again asked the minister of war to take action.[74] The effect of the council's letter is difficult to ascertain. What seems to have made the difference was a report to the minister of war from General Deschamps. After pointing out the fact that the strength of the Irish Regiment was little more than that of a battalion, and reminding the minister that the decree of 3 August called for a regiment of four battalions, he strongly urged that recruiting should once again be authorized. In the margin of this report the minister of war wrote "Approved".[75] This was the most important step in the revitalization of the Irish Regiment. With the return of the officers and noncommissioned officers of the 2nd Battalion from Spain, the naming of William Lawless as colonel and commanding officer, promotions, and the formation of two new battalions, the Regiment once again became combat ready. However, these events did not occur quickly. A full year was to elapse between the time recruiting was authorized and the Regiment was ready to take the field.

It is interesting to take note, at this point, that at a time when the Irish Regiment was in extremely poor condition, Napoleon once again seemed to have given serious thought to sending an expedition to Ireland. On 11 March 1811 he ordered the minister of war to "Make me a very detailed report that will inform me if the officers and noncommissioned officers of this corps [the Irish Regiment] are Irish, and if it is possible to create an Irish regiment by recruiting principally Germans. This regiment [he continued] would be of use in case of an expedition to Ireland."[76] This undoubtedly helps to explain why the Regiment was expanded from two undermanned battalions in the late summer of 1811 to three war-strength battalions, plus the nucleus of a fourth, by the beginning of the summer of 1812. But the French were out of touch with conditions in Ireland in 1811. Napoleon's attention had been consumed with affairs on the Continent since 1805, and it was necessary to know if there still existed a party, or faction, in Ireland that would rally to the support of a French landing accompanied by Irish officers. General Arthur O'Connor, who had been doing very little in the way of service to France, or Ireland, the past five years, was asked to report on the situation in his native land. His lengthy report, dated 1 September 1811, was reassuring, but lacked the first hand touch of someone who had recently been in Ireland.[77] O'Connor had not been back himself since 1798. To acquire a full and reliable picture of conditions in the country the minister of war was ordered to send someone to Ireland who would return with the desirable information. The minister chose Lieutenant Luke Lawless, a member of the Irish Regiment who was the nephew of Major William Lawless.[78]

Charged to gain political and military information on conditions in Ireland, Lieutenant Lawless crossed over to Sandgate and made for Dublin by way of London. He reached Ireland on 24 September and remained for more than a month. Upon his return to France, and having arrived in Paris on 20 November, Lawless wrote a lengthy report for the emperor. He was rewarded for his successful mission with the rank of captain. In his report he analyzed Irish society, put the number of English troops on the island at 12,100 plus an artillery corps, and expressed the opinion that a French Army of 30,000 men would be the minimum necessary for a successful invasion.[79] In the winter of 1811–12 the Irish Regiment was not ready to undertake a campaign of any kind, and Napoleon was quite absorbed with his preparations for the forthcoming invasion of Russia. Rather than an offensive strike against Ireland in the west, he would settle for a defensive position, as he had in 1809, while the Grand Army operated in the east.

Early in January 1812, the Regiment found itself doing garrison duty in the lowlands of Holland. *Chef de Bataillon* Tennent's 1st Battalion was on the islands of the lower Scheldt, while Ware's recently formed 3rd Battalion had moved to Williamstadt [Willemstade] in the first week of the month, the skeleton of the 4th Battalion was at the depot at Bois-le-Duc, and officers and noncommissioned officers of the 2nd Battalion were marching through Spain on their way to join their comrades in the Netherlands. Efforts were being made to raise the strength of the Regiment to four war battalions. Prisoners of war, mostly Germans, were being sent to Bois-le-Duc to fill the ranks, while promotions of both noncommissioned officers and officers were being made in extraordinary numbers. In the last week of February alone, Lawless recommended the promotion of eleven lieutenants to captain and eighteen second lieutenants and noncommissioned officers for the brevet of lieutenant or second lieutenant. With few exceptions they were all approved.[80] It was at this same time that William Lawless and John Mahony were also promoted.

Lawless was promoted to the rank of colonel on 8 February 1812 and named commanding officer of the 3rd Foreign Regiment. The Irish officers, especially those who had joined the Legion in the early years, were exceedingly pleased. For the first time since its formation they felt that the commander of the Irish Corps had been chosen from their ranks. It is true that both MacSheehy and O'Meara were "Irishmen," but both men were first and foremost "French" army officers. Neither had fought for Ireland in the troublesome days of the 1790s. William Lawless, on the other hand, had been a United Irishman who was among the first to join the Irish Legion in 1803 to fight for Ireland. Born in Dublin in 1772, young Lawless had studied medicine, and in 1798 "he was professor of anatomy in Dublin College of Surgeons."[81] As a member of the Society of United Irishman he had been a close friend of Lord Edward Fitzgerald, its military commander. A member of the society's executive committee in 1798, he fled to France in order to avoid arrest. When General Brune led a French army against the Anglo-Russian invasion force in Holland in 1799, Lawless accepted a commission and served for the duration of the campaign. He then returned to Paris and civilian life until the Irish Legion was created.[82] Miles Byrne, who first met Lawless in Paris in the fall of 1803, and was associated with him until his death in Paris on 25 December 1824, wrote of him that he "was the most agreeable, kind, companionable man possible; highly educated, well versed in almost every branch of science, speaking fluently and well, both French and English; in short, had his country obtained her freedom, he would have shone in her senate as a first rate orator."[83]

Chef de Bataillon John Francis Mahony was also promoted at this time. He was named major of the Regiment in place of Lawless. With Colonel Lawless in place and the Regiment united, the importance and the duties of Major Mahony were greatly limited in comparison with those of the former major. After serving on General Junot's staff during the Portuguese Campaign, Mahony had been sent back to his regiment in the fall of 1811. There was some question as to his duties and his position in the Regiment upon his arrival in Holland. He had not been a good battalion commander, and making him the regimental major was the means by which the minister of war was able to give his old friend employment while causing as little trouble as possible within the officer corps.[84]

In the early months of 1812, morale in the Irish Regiment was still a problem. The formation of two new battalions was interpreted by the officers and men of the Regiment as holding out to them great possibilities for promotion. Indeed, there were numerous promotions for those who had been serving in its ranks. But vacancies in the officer corps and in the ranks of the noncommissioned officers were also filled by non-Irish from the outside. In particular, this vexed the junior officers and sergeant majors who felt unjustly passed over.[85] The War Ministry singled out particularly the grades of sergeant and *Fourrier* or sergeants who were assistants to the quartermaster sergeant. These were to be filled by Frenchmen. This was not well accepted by the rank and file of the Regiment, more so because it was from the ranks of first sergeant that new second lieutenants were chosen. Lawless complained that this new regulation was having a negative effect upon morale. He further complained, and with even more justification, of the quality of the sergeants who were being sent to his regiment. The French regiments were sending incompetent men, "most of whom could neither read nor write, and those who could were troublemakers whom I had to put to public work and find someone else to take over their duties. . . . I hope further [he continued] that your Excellency will take measures so that the noncommissioned officers who will be sent to our corps in the future will not be the rejects to the regiments from which they would come. It is also necessary that Your Excellency decide what I am to do with the sergeant major and *Fourriers* of the Regiment who are useless to us."[86] The Irish Regiment had become a dumping ground where French regiments could rid themselves of undesirable noncommissioned officers. It is understandable that Lawless and his officers were provoked, for not only was morale affected but discipline and the efficiency of the entire corps had declined.

On 11 April 1812, the officers and noncommissioned officers of the 2nd Battalion arrived from Spain at Bois-le-Duc. Their arrival coincided with that of 1,500 Germans and other foreign nationals, many of whom had been serving in the Dutch army. Eight hundred of those men were immediately assigned to the 2nd Battalion. It was only necessary to add a few officers and promote a few noncommissioned officers to bring the Battalion up to full strength. One of the officers promoted at this time was a recently returned prisoner of war. Second Lieutenant Charles Ryan had been taken prisoner at Flushing in 1809. He escaped from England in 1812 and was promoted to lieutenant upon rejoining the Regiment. In point of fact, Byrne says that all of the officers of the 2nd Battalion were promoted except Captain Austin O'Meally and himself. On 18 April the 2nd Battalion left Bois-le-Duc and marched to Bergen op Zoom, where it took up garrison duties and trained for what the men believed was preparation to join the Grand Army in eastern Europe.[87]

Fortunately, in light of the horrible losses and hardships the Napoleonic army suffered during the Russian Campaign of 1812, the Irish Regiment remained in Holland until February 1813. On the other hand, they occupied the most unhealthy district in all of Europe. The islands of Goree, Bergen op Zoom, and Willemstad were all three in the low-lying, malaria-stricken district of southwest Holland. The men suffered the same fever that had killed so many in 1808–9 on the island of Walcheren. In June 1812, Lawless reported that even before the bad season arrived a large number of the men were in the hospital, and an even larger number were sick but were afraid to enter the hospital because so few of their comrades who had entered ever returned. The fall of 1811 had taken a heavy toll on the 1st Battalion. When Napoleon visited the district in early October, he took lunch at Willemstad on the fourth. Despite the enthusiasm of the troops, only 160 men of the Battalion were well enough to muster under arms. For six weeks during that fall there were not enough officers or men to post guard adequately at the gates of Willemstad. "If the enemy had presented himself [Lawless wrote to the minister of war] he would have found only ghosts in place of soldiers."[88] Among the officer corps, the fever not only adversely affected health but also morale. Better to die from enemy fire on the field of battle, they declared, than in bed from the "fever." Lawless was deluged with requests for transfers just as *Chef de Battaillon* Petrezzoli had been in 1805 under very similar circumstances. In 1805 the Grand Army had marched from its camps along the northwest coast on to the Danube and the Battle of Austerlitz, leaving the embryo of the Irish Legion in Brittany. In the first half of 1812, the Grand Army was assembling in eastern Europe and on 22 June crossed the Niemen River and invaded Russia. Clearly, promotion, glory, honor, and reputation were to be found in the east, not in the west. Although Lawless tried his best to appease the officers under his command, he could not convince them that they were receiving the same consideration as the men in the Grand Army. They felt that they were forgotten and wasting their time, energies, and even their lives in an insignificant fever-laden part of Europe. Bored, disgruntled, and ill, the men of the Irish Regiment cursed their fate and longed for a change.[89]

Lawless was primarily concerned about the health of the men under his command, but he also worried about low morale and poor discipline. To be sure, he saw a direct relationship between the three and proposed to the minister of war a solution to the health problem, which he believed would affect in a positive manner morale and discipline. Early in June he suggested that the bulk of the three battalions be moved away from the low coastal regions to the vicinity of Utrecht. He pointed out that the region was significantly more healthy, the Regiment would be united, and the same services and vigilance could be maintained on Goree, Willemstad, and Bergen op Zoom. With the Regiment quartered in the healthy climate of Utrecht it could rotate companies in and out of the feverish posts assigned to it, so that the men would be exposed to malaria for only brief periods and could recuperate at a safe distance. Should they be needed, the battalions would be within a day's march. There was no need, Lawless continued, for the entire Regiment to live continually with the fever when at any one time only a small number was required. Furthermore, with better health and the battalions united for the first time since 1807, morale and discipline would quickly improve. Summing up his proposal Lawless wrote: "It offers an occasion to establish, for the first time, discipline and an environment of a more honorable manner as are the other regiments of the army."[90] It should finally be pointed out that the massive influx of noncommissioned officers and soldiers and the large number of new and recently promoted officers had not been conducive to either high morale or good discipline. Lawless' proposal to unite the Regiment at Utrecht was sound and wise, but it met deaf ears in Paris. Unfortunately, the three battalions remained in place, and just as he had predicted, the summer brought an increase in the number of deaths and illnesses.[91]

All eyes in Europe were focused east in the summer of 1812 as the massive Napoleonic army marched towards Moscow. It is not surprising that little attention was paid to the Irish Regiment. Yet in addition to the routine matters involved in doing garrison duty in a most unhealthy climate, Lawless had to handle some rather sensitive problems. For example, there was the time that Captain Joseph Parrott took offense at the fact that Captain Terence O'Reilly was given command of the company of carabiniers in the 2nd Battalion. Parrott, who had commanded that company in Spain, believed himself slighted and handed in his resignation. "Upon my return to France [he complained] I had expected some reward for my fatigue [three years of campaigning in Spain and Portugal], but instead my company was given to another officer."[92] Lawless, under whom Parrott had never served, apparently did some fast talking and diplomatic maneuvering. He convinced Parrott to withdraw his resignation and to accept a staff position, that of adjutant major of the 3rd Battalion, and O'Reilly kept the company of carabiniers.[93]

The regimental commander also had to face the problem of troops, entering and leaving the corps. A number of Dutchmen had been enlisted into the Regiment after Holland had been incorporated into the French state. The issue was raised as to whether they were Dutch and therefore eligible for a "foreign" regiment, or French and thus should be sent to a French regiment. The men were allowed to remain in the Irish Regiment, but Lawless was told to stop recruiting in Holland.[94] Men were also leaving the Regiment. In June, fourteen soldiers were discharged. All of them had seen active service and received wounds in an army other than the French. They were no longer deemed fit for active duty. Because they had served some time in the Irish Regiment, eleven of them received a single payment of 100 francs each upon discharge, while the other three, having much less claim on the French government, received lesser amounts.[95] An additional thirteen men were sent away. The Regiment had received a number of prisoners of war who had been captured in Spain. However, they were not fit for service at the time they had arrived, and Lawless had them removed. As they were all natives of the Austrian Empire, a French ally in the summer of 1812, they were simply sent home.[96] Men of such poor quality were still being sent to the Irish Regiment. This seemed to verify the claims made by Lawless that the Regiment was still being used as a dumping ground. Yet there were also bright and enthusiastic young men seeking to enter the corps. Captain Luke Lawless of the Regiment had a younger brother who wished to enter the Irish Regiment with the rank of second lieutenant. However, as the younger Lawless was only seventeen years of age, and army regulations required that one be eighteen in order to be commissioned an officer, he had to enter as a noncommissioned officer with the understanding that he would be commissioned after he became eighteen.[97]

New recruits continued to arrive through the summer and fall of 1812, and requests for promotions to fill vacancies were approved. The three battalions were brought up to near full strength and the skeleton of a fourth battalion was formed at Bois-le-Duc.[98] There was some grumbling among the officers when Captain W. Edward Hayne of the 20th Regiment, then serving in Italy, was promoted to *chef de battaillon* and given command of the new 4th Battalion. It was not that they felt him unworthy of the promotion, rather that they wanted a captain from the Regiment promoted and given the command.[99] By December the three battalions of the Regiment were ready to march, but still the hoped for orders did not arrive. It was too late to make any difference on the eastern front. Napoleon had reached Moscow in September but had failed to destroy the Russian army or the tsar's will to resist. The withdrawal that began in mid-October became a retreat in early November and finally a disaster in December. By mid-December there no longer was a Napoleonic army in the field in eastern Europe, only a rabble fleeing to the west. The emperor arrived back in Paris on 18 December and immediately began preparations to reestablish his hold on central and east-central Europe. The Irish Regiment was to play a role, eventually a tragic one, in this new campaign.

The Regiment was in reasonably good condition as the year 1812 drew to a close. The 1st Battalion was commanded by *Chef de Battaillon* John Tennent, who had become quite ill in the previous summer and had to spend three months recuperating at Brussels.[100] It consisted of nineteen officers and 604 noncommissioned officers and men. The 2nd Battalion, commanded by *Chef de Battaillon* Auguste Dillon, had twenty-two officers and 604 noncommissioned officers and men. The 3rd Battalion was commanded by *Chef de Battaillon* Hugh Ware and was made up of twenty-one officers and 510 noncommissioned officers and men.[101] The three battalions thus consisted of sixty-two officers and 1,718 noncommissioned officers and soldiers. The Regiment also included seven officers assigned to the 4th Battalion and nine officers in a fifth battalion. However, these last two battalions did not seem to have any noncommissioned officers or soldiers and existed only on paper, although the sixteen officers were listed as "present" at Bois-le-Duc at the end of June 1812.[102] In order to complete the total count of the 3rd Foreign Regiment, one must include Colonel Lawless and the five officers of his staff for a grand total of eighty-four officers and 1,787 noncommissioned officers and men.

On 11 and 12 November 1812, each of the three battalions of the Regiment submitted a breakdown of the officers and men by nationality. The documentation in the archives does not give any indication as to why this information was compiled, but it provides an unusual profile of the ethnic composition of the "Irish" Regiment at that point in time. Exactly 50% of the officers were Irishmen, either native-born or sons of native-born. Thirty-two percent were Frenchmen, and the remaining 18% were primarily German. The breakdown of the 18% was ten Germans (15%), one Pole, and one Austrian. The composition of the noncommissioned officers and soldiers was completely different from that of the officers. Only 4.8%, that is eighty-six out of 1,718, of them were Irish and 6.5% French. The majority of the men, 52.3%, spoke German: 17% Prussians; 13% Austrians; 7.2% Westphalians; 5.4% Saxons; and 9.7% from the lesser German states. Of the remaining noncommissioned officers and soldiers, 13% were Hungarians and 12.5% were Poles. Then there was an assortment that represented seventeen nations or provinces. There were, for example, fifteen Russians, seventeen Bohemians, eighteen Moravians, and one Dane. Most interesting, perhaps, is the listing of five citizens from the United States and four others who gave their nationality as "American."[103]

The three battalions were not similar with respect to their national makeup. The 2nd Battalion had the greatest number of Irish officers— fourteen out of twenty-two, or almost two-thirds. But there were only two noncommissioned officers and seven soldiers who were Irish. The large number of officers was the result of the Battalion's having been formed in 1808 when the officer corps of the Irish Legion was predominantly Irish. Those officers returned from Spain in 1812 and were assigned to reorganize the 2nd Battalion. The noncommissioned officers from Spain, a majority of whom were never Irish, also returned but were assigned to any battalion. The soldiers who were placed in the Battalion in April 1812 were Poles, Austrians, Hungarians, and Germans. The 1st Battalion had eleven Irish officers out of nineteen. Three officers were French, three were Germans, and two can only be classified as non-Irish. There were sixty-five noncommissioned officers and soldiers who were also Irish. The remaining noncommissioned officers and soldiers represented all of Europe and the United States. Again this reflects its formation. The 1st Battalion was re-established in 1810 after the disaster at Flushing. Some of the officers of the original 1st Battalion had escaped from Flushing and were placed in the new battalion. Furthermore, during the years 1809–10 the Irish Regiment recruited in the English prisoner of war camps and those recruits, some of whom were Irish, were put into the new 1st Battalion. The 3rd Battalion was hastily organized in the fall of 1811 when recruitment was again authorized for the Irish Regiment. The result was that only six officers were Irish, six officers were French, five were German and one was Polish. The nationality of almost half of the rank and file of the Battalion was listed as being "Prussian."[104]

The Irish then made up about 6.4% of the 3rd Foreign Regiment after it was reorganized in 1812. It is true that the colonel and the three battalion commanders were Irish, as was half of the officer corps, but it is very questionable as to whether or not that constitutes an "Irish" regiment. Yet there was no doubt in the minds of those Irish officers. They continued to refer to the Regiment as the "Irish Regiment" in their correspondence as did the minister of war. Even Napoleon, as late as 1811, used that terminology when he wrote, "Monsieur the Duke of Feltre [General Clarke, minister of war], I received your report on the Irish Regiment."[105]

Whatever its make-up, the Regiment was ready for combat. It was well equipped, rested, and eager to join the French army that Napoleon was assembling behind the Elbe. Most of its officers had seen combat, some had spent four years in the Iberian Peninsula. The vast majority of its noncommissioned officers and soldiers had been trained in either the Prussian or Austrian armies and had seen combat before joining the French army. Even the general health of the officers and men had improved by February, as it did each winter when the fever was less rampant. There was, in fact, general rejoicing when orders came for the Regiment to march into Germany and join the field army for the projected spring campaign of 1813.

7

The Year of Disaster: 1813

The year 1813 was a disaster not only for Napoleon and France, but also for the Irish Regiment. The near-total loss of two war-strength battalions in Silesia virtually transformed the Regiment into a battalion as the result of one battle. For Napoleon the Leipzig campaign ended his control and influence in central Europe and Italy. The Russian campaign of the previous year had heralded the beginning of the end of the empire. This foresight, however, was not universally recognized or accepted. Napoleon himself blamed "General Winter" for the tragic destruction of his army. General Mikhail Golenischev Kutusov, the Russian field commander, was not convinced that Napoleon was finished, only driven from Russia and in a difficult position at the beginning of 1813. It is true that Prussia renounced its treaty with France and again entered into an alliance with Russia and England after the French had been driven from Berlin. But there was hesitation on the part of Austria and the lesser German states. They were not at all sure that Napoleon's control of the Continent had been broken. In France itself, while there were those who feared the end might be approaching, there was still ample support for the emperor. The war was, after all, in central and eastern Germany. The emperor would raise another army and once more find a military solution that would reestablish French dominance in Europe. Another Marengo, Austerlitz, Jena-Auerstadt, Friedland, or Wagram would correct the temporary setback of the Russian campaign.

Certainly Napoleon himself believed in a military solution in 1813, and even before he reached Paris on 18 December 1812, he had begun his preparations for the spring campaign in Germany that would keep Austria and the lesser German states in line and send the Russians reeling back across the Niemen. To accomplish these ends, the emperor spent the first four months of 1813 building a new army of 200,000 men in central Germany. It was necessary to call up the recruits of the year 1814 a full year early, withdraw divisions from Spain, activate reserve national guard units, and strip the coastal defense units to the bare bones. This latter action affected the Irish Regiment in southwest Holland.

The men of the Irish Regiment had been disappointed in the summer of 1812 when 420,000 men had invaded Russia and they had been left in the fever-ridden islands and lowlands of Holland. With the loss of that army, Napoleon had no choice but to use the Regiment in 1813. In the second half of January, Lawless was ordered to merge the three existing battalions of the Regiment into two full-strength war battalions.[1] Command of the 1st Battalion went to *Chef de Bataillon* John Tennent and that of the 2nd Battalion to *Chef de Bataillon* Hugh Ware. The Regiment had two other officers with the rank of *chef de bataillon*, August Dillon and William Hayne. Dillon was named commander of the *cadre* of a third battalion that had a number of officers but few rank and file. As new recruits arrived at the depot throughout 1813, the reconstructed 3rd Battalion took real form. There was also a 4th Battalion, and Hayne was its commander, but in name only for it never became a true military unit.[2]

Even before the fusion of the three battalions into two, but especially as it took place and in the months afterwards, there were problems with respect to the naming of captains to command the elite companies, the carabinier and voltigeur. Not only was it an honor to command an elite company, but it was considered a stepping-stone to promotion to battalion commander. For these reasons the command of the elite companies was allocated on the basis of seniority in rank. There had been no serious problem on this account during the years that the 2nd and 3rd Battalions were serving in Spain, and the 1st and 4th Battalions were at Flushing and Landau. The separate battalions, in Spain and in northern Europe, calculated their respective seniority on a local basis rather than on the whole. But when the officers from Spain rejoined the Regiment late in 1812 and the number of battalions was reduced first to three and then to the two that would join the army in Germany in 1813, there developed a rivalry among the senior captains.

Captains Terence O'Reilly and Edmond St. Leger claimed seniority over Captains John Allen and Miles Byrne and thus entitled to command of an elite company before their fellow officers. Both Allen and Byrne had commanded elite units for several years in Spain. They both had three years of combat experience and quite naturally expected to command a company of carabiniers or voltigeurs when the Regiment again took the field. O'Reilly had commanded an elite company, but not in combat. Nevertheless, he and St. Leger both pressed their claims to the minister of war. St. Leger based his on the grounds that he had been named second lieutenant,

lieutenant, and captain on the same days as Byrne and had been in the French army as a noncommissioned officer before Byrne. O'Reilly's claim was that he had been an acting captain during the siege of Flushing before Allen or Byrne had been promoted to that rank.

The whole affair was not one that Lawless wanted to settle himself, and he was quite pleased to send all of the correspondence, and the problem itself, to Paris to be sorted out at the War Ministry. In the end, everyone was satisfied except St. Leger. Byrne and Allen were given command of the carabinier and voltigeur companies respectably in the 2nd Battalion—the same positions they had each held in the old 2nd Battalion in Spain. O'Reilly was given the company of voltigeur in the 1st Battalion after Captain MacCarthy gave up the company to become aide-de-camp to General Casterole. St. Leger had to be content with the 1st Company of the 1st Battalion.[3]

Recruitment continued to be a problem for the Regiment in 1813. The 3rd Battalion was cannibalized in late January and early February to create two battalions of one thousand men each. At the same time, the Regiment was instructed to rebuild the 3rd Battalion. However, the quality of the recruits being sent from the prisoner of war camps had been declining during the winter of 1812–13, and Major Mahony had to take up the matter with the minister of war. Men were being sent to Bois-le-Duc who were not fit for military service, and the Regiment did not have the option of rejecting them. The result was that they were carried on the roster, and not only were they of no use to the Regiment, but they had become a drain on its resources and gave an inflated impression of the strength of the battalion to which were assigned. When the three battalions were reorganized into two, those men who were unfit for campaigning were removed from the war battalions and assigned to the depot. Mahony asked for, and later received, permission to reject new recruits whom the Regiment considered unfit, and eventually those who were already with the Regiment were sent back to the prisoner of war camps.[4]

Marching orders for the Irish Regiment reached Bois-le-Duc on 30 January 1813. The 1st and 2nd Battalions had been ready to move for several days so anxious were the officers and men to leave Holland and join the army in Germany. Their destination was Magdeburg on the Elbe, and they broke camp on 1 February for the long winter march. *Chef de Bataillon* Ware's 2nd Battalion turned its back on Bergen op Zoom and marched to Munster by way of Breda, Grave, and Nijmegen. Tennent's 1st Battalion left the island of Goree on the same day and by a series of parallel marches arrived at Munster at the same time as Ware. It was the first time in four years the officers of the two battalions had met, and Captain Byrne remembered the occasion as being "very agreeable to all."[5] The united

Regiment continued its march through Hanover and Brunswick and on to Magdeburg arriving on the last day of February.[6]

The Regiment was warmly received at Magdeburg, which was commanded by an Irishman, Colonel William O'Meara, the twin brother of the former commander of the Irish Regiment, Daniel O'Meara. On 1 March, General Alexandre Jacques Bernard Lauriston, who commanded the reorganized 5th Corps, reviewed the two battalions and was exceedingly pleased to find units in such good condition. Despite the winter march through Holland and Germany, the two thousand men of the Regiment were in fine shape, fully equipped, and eager to meet the enemy.[7] What a contrast they must have been to the beleaguered, war-weary veterans of the Russian campaign who had found their way back to the Elbe. The Regiment formed a part of General Joseph Lagrange's 3rd Division of the 5th Corps. So impressed was General Lauriston with the officers of the Irish Regiment that he instructed Colonel Lawless to draw up a list of the captains under his command who were in line for promotion to *chef de bataillon*. Lawless was somewhat concerned over this request. Although he did not wish to stand in the way of the advancement of any of his officers, he feared the loss of his best company commanders just as his battalions were about to take the field against a formidable enemy. He suggested that *Chef de Bataillon* Dillon, a good officer, who had been left behind at Bois-le-Duc to organize the new 3rd Battalion of the Regiment, was more accustomed to serving in a French regiment, and if there was a need for battalion commanders outside of the Regiment that he should be considered. Captains Allen and Byrne, in his opinion, should remain in the *Irish* Regiment and be promoted as openings would occur. Allen, whom he believed to be next in line for promotion, could replace Dillon in command of the 3rd Battalion, and the latter could be given a command in a French regiment. In point of fact, Dillon was extremely displeased that he had been left behind when the Regiment went to war. Even his mother, the widow of General Theobald Dillon, wrote to the minister of war, whom she knew personally, in order to secure her son a combat command.[8] Lawless also singled out Captains MacCarthy, St. Leger, and Osmond as worthy of promotions, and he felt that they were suited to serve in French regiments. But the colonel was clearly not anxious to lose any of these senior company commanders at such a critical time.[9]

When the Irish Regiment arrived at Magdeburg, Prince Eugene was struggling desperately to hold the west banks of the Elbe-Saale line. The remains of the once mighty army that had invaded Russia the previous summer, plus reinforcements, was less than 50,000 men. The combined forces of the Russian and Prussian armies were perhaps twice that number.[10]

The months of March and April were spent by Eugene in preventing the allies from penetrating further west into Germany than the Elbe-Saale. Fortunately for him, Kutusov, who was already deathly ill—in fact he died on 25 March—was in no hurry. Despite the aggressive actions taken by the Prussian commanders, General Gebhard Leberecht Blücher and General Friedrich Wilhelm Bulow, as well as the cossack light cavalry, Eugene was able to stop the French retreat and hold his position in central Germany until the emperor and the new army arrived in late April.

So pressed were the French in the early spring that the Irish Regiment was immediately deployed. On 3 March the battalions were posted north to Stendal to guard against an attempted crossing of the Elbe by the Russians. During the next several weeks the Regiment took part in several engagements, and for a brief period even served under the orders of one of Napoleon's greatest marshals, Louis N. Davout, prince of Eckmühl, duke of Auerstädt. On 20 March, Colonel Lawless commanded the infantry under General of Brigade Montburn (brother of General Louis Pierre Montburn, the renowned cavalry general killed at the Battle of Borodino) and drove an enemy raiding party back across the Elbe at Werben. On the twenty-fourth the Regiment played an important role in capturing Seehousen. In April, the two battalions, under different commanders, fought a number of skirmishes, the most serious being at Uelzen on the twenty-second. During these two very active months, the Irish battalions received their baptisms of fire and were welded into combat units. It is true that a majority of the officers were already combat veterans, and a large majority of the noncommissioned officers and men, former prisoners of war, had been under fire while serving in other armies. Nevertheless, the months of March and April provided an opportunity for officers and men to fight together and to gain a mutual respect for one another under enemy guns.[11]

Napoleon left Saint-Cloud early on the morning of 15 April and reached Mainz in just forty hours. After directing the movement of his new army onto the Elbe-Saale, he took personal command in the last week of April.[12] By 1 May, the emperor was on the Elbe with 200,000 men, 372 guns, but weak cavalry support. The allied army facing west on the Elbe-Saale in the last week of April numbered only about 110,000 men. Napoleon's master plan called for an advance on Berlin and the lower Oder River to relieve the garrisons that had been left behind as the army retreated west. However, when the Allies concentrated their forces south of the Elbe and east of the Saale, he temporarily altered his plan. He would advance through Leipzig to Dresden and sever Allied communications with Berlin and Silesia, thus forcing the enemy army to fight a major battle on French terms. To carry out this strategic maneuver, the French army crossed the Saale at

Merseburge, and while Marshal Ney's 3rd Corps occupied Lützen and sent patrols south of the town, Laureston's 5th corps and Marshal Jacques Alexandre Macdonald's 11th Corps made for Leipzig. The emperor thought that the Allied army would retire east towards Dresden when it realized he was moving on Leipzig with superior numbers. He was surprised when General Ludwig Wittgenstein, the Allied field commander, attacked what he believed to be Ney's isolated corps, which was extended and in a poor defensive position south of Lutzen. Only the quick reaction on the part of Napoleon and his corps commanders turned the Battle of Lützen into a French victory on 1 May, 1813.[13]

The defeated Allied army retreated east through Dresden to Bautzen. Napoleon reorganized his army and divided it into two parts. Three corps (2nd, 3rd, and 7th) plus cavalry (2nd Corps and a light division) were placed under Marshal Ney and ordered across the Elbe towards Luckau to threaten Berlin and the lower Oder river. Napoleon, with the larger part of the army (the 4th, 6th, 11th, 12th Corps, the Imperial Guard, and the 1st Cavalry Corps) would pursue Wittgenstein's army to Dresden and occupy Saxony. General Laureston's 5th Corps, which was strictly speaking a part of Ney's command, was to serve as the connecting link between Napoleon and Ney. Thus he was neither with Ney nor Napoleon as the army moved east in the first two and one-half weeks of May. Then on 16 May, Marshal Macdonald came upon the Allied army at Bautzen. Napoleon immediately rushed the army corps with him to the point of contact and sent orders to Ney to come with two of his corps, but to leave the 2nd and 7th Corps facing Berlin. There was some confusion in the orders and their interpretation. Ney came south with his entire command, including Lauriston's 5th Corps.

The Irish Regiment had been detached from the 5th Corps in April. When the campaign truly began on 1 May, it was serving under General Jacques Pierre Marie Puthod in the vicinity of Brunswick and Celles. On 5 May the two battalions marched from Brunswick to Halberstadt. It was only when they arrived at the latter town on 8 May that the Irish learned of the emperor's victory at Lützen. The Regiment then received orders to rejoin the 3rd Division of the 5th Corps, to which it officially belonged. It reached Bernburg on the fifteenth and Dessau on the seventeenth. On the march to Bautzen, the Regiment again made up a part of General Puthod's 2nd Division of the 5th Corps.[14]

The Battle of Bautzen took place over two days. Napoleon was in the presence of the enemy on 19 May, but as Ney was unable to arrive on the field until late on the twentieth, he delayed his attack one day. However, Wittgenstein, who had received captured dispatches addressed to Lauriston, sent Generals Michael Barclay de Tolly and H. D. L. Yorch north to intercept the 5th Corps and prevent it from taking part in the pending battle. The Allied commanders did not know that Lauriston was supported by three army corps, and while the 5th Corps drove Yorch's divisions from the field, Ney's advance guard sent Barclay to the rear. Both Allied commanders retreated in reasonable order to their former positions at Bautzen.[15]

Napoleon opened the battle about 3:00 P.M. on the twentieth with a frontal attack to pin the enemy in place. The fighting on that day was not conclusive, although by dark the French were firmly established on the east bank of the Spree River. On the second day of the battle, Napoleon opened by threatening the Allied left so as to distract attention from their right. He planned for Ney to outflank the Allied army on its right and to cut its line of retreat. However, there was confusion on Ney's part, and instead of the 3rd and 5th Corps' going behind the enemy's right and severing its retreat, they attacked its right flank and simply became a part of the battle, forming an extended French left.[16]

The Irish Regiment arrived on the battlefield during the morning of 21 May while Lauriston's corps was fully engaged with the enemy. It had not taken part in the fighting on the twentieth, and although it had been making forced marches in order to arrive in time for the battle, the two battalions were still in fine condition. The Regiment, at the head of Puthod's Division, advanced against Barclay's Corps on the extreme Allied right. While Ney spent the afternoon capturing the village of Preititz, Lauriston drove Barclay from Baruth and the French center slowly advanced. Wittgenstein was fortunate that his army was not destroyed. Skillful operations on the part of Blücher and errors made by Ney turned what might have been an outstanding victory into just a victory. The losses on both sides were about equal, but the Allied army slipped away to the east to fight again on another day.[17]

Napoleon's lack of cavalry prevented an all-out pursuit of the retreating enemy, but the army corps pressed eastward as best they could. While the Allied commanders had little desire to again engage their foe, they were still quite capable of serious harassment. The 5th corps advanced through Bunzlaw on 24 May and reached Haynau on the twenty-fifth. Its leading division, that of General Nicolas Joseph Maison, passed through the town and bivouacked half a mile to the east. Puthod's 2nd Division and General Lagrange's 3rd Division, of which the Irish Regiment was a part, camped west of the town. As the French were preparing to settle down for the night, enemy cavalry attacked Maison's isolated division. Puthod and Lagrange immediately rushed to his aid and a rather confused engagement took place in the hours before dark. The Irish Regiment had just arrived at Haynau when the fighting began. Being still under arms and all present, it was the first to the assistance of its comrades. When the Corps' artillery was brought into play, the enemy cavalry was driven off, but Maison's Division had suffered heavy losses and Lawless' Regiment remained under arms all night as the 5th Corps' most advanced unit.[18]

When Napoleon received word that the enemy had turned about and attacked his forward corps, he rushed to Haynau and at dawn on 26 May placed himself at the head of the Irish Regiment and moved forward to engage the foe. With Lauriston's Corps at it back, the Irish Regiment made contact with the enemy and drove him several miles to the east. The action was not a battle, but it was the only time in its history that the Irish Regiment actually fought directly under the orders, and the eyes, of the emperor. The Irish were rewarded by being given the honor of posting guard at the town of Lignitz for Napoleon until the Imperial Guard arrived and relieved them.[19]

The Allied army continued its retreat toward the upper Oder River in Silesia. The French army, with the 5th Corps at its head, reached Breslau on the Oder on 1 June, and Lauriston bivouacked his men five miles east of the city. The next morning news of a temporary cease-fire reached corps headquarters and the fighting was halted. During the next few days arrangements were made with the Russians and Prussians, and the 5th Corps retired first to Breslau and then back across the Oder and into a more permanent summer cantonment in the vicinity of Goldberg, some sixty miles west of Breslau.[20]

An armistice was arranged through the mediation of Austria and was actually signed and put into effect on 4 June 1813. Both the Allied commanders and Napoleon needed time to bring up badly needed supplies and reinforcements, as well as to rest and regroup their weary armies.[21] The Grand Army was not composed of campaign-hardened veterans as it had been in the past. The enormous losses of 1812 had resulted in a new army of inexperienced recruits and a serious shortage of cavalry. Napoleon hoped to rest and resupply his troops, who were unaccustomed to living off the land during a long campaign. He also expected to take advantage of the lull to bolster his cavalry, the weakness of which contributed to his inability to destroy the enemy even though he was able to defeat him on the battlefield. The armistice remained in effect until 16 August, when the French army was rested and resupplied. The cavalry was somewhat strengthened, but remained inadequate throughout the campaign.

The Irish Regiment, which had left Breslau on 6 June, arrived at the small village of Holberg just a little more than a half mile from Goldberg. The men spent the next days building huts and making the encampment livable. Miles Byrne described the way in which the men passed the months of June and July.

> The interval of the armistice was employed in exercising and maneuvering the troops twice a day. The formation into hollow squares was particularly recommended to the regiments. From the want of cavalry, this order of battle became more urgent. The soldiers were also employed digging entrenchments and filling them up, to accustom them to this kind of work, and every day something being done to embellish the camp, it soon became quite a nice little town. From being so near Goldberg, it was well supplied by the inhabitants with provisions, etc. The evenings were spent gaily, particularly on Sunday, when there was dancing and various amusements carried on with the people of the town and country and villages around.
> During the month of July, a quantity of ball cartridges were distributed to each regiment that the soldiers might practice at the target.[22]

Shortly before the armistice ended, General Lagrange's 3rd Division was disbanded, and the Irish Regiment was assigned to Puthod's 2nd Division. It left its encampment and joined Puthod about three miles from Goldberg.

During this lull in the campaign, Captains John MacCarthy and Achille Magrath gave up their companies in the Regiment to become aides-de-camp to General Casterole, who was a cousin of General Lauristan's. MacCarthy had commanded the carabiniers of the 1st Battalion and his departure enabled Captain O'Reilly to take command of that elite company.[23] The Regiment had already lost Lieutenant Augustin Osmond who had become aide-de-camp to General Vacherau. On 18 June, Napoleon named six officers of the Regiment knights of the Legion of Honor. The men so honored were Battalion Commanders Tennent and Ware, Captains Byrne, Saint-Leger, and Parrott, and Lieutenant Osmond.[24]

The celebration of the emperor's birthday was moved up five days from the fifteenth to the tenth of August that year for the army in eastern Europe. The reason for this was that the armistice was about to be terminated and to be sure that the festivities would not be disrupted by a surprise advance on the part of the enemy the celebration was held early. Again Byrne described the event in his *Memoirs.*

> As no expense was spared, and as the preparations began several days before, it proved very splendid.—General Puthod reviewed his division that morning, and made it perform various evolutions: maneuvering in hollow squares, by echelons, firing blank cartridges, etc.
> Ten thousand soldiers and four hundred officers dined at the same table and each man having his glass filled, drank to the health of the emperor, etc., the general giving the signal.—In the evening the camp was illumi-

nated, and many curious allegorical figures of victory etc., with the emperor effigy, were exhibited in transparent paintings.—Between the dinner and the illuminations, there were races and other amusements.[25]

The armistice officially ended 16 August 1813, and hostilities resumed. However, there was one major, and perhaps decisive, event that had taken place in mid-August. After fruitless negotiations through the summer at Prague had failed to produce a permanent peace between France and the Allies, Austria had declared war on France. Napoleon still believed that he could gain a favorable solution on the battlefield to the problems he faced in central and eastern Europe. However, Tsar Alexander I of Russia and King Frederick William III of Prussia believed otherwise. With the addition of 240,000 men the Austrians would put into the field, Napoleon would be outnumbered in eastern Europe. Sweden had also joined the Allies, and Prince Charles-John, the former Marshal Jean-Baptiste-Jules Bernadotte, was in Swedish Pomerania with 20,000 men. Thus the alliance against Napoleon was formidable in mid-August and renewed fighting promised to be bitter with the shape of Europe hanging in the balance.

Command of the Allied armies was given to Prince Karl Philipp Zu Schwarzenberg; but in fact, as the emperors of Russia and Austria and the king of Prussia were all present with the army, decisions were made by committee. Schwarzenberg was in northern Bohemia with 240,000 men; Bernadotte, with 120,000, was in the vicinity of Berlin and Blücher, with 95,000, was in Silesia. The basic strategy was for Schwarzenberg to make the principal effort against Napoleon's lines of communication west of the Elbe River. But the Allies adopted the so-called Trachenberg Plan, which seems to have been an unwritten agreement not to give battle if Napoleon was present on the field and in command of the French troops. Instead, the army facing Napoleon would retire while the other armies would advance. This would frustrate the French emperor by depriving him of the possibility of a major victory. The campaign would become a war of attrition which the Allies believed they could win in central Europe.[26] Napoleon planned to renew the campaign by sending Marshal Oudinot to the north with 100,000 men (he would actually command only 66,000) to capture Berlin, and Macdonald, with several corps, to the west to hold Blücher in check, while he maneuvered against Schwarzenberg's rear with the main French army. If Schwarzenberg advanced north towards Leipzig or west towards Munich, he would strike south and capture Prague thus placing the main Allied army in great peril. However, it was not Schwarzenberg but Blücher who was first to advance. The Prussian commander did not wait until 16 August to renew the war. On the fourteenth he advanced to the northwest on a front between the Austrian border and the Oder River. Thus the first serious fighting took place in Silesia, and the Irish found themselves in the thick of the action.

The Regiment was one of three that made up General Vacherau's Brigade in Puthod's Division. Together with the 134th Regiment and the 143rd Regiment, it spent the last days of peace preparing for the renewal of hostilities. The sick were sent to the rear with the heavy baggage, and on 16 August Puthod's Division assembled at Goldberg. On the eighteenth Blücher's cavalry made contact with Puthod and he retired on Lowenberg. The Irish Regiment bivouacked on the banks of the Boder River. Early on the morning of the nineteenth, General Lauriston led Vacherau's Brigade forward to a point where the ground was higher than the bottomlands around it and formed the three regiments into hollow squares. Lawless' two battalions were in the center and farther advanced towards the enemy. No sooner than that brigade had taken up its position, the enemy cavalry appeared. As the enemy cavalry advanced in preparation for its attack, Lauriston sent orders for General M. J. Rochambeau[27] to bring up his division as quickly as possible, as Vacherau's Brigade had neither cavalry support nor artillery.[28]

The enemy cavalry, which was greatly superior in numbers, fell upon the Brigade with a fury. The squares held fast, and after a number of attempts to break them, the enemy backed off and brought forward artillery. Without the ability to challenge the enemy's guns, the Brigade suffered heavy casualties. A battery of artillery was brought to bear on the Irish Regiment, and the combination of grapeshot and cannonball tore great holes in its square. The Irish quickly closed ranks each time so that the enemy cavalry was never able to exploit a weakness in their ranks. At last Lawless was ordered to retire into a wooded area about a half mile to his rear. The Regiment moved back in good order stopping every few minutes to fire a volley so as to prevent the enemy cavalry from becoming too bold. As they reached the safety of the woods, Rochambeau's Division appeared on the field with its artillery and the enemy hastily withdrew.[29]

This affair was the most bloody that the Irish Regiment had seen since it had joined the army in March. Three hundred men had been killed or wounded. Two officers had lost their lives: *Chef de Bataillon* John Tennent and Captain John Evens. Ten other officers were wounded: *Chef de Bataillon* Hugh Ware, Captains Christian Eckardt, Joseph Parrott, and John Elliot, Lieutenant William MacGauley, and Second Lieutenants Auther Deral, Samuel Stephens, Thomas Brown, Phillip Petters, and Felix H. Noel.[30] Captain Byrne, who commanded the company of carabiniers in Ware's Battalion wrote the following account of the death of Tennent:

Commandant [*sic*] Tennent was cut completely in two; the cannon ball striking a belt in which he carried his money served as a knife to separate the body. The soldiers dug his grave with their bayonets, and when burying him found several pieces of gold that fell out of his entrails and a part of his gold watch . . . poor Tennent was giving orders to have the ranks closed and the gaps filled, which had been opened by the artillery, when he fell; his horse feeling he had lost his rider, dashed through the ranks and caused a still greater opening in the hollow square.[31]

During the Brigade's withdrawal to the wooded area Lieutenant August St. Leger, younger brother of Captain Edmond St. Leger, saved the life of General Vacherau. The general's horse had been killed under him while he was giving orders from the center of the Irish square and he had to fall back on foot. Enemy cavalry attacked just as they reached a farmyard that was surrounded by a stone wall. Lieutenant St. Leger picked up the general and threw him over the wall into the farmyard. Vacherau escaped injury, as did St. Leger, but Lieutenant Elliot was wounded at that moment by a cavalryman's saber stroke before he was able to reach the safety of the farmyard.[32]

The Irish Regiment bivouacked that night on the same ground as it had the previous night. On 20 August, Lauriston ordered his entire corps to fall back on Lowenberg where it spent the night. But on the twenty-first, the French army took the offensive. When Schwarzenberg was slow in mounting an advance out of Bohemia and Blücher seemed anxious for a fight— with Macdonald—Napoleon quickly marched east into Silesia. He arrived at Lowenberg about noon on the twenty-first and immediately ordered a general advance. The emperor had brought with him the Imperial Guard and General Marie Victor Nicolas Latour-Maugourg's cavalry. This counter-attack drove the enemy back and when Blücher became convinced that Napoleon was in command of the army before him, he quickly retreated in accordance with the Trachenberg Plan.[33]

The Irish Regiment led Lauriston's 5th Corps into the battle. It did not suffer the heavy casualties it had on the nineteenth, as the enemy did not stand long and fight. However, Colonel Lawless was seriously wounded and forced to give up his command of the Regiment. While at the head of his advancing Regiment, he was struck on the leg by a cannonball. He was carried on a door by six grenadiers back to the village that was serving as Napoleon's field headquarters, and the emperor ordered his personal surgeon, Baron Dominique-Jean Larrey, to attend to his wound. The leg was so badly damaged that Larrey at once amputated the limb. It was the end of the war for William Lawless, who was certainly more fortunate than poor Tennent. After recovering from his wound, he retired to his home at Tours.[34]

Within three days the Regiment's commanding officer and both of its battalion commanders had been either killed or wounded. The death of Tennent and the removal of Lawless resulted in a number of acting commanders. *Chef de Bataillon* Hugh Ware, although wounded, was named acting commander of the Regiment. Captain Byrne was given command of Ware's 2nd Battalion and Captain St. Leger command of the 1st Battalion. Lieutenants were moved up to command companies that had lost their captains to enemy fire or promotion. Clearly the ranks of the officer corps, as well as the rest of the Regiment, were thinning as the fighting became intense.

By the evening of 21 August, the enemy had been driven more than five miles southeast of Lowenberg. On the twenty-second Lauriston continued the advance. There was heavy fighting on the twenty-third, and again the Irish suffered casualties. Lieutenant Patrick Lench was the only officer of the Regiment who was wounded, but General Vacherau was killed early in this battle while at the head of the Irish Regiment. General Puthod was so pleased with the performance of the officers and men of the Regiment that on the twenty-fourth he recommended eleven of its members for the Legion of Honor. Captain Parrott, who was already a knight in the order, was recommended to be an officer in the legion. At the same time Puthod requested promotions for Ware, to colonel, and Byrne, St. Leger, Allen, and O'Reilly to *chef de bataillon*. All of these recommendations were strongly backed by General Lauriston.[35]

Puthod's Division was inactive on 24 August, except for the burial of General Vacherau. Napoleon, the Imperial Guard, and Latour-Maugourg's cavalry marched back west to Dresden, which was being threatened by the advancing Prince Schwarzenberg. When the Allied leaders learned that Napoleon was in Silesia, they decided to move against Dresden and sever his lines of communication. As the major portions of both armies converged on Dresden, Macdonald was ordered to keep Blücher in check on the Katzbach River. However, in violation of his orders, the marshal did not take up a defensive position on the river. Unaware of the Trachenberg Plan, he thought that Blücher had been beaten on the twenty-second and hoping to take advantage of the situation, he ordered his newly created "Army of the Bober" forward on the twenty-sixth. Advancing on a wide front between the Oder on his left and the mountains that formed the Austrian boundary on the right, he made contact with the enemy. The 3rd Corps of General J. Souham and the 11th Corps commanded by General Maurice Etienne

Gérard, supported by General Bastien Horace François Sebastiani's cavalry, crossed the Katzbach and engaged Blucher's army in battle. Lauriston's 5th Corps formed Macdonald's far right and was not in direct communication with the other army corps on the twenty-sixth. Lauriston advanced southward between the Bober, on his right, and the upper Katzbach, on his left. In the course of the battle that took place between Blücher and Macdonald at the Katzbach, the Prussians had the best of the fighting. Heavy rain made the muskets of the infantry useless, and Blücher's superiority in cavalry won the day. Souham, Gérard, and Sebastiani fell back with the Prussian cavalry hard on their heels. However, Lauriston, who received no news of the events on his left, continued his advance. When at last he realized the true picture on 27 August, he had Prussians on two sides and the Bober at his back.[36]

Puthod's Division was on Lauriston's extreme right and when the Corps was ordered to retreat, it became isolated from the rest of the army. It reached Hirschenberg on the Bober the evening of the twenty-seventh, but the river had risen out of its banks from the heavy rains and the bridges were under water. The ordinarily small river was one-half mile across and quite impassable. The Division had to camp on the east bank and hope that the water would quickly recede. On the twenty-eighth Puthod retreated down the Bober to Lowenberg where he expected to find Lauriston and the 5th Corps. He was now pressed hard by Prussian cavalry, and the roads had disintegrated into strips of mud. The regiments bivouacked several miles south of Lowenberg, and on the morning of the twenty-ninth reached the town. Puthod's Division had been reduced to six thousand men and twelve pieces of artillery. It took up the best position it could find with its back against the river. All of the bridges had been washed away, and there was no possibility of constructing a bridge with the river flooding its banks on both sides. There were Westphalian troops on the west bank, but they were not able to be of any assistance to Puthod. A combined Russian and Prussian army of overwhelming superiority[37] faced the Division on three sides. The battle began at 8:00 A.M. and lasted until after 4:00 P.M. When the Division had expended the last of its ammunition, the enemy attacked and overran its position.

There were few choices available to the men of the Irish Regiment on the afternoon of 29 August. Surrender and Siberia was one, but it appealed to no one. The Bober River was the other. Most of the officers waded into the river and swam to the opposite shore. The riverbed itself was not terribly wide although the current was strong. They were able to wade about half the distance, swim a short way, and walk through the water to dry land. Nevertheless, in order to pass the Bober one had to be able to swim, and many, including Brigadier General Scibie, who attempted it, drowned.[38] Only three officers of the Irish Regiment were taken prisoner on that day.[39] The others escaped across the river. Byrne gives the following account:

> Eight officers and thirty men of the Irish regiment with commandant Ware and the ensign who saved the Eagle of the regiment, had the good fortune to get out of the bed of the river, but had to wade through a sheet of water which covered the other side for more than half a mile under the fire of the enemy.[40]

Captain Byrne was one of those Irish officers who swam the Bober that day, and he was certainly in a position to report what took place. But only three officers are listed as having been captured by the enemy and none are shown as having been killed or wounded. The roster of officers of the two battalions and the *Etat-Major*, signed by Lawless and dated 1 July 1813,[41] listed forty-two present and under arms. All of those officers, except nine,[42] are also listed on Colonel Lawless' "Etat des Officiers" on 18 October 1813.[43] It cannot be determined how many of the nine, if any, were with the Regiment on 29 August, and if so what became of them. Even if some of them were recovering from their wounds and others were ill in a hospital, there would be more than eight who crossed the Bober that fateful day. Yet if it is difficult to keep track of the officers of the Regiment, for whom reasonable records were kept and preserved, it is totally impossible to keep track of the noncommissioned officers and soldiers. Again, Byrne says that thirty of them escaped the disaster of the twenty-ninth. Four weeks later, on 1 October 1813, Ware, still acting commander of the Regiment, listed by name and rank ninety-four noncommissioned officers and soldiers who had survived the campaign and were on their way back to the regimental depot at Bois-le-Duc.[44] Undoubtedly, many of the ninety-four men listed had been wounded in action before the twenty-ninth and were not with the Regiment on the Bober. This could account for the difference between what was most likely an estimate on the part of Byrne and the exact number given by Ware.

Whatever the exact figures might be, one conclusion is inescapable. The campaign, and particularly 29 August at the Bober, was a total disaster for the Irish Regiment. It no longer existed as a fighting unit. Early in September 1813, Napoleon ordered acting commander Ware to gather together the men of the Regiment who were able to march and return to Bois-le-Duc.

Ware had saved the regimental eagle when he swam the Bober, as

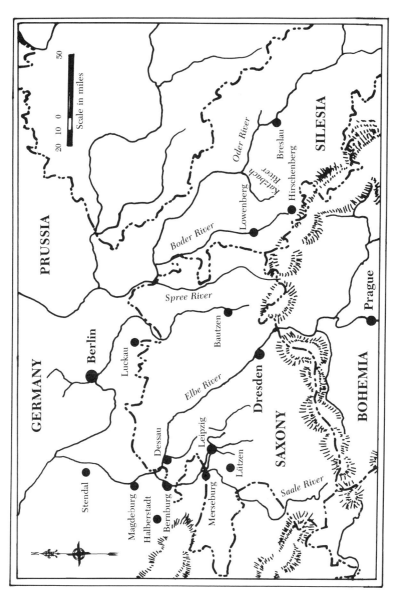

5. The Campaign of 1813

Lawless had saved it at Flushing in 1809. The small, wet band of men who had saved themselves on the twenty-ninth spent that night at Laubau. They then marched on to Goerlitz where they remained for several days while Macdonald's army recovered from its defeat at the Katzbach. Then on 3 September, the army retreated to Bautzen, at which town Napoleon had already arrived. Together with the sick and wounded who could march, the remnants of the once-fine Regiment started the long journey back to France. They passed through Dresden, where Napoleon had defeated Schwarzenberg on 26 August while Blücher was defeating Macdonald. The small band pushed on to Leipzig where it met Colonel Lawless and a number of other wounded men from the Regiment. Ware was forced to remain several days at Leipzig because the roads were not safe for any but large detachments due to roving bands of cossacks and partisans who infested the countryside. Finally, in the company of other units marching west, Ware, and all of the men of the Irish Regiment who could march, left Saxony behind and made their way to the Rhine. Lawless, although in great pain from the loss of his leg, traveled in a carriage with his troops. Once back into central Germany, the small detachment could travel on its own. Ware rested his men at Paderborn and Munster. The latter town was commanded by General Harty, who had been instrumental in the formation of the Irish Legion in 1803–4. He received his fellow countrymen graciously and wined and dined them. Marching by way of Wasal, Ware and his beleaguered little band reached the regiment depot at Bois-le-Duc early in October.[45]

Twenty-three officers[46] out of 47 and 94 noncommissioned officers and soldiers[47] returned from the campaign of 1813. Out of approximately 2,000 men who had marched to join the Grand Army eight months earlier, only 117 were left.[48] The 3rd Battalion, which had remained behind, had been stripped to the bone in the summer to send replacements to the 1st and 2nd Battalions, which were with the Grand Army. Even with the men who returned, the Regiment was only 64 officers and 300 to 400 soldiers.[49] On 6 October, the first orders were penned for the restructuring of the Irish Regiment. It was authorized to recruit Prussian and other northern Germans, but not Austrians or Hungarians.[50] However, this proved inadequate as there were too few northern Germans who were deemed reliable to serve in the French army. The Infantry Bureau suggested to the emperor that the 3rd Foreign Regiment be reorganized into the "1st Foreign Battalion," but Napoleon rejected this idea and ordered that the Regiment should be reformed with four fighting battalions and a battalion at the depot.[51] On 27 October, Major Mahony, who was acting commanding officer of the Regiment while Colonel Lawless was convalescing in Paris, was given authority to recruit Germans at the prisoner of war camp at Deux Ponts. On 3

November, he sent Captain Henry Thompson and two noncommissioned officers to Deux Ponts with instructions to recruit only good men who had deserted from the Allied army.[52] But this effort also fell far short of the manpower needs of the Regiment.

The officer corps of the Regiment was reorganized during November and December of 1813. By December it had been determined that Major Mahony would be promoted to the rank of colonel and assume full command of the 3rd Foreign Regiment. Colonel Lawless was to be promoted to general of brigade and reassigned once he was fit for active duty. The convalescing colonel recommended Hugh Ware to become the regimental major, the position to be vacated by Mahony, and Captain John Allen to be promoted to *chef de bataillon* to replace Ware at the head of the 1st Battalion. Lawless also mentioned Captains Byrne, O'Reilly, and St. Leger as worthy of promotion. Only a part of his recommendations were accepted, and these in the course of time. Allen received his brevet of *chef de bataillon* in March 1814, and Ware was named major in the same month. The Regiment also lost several good officers at this time. *Chef de Bataillon* Dillon was transferred to a French Regiment in accordance with his wishes and the recommendation of Lawless. He saw little possibility for advancement in the 3rd Foreign Regiment. St. Leger was called to Paris by the minister of war and assigned to the staff of General N. Maison. He never rejoined the Regiment.[53]

The reorganization of the Regiment, and the attempt at reconstructing several battalions that could rejoin the army, was plagued with problems. One such problem, which was reminiscent of the great purge of the summer of 1810, was the transfer of officers and men out of the Regiment on the basis of nationality. By an imperial decree dated 25 November 1813, the 3rd Foreign Regiment was ordered to remove all officers, noncommissioned officers, and soldiers who were Russian or German by nationality and to send them to a pioneer regiment.[54] After Napoleon had been defeated at Leipzig on 18 October 1813, the French army had quickly retreated behind the Rhine. With Prussia and Austria already in the Allied camp, the lesser German states, many of them former French allies, quickly fell into line and joined the victorious side. With the once-invincible French army on the run, it was assumed that Germans and Russians could not be trusted in battle against their countrymen fighting on the other side.

The German officers of the Irish Regiment were angered and frustrated by this decree. "We entered the Irish Regiment in 1806," wrote Lieutenants William Keller and G. Ruff, and Second Lieutenant Jean Klemps to Colonel Lawless, "made the campaigns of Spain and Portugal, and even had the honor of serving with the Grand Army [1813]. Our colonel has spoken of us with dignity and honor. . . . Why then must we suffer a disgrace that we do not deserve? . . . We wish to serve France with dignity, to fight and die for her."[55] They concluded their letter by asking if they were not permitted to remain in the Irish Regiment that they be sent home.[56]

At the same time five other German officers[57] in the Regiment wrote the minister of war also protesting their removal and requesting that they be allowed to remain in the Irish Regiment.

> We have served France for eighteen years, and we have made all of the campaigns. We might add that we have served with honor and the greatest devotion. This service is of no use to us today because we are Germans. May we remind Your Excellence that in December, 1811 when we passed from the 33rd Light Infantry Regiment to the 3rd Foreign [Regiment], his Majesty decreed that all foreigners who had served France for eight years, or who had made the Ulm Campaign [1805] . . . would be regarded as French subjects. The benefits of that decree apply to us.
>
> Therefore, Monseigneur, it is irrevocably proven that the dispositions of the decree of 29 [sic] November [which excluded all Russians and Germans from the 3rd Foreign Regiment] does not apply to us in any way. We thus implore Your Excellence, that as French subjects you allow us to remain in our Regiment. A decision contrary to our request could only be considered as an attack upon our honor, and in that case we would be in the unhappy position of requesting our discharge and that the necessary measures would be taken for us to return to our [native] country.[58]

Despite the pleas of the German officers the purge was carried out. Under the supervision of General Fanconnet, ten officers[59] and three hundred and nineteen men were sent from Antwerp, where the Regiment was stationed in mid-December, to join a pioneer regiment of foreigners.[60] There were no Russian officers in the Irish Regiment, but there must have been a few Russian noncommissioned officers and soldiers among those expelled at that time.[61]

The same decree that ordered the purge of the Irish Regiment also abolished the 4th Foreign Regiment and the 1st Foreign Battalion, both of which were German units. All of the Germans and Russians, the vast majority of the officers and men were sent to form a foreign pioneer regiment. The French, Swiss, Poles, Italians, and Irish of the Regiment and the Battalion were sent to Antwerp to be incorporated in to the 3rd Foreign Regiment.[62] There is no indication as to how many of those men were Irish, but the number was undoubtedly very small as it was general policy to send Irishmen to the 3rd Foreign Regiment.

The incorporation of the non-German noncommissioned officers and men from the disbanded foreign units caused more problems than it solved. To be sure, it increased the numbers in the understrength battalions of the

Irish Regiment, but the quality of the new troops left much to be desired. "The Major of the 3rd Foreign Regiment," wrote General Deschamps, chief of the Bureau of Infantry, "says that the new composition of the Corps, into which Irish, French, Italians, Poles, and Swiss of the old foreign regiment have been incorporated, has left him with men who cannot be counted upon, notable the Irish soldiers of whom many have deserted to the enemy with their arms and baggage."[63] At the same time Mahony himself wrote to the minister of war:

> The reorganization has resulted in the Regiment receiving a certain number of undesirables who because of their bad service and poor morale can not be employed at the advance posts because they will desert with their arms and baggage. They must be used in the interior of the city. . . . I am speaking of the Irish soldiers. . . . There is not one Irish officer here who does not regard as bad soldiers the majority of the men of his native [Ireland] who are found in this corps.[64]

Mahony requested that the unreliable soldiers in the Regiment, whom he had to station within the fortifications of Antwerp, be removed. He complained that they compromised the effectiveness and the reputation of the Regiment, and suggested that they be sent to the rear to be employed in a pioneer regiment. However, the minister of war ordered that they be sent into France to English prisoner of war camps.[65]

By the end of the year 1813, the 3rd Foreign Regiment was organized into four skeleton battalions. There were sufficient officers for such an organization, but the shortage of soldiers to fill the ranks was so great that it limited the type of service that the Regiment could be expected to render.[66] As it was in no condition to join the main army, it was assigned to the command of General N. J. Maison and posted at Antwerp. Although the Allied armies did not reach the Scheldt River in strength by the end of the year 1813, their advance units were skirmishing with the French in the vicinity of Antwerp, and the defenders of outposts were under frequent attack. Mahony and regimental headquarters were in the city while three battalions were stationed in the vicinity and the depot was at Lille.

In the first week of January 1814, General Charles François Lebrun, duke of Paisance, who was the military governor at Antwerp, reported that "the 3rd Foreign Regiment was only a battalion of 3 to 400 men, sixty-four of whom were very distinguished officers."[67] During the month of January the Irish Regiment was given various duties and assignments. Detachments escorted provisions to semiblockaded garrisons, notably at Bergen op Zoom. Other units were stationed at outposts. On 13 January Ware's Battalion was heavily engaged with the enemy and suffered a number of casualties. By the end of the month Bernadotte was laying siege to Antwerp on three sides, which left open communications only across the Scheldt. Eventually the enemy occupied the west (left) bank of the river, and the city came under a state of total siege. However, just before the Allied army arrived before Antwerp in strength, General Maison assigned 1,400 men to garrison the city and withdrew with the rest of the 1ˢᵗ Corps to Louvain and Brussels. The Irish Regiment remained at Antwerp where General Lazare-Nicolas Carnot, the "Organizer of Victory" in 1793–94, arrived and took command.[68]

As the year 1814 began, the overall military situation was bleak from the French point of view. After the defeat at Leipzig (16–19 October) Napoleon retreated behind the Rhine. The French continued to hold some key cities in Germany. One of the most important of these was Hamburg where Marshal Davout's stand became legendary. Once back in France, Napoleon worked tirelessly to reorganize and rebuild his army in preparation for the campaign that would decide the fate of France, as well as that of his own throne. The Allied armies had suffered heavy losses in the Leipzig Campaign and were slow to recover and advance to the boundaries of France. Nevertheless, they were across the Rhine at several points in the first week of January; and by the second half of the month, the Campaign of France was well under way.

At Antwerp, the fighting was not intense. The city was well supplied and heavily fortified. There were skirmishes and sorties by the garrison, but no major attempt was made to take the city by assault. The Irish Regiment, while performing its duties, had also to cope with internal problems. There was, for example, a surplus of officers in the Regiment for the number of troops. In mid-January Mahony was ordered to send ten captains and ten lieutenants to Paris as they were needed for service in line regiments.[69] These twenty officers, none of whom were Irish,[70] were dispatched at once before Antwerp was fully blockaded. This departure of twenty officers, most of whom were French, was timely from the point of view of many of the officers in the Regiment. Several of them who had been transferred into the 3ʳᵈ Foreign Regiment from the old 4ᵗʰ Foreign Regiment were dissatisfied and had already requested to be transferred to a French regiment.[71] Furthermore, the officers who had served in the Regiment before the reorganization at the end of 1813 were complaining that the new officers were receiving preferential treatment and the better assignments. This was causing friction within the officer corps, which Mahony was most pleased to solve, at least in part, by sending twenty officers to Paris.[72] At the same time the minister of war ordered officers to Paris, he also ordered all French noncommissioned officers in the Irish Regiment to be sent to the capital as there was a notable shortage of noncommissioned officers to train and lead the new recruits being raised in France.[73]

The removal of Colonel Lawless and the decision to promote Major Mahony to replace him caused several problems in the Regiment. The first was the filling of the vacant position of major. Clearly *Chef de Bataillon* Hugh Ware had every reason to believe that he would be chosen. He was, after all, the senior battalion commander. He had been recommended for the position by Lawless, and he had an outstanding military record, first as a battalion commander and then as acting regimental commander during the last campaign (1813). Nevertheless, in his administrative wisdom, the minister of war named *Chef de Bataillon* Kenlan to fill the vacancy. At the end of January, Ware secured permission to go to Paris and make a personal appeal to the minister. With the support of Colonel Lawless, soon-to-be Colonel Mahony, the officers of the Regiment, and the chief of the Bureau of Infantry, Ware was promoted to major and sent back to the Regiment. Major Kenlan was transferred to a French regiment. Unfortunately, it was late February before the affair was settled, and Ware was unable to reach Antwerp because of the tight blockade. He thus went to the regimental depot at Lille, where he remained until the Regiment joined him in May.[74]

Ware's promotion to regimental major left his 1st Battalion without a commanding officer, and this posed the second problem. When he left Antwerp to go to Paris, Captain Byrne, the senior captain of the Battalion, became the acting commander and logical successor. However, Lawless recommended that Captain O'Reilly be promoted and given Ware's Battalion.[75] But neither of those two hopefuls were given the command. Captain John Allen, longover due for promotion as the result of his outstanding service in Spain, was promoted to *chef de bataillon* and given the 1st Battalion. Unfortunately, with all communications severed between Antwerp and France, Allen did not receive news of his promotion until after Napoleon had abdicated and the war had ended.[76] Captain O'Reilly did receive his brevet of *chef de bataillon* in March 1814, but not a command in the Irish Regiment. He had been ordered to Paris and joined the staff of the War Office just before the city of Antwerp was sealed off by the Allied army; however, he did not receive a field command before the war ended in April.[77] Captain Byrne, who remained at Antwerp, was not promoted. He always believed that O'Reilly had been promoted because he was in Paris, while he, having remained on active duty in a besieged city, was not. For Byrne it was no small matter, for when the Irish officers were retired on half pay after the Hundred Days, he had to live on half of the pay of a captain.[78]

The question of the German officers, who were sent away from the Regiment in December 1813 as the result of the imperial decree of 25 November of the same year, was kept alive in the early months of 1814. The protests and requests for their return on the part of the Regiment were picked up in January, 1814 by General Maison, commander of the 1st Corps. In asking that they be sent back to Antwerp, he pointed out that they had all served in the last campaign with distinction and that most of them had been wounded in combat. If they were not to be returned to their Regiment, he asked that they be treated well.[79] Then on 20 January, Napoleon authorized Maison to discharge "the eight officers."[80] Finally in February the emperor gave way to the pressures from all sides and to military necessity. They were too high in quality as officers to be discarded at a time when he was fighting a last desperate campaign. The eight German officers, Buhlmann, Eckardt, Gassling, Keller, Klimps, Ruff, Ram, and Schroder, were ordered to rejoin the Irish Regiment.[81] The siege of Antwerp prevented them from resuming their previous commands in the various battalions, but they reported to the depot at Lille and were once again included on the regimental list of officers dated 1 March 1814.[82] Finally, there remains the question of how many German officers were involved. Clearly the *Procès verbal*, dated 19 December 1813, states that there had been ten officers removed from the Regiment. Yet only eight can be identified by name. Then all of the correspondence in January and February 1814 concerning their return to the Regiment refer to only eight. Since the two officers in question cannot be identified, the question remains: were ten officers removed and eight returned, or were only eight actually removed and thus all returned?[83]

The Irish Regiment remained in the besieged city of Antwerp until the war ended with the abdication of the Emperor Napoleon. It took part in the skillful defense of the city under the old republican, General Carnot. The fighting was of a more routine nature for a city under siege. However, there was one serious episode that involved the Regiment. Colonel Mahony was arrested and confined to his quarters by Carnot when his correspondence with the enemy was intercepted and presented to the commanding general. Mahony, it will be recalled, had served in the English army before he had entered the service of France. Realizing that Napoleonic France was about to collapse, he opened communications with the Allies to ensure a favorable reception by the new regime. Needless to say, the Irish officers of the Regiment, with whom he had never been popular, were delighted to see him removed. *Chef de Bataillon* William Hoyne, who was Irish by birth, was named to replace him as regimental commander.[84]

The news of Napoleon's abdication on 6 April first reached Antwerp four days later on the tenth. Carnot, to make sure that it was not some trick on the part of the Allies to gain control of the city, which they could not otherwise capture, requested and was granted permission to send two of his own aides to Paris in order to confirm the change of government from the emperor to a provisional regime. Upon their return with the confirmation of Napoleon's abdication, Carnot signed an armistice with the English General Graham. However, he maintained French control of the important city of Antwerp. Then on 18 April news arrived that Louis XVIII had been proclaimed king of France. The following day the garrison was assembled, and the men replaced the tricolored cockade with the white of the house of Bourbon and swore allegiance to the new king.[85]

When the war ended in April 1814, the officer corps of the 3rd Foreign Regiment consisted of eighty-seven men.[86] Of that number thirty-one of them, that is thirty-six percent, were Irish and forty-seven, fifty-four percent, were French. The remaining nine were one Swiss, three Poles, two Swedes, one Italian, one Bohemian, and one from the Duchy of Nassau.[87] These figures represent the make-up of the officer corps after ten captains and ten lieutenants, all of whom were French, had been sent to Paris for duty with the main army. Even so, the number of Irish officers had dropped below fifty percent. The principal reason for that decline was the number of officers lost in the campaign of 1813. Although a few Irish noncommissioned officers had been promoted to second lieutenant, most of the replacements had been French. The nationality of the noncommissioned officers and soldiers cannot be determined at this time as the documentation gives only numbers for each grade. There were two hundred noncommissioned officers, but only four hundred and seventy-seven soldiers in the Regiment. Furthermore, twenty-five percent of the soldiers were in the hospital. Thus while the Regiment had a large number of officers and a sufficient number of noncommissioned officers, there were only three hundred and nineteen men on active duty.[88] The Irish Regiment in April 1814 was at best an understrength battalion.

8

The Restoration and Disbandment of the Legion

The fall of Paris, or perhaps more correctly the surrender of Paris by Marshal Auguste-Frédéric-Louis Viesse de Marmont, on 31 March 1814, confirmed the end of the empire. Napoleon did not abdicate his throne until 6 April, but the war had been lost. The French nation longed for peace. After twenty-two years of almost continuous warfare France had had more than enough. The casualties of the Russian Campaign of 1812 and the Leipzig Campaign of 1813 had shocked the nation into the realization of the price of war without victory. The Allies allowed Napoleon to keep his title of emperor, empty as it was, and gave him the Island of Elba off of the west coast of central Italy. He set up court in his tiny kingdom, and while he reorganized the government, he watched events on the Continent.

A provisional government filled the vacuum in Paris even before the emperor had abdicated at Fontainebleau. Led by men like the ex-bishop Charles-Maurice de Talleyrand-Périgord and the regicide Joseph Fouché, and faced with the Allied armies of occupation, the provisional government both accepted and invited the Comte de Provence to reign as king of France. The younger brother of the executed Louis XVI, the new king styled himself Louis XVIII.[1] Arriving in Paris late in April after twenty years in exile, Louis installed a new government. The man who was named minister of war to replace General Clarke was General Pierre Dupont de l'Etang. Although of noble birth, young Dupont had remained in the army during the years of the Revolution and had risen in the ranks. He was already a major general when Napoleon came to power. A good solider, he had fought at the battles of Marengo, Ulm, Jena, and Friedland, and had been awarded the grand cordon of the Legion Honor. Sent to Spain in 1808 he had the misfortune of being surrounded at Baylen where he surrendered more than half of his army. Although he had been repatriated, Napoleon never forgave him for Baylen. In 1814 he formed that necessary link between the army and the new Bourbon government.

The army was not popular with the returning royalist nobility. It was viewed by them, and quite correctly, as a "Napoleonic" army, the creation of a man they despised and loyal to him. Faced with the reality of the loss of the war, the army accepted the removal of the emperor and his replacement by the king. However, there continued to be an uncomfortable relationship between the king and his government on the one hand, and the army on the other. France was now at peace with the nations of Europe and did not need a large army. Many officers, who had hoped to make the military their career, were retired on half pay with few prospects of finding another means of income. Most of the rank and file who were discharged were eager to return to civilian life, but even some of these men had also hoped to make the army their home. The Irish officers, almost to a man, wished to remain in the army and to continue their careers. Those who had been exiled from Ireland could still not go home, and even the sons of Irishmen, themselves born in France, had entered the army at an early age with the intention of becoming career officers. Few of the Irish officers had any future outside of the military life. There were serious concerns, even fears, on the part of these officers that with the reorganization of the army under this first restoration that they would be discharged. Most of them, already middle aged, would be faced with the prospect of living on half pay the rest of their lives.

The new government had hardly had time to unpack when Colonel Mahony, who began to style himself "Chevalier Mahony,"[2] suggested to the minister of war that the old Irish Brigade be reorganized out of the 3rd Foreign Regiment, which he commanded. Mahony had begun his military career in the Dillon Regiment of the Brigade.[3] He undoubtedly saw himself as commander of such a brigade, a position which had carried the rank of general of brigade. His proposal was not acted upon favorably. Miles Byrne makes the point in his *Memoirs* that it was not the king, nor the minister of war, who opposed the reestablishment of the Brigade, it was Robert Stewart Castlereagh, the English foreign minister.[4] The Irish Brigade in the French army had been a direct affront to England from its origins in the late seventeenth and early eighteenth centuries, down to its stepchild the Irish Legion in the early nineteenth century. The recreation of an Irish Brigade would have offended the French king's English supporters and strained relations between the two countries at a time when the new French government needed all of the friends it could get. Thus not only was the Brigade not resurrected, but the 3rd Foreign Regiment was no longer allowed to style itself "Irish."[5] In point of fact, the vast majority of documents, and most correspondence, no longer added "Irish" to the Regiment's title. The Irish officers in the Regiment, who had still been appending "Irish" to its title, were disappointed and felt that they had lost an important part of their identity.

The 3rd Foreign Regiment remained at Antwerp until the first week of May. It then withdrew from that territory, which became a part of Holland, to Dunkirk. When it arrived on the coast Colonel Mahony obtained a leave of absence to go to Paris, and *Chef de Battalion* Hayne took over command of the corps. In the second week of May the Polish members of the Regiment were ordered removed. One officer and thirty noncommissioned officers and soldiers, in accordance with orders received from the minister of war, set off for St. Denis, a suburb of Paris. Tsar Alexander I, who was annexing the greater portion of the duchy of Warsaw with the consent of the great powers of Europe, had requested that the Poles from all over France be returned to Russia. Those at Dunkirk were paid through 12 May, and they left the Regiment the following day.[6] Another decision of the new government that had an effect upon the Regiment was one which allowed French-born officers in a "foreign" regiment to transfer into a regular line unit. Several officers of the 3rd Foreign Regiment took advantage of this offer, which they believed would further their careers. Those officers who were not on good terms with Colonel Mahony, in particular Captain Brevelet, Lieutenants Jean-Baptiste Sauland, Tumoral, and Kerthen, and Second Lieutenant Jean-Baptiste Lagrange, took advantage of this opportunity to leave the Regiment.[7]

From Dunkirk the Regiment marched to Lille and arrived there on 16 May. Major Ware was waiting at Lille, the Regiment's depot, with a number of officers and men who had gathered there since the blockade at Antwerp had become effected early in February. The major assumed command of the Regiment as the senior officer in the absence of Colonel Mahony. However, the Regiment remained at Lille only five weeks before it received orders to go to Avesnes and take up garrison duties. It left Lille on 25 June for its new destination—Avesnes. To the relief of the officers and men, who had been on campaign, besieged at Antwerp, and in temporary quarters for more than six months, they settled into their routine duties in the anticipation that this would be a more permanent assignment.[8]

The Regiment went through yet another reorganization in the summer of 1814 after its arrival at Avesnes. There had been reorganization in May and June, but the personnel had continued to change through the spring and early summer. Germans had been removed from the corps, then returned, and removed a second time. The Poles had been removed, and some of the French-born officers had transferred to other regiments. Finally there was the problem of returning prisoners of war. It was a problem because no one knew how many officers, or of what rank, would be returning. Furthermore, they arrived back in France over a period of six to nine months after the war had ended. They were coming from as close as eastern England and from as far away as central Russia. Upon arriving back in France they tended to make their way to the city that had been their regiment's depot at the time they were taken prisoner. Thus the returning officers went first to Bois-le-Duc, and then had to catch up with a regiment that was moving every four to five weeks. For the Prussians and Germans who had served in the 4th Foreign Regiment, the problem was compounded by the fact that Napoleon had disbanded their regiment shortly before the war ended and incorporated the remnants into the 3rd Foreign Regiment. This caused great difficulties in determining seniority and in placing the new arrivals into the framework of a regiment that already had too many officers.[9]

Several of the former prisoners of war were not at all pleased to find that their old regiments no longer existed, and that they were assigned to the "Irish" regiment. Lieutenant Jean-Frédéric Mundt and Second Lieutenant François Charles Emanuel Junot, both of whom had served in the Prussian Battalion and had been taken prisoner at Flushing in August 1809, returned from England to find themselves assigned to the 3rd Foreign Regiment. They wrote to the minister of war requesting transfers.[10] Four more German officers, and one Polish, also returned from English prisoner of war camps in May.[11] Then in July, three officers and one hundred and nine noncommissioned officers and men, most of them German, returned to France and were sent to the 3rd Foreign Regiment. This group of men had been a part of General Dupont's army that had surrendered at Baylen in Spain in 1808.[12]

In some instances officers did not return until 1815. Three Irish officers, Captain Charles Mullein, Lieutenant Patrick Lynch, and Lieutenant Anthony Doyer, returned to the Regiment in that year. All three men had been taken prisoner on 3 September, 1813 in the confusion that had taken place after Marshal MacDonald's defeat on the Katzbach.[13] Unfortunately, from their point of view, there had just been a major reorganization of the Regiment and there was no place for them. They were placed on half pay without command, and it seemed unlikely that they would be reinstated in the near future. However, Colonel Mahony and the other Irish officers made a special plea on behalf of these men. It was pointed out to the minister of war that they were Irish by birth and had no other means of a honorable livelihood than the army. No provisions had been made for returning prisoners of war in the latest reorganization of the army. Thus, they requested that the three be allowed to remain with the Regiment until such time as openings would present an opportunity for them to be employed.[14] The request was granted and on 11 March 1815, just before Napoleon reached Paris on his return from Elba, all three officers were reinstated on active duty with full pay, but without being placed in a battalion.[15]

The returning Prussian and German officers, together with those officers from the remnants of the 2nd and 4th Foreign Regiments, caused concern and ill feeling within the 3rd Foreign Regiment. The Irish officers perceived that the Prussians were receiving preferential treatment in the reorganizations taking place under the new regime.[16] Perhaps it was the fact that Napoleon had become suspicious of the loyalty of the Prussians and Germans. He had, after all, disbanded their regiments after Prussia and some of the lesser German states had declared war upon France. On the other hand, the loyalty of the Irish officers had not been questioned at that time. The Bourbon government may well have preferred the German officers, who had some cause to be anti-Bonapartist, to the Irish who owed everything to the ex-emperor.

One of the first acts of the new government was to promote Captain Geith, a Prussian officer from the old 4th Foreign Regiment, to *chef de bataillon* and to place him in the 3rd Foreign Regiment. At the same time *Chef de Bataillon* John Allen, himself recently promoted, but senior to Geith, remained in the Regiment without a command and seemingly less opportunity of receiving a battalion. Then Captain Joseph Parrott lost command of the elite company of grenadiers, which he had commanded for several years, to Captain Maurice St. Colomb, formerly of the 2nd Foreign Regiment (Isenberg), who had never commanded an elite company until he received this appointment. Even St. Colomb, much to his credit, recognized the injustice of this decision and went to General Jean R. C. Bourke to speak on behalf of Parrott. However, this only infuriated the general who refused to take further action on the matter.[17] The Irish officers viewed such affairs as clear indications of the treatment they might expect from the Bourbon government in the future.

The incident that caused the Irish the most concern, and the one that struck at the heart of their fears, was the forced retirement of *Chef de Bataillon* William Hayne. A native-born Irishman with twenty-eight years of service in the French army, he was placed on half pay on 13 March 1815.[18] Had he been allowed to remain on active duty for little more than a year, he would have received full retirement and been able to live comfortably in his declining years. His health was still quite good and he was fit for active service, but his relationship with his commanding officer, Mahony, left much to be desired.[19]

The Irish officers were not only apprehensive about their relationship with the government, but there was also an extremely poor relationship between themselves and their commanding officer. John F. Mahony had never been popular with the officers of the Irish Regiment. They had considered him to be an incompetent battalion commander in Spain in 1810. They had regretted his promotion to major, and felt that either Tennent or Ware should have been named second in command. Nevertheless, there seemed to be little damage he could do at the depot in 1813. When he received his brevet of colonel and was named to replace Lawless, the men of the Irish Regiment knew that all would not go well. They had hoped that *Chef de Bataillon* Ware, by far a more capable officer, would have stepped into the vacuum created by Lawless' untimely departure. But although Mahony was lacking in ability, he was not lacking in friends in high places. General Clarke liked him and had promoted his career over the years. It was the minister of war who had secured his promotions to *chef de bataillon*, major, and colonel. With the restoration of the monarchy, Mahony again found favor with his superiors. He embraced the new regime immediately and wholeheartedly. He even began to sign himself first as "chevalier" and then in March 1815, as "Count O'Mahony."[20] As Byrne later reported in his *Memoirs*: "This was the first intelligence which the officers had of his being a count."[21]

In August 1814 an incident took place that greatly increased the tension between the Irish officers and their commander. On the twenty-fifth of the month the officers of the Regiment gave a dinner and a ball to celebrate the feast of St. Louis and the king's birthday. Byrne wrote the following account of the events of that night and next few days:

> Unfortunately at the opening of the ball, colonel Mahony insulted Captain [Hugh] Lawless with the grossest language and then ordered him away under arrest. On lieutenant-colonel [*sic*] Ware however observing to the colonel, that on a day of rejoicing like that they were then celebrating, it would be better if it passed over without having any one punished, he consented to raise the captain's arrest, and to allow him to remain at the ball, for which lieutenant-colonel [*sic*] Ware thanked him; but in less than fifteen minutes after, on colonel Mahony meeting captain Lawless he again insulted him worse than before, and ordered him to quit the room immediately. Lieutenant-colonel [*sic*] Ware wishing to demonstrate, the moment he spoke, colonel Mahony ordered him also under arrest. Upon which lieutenant-colonel [*sic*] Ware said to him: "I will go home and guard my arrest, but I must tell you, before I go, that your conduct this evening is unworthy of a gentleman; and it is both cowardly and scoundrelly [*sic*] of you to insult an officer like captain Lawless, whom you know cannot bring you out. . . . " The ball became rather dull in consequence of this

unpleasant affair, for almost all the Irish officers went away when they heard of colonel Mahony's insolent conduct.[22]

The day following Ware's arrest he was freed, and went straight to Mahony and challenged him to a duel. The Colonel chose pistols as the weapons and both men secured seconds. *Chef de Bataillon* Allen and Captain Parrott acted as seconds for Ware, while Mahony had to select two Frenchmen, Captain de Tressan and a certain colonel who was married to Mahony's cousin. They exchanged shots without drawing blood, and the colonel declared that he was satisfied, despite the fact that Ware refused to apologize. The officers of the Regiment thought the affair behind them, but on the following Sunday it began anew. With the officer corps assembled waiting on General Bourke, who was visiting the Regiment and who had observed from a distance the events at the ball, Mahony lashed out at Ware. He declared that the major had no right to speak to him as he had and that he should have him court-martialed. There had been little love between the Irish and Mahony before this affair, but after it there was only contempt for the man under whose orders they had to serve.[23]

Throughout the summer and into the fall of 1814 the French army underwent major reorganizations. The aspect that affected the former Irish Regiment took place in July and early August. Under the direction of General Bourke three foreign regiments were organized. The former Latour-d'Aubergne Regiment became once again the 1st Foreign Regiment; the Isenberg Regiment, disbanded by Napoleon late in 1813, was reconstituted as the 2nd Foreign Regiment; and the ex-Irish Regiment continued to be the 3rd Foreign Regiment.[24] This organization took place at Avesnes where the 3rd Regiment remained until mid-December. The 1st and 2nd Foreign Regiments left Avesnes shortly after the completion of their organization and marched south to do garrison duty. Then in mid-December the 3rd Foreign Regiment was moved from Avesnes to Montreuil-sur-Mer, where it was inspected by General Bourke.

The general's report shows that the make-up of the officer corps had continued to fluctuate through the fall of 1814. Twenty-six of its German officers had been sent to the 1st and 2nd Foreign Regiments or retired on half pay. Two Irish officers returned from prisoner of war camps and rejoined the Regiment.[25] Eighty-five officers are listed by name and rank in General Bourke's report. Sixty-eight of them held positions in the three battalions that made up the Regiment or on the regimental staff. The remaining officers, six captains, five lieutenants, and six second lieutenants were carried "à la suite" without command. The Irish in the Regiment's officer corps numbered thirty, or thirty-five percent. However, if their numbers had been declining over the years, eight-five percent in 1805, fifty percent in 1813, the Irish held most of the upper ranks. Nineteen out of the thirty Irishmen held the rank of captain or higher.[26]

The regiment was in fact only three skeleton battalions. It is true that it had too many officers, but it had almost no soldiers. When the last reorganization was completed at the end of 1814, there were only two hundred ninety noncommissioned officers and soldiers under arms in all three battalions. The organizational charts prepared for the minister of war on 1 January 1815 show that each battalion had between twenty-two and twenty-five noncommissioned officers, four drummers, and sixty-three men.[27] The Regiment should have had 1,312 noncommissioned officers and troops, thus it lacked 1,027 men to be brought up to *peacetime* strength. To be sure, the Bourbon government had no plans to go to war and thus did not need, nor did it wish to support, a large army. Yet the manpower of the entire Regiment equaled less than three good war-strength companies.

At the beginning of the year 1815 the officer corps of the 3rd Foreign Regiment pledge its loyalty to Louis XVIII in the most glowing terms: "The 3rd Foreign Regiment . . . " they wrote, "lays at the feet of the best of kings, the homage of its devotion and its fidelity. . . . The colonel, major, battalion commanders and officers of all grades animated by sentiments of the most profound admiration for Your Majesty, wish only to prove how much they deserve the honor which had been bestowed upon them. . . . "[28]

Towards the end of February and during the month of March the 3rd Foreign Regiment received a number of returning prisoners of war who did not wish to remain in the French army. None of these men were French or Irish, but had been drafted into the Napoleonic army from Belgium, Italy, Holland, and Germany. They wished to be discharged and allowed to return to their homes. As can be best determined, most, if not all, of these men were allowed to leave the army.[29] Not all of the non-French ex-prisoners wanted to quit the service. Exact numbers are not available, but the vast majority of the rank and file of the Regiment was made up of foreigners, many of them returned prisoners of war.[30]

The morale of the Irish officers in the 3rd Foreign Regiment had been declining since the restoration of the Bourbon dynasty. They had every reason to believe that their position in the king's army would continue to deteriorate, as it had over the past eleven months. Their relationship with Colonel Mahony could hardly have been worse, even though he was Irish, and they feared that English influence at court might even lead to their forced retirement. Thus, one can well imagine the joy with which they received the news of Napoleon's landing in southern France.

The emperor landed at Cannes on 1 March, and avoiding Marseilles, a

Bourbon stronghold, he marched north through the mountains to Grenoble. The small party then moved on to Lyons and north again to Paris. By the time he reached the capital on 20 March, the king and his supporters had departed for Belgium. The French people, and in particular the army, welcomed him back. The Bourbons had made few friends in the eleven months since Napoleon's abdication. The nation did not want a renewal of the war, but neither did it want a restored monarchy that looked too much like the old regime it had overthrown in the early 1790s. Thus the bloodless restoration of the emperor took place amidst guarded joy and apprehension of what the future would bring.

Colonel Mahony had been given a leave of absence in February 1815 so that he could be married in Paris. However, the news of Napoleon's return to France caused him to postpone his wedding and return to his Regiment. Reaching Montreuil-sur-Mer on 15 March he was in command of the Regiment when news arrived that the king was on his way to Belgium (he would establish his court at Ghent), and the emperor had installed himself in Paris. The Irish officers, who followed these events in the local newspapers, took a neutral course of action despite their inner feelings. As foreigners in France they were determined to be loyal to the existing government. Thus they did not at once declare for Napoleon but waited for events to run their course. Enthusiasm in the town of Montreuil-sur-Mer ran so high in favor of the emperor's return that the commander, Colonel Tobin, asked for a battalion of the Regiment to be moved into the citadel to ensure order. Mahony sent Allen's battalion (he had replaced the retired Hayne), and its presence was sufficient to maintain tranquillity.[31]

No orders were received at Montreuil-sur-Mer for almost a week after Napoleon had reached Paris. It was necessary to reorganize the entire government. Marshal Louis N. Davout, reluctantly consented to serve as minister of war and began at once to put the affairs of the army in good order. This was not an easy task in light of the resignation of some officers who declined to serve the returned emperor.[32] In the provinces each district and each barracks was left pretty much on its own. On 25 March Colonel Mahony assembled the officer corps of his Regiment and told them that the king was on his way to the Belgian coast and wanted to know their feelings and attitudes on the events that were taking place. Major Ware answered for the Regiment in the following manner: "Colonel, give your orders and they will be executed. If the king wants an escort to the frontiers, he may rely on the regiment doing its duty. But we Irish patriots will never go to the enemy's camp, to fight against France, our adopted country."[33]

Mahony could hardly have expected a reply different from that which he received. He then informed his officers that he would follow the king into exile and he considered that it be *"le chemin de l'honneur."* Then he added that he would never again serve the emperor after the manner in which he had been treated at Antwerp during the siege of 1814. Having thus made his intentions and his reasoning clear, Mahony turned over command of the Regiment to Major Ware and sent the military chest to his quarters.[34]

The departure of Colonel Mahony did not change the situation at Montreuil-sur-Mer vis-à-vis the new government at Paris. But on the morning of 26 March, the civil authorities received orders from the prefect of the department of Pas-de-Calais to recognize Napoleon as head of state. The military orders from Marshal Adolphe-Edouard-Camimir-Joseph Mortier governor of the 16th Military Division at Lille, arrived several hours later. Thus, on the afternoon on the twenty-sixth the civil authorities, the national guard, and the officers and men of the Regiment assembled in the main square and "the Emperor Napoleon was proclaimed with the greatest expressions of satisfaction and joy."[35] On this occasion the Irish proudly displayed their imperial eagle, which they had kept hidden during the eleven months of the Bourbon restoration, and there was good will between civilian population and the men of the Regiment. The rejoicing was not, it must be said, universal. Ware, then acting commander, called upon any officer who in good conscience did not feel that he could serve the emperor to leave the Regiment. He assured anyone who would depart that their integrity would be respected and they were free to leave. Two men availed themselves of the major's offer, Captain John Ferguson and Lieutenant Robert Gordon. All of the others swore allegiance to Napoleon. Byrne actually names three officers whom he says left the Regiment. The names of Captain Ferguson and Lieutenant Gordon can be confirmed as they are listed on the regimental rosters in January, February, and March 1815, and then missing in April, May, and June. However, he also mentions a Captain Bonan, no first name, as having left the Regiment rather than serve the returned emperor. Captain Bonan's name is not to be found on any of the regimental lists in 1815.[36]

The joy and celebration of the Irish officers was short-lived. The following day, 27 March, Colonel Mahony returned to Montreuil-sur-Mer and demanded that Ware give back to him the military chest and command of the Regiment. The major refused and told him that he would never again serve under his orders. Mahony went to Colonel Tobin, the military governor of Montreuil-sur-Mer, and the colonel gave him his support by ordering Ware to accept the authority of Mahony. Rather than do so, Ware gave his sword to Tobin and placed himself under house arrest. When the officers of the Regiment heard what had taken place, they went to Tobin's residence

and all, save one, surrendered to him their swords, thus relieving themselves of duty. Despite support from General Pellet, who arrived that
evening and implored the officers to take back their swords, and the fact
that Tobin went himself to Ware's lodgings and took possession of the
military chest, the officers refused to serve under Mahony. When the
general explained the situation to Mahony and the likely consequences of
the affair, the Colonel once again decided to follow the *"chemin de l'honneur."* This time, however, he did not start for Ghent and the king, but for
Paris where he planned to plead his case before Marshal Davout. Fortunately, for the officers of the Regiment, General Carnot was in Paris at the
time and a few words from him to the minister of war sealed the fate of
Colonel Mahony. Had General Clarke been minister of war at that time,
Mahony would have received a much more friendly ear, and the outcome
could have been quite different and much less pleasing to the officers of the
Regiment. But Davout was a man of integrity, principles, and loyalty to
Napoleon, who cared little for the likes of John F. Mahony. With the final
departure of the colonel, the officers of the Regiment took back their swords
and Ware resumed command. The affair was thus settled "to the great
satisfaction of the Irish officers."[37]

With the emperor back in Paris and the "Iron Marshal" (Davout) at the
war ministry, changes began to take place. Colonel Tobin, who was no friend
of the Irish officers, was replaced by Colonel Peltier as military governor at
Montreuil-sur-Mer. Peltier had held that post before the Bourbon restoration
and was a strong Bonapartist. He quite understood, and approved of, the
actions taken by the officers of the Regiment. Then *Chef de-Bataillon* Hayne
was restored to active duty and reassigned to his old regiment. Even though
he did not rejoin the Regiment during the Hundred Days, this action pleased
the Irish officers very much. Captain Parrott was given back his elite company
of grenadiers and Captain St. Colomb took command of the 1st Company in
the 3rd Battalion.[38] Then in May, Major Ware was promoted to the rank of
colonel and named commander of the Regiment.[39] Finally, the Regiment was
allowed once again to add "Irish" to its title, and the tops of documents once
again read "3me Regiment Etranger (Irlandais)."[40]

When the news of Napoleon's return to France and the flight of Louis
XVIII reached the capitals of Europe, the grand alliance of 1813–14 was
reconfirmed, and the monarchs pledged once again to make war on the
emperor. Despite Napoleon's declarations of peace and willingness to accept
the settlements reached at the Congress of Vienna, Europe believed that
his return meant war. Faced with the hostility of Prussia, Austria, Russia,
and England (who found Napoleon's presence on the throne of France, or
perhaps, more worrisome, his presence at the head of the French army,

unacceptable), the emperor threw himself with much energy into rebuilding
the army. The Bourbon government had greatly reduced its numbers and
had allowed it to decline in terms of war-readiness. If France was again to
face an alliance of the great powers of Europe, its military forces needed
immediate and energetic attention. One of the measures taken was the
rebuilding of the Irish Regiment.

A fourth battalion was added to the Regiment and all of the officers who
had been carried on the regimental list without command were used to staff
its companies.[41] At the beginning of the Hundred Days the Regiment had
three battalion commanders, Charles de Fectze, Anthony Braun, and John
Allen.[42] By June, *Chef de Bataillon* de Fectze was no longer on the regimental list.[43] Despite the fact that *Chef de Bataillon* William Hayne never
rejoined the Regiment, his name was back on the list as senior battalion
commander on 1 August 1815. Furthermore, although Ware was promoted
to colonel, no new major was named to replace him.[44] Thus the upper ranks
of the officer corps were at least in a mild state of disarray. There was a
colonel, but no major, two battalion commanders on active duty for four
battalions, one battalion commander at Paris who never took command,
and one vacancy. To fill the ranks of the battalions, which were grossly
undermanned in March 1815, Davout sent a steady stream of men, a few
of them officers, who had been put on half pay by the previous government.
Captain Paul Murray, who had been retired under the restored Bourbons,
rejoined his comrades and was welcomed with great joy.[45]

On the lighter side, although it was taken very seriously by the Irish
officers, was the question of the color of the uniform of the Regiment. By
a decision on the part of the ministry of war during the restoration, the
green coats worn by the Irish since the formation of the Legion in 1803 had
been ordered replaced by blue coats. In early April, Ware requested that
the officers and men be allowed to go back to their traditional green.
Although the emperor was sympathetic, there was little money to be had
for such cosmetic changes.[46]

The Irish Regiment was not to see combat again. When the French
army marched across the northern frontier of France to attack General
Blücher's Prussian army in Belgium it remained tranquil at Montreuil-sur-
Mer. In the first place, its four battalions were still greatly under-strength
and thus not combat-ready. Furthermore, there were rumors to the effect
that the English were preparing to land 6,000 men on the French coast as
soon as the French army crossed the frontier. Napoleon designated the
Irish Regiment and the local national guard as a coastal-defense force to
deal with such a landing.[47]

With the coalition of Prussia, England, Austria, and Russia reaffirmed,

Napoleon faced the prospects of overwhelming odds if he waited for the Allies to converge on France. If, on the other hand, he took the initiative before the Austrians and Russians were able to reach the Rhine, he would have only the English army commanded by Wellington and the Prussian army commanded by Blücher, with which to contend. Moreover, although those two armies were in Belgium, they were not united. If the emperor moved in mid-June, he had the opportunity to strike first one and then the other before help from the east could arrive. Consequently, he opened the Waterloo Campaign on 15 June by crossing the Belgan frontier and marching on Charleroi. On the sixteenth he attached Blücher's army at Ligny and sent it reeling back in some disorder. He then swung to his left and marched against Wellington. The English general took up a defensive position at Waterloo, and although on 18 June the French pressed him all along the front, his lines held until Blücher arrived in the late afternoon and won the day. The French army was broken and retreated south in great disorder. Napoleon returned to Paris despondent, and for the second time in as many years, abdicated. This time he put himself into the hands of the English, and they sent him to the island of St. Helena where he died in 1821.

On the eve of the last Napoleonic campaign there were some defections from the Irish Regiment. Three officers, who had sworn allegiance to the emperor in March, deserted and went over to the royalists. Captain Maurice St. Colomb left Montreuil-Sur-Mer on 10 June and Captain Henry Thompson left two days later on the twelfth. Both men were French emigrants who had returned in 1814 and had been placed in the 3rd Foreign Regiment. St. Colomb had received favorable treatment under the restoration, but as a staunch loyalist he could not expect rapid promotion, even in time of war, by the restored Bonapartist regime. Captain Hercule La Roche, another returned French emigrant also left the Regiment in June.[48] These three officers who went over to the king had never been Bonapartists, and their actions are quite understandable. But Captain Patrick Magrath's behavior is another question. An Irishman by birth, he was fifty years of age in 1815. He had made the campaign of 1813 as the Regiment's quartermaster officer, but found himself without a command when Napoleon returned to France from Elba. During the Hundred Days he was in correspondence with the king's agents at Ghent. Neither in Byrne's *Memoirs* nor in the available documents is there any clue as to his motives. Whatever they might have been, they were unacceptable to the Irish officers of the Regiment. Byrne wrote the following account of this affair:

> In Consequence, captains of the regiment waited on captain Magrath and reproached him with his infamous and dishonorable conduct. He could

not deny that he corresponded with the Bourbon party at Ghent, nor that he had accompanied captain Saint-Colomb on the road the day he deserted. The eight captains told Magrath that they were resolved not to serve with traitors, and said he must resign.[49]

Despite the furor caused by his behavior, Magrath was still carried on the regimental list on 1 August. Napoleon's second abdication and the disbandment of the Irish Regiment resolved this affair with the retirement of all of the Irish officers.[50]

The news of Napoleon's victory over the Prussians at Ligny on 16 June had been received at Montreuil-sur-Mer with great joy. However, it was followed within a few days by the grim details of the disaster at Waterloo. In one sentence in his *Memoirs* Byrne summed up the forlorn reality of that event when he wrote: "But the loss of the Battle of Waterloo on the 18th of June, with the other unhappy circumstances which followed Napoleon's abdication, put an end to their [the Irish officers] career, and to all further hopes of aid from France to relieve Ireland from her bondage."[51]

When the extent of the French defeat at Waterloo became known in Paris, the minister of war ordered the various military units in the north of France to assemble before the capital to defend the city. His intention was to gather all French forces about Paris, thus presenting a formidable military force that would give the French government, whether Napoleon or a provisional government, a better bargaining position for ending the war.[52] That this strategy did not work can be seen in the reaction of local military authorities. At Montreuil-sur-Mer, Colonel Peltier, the local military governor, did not transmit Davout's instructions to Colonel Ware. Thus the Irish Regiment, which would have marched immediately to Paris, remained idle in its barracks as the Allied armies converged on the capital.[53]

With Napoleon's final departure, Louis XVIII again returned to Paris in the "baggage of the Allied army." On 12 July, in accordance with orders from the minister of war, the officers and men of the Irish Regiment again proclaimed Louis king and swore to him allegiance. There was none of the enthusiasm, joy, and celebration that had accompanied the swearing of allegiance to Napoleon just three months earlier. The Irish knew well that the future would hold little promise for their careers under the Bourbon regime. But they had few choices. Their situation had not changed since Napoleon's first abdictaion. They could not return to Ireland, and there was little that they could do outside of the military life. Several of them, including Colonel Ware, went to the new commander of Montreuil-Sur-Mer and expressed "their hesitation at continuing in the service under so many changes."[54] But in the end they really had nowhere else to go. On 13 July Ware drew up an address to the king, which was made available for all officers to sign. It declared their loyalty to the king, and their desire to continue to serve in the army. However, trouble arose when *Chef de Bataillon* Antoine Braun, a Prussian who had served in the 4th Foreign Regiment until it was disbanded in 1813 and he was sent to the 3rd Foreign Regiment, drew up a second address to the king. Braun's address, which was signed by the German officers in the Regiment, proclaimed loyalty and attachment to the Bourbon monarchy in much stronger terms than the one written by his commanding officer. Ware's address was signed by all of the Irish officers, but not by the Germans. Thus it actually became a strike against the Irish to have signed Ware's address instead of a point in their favor. Needless to say, when the Irish officers found out what had happened it created very bad feelings between themselves and the German officers of the Regiment.[55]

There was one slight gleam of hope to which the Irish eagerly grasped. The returning Bourbons appointed General Clarke once again to be minister of war. The Irish at once put their hopes in the hands of this son of an Irishman. They hoped for better treatment than they had received under the first restoration. They drew up a letter to the new minister in which they welcomed him back and implored him to tell the king that they wanted to continue to serve. "You know the history of our unhappy country better then any other person. . . . We implore you to take into consideration . . . that we have no other homeland other than France and no resource other then the good will of the King."[56] The letter concluded by the Irish placing their destiny in the hands of the minister, whom they asked to intercede for them with the king. Unfortunately, General Clarke had neither a sufficient amount of influence at court or the desire to help the Irish officers. His own position as minister of war was on shaky ground and he had no intention of taking up such an unpopular cause as the fate of the Irish officers.

There was most likely nothing that could be done to save the Irish Regiment. The monarchists had only allowed it to exist during the first restoration with reluctance. Its officers were perceived, and correctly it should be added, as being Bonapartists with republican undercurrents. A victim of the "White Terror," brought about by the frustration and humiliation of the Hundred Days, the Regiment was officially disbanded on 28 September 1815.[57] The Irish themselves believed that it was Lord Castlereagh (Robert Stewart), himself an Irishman, and English influence in general at the court of Louis XVIII, that brought an end to the Regiment and their careers in the French army.[58] It certainly was not the desire of those men to be retired on half pay in the prime of life. They desperately wished to remain on active duty. Collectively and individually they wrote to the minister of war declaring their loyalty to the king and their deep desire to serve. They reminded him that as Irish exiles they had no other country except France.[59]

These men, who had been United Irishmen, rebels, expatriates, and Napoleonic soldiers, were now willing to become monarchists in the service of Louis XVIII. It was an ironic transformation only understood by the course of events that had taken place over the previous twenty years. Each step of the way seemed quite logical, if not always desirable, at the time. This evolution reflects the sad course of Irish history under the direct control of England in the eighteenth century. These individuals represent the last chapter of "Wild Geese"—the legacy of the Treaty of Limerick and the Irish Brigade. Men like William Lawless, John Allen, Terence O'Reilly, and Miles Byrne could hardly have been ideologically happy serving the Bourbons, even if serving the Emperor Napoleon had been somewhat of a transition from their republicanism of the 1790s. Nevertheless, what choices did they have? Retirement in their mid-thirties on half pay did not offer a bright future. Lawless might live on his pension, but Captain Byrne would have financial problems. They had virtually no family money and no other profession or occupation other than that of the military. Thus, unpleasant as it may have been, the Irish officers tried hopelessly to remain in the army.[60]

The non-Irish officers, most of whom were Germans who had served in the 4th Foreign Regiment (the former Prussian Regiment), were transferred to other units of the French army. The noncommissioned officers and soldiers of the Irish Regiment, who did not ask to be discharged, were sent to Toulon where a foreign regiment was being formed.[61] The Irish officers were not given a choice of remaining in the army. The only choice they had was as to the town or city in which they wished to reside following their discharge.[62] Only the members of the Regiment's Council of Administration (Commander Ware, *Chef de Bataillon* Antoine Braun, Captains Byrne and Patrice d'Owitzky, and Gugelot[63])[64] remained at Montreuil sur Mer to handle the paperwork and to supervise the final distribution of the effects of the Regiment. This included, among other things, the destruction of everything bearing imperial markings. To this end the flags of the 2nd and 3rd Battalions were burned and the regimental eagle destroyed.[65] These men received two-thirds pay until they completed their task early in 1816.

The disbandment of the Irish Regiment in September 1815 did not end the drama for all of the Irish officers. Six of the ex-officers were singled out as dangerous individuals. The six men against whom accusations were made were John Allen, Miles Byrne, Luke Lawless, Thomas Jackson, William David Towne, and Laurent Esmonde.[66] Of this number, three were forced into exile, Lawless, Jackson and Towne, while the other three, after serious harassment, were allowed to remain in France.

John Allen was one of the most outstanding and respected officers to serve in the Irish Legion. A member of the Legion of Honor, he had been several times wounded in combat during the course of twelve campaigns that had taken him from Portugal to Poland. At age thirty-eight he had served twelve years in the French army and risen from second lieutenant to *chef de battalion*. Truly, Allen's military career had been distinguished, but this was not being questioned in 1815. Rather it was his political affiliations. The chief of the Bureau of Infantry, in a report to the minister of war, wrote the following concerning him: .

> This officer has a great deal of ability, and this makes him all the more dangerous. He is a compulsive Jacobin, capable of taking every measure possible to survive. One can never trust him. He is not capable of serving the King with zeal and fidelity, . . . He was a zealous partisan of the usurper. It is necessary to place him under strict surveillance.[67]

Allen was arrested in Paris and ordered to leave the country at once. He was not charged with any crime or wrongdoing, and he was not to be given a trial. Fortunately for this brave soldier, General O'Connor came to his aid. It is to O'Connor's credit that he supported a man in 1815 who had not supported him in 1804. But the old Irish political problems had faded, and what the general saw was a helpless Irish expatriate being wronged in the heat of French political turmoil. He went to the minister of war and spoke personally to him on Allen's behalf. As a direct result of this strong intervention on the part of O'Connor, the minister relented. Allen was released and allowed to retire to Tours where he lived quietly on half pay for a number of years. He died at Caen in 1855.[68]

Miles Byrne, like Allen, had joined the Irish Legion when it was created in 1803. He, too, had served in Spain and Portugal for four years and made the Campaign of 1813, and he was a member of the Legion of Honor. Although he was still a captain, he had been nominated for the rank of *chef de bataillon* in the waning months of the empire, and would surely have been promoted but for the abdication of Napoleon in 1814. Again like Allen, it was not his military service or his conduct that were brought into question in the fall of 1815, but his politics. His condemnation reads: " . . . *méchant* and very dangerous; has been a fervent partisan of Bonaparte who will never change. He should be placed under strict surveillance at his home."[69] However, unlike Allen, Byrne was not immediately arrested. Perhaps it was because he remained on active duty until early 1816. When, at that time, he retired to Tours and took up residence, he was placed under police surveillance. Then in 1817 he was actually ordered to leave France, but he was able to go to Paris and secure the revocation of the order. He lived in retirement in Tours until 1828 when, much to his surprise and great pleasure, he was recalled to active duty and sent to Greece. He was still in Greece when the July Revolution of 1830 took place. The new regime of Louis-Philippe promoted Byrne and ordered him back to France. He remained in the army until 1835 at which time he retired and took up residence in Paris where he died on 24 January 1862.[70]

Laurent Esmonde was also placed under surveillance rather than exiled. Born in Ireland in 1792, he had joined the Irish Regiment with the rank of second lieutenant in 1812. After the campaign of 1813, he had been promoted. He was denounced as a Bonapartist and a Jacobin. "This man, although young," reads the accusation, "is dangerous. He is capable of anything and must be closely watched."[71]

Luke Lawless was the nephew of William Lawless. Born in Dublin in 1786, he had joined the Irish Regiment in February 1811 with the rank of lieutenant and was promoted to captain in December of the same year. The externally quick advance in rank for one who had never been on campaign was most likely brought about by his relationship to the then Major Lawless, who was acting commander of the Regiment, and the fact that General Clarke took a liking to him. Immediately following his promotion the minister of war attached Luke Lawless to his staff in Paris. Thus he did not make the terrible Campaign of 1813, and, in fact, young Lawless never served in combat. The report to the minister of war declared that he was "extremely dangerous," and "an irrevocable enemy of the King." But in his case, unlike those of Allen, Byrne, and Esmonde, there was a specific incident mentioned to back up the charges. "He is one of six dangerous officers," the report states, "who used violence to remove the white [Bourbon] flags which the inhabitants had placed in their windows the day when the king passed through the town on his return from England, and this was done almost before his eyes. It is absolutely indispensable to put him under the closest surveillance. He is totally unworthy to serve the king."[72] In spite of Lawless' personal acquaintance with the minister of war, or perhaps because Clarke knew him so well, he was ordered to leave France. Luke Lawless eventually sailed to the United States and took up residence in St. Louis, Missouri, where he became a prominent lawyer.[73]

Born in Ireland in 1786, Thomas Jackson had joined the Irish Regiment in 1809 and made six campaigns. His condemnation declared that he "shared with the others the same principles, the same spirit, and like them should be placed under close surveillance. Bonapartist to the core, this is a very dangerous man, and entirely incapable and unworthy to be employed in the army."[74] Jackson was also eventually ordered to leave France, and, without influence in Paris, he sailed to the United States early in 1816.

The sixth officer denounced was William David Towne. Born in England in 1788, he had joined the Irish Legion in 1807 as a lieutenant and was promoted to captain in April 1813. He had taken part in eight campaigns and was a good officer. "An extreme Bonapartist and Jacobin," reads his denunciation, "a dangerous man, entirely unworthy to serve the king." He is then singled out as "the leader of the revolutionary party in the Regiment," and as the one "who led the insurrection in March," 1815, against Louis XVIII and in favor of the returning emperor. He is further accused of stamping on the king's flag while shouting "Vive l'Empereur."[75] Towne is indeed portrayed as the ringleader of the anti-Bourbon sentiment in the Irish Regiment. It is more surprising that he was not court-martialed than that he was sent into exile. At the time of his denunciation, in September, Captain Towne was on his way to Toulon. He had been put in command of the detachment of one hundred and seventeen noncommissioned officers and soldiers who were to become a part of the foreign regiment being formed. On the basis of the report received from the Bureau of Infantry, Clarke ordered Towne removed from his command and placed under strict surveillance until he left the country.[76]

John Allen's name was removed from the list of six in October as the result of O'Connor's intervention. But the correspondence continued concerning the other five. On 12 December, the minister of war ordered M. De Cazes, minister of police, to take the necessary measures to see that they would leave the country.[77] Then on 14 December, M. Deboulard, who signed himself "le Lieut. de Roi," wrote to General Baron Destabemath, commander of the 15th Military District, that he had investigated Lawless and Jackson and found nothing that would warrant suspicion. "To confirm my opinion of them," he continued, "I wrote to the Chief of Police of the city [Rouen] who had the means of surveillance unavailable to me . . . , and he responded that there were no unfavorable comments on them in their files. Their conduct is prudent, they seldom go out, and they only have visitors permitted by their situation."[78] Furthermore, on 16 December, Destabemath reported some nonincriminating information directly to the minister of war.[79] Nevertheless, and despite several appeals from Lawless and Jackson on 18 December to allow them to serve in the "Royal Foreign Regiment at Toulon,[80] Clarke went forward with their expulsion from France.

9

Conclusion

The Irish Legion was the product of the needs of General Bonaparte and the Irish exiles on the Continent. Bonaparte wished to end the conflict with England by invading and conquering the island kingdom. As a part of that plan he wanted to send a smaller force to Ireland as a distraction from the English invasion and thus tie down English regiments in the west that otherwise could be used to face his principal force, which would then cross the Channel. However, unless such an expedition to Ireland was supported by Irishmen, it might fare no better than those of 1796 and 1798. More specifically, it was the plan of the then-First Consul to train Irishmen in the French army to be officers so that they would be able in turn to train and lead Irish volunteers once the French had landed in Ireland. The Irish who would accompany the expedition should have political influence in Ireland and military training. Bonaparte wanted native-born Irishmen, or the sons of Irishmen, who were of good families and had social and political status and influence in Ireland. This tended to be equated with men who had been members of the Society of United Irishmen, and thus still had political ties and presumably that desired influence, in their native land. There is little indication that Bonaparte cared at all about the fate of Ireland, despite the lip-service he gave to independence and republicanism. Certainly he was not himself a republican and, therefore, did not share the political aspirations and ambitions of the United Irishmen to establish an Irish republic. Nevertheless, an Irish expedition, even if it resulted in an independent republic, would have served the purpose of harming England. Finally, even if the Irish expedition should be a failure and the Anglo-Irish forces would maintain their control, it would have tied down military forces that could otherwise have been used against the main French invasion of England. From Bonaparte's point of view the Irish Legion and its role in the grand strategy for war against England was wise, and had there been an invasion, it would have made a major contribution to the overall French effort.

The creation of the Irish Legion was also advantageous from the point of view of the Irish exiles, as well as for the cause of Irish independence. While it is true that the 1780s and 1790s had produced political organizations and political leaders in Ireland, the Irish people had no serious military organization and few military leaders. This was most obvious in the great rebellion of 1798 and in the brief campaign of General Humbert in the west of Ireland in August of the same year. If Humbert had brought with him trained Irish officers, the hundreds of Irishmen who joined the French might have been of real use to the French commander and perhaps even have changed the outcome of that ill-fated expedition. It was quite clear that the Irish would gain their freedom only on the battlefield. The English would not permit the training of Irish officers, while those who had been trained in the Irish Brigade of the French army were monarchists. Thus Irish nationalists, most of whom were republicans, welcomed the opportunity to join the French army with a commission. They would form the cadre of a future Irish army. Furthermore, some were in financial need in 1803 having fled from Ireland with little more than the clothing on their backs. Others were employed beneath their former station in life in Ireland. Only a small number were living comfortably on income from home or money they had brought with them. What they had in common was a hatred of England and the Anglo-Irish government and a desire to return to their homeland and establish an independent nation. The failure of 1798 had convinced the vast majority of exiles that their aims could be achieved only with French support. Thus the Legion was viewed by both the French and Irish as a solution, or, in the case of Bonaparte, a contribution to a solution, of their respective problems. For Bonaparte it was a small part of a very large and complex plan. For the Irish it was the only game in town.

The Legion was beset by problems from the very beginning. Commissions and rank were given on the basis of political favor and influence rather than military experience or ability. From its inception the Legion was as much a political organization as it was military. Leadership in the persons of Adjutant Commander MacSheehy and *Chef de Bataillon* Blackwell was weak, and when Arthur O'Connor was named general of division, rivalry, quarreling, and dissension tore at the very foundation of the Legion. But it was the cancellation of the long awaited expedition to Ireland in 1805 that marked the real beginning of the transformation of the Irish Legion into a Foreign Legion. Some men resigned their commissions and settled in France or sailed for America. Most had no place to go and little to look forward to as civilians in a foreign land. Still others clung to the hope that

Napoleon would return to his original plan for an invasion of England and Ireland. Thus the great majority of the men of the Legion remained in the French army and gradually became professional soldiers.

For Napoleon the Legion became just another regiment of foreign troops to be used in Spain, Holland, or Germany. For the Irish the French army became their new home. In place of the expedition to Ireland, they sought promotions, reputations, and honors on battlefields from Lisbon to the Oder River. Despite the fact that the foreign legions in the French army tended to be treated as second-class units, the Irish fought bravely and with distinction throughout the Napoleonic wars. They served in the Iberian Peninsula for four years and established an enviable reputation at the siege of Astorga when one of its elite companies made a significant contribution to the capture of the city by storming the breech made in the wall. On the island of Walcheren, in southern Holland, they contributed a battalion that distinguished itself against an overwhelming English force and suffered heavy casualties before the French force surrendered. In 1813 the Irish Regiment, which consisted of two war-strength battalions of 1,700 men, again served with distinction at the Battle of Bautzen and in Silesia, where after heavy losses in lesser engagements with the enemy it was finally destroyed on the banks of the Bober River. The Regiment was reorganized in the winter of 1813–14, but with a dwindling number of Irishmen. Yet those Irishmen remained loyal to France and the Emperor Napoleon until his abdication in April 1814, and when he returned the following year, they gave him their full support.

The transition from Irish republican nationalist to Napoleonic professional soldier took place over a period of years. However, it was never complete. Men like Byrne, Allen, and Lawless did not lose their love of Ireland, nor the hope, never fulfilled, that one day they might return to their native land as a part of a French military expedition. They served well Napoleon and France, but never gave up their dream. Napoleon rewarded them with promotions and decorations, and they were not ungrateful. Some gave their lives, most shed their blood, all contributed to the glory of Napoleon and France. The Legion wrote a proud chapter in Irish military history as the last of the Wild Geese.

Notes

Bibliography

Index

.

Notes

1. Introduction

1. On the Treaty of Amiens and the renewal of hostilities see Jean Thiry, *L'Avenement de Napoléon*, pp. 65–100; and Georges Lefebvre, *Napoleon: From 18 Brumaire to Tilsit 1799–1807*, pp. 110–5; 162–79. The French historian Georges Lefebvre summed it up in the following manner: "The English capitalists learned that the economic struggle would continue, and they became disgusted with a peace which profited them nothing." *Napoleon from 18 Brumaire to Tilisit*, p. 170.

2. On James II and Ireland see J. G. Simms, *Jacobite Ireland, 1685–91*; and R. H. Murray, *Revolutionary Ireland and its Settlement*.

3. See John Cornelius O'Callaghan, *History of the Irish Brigades in the Service of France*, p. 9.

4. On the formation of the Irish Brigade see O'Callaghan, *History of the Irish Brigades*, pp. 6–33; and Maurice N. Hennessy, *The Wild Geese: The Irish Soldier in Exile*, pp. 19–28.

5. On the Treaty of Limerick see J. G. Simms, *The Treaty of Limerick*; Hennessy, *The Wild Geese*, pp. 16–19; and O'Callaghan, *History of the Irish Brigades*, pp. 21–32.

6. On the Penal Laws and the Treaty of Limerick see M. Wall, *The Penal Laws, 1690–1760*.

7. On the Irish and the Battle of Fontenoy see Hennessy, *The Wild Geese*, pp. 60–72; and O'Callaghan, *History of the Irish Brigades in the Service of France*, pp. 350–67.

8. See W. S. Murphy, "The Irish Brigade of France at the Siege of Savannah, 1779," *Georgia Historical Society*, vol. 38, no. 4, December 1954, pp. 307–21: and O'Callaghan, *History of the Irish Brigades*, pp. 621–22.

9. Hennessy, *The Wild Geese*, p. 102.

10. Hennessy, *The Wild Geese*, pp. 102–3.

11. On the Penal Code during the eighteenth century see James Camlin Beckett, *The Making of Modern Ireland, 1603–1923*, pp. 151–79.

12. Marianne Elliott, in *Partners in Revolution: The United Irishmen and France*, p. 22, lists the eleven as: Samuel Neilson, Samuel McTier,

William Sinclair, William McCleery, William and Robert Simms, Henry Haslett, William Tennent, Thomas McCabe, Gilbert McIlveen, and John Campbell.

13. See Richard R. Madden, *The United Irishmen, Their Lives and Times*, pp. 585–86.

14. See Madden, *The United Irishmen, Their Lives and Times*, on the formation and early years of the United Irishmen, pp. 216–26.

15. *Life of Theobald Wolfe Tone*, ed. T. W. Tone, vol. 1, pp. 367–68, as quoted in Elliotte, *Partners in Revolution*, p. 23.

16. *Northern Star*, vol. 1, no. 3, as quoted in Elliott, *Partners in Revolution*, p. 23.

17. Madden, *The United Irishmen, Their Lives and Times*, p. 263.

18. See Elliott, *Partners in Revolution*, pp. 108–9.

19. Elliott, *Partners in Revolution*, p. 108.

20. See Madden, *The United Irishmen, Their Lives and Times*, pp. 264–66.

21. See Madden, *The United Irishmen, Their Lives and Times*, p. 282.

22. This lower figure was the estimate of Lord Edward Fitzgerald. See Madden, *The United Irishmen, Their Lives and Times*, p. 284.

23. Elliott, *Partners in Revolution*, p. 52.

24. See Madden, *The United Irishmen, Their Lives and Times*, p. 270.

25. Elliott, *Partners in Revolution*, p. 104.

26. Edouard Desbrière, *Projets et tentatives de débarquement aux Iles Britanniques*, vol. 1, p. 170. Elliott, *Partners in Revolution*, gives the number of men at 14,450 (p. 111).

27. Desbrière, *Projets et tentatives de débarquement aux Iles Britanniques*, vol. 1, pp. 200–201. Elliott gives the figure of 6,450 men, *Partners in Revolution*, p. 113.

28. On the Hoche expedition of 1796 see Desbrière, *Projets et tentatives de débarquement aux Iles Britanniques*, vol. 1, pp. 135–232; and Elliott, *Partners in Revolution*, pp. 85–123.

29. On conditions in Ireland in 1797 see Elliott, *Partners in Revolution*, pp. 124–62; and Madden, *The United Irishmen, Their Lives and Times*, pp. 406–587.

30. See Elliott, *Partners in Revolution*, pp. 165–213.

31. See Thomas Addis Emmet, *Memoir of Thomas Addis Emmet and Robert Emmet with Their Ancestors and Immediate Family*, vol. 1, p. 317.

32. Elliott, *Partners in Revolution*, p. 170.

33. The other members of this executive were William Lawless, John Sheares and Henry Sheares. See Elliott, *Partners in Revolution*, pp. 194–95.

34. On the Kilmainham Treaty see Elliott, *Partners in Revolution*, pp. 208–13; and Charles Hamilton Teeling, *History of the Irish Rebellion of 1798 and Sequel to the History of the Irish Rebellion of 1798*, pp. 352–76.

35. See Desbrière's chapter on Ireland, *Projets et tentatives de débarquement aux Iles Britanniques*, vol. 1, pp. 135–323; and Elliott, *Partners in Revolution*, pp. 163–240.

36. Las Cases, Marie Joseph Emmanuel, comte de, *Le Mémorial de Sainte-Hélène*, vol. 2, p. 335 (ed. 1823), as quoted in W. E. H. Lecky, *A History of Ireland in the Eighteenth Century*, vol. 5, p. 39.

37. Lecky, *A History of Ireland in the Eighteenth Century*, vol. 5, pp. 46–50.

38. On the Irish prisoners see Lecky, *A History of Ireland in the Eighteenth Century*, vol. 5, pp. 63–64 and 99–101.

39. On Morres see Elliott, *Partners in Revolution*, pp. 229 and 261; and Lecky, *A History of Ireland in the Eighteenth Century*, vol. 5, p. 73. He had been an United Irishman leader in Tipperary, and tried to cooperate with Humbert in the summer of 1798. After Humbert's surrender, Morres fled to Hamburg and was living in the American Arms Hotel along with Tandy, Corbet, and Blackwell.

40. On Tandy see Lecky, *A History of Ireland in the Eighteenth Century*, vol. 5, pp. 68–74; and Elliott, *Partners in Revolution*, pp. 260–64.

41. On John Hardy see Miles Byrne, *Memoirs of Miles Byrne*, vol. 2, pp. 16–18.

42. Tone's execution was scheduled for 12 November, but it was postponed on a technicality, and he died before he could be hanged. He had asked for a military death, that is to be executed by a firing squad. When this request had been denied, he cut his throat with a knife that he had concealed. On Tone see Frank MacDermot, *Theobald Wolfe Tone and His Times*, pp. 247–79; and Lecky, *A History of Ireland in the Eighteenth Century*, vol. 5, pp. 74–82.

43. See Madden, *The United Irishmen*, p. 272.

44. Lecky, *A History of Ireland in the Eighteenth Century*, vol. 5, p. 98. Lecky footnotes this statement as follows: "Cornwallis Correspondence, ii, 425, 430; Castlereagh Correspondence, i, 394–96."

45. Miles Byrne, in his *Memoirs of Miles Byrne*, states that the Irish prisoners were "sold" to the Prussians. See vol. 3, pp. 163–64. Lecky writes that on September 8, 1799, 318 Irish prisoners were sent to Prussia, but he says that they went voluntarily, and at the request of the Prussian government, vol. 5, p. 103.

46. See Lecky, *A History of Ireland in the Eighteenth Century*, vol. 5, p. 100; and Elliott, *Partners in Revolution*, p. 251.

47. See Emmet, *Memoir of Thomas Addis Emmet and Robert Emmet*, vol. 1, pp. 317–19, and 327.

48. Emmet, *Memoir of Thomas Addis Emmet and Robert Emmet*, vol. 1, p. 336.

49. Emmet, *Memoir of Thomas Addis Emmet and Robert Emmet*, vol. 1, p. 336.

50. On the relations between Emmet and O'Connor see: Emmet, *Memoir of Thomas Addis Emmet and Robert Emmet*, vol. 1, pp. 318–19; and Elliott, *Partners in Revolution*, pp. 323–36.

51. See Emmet, *Memoir of Thomas Addis Emmet and Robert Emmet*, p. 328.

52. Emmet, *Memoir of Thomas Addis Emmet and Robert Emmet*, pp. 327–28.

53. See Byrne, *Memoirs of Miles Byrne*, vol. 3, pp. 5–6; and Emmet, *Memoir of Thomas Addis Emmet and Robert Emmet*, pp. 330–40.

2. The Formation of the Irish Legion

1. On the life of Arthur O'Connor see Madden, *The United Irishmen: Their Lives and Times*, vol. 4, pp. 3–171.

2. Lord Edward Fitzgerald and Bartholomew Teeling were dead, Robert Simms was living in Belfast, and Richard McCormick, MacNeven, T. A. Emmet, Joseph Orr, and Alexander Lowry were in exile. O'Connor himself was the ninth member of the executive committee (the directory).

3. On the projected invasion of England and Ireland in 1803–4 see Desbrière, *Projects et tentatives de débarquement aux Iles Britanniques*, vol. 3, pp. 571–618.

4. On the conversation between Emmet and Dalton see Emmet's "Diary" in Emmet, *Memoir of Thomas Addis Emmet and Robert Emmet*, vol. 1, pp. 340–42. Emmet kept a diary of his negotiations with the French while he was in Paris in 1803–4. The first entry, which detailed his interview with Dalton, was dated 30 May. The last entry was on 10 March of the following year. See Emmet, vol. 1, pp. 340–80.

5. Pat Gallagher was actually Lord Edward's bodyguard and close associate until the latter was killed. On Fitzgerald see R. R. Madden, *The United Irishmen, Their Lives and Times*, vol. 4, pp. 172–298, and vol. 5, pp. 3–161.

6. See Emmet's "Diary," *Memoir*, vol. 1, p. 342.

7. On Harty see Richard Hayes, *Biographical Dictionary of Irishmen in France*, pp. 113–15.

8. Emmet's, "Diary," *Memoir*, vol. 1, p. 349.

9. See Harty to MacGuire, 8 July 1803, Service Historique de l'Etat-Major de l'Armée, Château de Vincennes (hereafter referred to as Arch. Guerre) X^h 16C.

10. See Emmet's "Diary," *Memoir*, vol. 1, pp. 350 and 352.

11. On Corbet's conversations with Emmet and the conversation between Emmet and O'Connor on 18 September 1803, see Emmet's "Diary," *Memoir*, vol. 1, pp. 359, 365, and 370.

12. See Emmet's "Diary," *Memoir*, vol. 1, pp. 344 and 379.

13. Emmet's, "Diary," *Memoir*, vol. 1, p. 370.

14. Miles Byrne, *Memoirs*, vol. 3, pp. 11–12.

15. See Desbrière, *Projects et tentatives de débarquement aux Iles Britanniques*, vol. 3, pp. 339–446; and Napoleon to Admiral Denis Decres, minister of the Navy, 16 August 1803, *Correspondance de Napoléon Ier*, no. 7009, vol. 8, pp. 585–86.

16. See Emmet's "Diary," *Memoir*, vol. 1, p. 357.

17. See Emmet's "Diary," *Memoir*, vol. 1, p. 375.

18. See the memoranda written by Harty and Dalton recommending individual Irishmen for commission in the Legion in Arch. Guerre, dated vendémiaire (September–October), an 12, Arch. Guerre, X^h 14.

19. Emmet's "Diary," *Memoir*, vol. 1, p. 373.

20. See Emmet's "Diary," *Memoir*, vol. 1, p. 379.

21. See Emmet's "Diary," *Memoir*, vol. 1, p. 371.

22. On the so-called Emmet insurrection, see Elliott, *Partners in Revolution*, pp. 302–22.

23. See Emmet's "Diary," *Memoir*, vol. 1, p. 368–69.

24. Emmet's "Diary," *Memoir*, vol. 1 p. 372.

25. See "Order," 23 November 1803, *Corresp. Nap.*, no. 7304, vol. 9, p. 129; and Emmet's "Diary," *Memoir*, p. 374.

26. Emmet's "Diary," *Memoir*, vol. 1, p. 373.

27. Emmet's "Diary," *Memoir*, vol. 1, pp. 375–76.

28. For Emmet's rather lengthy discussion of the committee see his "Diary," *Memoir*, pp. 375–77.

29. Emmet's "Diary," *Memoir*, vol. 1, p. 379.

30. Emmet's "Diary," *Memoir*, vol. I, p. 360.

31. See the report signed by Adjutant Commander Bernard Mac-Sheehy, dated 17 May 1804, Arch. Guerre, X^h 14.

32. See the multitude of letters and documents signed by MacSheehy in Arch. Guerre, X^h 14 and C^1 2–20,

33. Byrne, *Memoirs*, vol. 3, p. 35.

34. Byrne, *Memoirs*, vol. 3, pp. 25–26.

35. On the conditions of the Irish exiles in Paris see Byrne, *Memoirs*, vol. 3, pp. 6–39.

36. Byrne, *Memoirs*, vol. 3, p. 8.

37. Byrne, *Memoirs*, vol. 3, p. 7.

38. Byrne, *Memoirs*, vol. 3, pp. 7–8.

39. See the service records of the Corbets, Arch. Guerre, X^h 14.

40. See Byrne's *Memoirs* for a lengthy account of the Irish in Paris in the fall of 1803 (vol. 3, pp. 1–29).

41. MacSheehy to Berthier, 24 July 1804, Arch. Guerre, X^h 14.

42. See "Etat Nominatif des Officiers de la Légion," signed General of Brigade Donzelot, 11 October 1804, Arch. Guerre, X^h 14.

43. Byrne, *Memoirs*, vol. 2, pp. 8–9.

44. MacSheehy to Minister of War, 24 July 1804, Arch. Guerre, C^1 15;

"Etat Nominatif des Officiers de la Légion," 11 October 1804, Arch. Guerre, X^h 14; and MacSheehy to Minister of War, 30 July 1804, Arch. Guerre, C^1 15.

45. See the roster of officers of the Legion dated 17 May 1804, and signed by Adjutant Commander MacSheehy, Arch. Guerre, X^h 14; and "Etat Nominatif des Officiers de la Légion," signed by General Donzelot, 11 October 1804, Arch. Guerre, X^h 14.

46. On the men of the Legion before 1803 see Richard Hayes, *Biographical Dictionary of Irishmen in France*; Byrne, *Memoirs*, vol. 3; and the notes on each officer in MacSheehy's list of officers dated 17 March 1804, Arch. Guerre, X^h 14.

47. See Byrne, *Memoirs*, vol. 3, p. 222; and Emmet's "Diary," *Memoir*, vol. 1, p. 374.

48. See Byrne, *Memoirs*, vol. 3, pp. 222–23.

49. On the daily routine, instruction, and life in general at Morlaix, see Byrne, *Memoirs*, vol. 3, pp. 231 and 263–67, and vol. 2, pp. 10–12.

50. See MacSheehy to Minister of War, 5 January 1804, Arch. Guerre, C^1 2.

51. See List of Officers of the Irish Legion, signed MacSheehy, 17 May 1804, Arch. Guerre, X^h 14.

52. Captain Patrick MacSheehy resigned his commission and quit the army in 1805. See Byrne *Memoirs*, vol. 2, pp. 34–35.

53. See MacSheehy to Minister of War, 18 January 1804, Arch. Guerre, C^1 3.

54. See MacSheehy to Minister of War, 18 January 1804, Arch. Guerre, C^1 3.

55. On Irish and English prisoners of war see the correspondence from MacSheehy to Minister of War in the Arch. Guerre dated 11 January 1804 (C^1 2); 18 January 1804; 26 January 1804; 27 January 1804 (C^1 3); and 1 February 1804 (C^1 7).

56. Donzelot to Minister of War, 31 March 1804, Arch. Guerre, C^1 7.

57. "Liste des Capitaines dans la Légion Irlandaise," no date, no signature, Arch. Guerre, C^1 7.

58. On the relationship between MacSheehy and O'Connor in 1804 see MacSheehy's correspondence with the minister of war and General O'Connor during the spring and summer of that year. More specifically: MacSheehy to Minister of War, 17 March 1804 (Arch. Guerre, C^1 7); and MacSheehy to O'Connor, 17 March 1804 (Arch. Guerre, C^1 7). See also Byrne's discussion of their relationship in his *Memoirs*, vol. 3, p. 112.

59. MacSheehy to O'Connor, 17 March 1804, Arch. Guerre, C^1 7.

60. MacSheehy to Minister of War, 17 March 1804, Arch. Guerre, C^1 7.

61. Minister of War to General Augereau, 6 March 1804, Arch. Guerre, C^1 6.

62. Byrne, *Memoirs*, vol. 3, p. 112.

63. Markey to MacSheehy, 28 March 1804, Arch. Guerre, C^1 7.

64. Donzelot to Minister of War, 31 March 1804, Arch. Guerre, C^1 7.

65. See Byrne, *Memoirs*, vol. 2, pp. 12.

66. MacSheehy to the Minister of War, 5 April 1804, Arch. Guerre, C^1 9.

67. Berthier to Augereau, 23 April 1804; and Berthier to MacSheehy, 23 April 1804, Arch. Guerre, C^1 9.

68. Augereau to Minister of War, 24 April 1804, Arch. Guerre, C^1 9.

69. Augereau to Minister of War, 25 May 1804, Arch. Guerre, C^1 9.

70. See "Les Officiers, Sous Officiers et Soldats de la Légion Irlandaise," signed by all of the officers and noncommissioned officers of the Legion, 14 June 1804, Arch. Guerre, C^1 12; "Paroles prononcé par l'adjudant-Commandant MacSheehy à la Tête de la Légion Irlandaise en lui présentant le Drapeau qui lui à été envoyé par le Ministre de la Guerre le 25 prairial, an 12," signed MacSheehy, 14 June 1804, Arch. Guerre, C^1 12; and Byrne, *Memoirs*, vol. 2, p. 12.

71. On 17 May 1804, the Irish Legion had fifty-five officers. See the list of officers, complete with their service records and comments, dated 27 florial, an 12, and signed by MacSheehy (Arch. Guerre, X^h 14). The number of noncommissioned officers and men was most likely less than twenty. By 10 September, when the number of officers had increased to sixty-six, there were only twenty-two noncommissioned officers and men. See General Donzelot's report on his inspection of the Legion on that date (Arch. Guerre, X^h 14).

72. See "Ordre de la Légion Irlandaise," signed MacSheehy, 2 June 1804, Arch. Guerre, C^1 12.

73. MacSheehy to Donzelot, 6 June 1804, Arch. Guerre, C^1 12.

74. MacSheehy to Donzelot, 6 June 1804, Arch. Guerre, C^1 12.

75. Patrick Powell was born in 1774, in County Mayo, Ireland. He arrived in France in 1801 and joined the Irish Legion as a lieutenant on 7 December 1803. See "Etat Nominatif des Officiers de la Légion," Arch. Guerre, X^h 14.

76. *Procès Verbal*, 4 June 1804, Arch. Guerre, C^1 12.

77. O'Meara, Gallagher, and Dowdal to MacSheehy, 6 June 1803, Arch. Guerre, C^1 13.

78. Gibbons, Read, Dupouget, MacKey, and Gibbons to MacSheehy, 6 June 1804, Arch. Guerre, C^1 13.

79. Blackwell to MacSheehy, 6 June 1804, Arch. Guerre, C^1 12.

80. See MacSheehy to Donzelot, 8 June 1804, Arch. Guerre, C^1 12.

81. See Tennent to MacSheehy, 4 June 1804, Arch. Guerre, C^1 12; "Rapport sur ce qui s'est passé à Carhaix, les 14 et 15 prairial, an 12, entre Mm Blackwell, Thomas Corbet, William Corbet, Sweeny, Gallagher et St. Leger, officiers de la Légion Irlandaise," signed General Donzelot, Arch.

Guerre, X[h] 14; and Thomas Corbet to MacSheehy, 5 June 1804, Arch. Guerre, C[1] 12.

82. Blackwell to MacSheehy, 6 June 1804, Arch. Guerre, C[1] 13.

83. MacSheehy to Donzelot, 8 June 1804, Arch. Guerre, C[1] 12; and Tennent to MacSheehy, 8 June 1804, Arch. Guerre, C[1] 12.

84. Tennent to MacSheehy, 8 June 1804, Arch. Guerre, C[1] 12.

85. "Rapport relatif à l'attaque fait par le Capitaine William Corbet sur le Capitaine Gallagher," signed MacSheehy, 8 June 1804, Arch. Guerre, C[1] 12.

86. Tennent to MacSheehy, 4 June 1804 Arch. Guerre, C[1] 12.

87. "Rapport relatif à l'attaque fait par le Captaine William Corbet sur le Capitaine Gallagher," signed MacSheehy, 8 June 1804, Arch. Guerre, C[1] 12.

88. On the clash between William Corbet and Gallagher see "Rapport relatif à l'attaque fait par le Capitaine William Corbet sur le Capitaine Gallagher," signed MacSheehy, 8 June 1804, Arch. Guerre, C[1] 12; and Tennent to MacSheehy, 4 June 1804, Arch. Guerre, C[1] 12.

89. Thomas Corbet to MacSheehy, 5 June 1804, Arch. Guerre, C[1] 12.

90. Thomas Corbet to MacSheehy, 6 June 1804, Arch. Guerre, C[1] 12.

91. Thomas Corbet to MacSheehy, 6 June 1804, Arch. Guerre, C[1] 12.

92. Thomas Corbet to MacSheehy, 8 June 1804, Arch. Guerre, C[1] 12.

93. Sweeny had not been on speaking terms with O'Connor when they were together in Fort George prison, in Scotland. See Emmet, *Memoir*, vol. 1, pp. 335–37.

94. Sweeny to MacSheehy, 5 June 1804, Arch. Guerre, C[1] 13.

95. Sweeny to MacSheehy, 5 June 1804, Arch. Guerre, C[1] 13.

96. On the internal problems of the United Irishmen see Elliott, *Partners in Revolution*, pp. 323–27.

97. When the empire was created in May 1804, Napoleon reestablished the title of "Marshal," which had not been used under the republic. He immediately named sixteen generals to the dignity of "Marshal of the Empire." General Augereau was one of the sixteen so honored.

98. Donzelot to Augereau, 7 June 1804, Arch. Guerre, C[1] 12.

99. Donzelot to Augereau, 9 June 1984, Arch. Guerre, C[1] 12.

100. MacSheehy to Augereau, 11 June 1804, Arch. Guerre, C[1] 12.

101. MacSheehy to Donzelot, 8 June 1804, Arch. Guerre, C[1] 12.

102. MacSheehy had written to Berthier of the events of 3–4 June on the eleventh of the month. See Berthier to MacSheehy, 27 June 1804, Arch. Guerre, C[1] 13.

103. Berthier to Augereau, 27 June 1804, Arch. Guerre, C[1] 13.

104. Berthier to MacSheehy, 27 June 1804, Arch. Guerre, C[1] 13.

105. MacSheehy to Donzelot, 28 June 1804, Arch. Guerre, C[1] 13.

106. MacSheehy to Donzelot, 28 June 1804, Arch. Guerre, C[1] 13.

107. "Raport sur ce qui s'est passé à Carhaix, les 14 et 15 prairial, an 12, entre Mm. Blackwell, Thomas Corbet, William Corbet, Sweeny,

Gallagher, et St. Leger, officiers de la Légion Irelandaise." Signed Donzelot. No date. Arch. Guerre, X^h 14.

108. "Rapport sur ce qui s'est passé à Carhaix." Signed Donzelot. No date. Arch. Guerre, X^h 14.

109. "Rapport sur ce qui s'est passé à Carhaix." Signed Donzelot. No date. Arch. Guerre, X^h 14.

110. "Rapport sur ce qui s'est passé à Carhaix." Signed Donzelot. No date. Arch. Guerre, X^h 14.

111. "Rapport sur ce qui s'est passé à Carhaix." Signed Donzelot. No date. Arch. Guerre, X^h 14.

112. "Rapport sur ce qui s'est passé à Carhaix." Signed Donzelot. No date. Arch. Guerre, X^h 14.

113. "Rapport sur ce qui s'est passé à Carhaix." Signed Donzelot. No date. Arch. Guerre, X^h 14.

114. "Notes Confidentielles," signed Donzelot, no date, Arch. Guerre, X^h 14.

115. Donzelot to Augereau, 23 July 1804, Arch. Guerre, C^1 15.

116. Donzelot to Augereau, 23 July 1804, Arch. Guerre, C^1 15.

117. See "Légion Irlandaise: Etat Nominatif des Officiers de la Légion," signed Donzelot, 11 October 1804, Arch. Guerre, X^{h}14.

118. Harispe to Donzelot, 11 July 1804, Arch. Guerre, C^1 14.

119. "Notes Confidentielles," signed Donzelot (presumed July 1804), Arch. Guerre, X^h 14.

120. Augereau to Berthier, 8 July 1804, Arch. Guerre, C^1 14.

121. O'Connor to Augereau, 14 July 1804, Arch. Guerre, C^1 14.

122. "Notes Confedentielles," signed Donzelot (presumed July 1804), Arch. Guerre, X^h 14.

123. Mayor of Carhaix to MacSheehy, 30 July 1804; and MacSheehy to Berthier, 31 July 1804, Arch. Guerre, C^1 15.

124. See Donzelot to Augereau, July 1804, Arch. Guerre, C^1 15.

125. MacSheehy to Berthier, 31 July 1804, Arch. Guerre, C^1 15.

126. See O'Connor to Augereau 21 August, 1804, Arch. Guerre, C^1 17.

127. MacSheehy to Berthier, 24 July 1804, Arch. Guerre, C^1 15.

128. Berthier to Augereau, 11 August 1804, Arch. Guerre, C^1 16.

129. Donzelot to Augereau, 8 September 1804, Arch. Guerre, C^1 18.

130. O'Connor to Augereau, 21 August 1804, Arch. Guerre, C^1 17.

131. Donzelot to Augereau, 8 September 1804, Arch. Guerre, C^1 18.

132. Berthier to Augereau, 18 September 1804, Arch. Guerre, C^1 19.

133. Donzelot to Augereau, 27 September 1804, Arch. Guerre, C^1 19.

134. Donzelot to Augereau, 8 September 1804, Arch. Guerre, C^1 18.

135. MacNeven's account is contained in the dispatch from Donzelot to Augereau, 27 September 1804, Arch. Guerre, X^h 14.

136. MacNeven's account is contained in the dispatch from Donzelot to Augereau, 27 September 1804, Arch. Guerre, X^h 14.

3. From Irish Patriots to French Soldiers

1. An example of such rumors is found in the letter from Second Lieutenant Patrick MacMahon to Captain Valentin Derry dated 23 July 1804, Arch. Guerre, C^1 16.

2. Emmet withdrew from an active role in Franco-Irish affairs shortly after O'Connor was named lieutenant general. However, he did not leave France for the United States until the fall of 1804.

3. See Sweeny to Minister of War, 11 September 1804, Arch. Guerre, X^h 14; and Byrne, *Memoirs*, vol. 3, p. 25.

4. See Richard Hayes, *Biographical Dictionary of Irishmen in France*, pp. 44–46; and Byrne, *Memoirs*, vol. 3, p. 39.

5. "Rapport fait au Ministre," 13 October 1804, Arch. Guerre, X^h 14.

6. MacSheehy to Augereau, 28 July 1804, Arch. Guerre, C^1 15.

7. See Byrne, *Memoirs*, vol. 2, pp. 32–35.

8. Donzelot to Augereau, 11 October 1804, Arch. Guerre, X^h 14.

9. Byrne, *Memoirs*, vol. 2, p. 13.

10. Byrne, *Memoirs*, vol. 2, p. 13.

11. Byrne, *Memoirs*, vol. 2, p. 14. The archival documents most often spell the Adjutant Major's name "Couasnan," although other spellings may also be found. Byrne's spelling—Caugnan—is found only in his *Memoirs*.

12. Byrne, *Memoirs*, vol. 2, p. 14.

13. There were two second lieutenants in the Legion at that time with the name of Landy. MacSheehy, in his memo, did not give a first name. Thus there is no way of knowing if the Landy mentioned was Michael or Richard.

14. See document signed MacSheehy, no date, Arch. Guerre, C^1 15.

15. Berthier to Augereau, 11 August 1804, Arch. Guerre, C^1 16.

16. MacMahon to Derry, 23 July 1804, Arch. Guerre, C^1 16.

17. Donzelot to Augereau, 11 October 1804, Arch. Guerre, X^h 14.

18. Donzelot to Augereau, 11 October 1804, Arch. Guerre, X^h 14.

19. "Etat Nominatif des Officiers de la Légion," signed Donzelot, 11 October 1804, Arch. Guerre, X^h 14.

20. "Etat Nominatif," signed Donzelot, 11 October 1804, Arch. Guerre, X^h 14.

21. Donzelot to Augereau, 11 October 1804, Arch. Guerre, X^h 14.

22. Donzelot to Augereau, 11 October 1804, Arch. Guerre, X^h 14.

23. See Donzelot to Augereau, 11 October 1804, Arch. Guerre, X^h 14.

24. On the questions of discipline see Donzelot to Augereau, 11 October 1804, Arch. Guerre, X^h 14.

25. "Etat Nominatif," signed Donzelot, 11 October 1804, Arch. Guerre, X^h 14.

26. These two documents are dated 2 and 4 December 1804, and are signed "P. O'Kelly." There is no indication as to whom they were addressed.

But by 5 December they were in the hands of Petrezzoli, and he reproduced one of them for Donzelot in the battalion commanders letter of that date. All of these documents are in Arch. Guerre, X^h 14.

27. Petrezzoli to Donzelot, 4 December 1804, Arch. Guerre, X^h 14.

28. Petrezzoli to Donzelot, 4 December 1804, Arch. Guerre, X^h 14.

29. There is no indication in the documents of the reason or nature of O'Kelly's attacks against Couasnon or Thyroux. See the correspondence in Arch. Guerre, X^h 14.

30. See Petrezzoli to Donzelot, 5 December 1804, Arch. Guerre, X^h 14.

31. See MacSheehy to Minister of War, 24 June 1804, Arch. Guerre, C^1 13; "Opinion du Général de division O'Connor sur le projet d'organisation de la Légion Irlandaise, proposé au Ministre de la Guerre par l'Adjudant Commandant MacSheehy," signed O'Connor, 6 August 1804, Arch. Guerre, C^1 16; and Donzelot to Augereau, 17 September 1804, Arch. Guerre, C^1 17.

32. Donzelot to Minister of War, 21 December 1804, Arch. Guerre, X^h 14.

33. See "Etat Nominatif des Officiers de la Légion", signed Donzelot, 11 October 1804, Arch. Guerre, X^h 14. The number of officers in the Legion constantly changed because of resignations and enlistments that were taking place almost weekly.

34. "Liste des Capitaines dans la Légion Irlandaise," presumed date, Summer 1804, Arch. Guerre, C^1 7. This document includes Thomas Corbet who was killed in September 1804, thus it must predate that event.

35. See Berthier to Augereau, 4 October 1804, Arch. Guerre, C^1 20.

36. Still the best work on Napoleon's projected invasion of the British Isles is Edouard Desbrière's *Projects et tentatives de débarquement aux Iles Britanniques*. See the last two volumes on 1804–5.

37. For a detailed breakdown of Augereau's army corps see "Rapport à l'Empereur," 12 October 1804, Arch. Guerre, C^1 20.

38. Berthier to Augereau, 4 October 1804, Arch. Guerre, C^1 20.

39. See MacSheehy to Minister of War, 20 January 1804, Arch. Guerre, C^1 3; MacSheehy to Minister of War, 28 January 1804, Arch. Guerre, C^1 3; and "Etat Nominatif des Officiers de la Légion," signed Donzelot, 11 October 1804, Arch. Guerre, X^h 14.

40. See Byrne, *Memoirs*, vol. 2, p. 15.

41. See "Etat Nominatif des officiers de la Légion," signed Donzelot, 11 October 1804, Arch. Guerre, X^h 14.

42. Derry to Minister of War, 3 May 1805, Arch. Guerre, X^h 16b.

43. "Rapport fait au ministre le 6 messidor, an 13, M^m Tyrrel, Capitaine, et Morisson, Lieutenant, ex-officiers au bataillon irlandais," Arch. Guerre, X^h 16c; and "Etat Indicatif de Lieux où les officiers ci-après désigné, ou déclaré se retirer," signed Petrezzoli, no date, Arch. Guerre, X^h 14.

44. "Etat Indicatif de Lieux où les officiers ci-après désigné, ou déclaré se retirer," signed Petrezzoli, no date, Arch. Guerre, X^h 14.

45. See "Rapport fait au ministre le 6 messidor, an 13," Arch. Guerre, X^h 16c; Petrezzoli to General Delaborde, 6 November 1804, Arch. Guerre, X^h 16c; and Byrne, *Memoirs*, vol. 3, p. 191.

46. See letter from the prefect of the department of the Côtes-de-Nord to General Delaborde, 31 October 1805, Arch. Guerre, X^h 16c.

47. Byrne, *Memoirs*, vol. 3, p. 191.

48. Byrne, *Memoirs*, vol. 3, p. 175.

49. See the lists of officers of the Irish Legion, dated 17 May and 11 October 1804, and two lists signed by Adjutant Commander MacSheehy that have no date, in Arch. Guerre, X^h 14.

50. Thomas Markey signed his name Markey-Johnston when he first joined the Legion, but dropped "Johnston" sometime after the end of 1804. He appears on all of the lists of officers and in correspondence as Markey. See the documentation in the Arch. Guerre, X^h 14–17.

51. Markey to Augereau, 25 July 1805, Arch. Guerre, C^1 15.

52. Markey to Augereau, 15 September 1804, Arch. Guerre, C^1 17.

53. Henry de Dillon to Marshal Berthier 24 June, 1804, Arch. Guerre, X^h 16b.

54. Harty to General Desjardin, 12 April 1805, Arch. Guerre, X^h 61c.

55. Dillon to Minister of War, 24 June 1804, Arch. Guerre, X^h 16b.

56. Thomas James to Minister of War, 16 January 1804, Arch. Guerre, X^h 16c.

57. MacSheehy to Minister of War, 8 July 1804, Arch. Guerre, X^h 16c.

58. MacGueken, for whom no first name is given, was an Irish refugee who expressed a desire to serve in the Legion. He was sent by the minister of war to Lesneven as a mere soldier. When he arrived, he refused to serve unless he was given the rank of second lieutenant. As his name does not appear on any of the battalion rosters, it may be assumed that he did not receive the desired rank. See Petrezzoli to Minister of War, 16 October 1805, Arch. Guerre, X^h 16c.

59. Donzelot to Minister of War, 26 August 1804, Arch. Guerre, X^h 16b.

60. "Etat Nominatif des Officiers de la Légion," signed Donzelot, 11 October 1804. Arch. Guerre, X^h 14.

61. "Bataillon Irlandais: Contrôle Nominatif de M.M. les Officiers au bataillon avec les notes du Commandant du Corps sur leur Instruction, leur Moralité et les langues que chacun d'eux parle," signed Petrezzoli, 9 December 1807, Arch. Guerre, X^h 14.

62. See Byrne on John Gibbon, *Memoirs*, vol. 3, pp. 58–59.

63. MacSheehy to Minister of War, 30 April 1804, Arch. Guerre, X^h 16c.

64. "Etat Nominatif des Officiers de la Légion," signed Donzelot, 11 October 1804, Arch. Guerre, X^h 14.

65. See Augereau to Minister of War, 11 December 1804; "Rapport Fait au Ministre," 6 October 1804; and MacCarthy to Minister of War, 10 December 1804, Arch. Guerre, X^h 16c.

66. Minister of War to MacSheehy, 16 March 1804, Arch. Guerre, X^h 16c.

67. See Burgh to Emperor, no date; Burgh to Minister of War, no date; and the Council of Administration of the Irish Legion to Minister of War, 2 December 1804, Arch. Guerre, X^h 16b.

68. See Byrne, *Memoirs*, vol. 2, pp. 17–18.

69. See Laroche to Minister of War, 8 July 1804, Arch. Guerre, X^h 14.

70. Byrne mentions by name eight officers who were ordered to Landernau: William Baker, Jerome Fitzhenry, Patrick MacMahon, Edward Masterson, Paul Murray, Edmond St. Leger, John Ware, and himself. He also indicated that there were others, but he did not give their names. See Byrne, *Memoirs*, vol. 2, pp. 16–18.

71. See "Bureau de l'Infanterie" to Marshal Joachim Murat, governor of Paris, 25 March 1805, Arch. Guerre, X^h 14; Petrezzoli to Minister of War, 27 February 1805, Arch. Guerre, X^h 14; and Byrne, *Memoirs*, vol. 2, p. 12.

72. See Petrezzoli to Minister of War, 27 February 1805; and Minister of War to Marshal Joachim Murat, 25 March 1805, Arch. Guerre, X^h 14.

73. See Minister of War to Murat, 25 March 1805, Arch. Guerre, X^h 14.

74. Byrne, *Memoirs*, vol. 2, pp. 18–19.

75. Byrne, *Memoirs*, vol. 2, p. 20.

76. Byrne, *Memoirs*, vol. 2, p. 19–20.

77. On the controversy over senority between Corbet and Tennent see: William Corbet to Minister of War, no date; Arch. Guerre, X^h 14; "Consul d'Administration du Bataillon Irlandais" to Minister of War, 28 July 1805, Arch. Guerre, X^h 14; General Harty to Minister of War, 29 July 1805, Arch. Guerre, X^h 14; Tennent to Minister of War, 8 August 1805, Arch Guerre, X^h 16d; and "Rapport Fait au Ministre," 31 August 1805, Arch. Guerre, X^h 14.

78. See Harty to Minister of War, 29 July 1805; and "Rapport Fait au Ministre," 31 August 1805, Arch. Guerre, X^h 14.

79. See Harty to Minister of War, 29 July 1805, and "Rapport Fait au Ministre," 31 August 1805, Arch. Guerre, X^h 14.

80. On Villeneuve and the final phase of the naval operations against Britain in 1805, see Desbrière, *Projets et tentatives de débarquement aux Iles Britanniques, 1793–1805*, vol. 5.

81. Joseph Parrott to Minister of War, 4 November 1805, Arch. Guerre, X^h 16d.

82. Lambert to Minister of War, 5 September 1805, Arch. Guerre, X^h 16c. See also Petrezzoli to Minister of War, 5 September 1805, Arch. Guerre, X^h 14.

83. On Lacy's request for a transfer and Petrezzoli's comments see Lacy to Minister of War, 2 September 1805, Arch. Guerre, X^h 16b.

84. On Lacy's defection see Ch. 5, pp. 117–19.

85. See Gillmer to Minister of War, 3 September 1805, Arch. Guerre, X^h 16b.

86. See Dowdall to Minister of War, 2 September 1805, Arch. Guerre, X^h 16b.

87. Petrezzoli to Minister of War, 5 September 1805, Arch. Guerre, X^h 14.

88. See Byrne, *Memoirs*, vol. 2, p. 23. Byrne also names one O'Morin as having made the journey, but the author is unable to find any reference to him in the documents relating to the Irish Legion.

89. See Byrne, *Memoirs*, vol. 2, pp. 22–23.

90. See Byrne, *Memoirs*, vol. 2, pp. 25–29.

91. See "Etat d'Officiers du Bataillon Irlandais," no date, Arch. Guerre, X^h 14; and Lambert to Minister of War, 2 March 1806, Arch. Guerre, X^h 16c.

92. No details are given on the discharge of this French officer. See "Etat d'Officiers du Bataillon Irlandais," no date, Arch. Guerre, X^h 14.

93. See Swanton to Minister of War, no date, presumed to be written about 4 June 1806, Arch. Guerre, X^h 16d. The presumption of the date is based upon a note in the margin of Swanton's letter signed by Petrezzoli and dated 5 June 1806. Such notes, which are found on almost all requests for discharges, are usually dated the day after the letters were written.

94. See "Rapport Fait au Ministre" approved by General Dejean, 13 June 1806, Arch. Guerre, X^h 16d.

95. Gibbons to Minister of War, 7 June 1806, Arch. Guerre, X^h 16b.

96. Petrezzoli to Minister of War, 7 June 1806, Arch. Guerre, X^h 16b.

97. See "Rapport Fait au Ministre", 6 August 1806, Arch. Guerre, X^h 16b.

98. See Byrne, *Memoirs*, vol. 3, pp. 39–47.

99. Markey to Minister of War, 4 April 1806, Arch. Guerre, X^h 16c.

100. See the general correspondence between Petrezzoli and Donzelot and Donzelot's reports to Augereau and the minister of war in 1805–6, Arch. Guerre, X^h 14.

101. Byrne, *Memoirs*, vol. 2, p. 38.

102. A report to the minister of war dated 10 February 1807 gives the strength of the "Irish Battalion" at 1,200 men. See Arch. Guerre, X^h 16b. Byrne, in his *Memoirs*, says that there were "1500 Poles . . . [and] a great number of Irish." See vol. 2, p. 40.

103. Byrne, *Memoirs*, vol. 2, p. 41.

104. Byrne, *Memoirs*, vol. 2, pp. 44–45.

105. See "Rapport Fait au Ministre," 10 February 1807, Arch. Guerre, X^h 16b.

106. See Burgess to Minister of War, 7 February 1807, Arch. Guerre, X^h 16b; Parrott to Minister of War, 7 February 1807, Arch. Guerre, X^h 16d; and Murray to Minister of War, 8 February 1807, Arch. Guerre, X^h 16c.

107. Burgess to Minister of War, 7 January 1807, Arch. Guerre, X^h 16b.

108. See "Rapport Fait au Ministre," 10 February 1807, Arch. Guerre, X^h 16b.

109. "Rapport Fait au Ministre," 10 February 1807, Arch. Guerre, X^h 16b.

110. On 23 April 1807, Lawless wrote to the minister of war: "It has been three months since I wrote to you . . . the object of which was to obtain permission to retire from the service." Lawless to Minister of War, Arch. Guerre, Dossier Lawless, No. 1804.

111. "Rapport Fait au Ministre," from the Bureau of the Infantry, 10 February 1807, Arch. Guerre, X^h 16b.

112. Petrezzoli to Minister of War, 7 April 1807, and Petrezzoli to Minister of War, 13 April 1807, Arch. Guerre, X^h 16c. See also "Rapport Fait au Ministre," 10 February, 1807 Arch. Guerre, X^h 16b.

113. Petrezzoli to Minister of War, 7 April 1807, Arch. Guerre, X^h 16c.

114. Petrezzoli to Minister of War, 7 April 1807, Arch. Guerre, X^h 16c.

115. Petrezzoli to Minister of War, 7 April 1807, Arch. Guerre, X^h 16c.

116. This rather detailed account of the affair is given in Byrne's *Memoirs*, vol. 2, pp. 49–51. Petrezzoli gives the bare details in his letter to the minister of war 13 April 1807, Arch. Guerre, X^h 16c.

117. Petrezzoli to Minister of War, 13 April 1807, Arch. Guerre, X^h 16c.

118. Petrezzoli to Minister of War, 13 April 1807, Arch. Guerre, X^h 16c.

119. Petrezzoli to Minister of War, 13 April 1807, Arch. Guerre, X^h 16c.

120. Petrezzoli to Minister of War, 13 April 1807, Arch. Guerre, X^h 16c.

121. Petrezzoli to Minister of War, 14 July 1807, Arch. Guerre, X^h 14.

122. See Elliott, *Partners in Revolution*, pp. 323–53.

123. See Richard F. Hayes, *Biographical Dictionary of Irishmen in France*, pp. 33–35.

124. E. Fieffé, *Histoire des troupes étrangères au service de la France*, pp. 184–85.

125. See Byrne, *Memoirs*, vol. 3, pp. 116–34.

4. Walcheren: The Loss of the 1st Battalion

1. Monnet to Minister of War, 9 December 1807, Arch. Guerre, X^h 14.
2. Burgess to Minister of War, 5 December 1807, Arch. Guerre, X^h 16b.
3. Byrne, *Memoirs*, vol. 2, p. 65.
4. Byrne, *Memoirs*, vol. 2, p. 66. "Jesuits' bark" was introduced into Europe by the Jesuit missionaries from South America. It is the bark of a species of cinchona from which quinine is extracted.
5. Monnet to Minister of War, 9 December 1807, Arch. Guerre, X^h 14. The chief of the bureau of inspection, whose signature is not legible, wrote a three-page report summarizing Monnet's inspection to the Minister of War. The document repeats much of this quote. See "Rapport Fait au Ministre," signed Le Chef du Bureau, 30 December, 1807 Arch Guerre, X^h 14.
6. The War Archives contain only two documents from this inspection. The letter from Monnet and a report written by Petrezzoli on the officers of the Legion which is entitled "Bataillon Irlandais: Contrôle nominatif de M. M. les Officiers du Bataillon avec les notes du Commandant du Corps sur leur Instruction, leur Moralité et les Langues que chacun d'eux Parle." Petrezzoli's report is signed and dated 9 December 1807. See Arch. Guerre, X^h 14.
7. "Rapport Fait au Ministre," Le Chef du Bureau d'Inspection (signature not legible), 30 December 1807, Arch. Guerre, X^h 14.
8. See "Bataillon Irlandais: Contrôle nominatif de M. M. les Officiers du Bataillon avec les notes," signed Petrezzoli, 9 December 1807, Arch. Guerre, X^h 14.
9. See "Bataillon Irlandais: Contrôle nominatif de M. M. les Officiers du Bataillon avec les notes," signed Petrezzoli, 9 December 1807, Arch. Guerre, X^h 14.
10. See "Rapport Fait au Ministre," 30 December 1807, Arch. Guerre, X^h 14.
11. Petrezzoli, in a report on the officers of the Legion between 1 May 1807 and 31 August 1808, noted the following of the men assigned to the 2nd Battalion: "Passed to the Army of Spain on 5 November." See "Bataillon Irlandais: Relève des mutations expouve par MM les officiers depuis le 1er Mai 1807, jusqu'au 31 août, 1808," Arch. Guerre X^h 14.
12. See Byrne, *Memoirs*, vol. 2, pp. 62–65.
13. See "Le Ministre d'Etat, Directeur général" to Minister of War, 10 February 1808, Arch. Guerre, X^h 14.
14. On all of these personal changes see "Bataillon Irlandais, . . . 1er mai, 1807, jusqu'au 31 août, 1808," signed Petrezzoli, Arch. Guerre, X^h 14.
15. "Bataillon Irlandais, . . . 1er mai, 1807 jusqu'au 31 août, 1808," signed Petrezzoli, Arch. Guerre, X^h 14, and Byrne, *Memoirs*, vol. 2, p. 74.

16. See "Rapport fait au Ministre," 25 July 1808, Arch. Guerre, X^h 16c.

17. Monnet to Minister of War (also signed by Petrezzoli) 9 October 1808, and "Rapport fait au Ministre," from the Bureau of Infantry, 30 August 1808, Arch. Guerre, X^h 16c.

18. See Monnet to Minister of War, 2 January 1808; and "Rapport fait au Ministre," 23 January 1808, Arch. Guerre, X^h 16c.

19. See General Delahais, director general of reviews, to Minister of State, 17 May 1809; Minister of State to Minister of War, 31 May 1809; Petrezzoli's signed statement on the affair dated 13 May 1809; and extracts from the proceedings of the meeting of the Council of Administration signed by Dowdall and Barker, 6 May 1809, Arch. Guerre, X^h 14.

20. See "Rapport fait au Ministre," 11 November 1809, Arch. Guerre, X^h 16c.

21. See General Delahais' statement to that effect in his letter to the minister of state, 17 May 1809, Arch. Guerre, X^h 14.

22. See "Rapport fait au Ministre," from the Bureau of Infantry, 19 December 1808, Arch. Guerre, X^h 14.

23. See Devereux, Reilly, and Brangan to Minister of War, no date, Arch. Guerre, X^h 14.

24. Minister of War to the commanding general of the army at Brest, 11 May 1809, Arch. Guerre, X^h 15. On the reorganization of the Irish Legion into a regiment see Chief of the 4th Military Division to M. Tabarie, chief of the 2nd Military Division, 3 May 1809, Arch. Guerre, X^h 14.

25. See "Régiment Irlandais—1er Bataillon: Etat nominatif . . . de juin, 1809," signed Petrezzoli, 1 July 1809, Arch. Guerre, X^h 14.

26. On Lipinski and Drimbinski see the following correspondence: Lipinski, "Mémoire," 25 April 1807, Arch. Guerre, X^h 16c; Drimbinski to General St. Cyr, 25 April 1807, Arch. Guerre, X^h 16b; Minister of War to Chief of Staff of the Army of the Coast of Boulogne, 13 May 1807; and the list of officers of the "Bataillon Irlandais" between 1 May 1807 and 31 August 1808, signed Petrezzoli, Arch. Guerre, X^h 14.

27. See the "Etat nominatif," signed Petrezzoli, 1 July 1809, Arch. Guerre, X^h 14.

28. See "Etat nominatif," signed Petrezzoli, March 1809, Arch. Guerre, X^h 14.

29. Chief of the 4th Military Division to General Tabarie, 3 May 1809, Arch. Guerre, X^h 14.

30. Chief of the 4th Military Division to General Tabarie, 3 May 1809, Arch. Guerre, X^h 14.

31. See "Etat nominatif," signed Petrezzoli, March 1809, Arch. Guerre, X^h 14.

32. See "Etat nominatif," signed Petrezzoli, 1 July 1809, Arch. Guerre, X^h 14.

33. See "Tableau de la situation des troupes que composaient la Garri-

son de Flessingue au 30 juillet, 1809," Arch. Guerre, C² 102. The actual figures given are 430 soldiers plus 39 in the hospital. But the table does not indicate how many of the sick were officers. Presumably most of the 39 were soldiers.

34. See O'Meara to Minister of War, 1 August 1809, Arch. Guerre, X^h 15; and "Rapport fait au Ministre," 15 May 1809, Arch. Guerre, X^h 14.

35. "Tableau de la situation des troupes qui composaient la Garrison de Flessingue au 30 July, et renforts que ont été dirigé sur cette Place jusqu'au 6 août inclusivement," Arch. Guerre, C² 102. The 349 men break down as follows: 130 Cannoneers, Coast Guard Company; 67 Cannoneers, Veterans, 8th Company; 100 men of the Regiment, Foot Artillery; and 52 men of the 6th Veteran Regiment, 2nd Battalion, 1st and 2nd Companies.

36. On the Scheldt expedition see Gordon C. Bond, *The Grand Expedition: The British Invasion of Holland in 1809.*

37. On English strategy and the failure to land on Cadsand see Bond, *The Grand Expedition*, pp. 53–80.

38. See page 1 of Pierre Jacque Osten's twenty-eight page "Rapport Fait par le Général de Brigade Osten à son Excelence Monseigneur la Ministre," Paris, 30 August, 1810, Arch. Guerre, C² 103. This report was written after Osten's return from England where he had been a prisoner of war since the surrender of Flushing. This manuscript is hereafter cited as "Osten's Report."

39. "Osten's Report," p. 2, Arch. Guerre, C² 103.

40. "Osten's Report," p. 2, Arch. Guerre, C² 103. For a detailed account of the movements of the English see the account of John Pitt, Earl of Chatham, "Journal of the Army," in the Chatham Papers, Public Record Office, 30/8/260; and Bond, *The Grand Expedition*, p. 53–57.

41. "Osten's Report," p. 3, Arch. Guerre, C² 103.

42. "Osten's Report," p. 4, Arch. Guerre, C² 103.

43. "Osten's Report," p. 4, Arch. Guerre, C² 103.

44. "Osten's Report," p. 4, Arch. Guerre, C² 103.

45. See "Tableau de la situation des troupes qui composaient la Garrison de Flessingue au 30 juillet," Arch. Guerre, C² 102.

46. See "Osten's Report," pp. 4 and 5, Arch. Guerre, C² 103.

47. See "Osten's Report," pp. 5–6, Arch. Guerre, C² 103; Chatham's "Journal of the Army," pp. 2–6, Public Record Office, 30/8/260; Bond, *The Grand Expedition*, pp. 54–59; and Lawless to Minister of War, 13 November 1809, p. 2, Arch. Guerre, X^h 15.

48. See "Osten's Report," p. 6, Arch. Guerre, C² 103; and Bond, *The Grand Expedition*, p. 56.

49. "Osten's Report," p. 6, Arch. Guerre, C² 103.

50. Lawless to Minister of War, 13 November 1809, Arch. Guerre, X^h 15.

51. "Osten's Report," p. 7, Arch. Guerre, C² 103.

52. "Osten's Report," pp. 7–8, Arch. Guerre, C^2 103.

53. Bond gives this figure in *The Grand Expediton* (p. 59) as well as a detailed breakdown of "The British Army sent to the Scheldt in 1809" (pp. 167–71).

54. See Bond, *The Grand Expedition*, p. 60.

55. "Osten's Report," p. 8, Arch. Guerre, C^2 103.

56. See Bond, *The Grand Expedition*, p. 64; and "Osten's Report," p. 10, Arch. Guerre, C^2 103.

57. "Tableau de la situation des troupes que composaient la Garrison de Flessingue au 30 juillet, 1809, et renforte que ont été dirigé sur cette Place jusqu'au 6 août inclusivement," Arch. Guerre, C^2 102.

58. Lawless to Minister of War, 13 November 1809, p. 1, Arch. Guerre, X^h 15.

59. Lawless to Minister of War, 13 November 1809, p. 2, Arch. Guerre, X^h 15.

60. Lawless to Minister of War, 13 November 1809, pp. 1–2, Arch. Guerre, X^h 15.

61. Lawless to Minister of War, 13 November 1809, p. 2, Arch. Guerre, X^h 15.

62. The names, in addition to O'Rielly and Gillmer, mentioned in his report of outstanding service on 1 August were: First Sergeant Goodchild, Sergeants Foster and Koepinski; Corporals Kepher, Smith, Kent, Barrington, Hood, and Norton. A second first sergeant was mentioned but the name is illegible. See Lawless to Minister of War, 13 November 1809, pp. 2–4, Arch. Guerre, X^h 15.

63. Lawless to Minister of War, 13 November 1809, p. 4, Arch. Guerre, X^h 15.

64. Bond, *The Grand Expedition*, p. 80.

65. See "Osten's Report," pp. 14–18, Arch. Guerre, C^2 103.

66. "I have given him [Monnet] the order," Napoleon wrote to General Clarke from Schonbrunn on 6 August 1809, "which you will repeat, to cut the dikes if that be necessary." *Corresp. Nap.*, vol. 19, p. 365.

67. See Bond, *The Grand Expedition*, pp. 98–99.

68. "Osten's Report," p. 21, Arch. Guerre, C^2 103. Gordon C. Bond has translated pages 11 to 26 of "Osten's Report," and together with an introduction and notes published "The Siege of Flushing" in *The Irish Sword*, vol. 11, no. 43, Winter 1973, pp. 118–28 (Hereafter referred to as Bond, "The Siege of Flushing"). This quote is from page 122 of Bond's article.

69. "Osten's Report," pp. 21–22, Arch. Guerre, C^2 103; and Bond, "The Siege of Flushing," pp. 122–23.

70. "Osten's Report," p. 22, Arch. Guerre, C^2 103; and Bond, "The Siege of Flushing," p. 120.

71. "Osten's Report," p. 22, Arch. Guerre, C^2 103; Bond, "The Siege

of Flushing," p. 123; and Lawless to Minister of War, 13 November 1809, p. 5, Arch. Guerre, X^h 15.

72. Lawless to Minister of War, 13 November 1809, p. 5, Arch. Guerre, X^h 15.

73. "Osten's Report," pp. 24–25, Arch. Guerre, C^2 103; and Bond, "The Siege of Flushing," p. 124.

74. See Colonel William Fyers, "Journal of the Siege of Flushing, 1809," *Journal of the Society for Army Historical Research*, vol. 13, 1934, p. 157; "Osten's Report," p. 24, Arch. Guerre, C^2 103; and Bond, "The Siege of Flushing," p. 124. Colonel Fyers commanded the English engineers during the siege.

75. See Lawless to Minister of War, 13 November 1809, pp. 6–7, Arch. Guerre, X^h 15.

76. See Lawless to Minister of War, 13 November 1809, pp. 7–8, Arch. Guerre, X^h 15; and Byrne, *Memoirs*, vol. 2, p. 87. Byrne states in his *Memoirs* (vol. 3, p. 236) that Lawless was also promoted to the rank of lieutenant colonel upon his return from Flushing. However, his service record, dated 24 June 1816, shows only that he received the rank of *chef de bataillon* on 10 July 1809, major on 18 February 1810, and colonel on 8 February 1812. See "Dossier Lawless," GB 2ème Serie, 1840, Arch. Guerre.

77. Byrne, *Memoirs*, vol. 2, p. 88.

78. See Byrne, *Memoirs*, vol. 3, p. 181.

79. See the note entitled "Irish Regiment," no signature, dated 1 May 1810, attached to Lawless' letter to the minister of war, dated 13 November 1809, Arch. Guerre, X^h 15; and Byrne, *Memoirs*, vol. 2, pp. 87–88.

80. Lawless to Minister of War, 13 November 1809, p. 5, Arch. Guerre, X^h 15.

81. See the memorandum to the minister of war, dated 22 November 1809, Arch. Guerre, X^h 16c.

82. On Koslowski at Flushing, as a prisoner of war, and his return to France, as well as his entire service record, see "Rapport Fait au Ministre," 11 November 1809, and the memorandum to the minister of war, dated 22 November 1809, Arch. Guerre, X^h 16c.

83. When Ryan arrived at Calais, he was questioned by the local authorities. A full account of his captivity and escape are found in a copy of the police interrogation dated 21 May 1812, Arch. Guerre, X^h 16d.

84. See "Projet de Classement de M.M. les Lieutenants du Régiment Irlandais par rang d'anciennete de Brevets et d'arrivée au Corps," no date (post 1 January 1811), Arch. Guerre, X^h 15.

85. Byrne, *Memoirs*, vol. 3, p. 59.

86. See "Etat nominatif de MM les Officers du l^{er} Bataillon du Régiment Irlandais, . . . de Juin 1809," signed Petrezzoli, 1 July 1809, Arch. Guerre, X^h 14.

87. "Etat nominatif de MM les Officers du ler Bataillon du Régiment Irlandais, . . . de Juin 1809," signed Petrezzoli, 1 July 1809, Arch. Guerre, X^h 14.

88. See Byrne, *Memoirs*, vol. 3, p. 71.

89. Byrne, *Memoirs*, vol. 3, p. 71.

90. Byrne, *Memoirs*, vol. 3, p. 72.

91. On recruiting in the summer of 1809, see O'Meara to Minister of War, 1 August 1809, Arch. Guerre, X^h 15.

92. See Commander of the 4th (Military) Division to Minister of War, 13 September 1809, Arch. Guerre, X^h 15.

93. See "Rapport Fait au Ministre," 15 May 1809; and "Régiment Irlandais, 4e Bataillon: Mémoire de proposition aux Place des officiers au dit Bataillon," signed O'Meara, 16 October 1809, Arch. Guerre, X^h 14.

94. See O'Meara to Minister of War, 15 November 1809, Arch. Guerre, X^h 15.

95. "Rapport Fait au Ministre," 15 May 1809, Arch. Guerre, X^h 14.

96. See Brown and Hamilton to Minister of War, 27 July 1809; General François Roguet, chief of the 3rd Division to Minister of War, 29 July 1809; and Roguet to Minister of War, 16 September 1809, Arch. Guerre, X^h 15.

97. Roguet to Minister of War, 16 September 1809, Arch. Guerre, X^h 15.

98. See "Rapport Fait au Ministre," 15 May 1809, Arch. Guerre, X^h 14.

99. See "Rapport Fait au Ministre," 28 August 1809, Arch. Guerre, X^h 16b.

100. See "Mémoire de proposition au Place d'officiers au dit Bataillon," signed O'Meara, 16 October 1809; and "Rapport Fait au Ministre," 6 November 1809, Arch. Guerre, X^h 14.

101. See "Rapport Fait au Ministre," 6 November 1809, Arch. Guerre, X^h 14.

102. See "Mémoire de proposition aux Place d'officiers au dit Bataillon," signed O'Meara, 16 October 1809; and "Rapport Fait au Ministre," 6 November 1809, Arch. Guerre, X^h 14.

103. On d'Arbon see d'Arbon to the general of the 4th Military Division, 3 October 1809; Minister of War to d'Arbin, 8 November, 1809; d'Arbin to Minister of War, 14 November 1809; and Commander of the 4th Division to Minister of War, 25 November, 1809, Arch. Guerre, X^h 16b.

104. Chef de la 4e Division (the Bureau of Inspection) to Général le Vicomte Tabarie, Chef de la 2e Division, 10 August 1809, Arch. Guerre, X^h 14.

105. On the projected strength of the Battalion see "Rapport Fait au Ministre," 21 June 1809, Arch. Guerre, X^h 14. On Napoleon's orders see O'Meara to Minister of War, 1 August 1809, Arch. Guerre, X^h 15.

106. Mahony to Minister of War, 3 September 1809 X^h 14.

107. Mahony to Minister of War, 3 September 1809, X^h 14.

108. "Rapport Fait au Ministre," no signature, 18 October 1809, Arch. Guerre, X^h 14.

109. "Rapport Fait au Ministre," no signature, 18 October 1809, Arch. Guerre, X^h 14; Minister of War to Mahony, 25 October 1809, Arch. Guerre, X^h 15; and Minister of War to Mahony, 9 November 1809, Arch. Guerre, X^h 14; Duc de Valmy (Marshal Kellermann) to Minister of War, 9 October 1809, Arch. Guerre, X^h 14.

110. "Rapport Fait au Ministre," 19 October 1809, Arch. Guerre, X^h 14.

111. Chef de la 3^e Division (General François Roguet) to General Tabarie, Chef de la 2^e Division, 30 October 1809, Arch. Guerre, X^h 14.

112. See Chef de la 3^e Division (General Roguet) to General Tabarie, Chef de la 2^e Division, 30 October 1809, Arch. Guerre, X^h 14; O'Meara to Minister of War, 31 December 1809, Arch. Guerre, X^h 15; and Minister of War to Mahony, 9 November 1809, Arch. Guerre, X^h 14.

113. See O'Meara to Minister of War, 15 November 1809, Arch. Guerre, X^h 15.

114. See Chef de la 4^e Division to General Tabarie, 10 August 1809, Arch. Guerre, X^h 14.

115. Chef de la 4^e Division to General Tabarie, 11 October 1809, Arch. Guerre, X^h 15.

116. O'Meara to Minister of War, 15 November 1809, Arch. Guerre, X^h 15.

117. O'Meara to Minister of War, 15 November 1809, Arch. Guerre, X^h 15.

118. O'Meara to Minister of War, 31 December 1809, Arch. Guerre, X^h 15.

5. The Peninsular Campaigns

1. See Byrne, *Memoirs*, vol. 2, pp. 60–61; Chandler, *Campaigns of Napoleon*, pp. 601–22; and Jean Baptiste Antoine Marcelin, Baron de Marbot, *The Memoirs of Baron de Marbot, Late Lieutenant-General in the French Army*. tr. by Arthur John Butler, (New York: Longmans, Gren, 1913), vol. 1, pp. 244–56.

2. Byrne, *Memoirs*, vol. 2, p. 61.

3. On Lacy see "Etat Nominatif des Officiers de dit Bataillon," signed MacSheehy, 17 May 1804, Arch. Guerre, X^h 14; "Etat Nominatif des Officiers de la Légion [Irlandais]," signed Donzelot, 11 October 1804, Arch. Guerre, X^h 14; and "Notes Sur les Officiers du Bataillon Irlandais," no signature, no date (presumed to be 1807 by virtue of the ages given for the officers), Arch. Guerre, X^h 14.

4. See "Prefet du Department de Finistère" to Minister of War, 23 May 1809, Arch. Guerre, X^h 16c.

5. On Fitzhenry, see "Etat des Officiers proposé par l'Adjudant com-mandant MacSheehy . . . avec les notes . . . sur ces Officiers par le Citoyen Dalton," no date (presumed to be 1804), Arch. Guerre, X^h 14; and Byrne, *Memoirs*, vol. 2, p. 74, and vol. 3, pp. 67–82.

6. See Fitzhenry to Minister of War, 26 November 1808, Arch. Guerre, X^h 14.

7. Fitzhenry to Minister of War, 26 November 1808, Arch. Guerre, X^h 14.

8. See "Contrôle Nominatif des officiers faisant Partie du 2ème Bataillon Irlandais actuellement en Espagne," signed Fitzhenry, cover letter dated 21 March 1809, Arch. Guerre, X^h 14; "Etat Nominatif des Officiers du dit Bataillon," signed Allen, MacGuire, and Fitzhenry, 15 January 1809, Arch. Guerre, X^h 14; and "Etat nominatif des M.M. les Officiers du dit Bataillon classe par Grad et Company à l'époque du 1 Decembre, 1809." signed Fitzhenry, Arch. Guerre, X^h 14.

9. On the Spanish campaign of 1808–9, see José Gómez de Arteche y Moro, *Guerra de la Independencia, Historia Militar de España de 1808–1814*, 14 vols.; Sir Charles W. C. Oman, *A History of the Penensular War*, 7 vols.

10. See Byrne, *Memoirs*, vol. 2, p. 75.

11. Byrne, *Memoirs*, vol. 2, pp. 77–78.

12. Byrne, *Memoirs*, vol. 2, p. 78.

13. Byrne, *Memoirs*, vol. 2, pp. 82–83.

14. "Les Officiers du Bataillon Irlandais à son Excellence le Ministre de la Guerre," 5 May 1809, Arch. Guerre, X^h 15.

15. See "Rapport Fait au Ministre," by the Bureau of Infantry, 8 May 1809, Arch. Guerre, X^h 15.

16. See Byrne, *Memoirs*, vol. 2, p. 83.

17. Byrne, *Memoirs*, vol. 2, pp. 91–92.

18. Byrne, *Memoirs*, vol. 2, p. 93.

19. See "Etat nominatif de M.M. les Officiers du dit Bataillon . . . du 1er Décembre, 1809," signed Fitzhenry, Arch. Guerre, X^h 14.

20. See "Etat nominatif de M.M. les Officiers du dit Bataillon . . . du 1er Décembre, 1809," signed Fitzhenry, Arch. Guerre, X^h 14.

21. See Fitzhenry to Minister of War, 20 November 1809, Arch. Guerre, X^h 15; and "Etat nominatif de M.M. les officiers du dit Bataillon . . . du 1er Décembre, 1809," signed Fitzhenry, Arch. Guerre, X^h 14. On requests for promotions see also Fitzhenry to Minister of War, 22 August 1809, Arch. Guerre, X^h 14.

22. Fitzhenry to Minister of War, 20 November 1809, Arch. Guerre, X^h 15.

23. The Battalion lacked two lieutenants and two second lieutenants. The *Etat Major* was complete with an adjutant major (Perry), a pay officer, (Giraund), and two surgeons, (Prevost and Bernhold). See "Etat nominatif

de M.M. les Officiers du dit Bataillon . . . du 1er Décembre, 1809," signed Fitzhenry, Arch. Guerre, X^h 14.

24. Fitzhenry to Minister of War, 1 January 1810, Arch. Guerre, X^h 15.

25. Fitzhenry to Minister of War, 1 January 1810, Arch. Guerre, X^h 15; and Fitzhenry to Minister of War, 25 January 1810, Arch Guerre, X^h 15.

26. 856 men left Landau in late July 1809, and an additional 500 men on 6 December of the same year. See chapter 4, pp. 00–00.

27. The 3rd Battalion of the Irish Regiment is shown as having a total strength of 445 officers and men on 15 July 1810. See "Situation des Troupes" of General Jean Baptiste Solignac's division of the 8th Corps, dated 15 July 1810. Arch. Guerre, C^7 26.

28. "1er Régiment Irlandais: 2e et 3e Bataillons, Etat nominatif . . . au 1er février, 1810," Arch. Guerre, X^h 15.

29. See Jean Jacques Pelet, *The French Campaign in Portugal, 1810–1811*, ed. and trans. by Donald D. Horward, p. 17.

30. See "8e Corps, 2e Division, Situation des Troupes," 15 July 1810, Arch Guerre, C^7 26.

31. See Junot to Solignac, August 1810, "Correspondance du Général Junot, Commandre le 8e Corps d'août, 1810 au 15 Mai, 1811," Arch. Guerre, C^7 19.

32. MacGuire to Division Commandant (Solignac), 23 March 1810, Arch. Guerre, X^h 16c.

33. See MacGuire to Minister of War, 23 March 1810; and MacGuire to Division Commandant (Solignac), 23 March 1810, Arch Guerre, X^h 16c.

34. See Byrne, *Memoirs*, vol. 2, p. 99.

35. Byrne, *Memoirs*, vol. 2, p. 103.

36. This account of the siege of Astorga is taken from Byrne's *Memoirs*, vol. 2, pp. 103–5. Throughout the siege Byrne commanded the 2nd Company of Fitzhenry's Battalion. See also the letter that Colonel O'Meara wrote to the minister of war praising the actions of Allen and Perry, dated 23 April 1810, Arch. Guerre, X^h 15.

37. See Byrne, *Memoirs*, vol. 2, pp. 103–5.

38. See O'Meara to Minister of War, 23 April 1810, Arch. Guerre, X^h 15.

39. See Byrne, *Memoirs*, vol. 2, pp. 105–6.

40. O'Meara to Minister of War, 10 May 1810, Arch. Guerre, X^h 15.

41. "1er Régiment Irlandais, 2e et 3e Bataillons: Etat nominatif de M.M. les Officiers . . . au 1er février, 1810," Arch. Guerre, X^h 15.

42. O'Meara to Minister of War, 10 May 1810, Arch. Guerre, X^h 15.

43. See Byrne, *Memoirs*, vol. 2, p. 97.

44. On Canton, see Commanding General of the 11th Military District to Minister of War, 11 August 1810, Arch. Guerre, X^h 15; and Minister of War to O'Meara, 2 August 1810, Arch. Guerre, X^h 15.

45. See Minister of War to colonel of the Irish Regiment, 2 August 1810, Arch. Guerre, X^h 15.

46. On the sieges of Ciudad Rodrigo and Almeida, see Donald D. Horward, *Napoleon and Iberia: The Twin Sieges of Ciudad Rodrigo and Almeida, 1810*.

47. On the action of 4 July 1810, see Horward, *Napoleon and Iberia*, pp. 159–63. On Captain Ware and these events see Byrne, *Memoirs*, vol. 2, p. 108.

48. See Horward, *Napoleon and Iberia*, pp. 249–58.

49. See Horward, *Napoleon and Iberia*, pp. 249–88; and Jean Jacque Pelet's *The French Campaign in Portugal, 1810–1811*, pp. 88–132.

50. Byrne, *Memoirs*, vol. 2, p. 106; and O'Meara to Minister of War, 24 August 1810, Arch. Guerre, X^h 15.

51. Minister of War to the Prince Vice Connétable, August 1810, Arch. Guerre, X^h 15.

52. See Byrne, *Memoirs*, vol. 2, pp. 106–8.

53. See O'Meara to Minister of War, 24 August 1810, Arch. Guerre, X^h 15.

54. Junot to Masséna, 14 September 1810, "Correspondance Junot," Arch. Guerre, C^7 19.

55. Junot to Masséna, 14 September 1810, "Correspondance Junot," Arch. Guerre, C^7 19.

56. Minister of War to the Prince Vice Connétable, August 1810, Arch. Guerre, X^h 15.

57. Minister of War to the Prince Vice Connétable, August 1810, Arch. Guerre, X^h 15.

58. Junot to Masséna, 14 September 1810, "Correspondance Junot," Arch. Guerre, C^7 19.

59. Junot to Masséna, 14 September 1810, "Corrersondance Junot," Arch. Guerre, C^7 19.

60. See Minister of War to Berthier, August 1810, Arch. Guerre, X^h 15.

61. These figures are given by Horward in his *The Battle of Bussaco*, pp. 39–40.

62. See Horward, *The Battle of Bussaco*, pp. 50–51.

63. See Horward, *The Battle of Bussaco*, pp. 53–55; and Pelet, *The French Campaign in Portugal, 1810–1811*, p. 164.

64. For the best account of the Battle of Bussaco, see Horward's *The Battle of Bussaco*, pp. 65–141.

65. See Horward, *The Battle of Bussaco*, pp. 172–73; Wellington's losses were 1,252 (pp. 174–75).

66. On Wellington and the Caramula Pass see Horward, *The Battle of Bussaco*, pp. 136–41.

67. See Pelet, *The French Campaign in Portugal, 1810–1811*, p. 199.

68. Masséna to Junot, 2 October 1810, Arch. Guerre, C^7 10, as quoted by Horward, in Pelet *The French Campaign in Portugal, 1810–1811*, p. 202, fn. 12.

69. See Pelet, *The French Campaign in Portugal, 1810–1811*, p. 205.

70. Pelet, *The French Campaign in Portugal, 1810–1811*, pp. 207–8, and Horward's footnotes numbered 16, 17, and 18, pp. 207–8; and Jean Baptiste Antoine Marcelin, Baron de Marbot, *The Memoirs of Baron de Marbot*, tr. Arthur John Butler, vol. 2, pp. 431–32.

71. In footnote number 6, page 229, the editor Horward states that "Wellington's disposable force behind the [Torres Vedras] lines included 20,000 Portuguese militia and *ordenanza* and 8,000 Spanish troops occupying the fortifications, while his field army included 35,000 English and 24,500 Portuguese troops by the end of October 1810" (Pelet, *The French Campaign in Portugal, 1810–1811*).

72. Earl of Stanhope, *Notes of Conversations with the Duke of Wellington*, 1889, as quoted in Michael Glover, *The Peninsular War, 1807–1814: A Concise Military History*, p. 141.

73. See Pelet's account of the campaign, *The French Campaign in Portugal*, pp. 277 and 300. *Chef de Bataillon* Jean Jacques Pelet was Masséna's first aide-de-camp on this campaign.

74. See Junot to Masséna, 18 November 1810, "Correspondance Junot," Arch. Guerre, C^7 19.

75. See Junot to Masséna, 14 January 1811; and Junot to Solignac, 27 February 1811, "Correspondance Junot," Arch. Guerre, C^7 19.

76. Junot to Masséna, 14 January 1811, "Correspondance Junot," Arch. Guerre, C^7 19.

77. See "Rapport Fait au Ministre," signed Deschamps, 13 December 1810, Arch. Guerre, X^h 15.

78. "Rapport Fait au Ministre," signed Alexandre [Berthier], 11 February 1811, Arch. Guerre, X^h 15.

79. "Rapport Fait au Ministre," signed Alexandre [Berthier], 11 February 1811, Arch. Guerre, X^h 15.

80. See the report on the 8th Corps of the Army of Portugal, 11 February 1811, Arch. Guerre, C^7 26.

81. See the report dated 1 January 1811, in Arch. Guerre, C^7 26.

82. Byrne, *Memoirs*, vol. 3, p. 79.

83. See Glover, *The Peninsula War, 1807–1814*, p. 144.

84. See Pelet's account of the withdrawal and retreat, *The French Campaign in Portugal, 1810–1811*, pp. 464–80.

85. Byrne, *Memoirs*, vol. 2, p. 111, and vol. 3, p. 78.

86. See Glover, *The Peninsular War, 1807–1814*, p. 145; and Pelet's account in *The French Campaign in Portugal, 1810–1811*, pp. 468–72.

87. On the conflict between Masséna and Ney see the memoirs of Pelet and Marbot. More specifically, on Ney's disobedience and Masséna's

relieving him of his command, see Pelet's account in *The French Campaign in Portugal, 1810–1811*, pp. 490–95, and Marbot, tr. Arthur John Butler, *Memoirs*, vol. 2, pp. 448–55.

88. See Byrne, *Memoirs*, vol. 2, pp. 111–12, and vol. 3, pp. 41–42.

89. See Byrne, *Memoirs*, vol. 3, pp. 41–42.

90. See Byrne, *Memoirs*, vol. 3, pp. 44–48.

91. Byrne, *Memoirs*, vol. 2, p. 113.

92. Byrne, *Memoirs*, vol. 3, pp. 89–90. On the role of Julian Sanchez and his guerrillas and their disruption of French Communication in the spring of 1811, see Sir Charles W. C. Oman, *A History of the Peninsular War*, vol. 4, pp. 201 and 289.

93. See Byrne, *Memoirs*, vol. 3, p. 80.

94. Byrne, *Memoirs*, vol. 3, p. 80–81.

95. Byrne, *Memoirs*, vol. 3, p. 81.

96. See Oman, *A History of the Peninsular War*, vol. 4, p. 199.

97. See Oman, *A History of the Peninsular War*, vol. 4, p. 201.

98. See Byrne, *Memoirs*, vol. 3, pp. 81–82.

99. Byrne, *Memoirs*, vol. 3, p. 82.

100. Lawless to Minister of War, 19 June 1811, Arch. Guerre, X[h] 16b.

101. Minister of War to Lawless, 17 July 1811, Arch. Guerre, X[h] 16b.

102. On the Battle of Fuentes de Onoro see Oman, *A History of the Peninsular War*, vol. 4, pp. 314–41.

103. On Brennier's escape from Almeida see Oman, *A History of the Peninsular War*, vol. 4, pp. 348–62.

104. On Marmont's army in the summer of 1811 see Oman, *A History of the Peninsular War*, vol. 4, pp. 434–60.

105. Byrne, *Memoirs*, vol. 2, p. 134.

106. See Oman on the lifting of the blockade of Ciudad Rodrigo in September 1811, *A History of the Peninsular War*, vol. 4, pp. 542–82.

107. On Dillon see Byrne, *Memoirs*, vol. 3, pp. 140–41.

108. See letter from "Les Membres du Conseil d'Administration du 2e Bataillon du Régiment Irlandais" to Minister of War, 5 November 1811, signed by O'Malley, Jackson, Byrne, and Dowling, Arch. Guerre, X[h] 16c.

109. See Byrne, *Memoirs*, vol. 2, pp. 142–44.

6. Recruitment and Desertion

1. On Tennent see "Notes sur les Officiers du Bataillon Irlandais," no date (presumed to be 1807), Arch. Guerre, X[h] 15; and Byrne, *Memoirs*, vol. 3, pp. 35–36.

2. See: "Conseil d'Administration du 4e Bataillon du Régiment Irelandais" to Minister of War, 15 February 1810, Arch. Guerre, X[h] 15: and "Les Membres du Conseil d'Administration du 4e Bataillon du Régiment Irlandais" to Minister of War, 15 January 1810, Arch. Guerre, X[h] 15.

3. O'Reilly to Minister of War, 20 April 1810, Arch. Guerre, X^h 15.

4. O'Reilly to Minister of War, 20 April 1810, Arch. Guerre, X^h 15.

5. General Delaroche, commandant of the 7th Military Division, to Minister of War, 11 May 1810, Arch. Guerre, X^h 15.

6. Lawless to Minister of War, 2 May 1810, Arch. Guerre, X^h 15.

7. Lawless to Minister of War, 2 May 1810, Arch. Guerre, X^h 15.

8. Lawless to Minister of War, 2 May 1810, Arch. Guerre, X^h 15.

9. "Note no. 9," Lawless to Minister of War, 2 May 1810, Arch. Guerre, X^h 15.

10. See "Les Membres du Conseil d'Administration du 4e Bataillon du Régiment Irlandais" to Minister of War, 22 January 1810, and "Régiment Irlandais, Contrôle nominatif de MM. les Officiers composant les 1er et 4e Bataillons et Dépôt à l'Epoque de 12 août, 1810," signed Lawless, Arch. Guerre, X^h 16b.

11. See Morfie to Minister of War, 22 January 1810, Arch. Guerre, X^h 16c. O'Meara's recommendation is in the form of a note in the margin of this letter, and dated 2 February 1810.

12. See Deschamps to Minister of War, 26 January 1810, Arch. Guerre, X^h 14.

13. See "Rapport Fait au Ministre," signed Deschamps, 9 May 1810, Arch. Guerre X^h 15.

14. "Le Ministre directeur de l'Administration de la Guerre, Ministre d'Etat," to Minister of War, signature not legible, 9 May 1810, and "Chef de la Division de l'Habillement" to Minister of War, 18 May 1810, Arch. Guerre, X^h 15.

15. Lawless to Minister of War, 6 June 1810, Arch. Guerre, X^h 15.

16. Mémoire du proposition . . . d'officiers du 1er Bataillon . . . du 9 Mai dernier [1810] . . . " to Minister of War, signed Lawless; and Lawless to Minister of War, 2 June 1810, Arch. Guerre, X^h 15.

17. See Lawless to Minister of War, 23 May 1810, Arch. Guerre, X^h 15.

18. See Byrne, *Memoirs*, vol. 3, p. 35.

19. See "Rapport Fait au Ministre," from the Bureau of Infantry, signature not legible, 18 June 1810, Arch. Guerre, X^h 15.

20. These figures are taken from "Régiment Irlandais, 4e Bataillon et Dépôt," signed Lawless, 6 June 1810, Arch. Guerre X^h 15.

21. Lawless to Minister of War, 8 June 1810, Arch. Guerre, X^h 15.

22. Lawless to Minister of War, 8 June 1810, Arch. Guerre, X^h 15.

23. "Régiment Irlandais, Contrôle nominatif de MM. les Officiers composant les 1er et 4e Bataillons et Dépôt à l'Epoque de 12 août, 1810," signed Lawless, Arch. Guerre, X^h 16b.

24. Lawless to Minister of War, 8 June 1810, Arch. Guerre, X^h 16b.

25. See Lawless to Minister of War, 8 June 1810, Arch. Guerre, X^h 15.

26. Lawless to Minister of War, 8 June 1810, Arch. Guerre, X^h 15.

27. Desbureaux to Minister of War, 19 June 1810, Arch. Guerre, X^h 15.

28. Desbureaux to Minister of War, 19 June 1810, Arch. Guerre, X^h 15.

29. Desbureaux to Minister of War, 19 June 1810, Arch. Guerre, X^h 15.

30. Deschamps to Minister of War, 14 July 1810, Arch. Guerre, X^h 15.

31. Deschamps to Minister of War, 14 July 1810, Arch. Guerre, X^h 15.

32. See "Conseil d'Administration du 1er Régiment Irlandais" to Minister of War, 27 June 1810, Arch. Guerre, X^h 15.

33. Deschamps to Minister of War, 14 July 1810, Arch. Guerre, X^h 15.

34. See Minister of War to Lawless, 4 July 1810, Arch. Guerre, X^h 15

35. Lawless to Minister of War, 10 July 1810, Arch. Guerre, Dossier Lawless.

36. See the "Rapport Fait au Ministre." signed Deschamps, 20 July 1810, Arch. Guerre, X^h 15; and Minister of War to Lawless, 24 July 1810, Arch. Guerre, X^h 15.

37. See Minister of War to Napoleon (no date) August 1810, Arch. Guerre, X^h 15.

38. See Desbureaux to Minister of War to Napoleon (no date) August 1810, Arch. Guerre. X^h 15.

39. See "Rapport à Sa Majesté l'Empereur et Roi," (no date) August 1810, Arch. Guerre. X^h 15.

40. "Récapitulation" (of the 1st and 4th Battalions of the Irish Regiment), signed Desbureaux, and counter-signed Lawless, 17 June 1810, Arch. Guerre, X^h 15.

41. "Situation Sommaire des Officiers, Sous-officiers et Chasseurs . . . du 12 août, 1810," Arch. Guerre, X^h 15.

42. Lawless to Minister of War, August, 1810 Arch. Guerre, Dossier Lawless.

43. Lawless to Minister of War, 9 August 1810, Arch. Guerre, Dossier Lawless.

44. Markey to Minister of War, 14 August 1810, Arch. Guerre, X^h 15.

45. Markey to Minister of War, 14 August 1810, Arch. Guerre, X^h 15.

46. Markey to Minister of War, 14 August 1810, Arch. Guerre, X^h 15.

47. See Lawless to Minister of War, 6 June 1810, Arch Guerre, X^h 15.

48. James Neill to Minister of War, 17 August 1810, Arch. Guerre, X^h 15.

49. O'Meara to Minister of War, 24 August 1810, Arch. Guerre, X^h 15.

50. Lawless to Minister of War, 13 August 1810, Arch. Guerre, X^h 15.

51. See notation in the margin of Lawless to Minister of War, 13 August. 1810, Arch. Guerre. X^h 15.

52. See "1e Régiment Irlandais, 1e et 4e bataillons," 1 January 1811, Arch. Guerre, X^h 15.

53. See "1ᵉ Régiment Irlandais, 1ᵉ et 4ᵉ bataillons," 1 January 1811, Arch. Guerre, Xʰ 15.

54. See Lawless to Minister of War, 18 January 1811, Arch. Guerre, Xʰ 15.

55. Lawless to Minister of War, 9 March 1811, Arch. Guerre, Xʰ 15.

56. Lawless to Minister of War, 9 March 1811, Arch. Guerre, Xʰ 15.

57. See "Régiment Irlandais, 1ᵉʳ Bataillon et Suite; Contrôle nominatif des Sous-officiers . . . ," 11 April 1811, Arch. Guerre, Xʰ 15.

58. "Régiment Irlandais, 1ᵉʳ et 4ᵉ bataillons. Etat nominatif de MM les Officiers . . . ," 1 January 1811, Arch. Guerre, Xʰ 15.

59. Lawless to Minister of War, 9 April 1811, and note in the margin of the same letter, dated 14 May 1811, Arch. Guerre, Xʰ 16c.

60. "Rapport Fait au Ministre," signed Deschamps, 3 May 1811, Arch. Guerre, Xʰ 15. On Napoleon's consent to recruit Germans and to increase the Regiment to five battalions see Napoleon to General Clarke, 11 March 1811, *Corresp. de Nap.* no. 17456, vol. 21, p. 548.

61. For a list of officers of the Irish Regiment with their rank and nationality see "Etat nominatif des Officiers du Régiment Irlandais . . . ," dated only 1811, Arch. Guerre, Xʰ 15.

62. For a complete listing of the noncommissioned officers of the 1ˢᵗ Battalion with their place of birth, rank, and date they joined the Regiment see "Régiment Irlandais, 1ᵉʳ Bataillon et Suite; Contrôle nominatif des Sous-officiers . . . ," 11 April 1811, Arch. Guerre, Xʰ 15.

63. "Rapport fait au Ministre," signed Deschamps, 3 May 1811, Arch. Guerre, Xʰ 15.

64. "Rapport fait au Ministre," signed Deschamps, 3 May 1811, Arch. Guerre, Xʰ 15.

65. See "Le Commissaire ordonnateur, Chef de la 4ᵉ Division [Bureau de l'Inspection] au Ministre de la Guerre," 14 May 1811, Arch. Guerre, Xʰ 15.

66. On this affair see the following correspondence; Lawless to Minister of War, 21 May 1811, and Deschamps to Minister of War, 3 July 1811, Arch. Guerre, Xʰ 15.

67. The document dated 10 August 1811, and signed by Lawless, is found in Arch. Guerre, Xʰ 15.

68. "Notes sur le Régiment Irlandais," signed Lawless, 10 August 1811, Arch. Guerre, Xʰ 15.

69. "Notes sur le Régiment Irlandais," signed Lawless, 10 August 1811, and "Rapport fait au Ministre," signed Deschamps, 18 September 1811, Arch. Guerre, Xʰ 15.

70. "Notes sur le Régiment Irlandais," signed Lawless, 10 August 1811, Arch. Guerre, Xʰ 15.

71. See Deschamps to Minister of War, 23 October 1811, Arch. Guerre Xʰ 15.

72. See Lawless to Minister of War, not dated, but as it is signed "Colonel" Lawless it was written after 8 February 1812, the date of his promotion to colonel, Arch. Guerre, X^h 16a.

73. Deschamps to Minister of War, 23 October 1811, Arch. Guerre, X^h 15.

74. See "Conseil d'Administration du 3e Régiment Etranger (Irlandais)" to Minister of War, 11 October 1811, Arch. Guerre, X^h 15.

75. "Rapport Fait au Ministre," signed Deschamps, 23 October 1811, Arch. Guerre, X^h 15.

76. Napoleon to General Clarke, duke of Feltre, minister of war, 11 March 1811, *Corresp. de Nap.*, no. 17456, vol. 21, p. 548.

77. See "Le Général O'Connor à Sa Majesté L'Empereur et Roi," 1 September 1811, National Library of Ireland, MS. 10961.

78. See F. W. Ryan's article "A projected Invasion of Ireland in 1811," *The Irish Sword*, pp. 136–37; Napoleon to Clarke, *Corresp. de Nap.*, 4 July 1811, no. 17875, vol. 22, pp. 350–51; and Napoleon to Clarke, 15 August 1811 *Corresp. de Nap.*, no. 18034, vol. 22, p. 477.

79. See "Memorandum of the civil, political and military state of Ireland, drawn up by order of the Emperor Napoleon, and presented to His Majesty on the 20th of November 1811 by Lawless, Lieutenant in the service of France," Archives de Ministère des Affaires Etrangères, Angleterre, Supplement 15, Folio 454–512; and F.W. Ryan, "A Projected Invasion of Ireland in 1811," *The Irish Sword*, pp. 136–41.

80. See Lawless to Minister of War, 21 February 1812; and "Rapport fait au Ministre," from the Bureau de l'Infanterie, Arch. Guerre, X^h 16a

81. Richard F. Hayes, *Biographical Dictionary of Irishmen in France*, p. 153; and J. D. H. Widdess, *The Royal College of Surgeons in Ireland and its Medical School, 1784–1984*, pp. 21–46.

82. See Lawless to Minister of War, 21 January 1812, and "Rapport fait au Ministre," signature not legible, 31 January 1812, Arch Guerre, X^h 16a.

83. Byrne, *Memoirs*, vol. 2, p. 27. Bryne wrote this glowing description of William Lawless thirty years after his death despite the fact that he still felt Lawless had not pressed forward his promotion from captain to *chef de bataillon* in the last year of the empire, and as a result Byrne had to live on the meager pension of a captain for twelve years rather than the more comfortable pension of a superior officer. See *Memoirs*, vol. 2, p. 27–28.

84. See "Rapport fait au Ministre," from the 1st Division (Bureau de la Solde), signed Quillet, 28 October 1811; "Rapport fait au Ministre," from the 2nd Division (Bureau de l'Infanterie) signature not legible, 31 January 1812; Military Police of Paris to Minister of War, 12 February 1812, Arch. Guerre, X^h 16a.

85. See Lawless to Minister of War, 1 February 1812, Arch. Guerre, X^h 16a.

86. Lawless to Minister of War, 2 April 1812, Arch. Guerre, X^h 16a.

87. On the reorganization of the 2nd Battalion see Byrne, *Memoirs*, vol. 2 pp. 146–47, and the table of organization of the 3rd Foreign Regiment, signed Colonel Lawless, no date (presumed summer 1812), Arch. Guerre, X^h 16a.

88. Lawless to Minister of War, 28 February 1812, Arch. Guerre, X^h 16a. On Napoleon's itinerary during his inspection of the coast see Louis Garros, *Quel roman que ma vie! Itinéraire de Napoléon Bonaparte (1769–1821)*, pp. 359–62.

89. See Lawless to Minister of War, 3 June 1812, and Lawless to Minister of War, no date (presumed summer 1812), Arch. Guerre X^h 16a.

90. Lawless to Minister of War, 3 June 1812, Arch. Guerre, X^h 16.

91. See Lawless to Minister of war, 3 June 1812; and Lawless to Minister of War, 2 April 1812, Arch. Guerre, X^h 16a.

92. Parrott to Minister of War, 14 August 1812, Arch. Guerre, X^h 16a.

93. See Lawless' notes on Parrott's letter to the Minister of War, 14 August, 1812 Arch. Guerre, X^h 16d; Lawless' "observation" on the undated document "3e Régiment Etranger, 1er, 2e et 3e bataillions, Situation de M. M. les Officiers de 1, 2, et 3e bataillons du dit Régiment," (presumed summer 1812), Arch. Guerre, X^h 16a; and "3e Régiment Etranger, 3e Bataillon . . . Situation de la Troupe," 11 November 1812, Arch. Guerre, X^h 16a.

94. See "Rapport fait au Ministre," signed Deschamps, 17 June 1812, Arch. Guerre, X^h 16a.

95. See "Rapport fait au Ministre," signed Romeson (of the 5th Division), 10 June 1812, Arch. Guerre, X^h 16a.

96. See "Rapport fait au Ministre," signed Deschamps, 1 July 1812, Arch. Guerre, X^h 16a.

97. See "Rapport fait au Ministre," signature not legible (chief of the Bureau of Infantry), 7 September 1812, Arch. Guerre, X^h 16a.

98. See Minister of War to Lawless, 24 June 1812, Arch. Guerre. X^h 16a.

99. See Byrne, *Memoirs*, vol. 2, p. 147.

100. See Lawless to Minister of War, 30 July 1812, Arch. Guerre, X^h 16d.

101. See "3e Régiment Etranger, 1e Bataillon: Situation sommaire du dit Bataillon à l'Epoque du 11 Novembre an 1812," signed C. Eckhardt (Captain Chrétien); "Situation Générale du 2e Bataillon," signed Dillon, 12 November 1812; and "3e Régiment Etranger, 3e Bataillon, Situation Générale du Bataillon," no signature, 11 November 1812, Arch. Guerre, X^h 16a.

102. See "3e Régiment Etranger, Infanterie Légère, Etat Nominatif des officiers du dit Régiment au 23 Juin, 1812 . . . ," signed Lawless, Arch. Guerre, X^h 16a.

103. See "3e Régiment Etranger, 1e Bataillon: Situation sommaire du dit Bataillon à l'Epoque du 11 Novembre an 1812" signed C. Eckharot; "Situation Générale du 2e Bataillon," Signed Dillon, 12 November 1812; "3e Régiment Etranger 3e Bataillon, Situation Générale du Bataillon," no signature, 11 November 1812; and "3e Régiment Etranger, Infanterie Lég-

ère, Etat Nominatif des officiers du dit Régiment au 23 Juin, 1812 . . . ," signed Lawless, Arch. Guerre, X^h 16a.

104. See "3e Régiment Etranger, 1e Bataillon: Situation sommaire du dit Bataillon à l'Epoque du 11 Novembre an 1812," signed C. Eckharot; "Situation Générale du 2e Bataillon," signed Dillon, 12 November, 1812; "3e Régiment Etranger, 3e Bataillon, Situation Générale du Bataillon," no signature, 11 November 1812; and "3e Régiment Etranger, Infanterie Légère, Etat Nominatif des Officiers du dit Régiment au 23 Juin 1812 . . . ," signed Lawless, Arch. Guerre, X^h 16a.

105. Napoleon to General Clarke, Minister of War, 11 March 1811, *Corresp. de Nap.*, no. 17456, vol. 21, p. 548.

7. The Year of Disaster: 1813

1. See Lawless to Minister of War, 21 January 1813, X^h 16a.
2. See "Etat de situation des Officiers composant le Régiment . . . dans le Mois de Juin, 1813," signed Lawless, 1 June 1813, Arch. Guerre, X^h 16a.
3. See Lawless to Minister of War, 14 January 1813, Arch. Guerre, X^h 16a; Allen to Lawless, 18 January 1813, Arch. Guerre, X^h 16a; Byrne to Lawless, 10 May 1813, Arch. Guerre, X^h 16b; St. Leger to Lawless, 26 June 1813, Arch. Guerre, X^h 16d; and Lawless to Minister of War, 3 June 1813, Arch. Guerre, X^h 16a. Also see the "Etat de situation des Officiers composant le Régiment . . . dans le Mois de Juin, 1813," signed Lawless, 1 June 1813, Arch. Guerre, X^h 16a.
4. Mahony to Minister of War, 3 March 1813, Arch. Guerre, X^h 16a.
5. Byrne, *Memoirs*, vol. 2, p. 155.
6. On the details of the Regiment's march to Magdeburg see Byrne, *Memoirs*, vol. 2, pp. 154–55.
7. On the condition of the Regiment upon its arrival at Magdeburg see Lawless to Minister of War, 2 March 1813, Arch. Guerre, X^h 16a.
8. See Madame Dillon to Minister of War, July 1813, Arch. Guerre, X^h 16a.
9. See Lawless to Minister of War, 12 March 1813, Arch. Guerre, X^h 16a; and Lawless to Minister of War, 14 March 1813, Arch. Guerre, X^h 16a.
10. On the strength of the two armies see Esposito and Elting, *A Military History and Atlas of the Napoleonic Wars*, p. 127; and Chandler, *The Campaigns of Napoleon*, pp. 872–75.
11. For a detailed account of the Irish Regiment between February and May see Byrne, *Memoirs*, vol. 2, pp. 154–63.
12. See Louis Garros, *Quel roman que ma vie: Itinéraire de Napoléon Bonaparte (1769–1821)*, pp. 411–13.
13. On the opening phase of the Campaign of 1813 and the Battle of Lützen see Jean Thiry, *Lützen et Bautzen*, pp. 151–92; and Chandler, *The Campaigns of Napoleon*, pp. 865–88.

14. On the movements of the Regiment in May 1813, see Byrne, *Memoirs*, vol. 2, pp. 162–65.

15. See Thiry, *Lützen et Bautzen*, pp. 219–20; Chandler, *The Campaigns of Napoleon*, pp. 890–91; and Esposito and Elting, *History and Atlas of the Napoleonic Wars*, p. 131.

16. See Thiry, *Lützen et Bautzen*, pp. 220–25; Chandler, *The Campaigns of Napoleon*, pp. 891–96; and Esposito and Elting, *History and Atlas of Napoleonic Wars*, p. 131.

17. On the Battle of Bautzen see Thiry, *Lützen et Bautzen*, pp. 215–41; Chandler, *The Campaigns of Napoleon*, pp. 890–97; Esposito and Elting, *History and Atlas of the Napoleonic Wars*, pp. 130–31; and Byrne, *Memoirs*, vol. 2, pp. 164–67.

18. See Byrne, *Memoirs*, vol. 2, pp. 168–169.

19. See Byrne, *Memoirs*, vol. 2, pp. 172–173.

20. See Byrne, *Memoirs*, vol. 2, pp. 171–173.

21. For a good discussion of why each side was willing and anxious for an armistice see Chandler, *The Campaigns of Napoleon*, pp. 898–903.

22. Byrne, *Memoirs*, vol. 2, pp. 174–75.

23. See "3ème Régiment Etranger: Etat de situation des Officiers composant le Régiment . . . pendant le Mois de Juin, 1813," dated 1 July 1813, signed Lawless, Arch. Guerre, Xʰ 16a.

24. Byrne, *Memoirs*, vol. 2, p. 174.

25. Byrne, *Memoirs*, vol. 2, pp. 175–76.

26. See Esposito and Elting, *History and Atlas of the Napoleonic Wars*, p. 133; and Chandler, *The Campaigns of Napoleon*, p. 910.

27. This seems to be the son of Marshal Jean Baptiste Donatien de Vimeur Rochambeau who died in 1807. Byrne refers to him simply as "General Rochambeau." See Byrne, *Memoirs*, vol. 2, p. 181.

28. See Byrne, *Memoirs*, vol. 2, pp. 180–82.

29. See Byrne, *Memoirs*, vol. 2, pp. 180–83.

30. See "3ème Régiment Etranger, Etat des Officiers existant au Régiment . . . du 18 Octobre, 1813," signed Lawless, 21 October 1813, Arch. Guerre, Xʰ 16a. Byrne also lists twelve officers who had been killed or wounded, but his account is somewhat different from that of Colonel Lawless' report. Byrne writes the following in his *Memoirs*: "Three hundred men were killed and wounded. Four officers were killed, viz: commandant Tennant [*sic*], captain Evans and lieutenants Osmond and MacCauley.— Eight officers were wounded, of whom commandant Ware received three wounds and had his horse wounded under him. The others were captains Parrott and Ecart [Eckhardt], lieutenants O'Brien, Elliott, Brown, Wall and Petters." (See vol. 2, p. 182.) This is one of the few occasions on which Byrne's account differs from the archival records.

31. Byrne, *Memoirs*, vol. 2, p. 182.

32. See Byrne, *Memoirs*, vol. 2, p. 182.

33. See Thiry, *Liepzig*, pp. 68–70; Chandler, *The Campaigns of Napoleon*, pp. 911–12; and Esposito and Elting, *History and Atlas of the Napoleonic Wars*, p. 133.

34. See Byrne, *Memoirs*, vol. 2, pp. 183–84; and Hayes, *Biographical Dictionary of Irishmen in France*, pp. 152–53.

35. See Byrne, *Memoirs*, vol. 2, p. 187.

36. See Thiry, *Leipzig*, pp. 54–59; and Byrne, *Memoirs*, vol. 2, p. 188.

37. Byrne says there were 30,000 enemy troops (vol. 2, pp. 189–90). This number may be high, but Puthod was certainly greatly outnumbered.

38. See Byrne, *Memoirs*, vol. 2, pp. 189–90.

39. See "3ᵉᵐᵉ Régiment Etranger, Etat des Officiers existant au Régiment . . . du 18 Octobre, 1813," signed Lawless, 21 October 1813, Arch. Guerre, Xʰ 16a.

40. Byrne, *Memoirs*, vol. 2, p. 190.

41. "3ᵉᵐᵉ Régiment Etranger, Etat des situation des Officiers composant le Régiment . . . dans le Mois de Juin, 1813," signed Lawless, 1 July 1813, Arch. Guerre, Xʰ 16a.

42. The nine officers listed on 1 July 1813 but not on 18 October 1813 are: Cptains Jacque Perrey, Achille MacGrath, and the surgeon Louis Demon; Lieutenants William Keller and Alexandre Pongis (surgeon's aid); Second lieutenants Pierre Ram, E. Wall, François Malisiux, and Henry Klopstoch.

43. "3ᵉᵐᵉ Régiment Etranger, Etat des Officers existant au Régiment . . . du 18 Octobre, 1813," signed Lawless, 18 October 1813, Arch. Guerre, Xʰ 16a.

44. See "3ᵉ Régiment Etranger, Cadre des 1ᵉʳ et 2ᵉ Bataillons, Contrôle nominatif des sous officiers et soldats composant le cadre au 1 Octobre," signed Ware, 1 October 1813, Arch. Guerre, Xʰ 16a.

45. See Byrne, *Memoirs*, vol. 2, 193–95.

46. See "Rapport fait au Ministre," signed Mahony, 22 November 1813, Arch. Guerre, Xʰ 16a.

47. See "3ᵉ Régiment Etranger, Cadre de 1ᵉʳ et 2ᵉ Batallions, Contrôle nominatif des sous officiers et soldats composant le dit cadre au 1ᵉʳ Octobre, 1813," signed Ware, 1 October 1813, Arch. Guerre, Xʰ 16a.

48. It is possible that some others who had been wounded made their way back, but if they did so, there is no record of proof.

49. See "Minute de la Note au Ministre," from the Bureau of Infantry (2ⁿᵈ Division), signature not legible, no date, Arch. Guerre, Xʰ 16a.

50. See "Rapport fait au Ministre," signed Deschamps, 20 October 1813, Arch. Guerre, Xʰ 16a.

51. See Mahony to Minister of War, 3 November 1813; and "Rapport fait au Ministre," signed Deschamps, 20 October 1813, Arch. Guerre, Xʰ 16a.

52. See Mahony to Minister of War, 3 November 1813, Arch. Guerre, Xʰ 16a.

53. See Lawless to Minister of War, 3 December 1813, Arch. Guerre, X^h 16a; and Byrne, *Memoirs*, vol. 2, p. 198.

54. See "3ème Régiment Etranger, Procès verbal des Militaires d'origine Russe et Allemand sortant du dit Régiment et de nouvelle Composition de ce Corps," 19 December 1813, Arch. Guerre, X^h 16.

55. Keller, Ruff, and Klemps to Colonel Lawless, 15 December 1813, Arch. Guerre, X^h 16a.

56. It is not clear from their letter if they wanted to be discharged from the army or to be sent to a military post close to where their families lived. See Keller, Ruff, and Klemps to Colonel Lawless, 15 December 1813, Arch. Guerre, X^h 16a.

57. Captains Jacque Buhlmann, Chrétien Eckhardt and George Gossling, Assistant Surgeon Christopher Schroder and Second Lieutenant Pierre Ram. See Buhlmann, Eckhardt, Gossling, Schroder, Eckhardt, and Ram to Minister of War, 16 December 1813, Arch. Guerre, X^h 16a.

58. Buhlmann, Eckhardt, Gossling, Schroder, and Ram to Minister of War, 16 December 1813, Arch. Guerre, X^h 16a.

59. Only eight of the ten officers removed from the Regiment at that time can be positively identified: Captains Jacques Buhlmann, Chrétien Eckhardt, and George Gossling; Lieutenants William Keller, Jean Klemps, and G. Ruff, Second Lieutenant Pierre Ram; and Assistant Surgeon Christopher Schroder. See Keller, Ruff and Klemps to Colonel Lawless, 15 December 1813; and Buhlmann, Eckhardt, Gossling, Schroder, and Ram to Minister of War, 16 December 1813, Arch. Guerre, X^h 16a.

60. See "3ème Régiment Etrangers, Procès verbal des Militaires d'origine Russe et Allemand sortant du dit Régiment et de nouvelle Composition de ce Corps," 19 December 1813, Arch. Guerre, X^h 16a.

61. There had never been any Russian officers in the Regiment, but there had been fifteen Russian soldiers when it joined the Grand Army in the spring of 1813. There is no way to determine how many of them survived the Campaign of 1813. See "3e Régiment Etranger, 1e Bataillon: Situation sommaire du dit Bataillon à l'Epoque du 11 Novembre an 1812," signed Captain Chrétien Eckhardt; "Situation Générale du 2e Bataillon," signed Dillon, 12 November 1812; and "3e Régiment Etranger, 3e Bataillon, Situation Générale du Bataillon," no signature, 11 November 1812, Arch. Guerre, X^h 16a.

62. See "Régiment Etranger Procès verbal des Militaires d'origine Russe et Allemand sortant du dit Régiment et de nouvelle Composition de ce Corps," 19 December 1813, Arch. Guerre, X^h 16a.

63. "Rapport fait au Ministre," signed Deschamps, 29 December 1813, Arch. Guerre, X^h 16a.

64. Mahony to Minister of War, 24 December 1813, Arch. Guerre, X^h 16a.

65. See "Rapport fait au Ministre," signed Deschamps, 29 December 1813, X^h 16a.

66. On the reorganization of the Regiment see Mahony to Minister of War, 3 December 1813, Arch. Guerre, X^h 16a.

67. Lebrun to Minister of War, 4 January 1814, Arch. Guerre, X^h 16a.

68. See Byrne, *Memoirs*, vol. 2, pp. 199–202.

69. See "Note pour le Ministre," signed Fanilly, 11 January 1814, Arch. Guerre, X^h 16a.

70. For the names of the twenty officers sent to Paris see "3e Régiment Etranger, Contrôle Nominatif des officiers de ce Régiment qui se rendent à Paris pour y être à la disposition de Son Excellence le Ministre de la Guerre," signed Lebrun, 16 January 1814, Arch. Guerre, X^h 16a.

71. See Lebrun to Minister of War, 4 January 1814, Arch. Guerre, X^h 16a.

72. See Mahony to Minister of War, 8 January 1814, Arch. Guerre, X^h 16a.

73. See "Inspecteur aux rêvues, Chef de la 4e Division du Ministre de la Guerre," (signature not legible; presumed to be General Fanilly) to General Denniée, Chief of the 2nd Bureau, 12 January 1814, Arch. Guerre, X^h 16a.

74. On this rather involved affair see "Note pour le Ministre [de la Guerre]", signed Fanilly, chief of the Bureau of Infantry, 22 February 1814, Arch. Guerre, X^h 16a; and Byrne, *Memoirs*, vol. 2, pp. 200–201.

75. See "Rapport fait au Ministre," signed Fanilly, 10 January 1814, Arch. Guerre, X^h 16a.

76. On the problem of replacing Ware as commander of the 1st Battalion see "Rapport fait au Ministre," signed Fanilly, 10 January 1814; "Note pour le Ministre," signed Fanilly, 31 January 1814, Arch. Guerre X^h 16a; and Byrne, *Memoirs*, vol. 2, p. 201.

77. See "Note pour le Ministre," signed Fanilly, 31 January 1814; "Note pour le Ministre," signed Fanilly, 22 February 1814, Arch. Guerre, X^h 16a; and Byrne, *Memoirs*, vol. 2, pp. 201.

78. See Byrne, *Memoirs*, vol. 3, pp. 29–30 and 225–26.

79. Maison to Minister of War, 6 January 1814, Arch Guerre, X^h 16a.

80. See "Inspecteur au rêvues, Chef de la 4e Division du Ministre de la Guerre," (signature not legible) to General Denniée, chief of the 2nd Division," 25 January 1814, Arch. Guerre, X^h 16a.

81. See Minister of War to the Council of Administration (of the 3rd Foreign Regiment), 23 February 1814, Arch. Guerre, X^h 16a.

82. See "3e Régiment Etranger, Contrôle Nominatif de M. M. les Officiers du dit Régiment à l'époque du 1er Mars, 1814," no signature, Arch. Guerre, X^h 16a.

83. See "3ème Régiment Foreigners, Procès verbal des Militaires d'ori-

gine Russe et Allemand sortant du dit Régiment et de nouvelle Composition de ce Corps," 19 December 1813, Arch. Guerre, X[h] 16a; "Inspecteur aux rêvues, chef de la 4e Division du Ministre de la Guerre," (signature not legible) to General Denniée, chief of the 2nd Division, 25 January 1814, Arch. Guerre, X[h] 16a; and "3e Régiment Etranger, Contrôle Nominatif de M. M. les Officiers du dit Régiment à l'époque du 1er Mars, 1814," no signature, 1 March 1814, Arch. Guerre, X[h] 16a.

84. See Byrne, *Memoirs*, vol. 2, p. 209.

85. See Byrne, *Memoirs*, vol. 2, p. 209.

86. The figure eighty-seven is taken from "3ème Régiment Etranger. Etat Nominatif de M. M. les Officiers du dit Régiment avec l'Indication du Pays et du Corps d'ou ils sontent fait à l'époque de sa nouvelle Organization, 1814," signed Mahony and verified by Kollen, no date, presumed to be January 1814, Arch. Guerre, X[h] 16a. There is a document dated 23 April 1814, signed by Mahony, which gives the strength of the officer corps at one hundred and two. However, there is not a list of names, and it shows that only ninety-two officers were "under arms." See "3e Régiment Etranger, 1er, 2e, 3e, 4e Bataillons de guerre et 5e Bataillon de Dépôt; Etat de Situation de ce Régiment au 23 Avril, 1814," signed Mahony, dated 23 April 1814, Arch. Guerre, X[h] 16a. Thus there is a discrepancy of five for which the author cannot account.

87. See "3ème Régiment Etranger, Nominatif de M. M. les Officiers du dit Régiment avec l'Indication du Pays et du Corps d'ou ils sontent fait à l'époque de sa nouvelle Organization, 1814," signed Mahony and verified by Kollen, no date, presumed to be January 1814, Arch. Guerre, X[h] 16a. These figures are based on the list of officers which contained ninety-eight names, less eleven of the ninety-eight who were sent to Paris in mid-January. See "3e Régiment Etranger, Contrôle Nominatif des Officiers de ce Régiment que se rendent à Paris pour y etre à la disposition de Son Excellence le Ministre de la Guerre," signed General Maison, 16 January 1814, Arch. Guerre, X[h] 16a.

88. See "3e Régiment Etranger, 1e, 2e, 3e, 4e Bataillons de guerre et 5e Bataillon de Dépôt; Etat de Situation de ce Régiment au 23 Avril, 1814," signed Mahony, 23 April 1814, Arch. Guerre, X[h] 16a.

8. The Restoration and Disbandment of the Legion

1. Upon the execution of Louis XVI in January 1793, the royalists recognized his imprisoned eight-year-old son as Louis XVII. The boy died in 1795.

2. Colonel Mahony began to sign himself "Chevalier Mahony" as soon as the Bourbon monarchy was firmly reestablished. See his correspondence from mid-April in the War Archives, X[h] 16a.

3. See Mahony to Minister of War, 23 April 1814, Arch. Guerre, X[h] 16a.

4. See Byrne, *Memoirs*, vol. 2, p. 220.

5. See Byrne, *Memoirs*, vol. 2, p. 220.

6. See Hayne to Minister of War, 13 May 1814, Arch. Guerre, X^h 16a; and Byrne, *Memoirs* , vol. 2, p. 214.

7. Byrne, *Memoirs*, vol. 2, p. 214. Byrne also listed Lieutenant François Marshal as having left the Regiment in the Spring of 1814 (vol. 2, p. 214), however, Marshal was still carried on the officer's list dated 1 September 1815. See "1me Régiment Etranger (Irlandais), Contrôle nominatif des M. M. les officers de Régiment au 1 Septembre, 1815," Arch. Guerre, X^h 16a.

8. See letter to Minister of War, signature not legible, 24 June 1814, Arch. Guerre, X^h 16a; and Byrne, *Memoirs*, vol. 2, p. 216.

9. See the correspondence on, and from, the returning prisoners of War in Arch. Guerre, X^h 16a.

10. Mundt and Junot to Minister of War, May 1814, Arch. Guerre, X^h 16a.

11. See "3ème Régiment Etranger, Dépôt, Etat nominatif de M.M. les officers du 4e Régiment Etranger, qui, rentrant des prisons de l'ennemi, . . . en vertu d'ordre superieur," signed Ware, 16 May 1814, Arch. Guerre, X^h 16a.

12. See "Rapport fait au Ministre," signed Deschamps, 5 July 1814, Arch. Guerre, X^h 16a.

13. See Bureau of Inspection to Minister of War, signature not legible, 2 March 1815, Arch. Guerre, X^h 16a.

14. See General S. R. Pill to Minister of War, 2 March 1815. Arch. Guerre, X^h 16a.

15. See "3me Régiment Etranger au service de France, Contrôle nominatif de M.M. les officers du Régiment à l'époque de 1er avril, 1815," signed by all of the members of the Council of Administration, Arch. Guerre, X^h 16a.

16. See Byrne, *Memoirs*, vol. 2, p. 219.

17. See Byrne, *Memoirs*, vol. 2, p. 219–22.

18. See "3me Régiment Etranger au service de France, Contrôle nominatif de M. M. les officers du Régiment à l'époque du 1er avril, 1815." signed by all of the members of the Council of Administration, Arch. Guerre, X^h 16a.

19. See Byrne, *Memoirs*, vol. 2, pp. 222–23.

20. See the bottom of page two of the letter from Lieutenant Chatelin and Second Lieutenant De Wall to Minister of War, 20 August 1815, Arch Guerre, X^h 16a. A copy of this letter was also sent to "M^r Le Comte O'Mahony" at his Paris address. Byrne wrote in his *Memoirs*: "Colonel Mahony returned to Montreuil-sur-Mer on the fifteenth of March 1815, and retook command of his regiment, and in the first order of the day that he gave, he signed himself 'Count O'Mahony' " (vol. 2, p. 223).

21. Byrne, *Memoirs*, vol. 2, p. 223.

22. Byrne, *Memoirs*, vol. 2, pp. 217–18. It should be noted that in his *Memoirs* Byrne equated the French rank of "major" in the the Napoleonic army to that of "lieutenant-colonel" in the English army.

23. See Byrne, *Memoirs*, vol. 2, pp. 218–19.

24. See "3me Régiment Etranger, Infanterie de Ligne. Procès verbal," no signature, 1 January 1815, Arch. Guerre, X^h 16a; and Byrne, *Memoirs*, vol. 2, p. 220.

25. See "3me Régiment Etranger au service de France, Etat nominatif des officers du dit Régiment et composition du cadre des Bataillons à l'époque du premier Janvier 1815 jour de la nouvelle organization, . . . ," signed General Bourke, 1 January 1815, Arch. Guerre, X^h 16a.

26. See "3me Régiment Etranger au service de France, Etat nominatif des officers du dit Régiment et composition du cadre des Bataillons à l'époque du premier Janvier 1815 jour de la nouvelle organization, . . . ," signed General Bourke, 1 January 1815, Arch. Guerre, X^h 16a.

27. See "3me Régiment Etranger au service de France, Composition de le Troupe," signed Bourke, 1 January 1815, Arch. Guerre, X^h 16a.

28. "Au Roi," signed by all of the officers present at Montreuil-sur-Mer, 1 January 1815, Arch. Guerre, X^h 16a.

29. See "3me Régiment Etranger, Contrôle, nominatif des Personniers . . . arrive à Montreuil le 5 février . . . ," signed Ware, February 1815; "3me Régiment Etranger, Contrôle nominatif des Militaries . . . au dit Régiment . . . le 24 février, 1815 . . . ," signed Ware, 24 February 1815; and "3me Régiment Etranger, Contrôle nominatif des Militaries. . . Etrangers le 22 Février, 1815 . . . ," signature not legible, 22 February 1815, Arch. Guerre, X^h 16a.

30. John Flanager was typical of one who returned to the Regiment from a prisoner of war camp and remained in the service. See Count d'Enlou, commander officer of the 16th Military Division (Lille), to Minister of War, 26 March 1815, Arch. Guerre, X^h 16a.

31. Byrne's *Memoirs* are the principal source for the events relating to the Irish and restoration of the emperor. See vol. 2, pp. 223–24.

32. On Marshal Davout as Minister of War, see John G. Gallaher's *The Iron Marshal: A Biography of Louis N. Davout*, chapter 14, "The Minister of War" (pp. 298–334).

33. See Byrne, *Memoirs*, vol. 2, p. 224.

34. See Byrne, *Memoirs*, vol. 2, p. 224.

35. See Byrne, *Memoirs*, vol. 2, p. 225.

36. See Byrne, *Memoirs*, vol. 2, p. 225. See the list of officers in Arch. Guerre, X^h 16a.

37. This account is based upon Byrne, *Memoirs*, vol. 2, pp. 226–28.

38. See "3me Régiment Etranger au service de France, Contrôle, nominatif des M. M. les officers du Régiment à l'époque du 1er Mai, 1815," signed

by Ware and the members of the Council of Administration, Arch. Guerre, X^h 16a.

39. Ware signed himself "Colonel" on 6 June 1815. See Council of Administration to Minister of War, signed by all of the members of the Council, Arch. Guerre, X^h 16a.

40. See for example "3me Régiment Etranger (Irlandais), Contrôle nominatif de M. M. les officers de Régiment à l'époque du 1 Juin 1815," signed by the members of the Council of Administration, 1 June, 1815; and Council of Administration to Minister of War, signed by the members of the Council of Administration, 6 June 1815, Arch. Guerre, X^h 16a.

41. See "3me Régiment Etranger (Irlandais), Contrôle nominatif de M.M. les Officers de Régiment à l'époque de l Août, 1815," signed by Colonel Ware and other members of the Council of Administration, Arch. Guerre, X^h 16a. It should be noted that there is some confusion with respect to the numbering of the Irish Regiment at this time. Some of the documents are entitled "1me Régiment Etranger (Irlandais)" while others are "3e Régiment Etranger (Irlandais)." See Arch. Guerre, X^h 16a. Byrne says in his *Memoirs*: "By another decree, the emperor allowed the regiment to resume its former number and name of 'premier régiment Irlandais,' which greatly gratified the Irish officers." See vol. 2 p. 230.

42. See 3me Régiment Etranger au service de France, Contrôle nominatif de M.M. les officers du Régiment à l'époque du 1er Mars 1815," signed Ware and the other members of the Consul of Administration, 1 March 1815, Arch. Guerre, X^h 16a.

43. See "3me Régiment à l'époque du 1 June, 1815," signed Ware and the other members of the Council of Administration, 1 June, 1815, Arch. Guerre, X^h 16a.

44. See the Regimental lists dated 1 April, 1 May, 1 June, and 1 August, 1815, Arch. Guerre, X^h 16a.

45. See Byrne, *Memoirs*, vol. 2, pp. 230–31.

46. See "3e Régiment Etranger, Etat Sommaire des effects d'habillement . . . à l'époque du 8 Avril 1815," signed Ware, 11 April 1815, Arch. Guerre, X^h 16a.

47. See Byrne, *Memoirs*, vol. 2, pp. 231–32.

48. All three officers are listed as present with the Regiment on 1 June 1815, but are not listed on the roll 1 August 1815. Furthermore, Byrne, in his *Memoirs* states that they had deserted. See "3me Régiment Etranger (Irlandais), Contrôle nominatif des M. M. les officiers du Régiment à l'époque du l Août 1815," signed Ware and the other members of the Council of Administration, 1 August 1815, Arch. Guerre, X^h 16a. Also see Byrne, *Memoirs*, vol. 2, pp. 232–33.

49. Byrne, *Memoirs*, vol. 2, pp. 232–33.

50. In addition to Byrne's *Memoirs* (vol. 2, pp. 232–33) on the Magrath

affair see "3me Régiment Etranger, Etat de situation des officiers composant le 5e Bataillon du 3e Régiment Etranger à l'époque du 25 Novembre 1813," not signed; and "1me Régiment Etranger (Irlandais), Contrôle nominatif des M.M. les officiers du Régiment à l'époque du 1e Août 1815," signed Ware and the other members of the Council of Administration, 1 August 1815, Arch. Guerre, X^h 16a.

51. Byrne, *Memoirs*, vol. 2, p. 233.

52. See "Circulaire aux Général Commandant les Divisions Militaires," signed Davout, 22 June 1815, *Correspondance du Maréchal Davout, Prince d'Eckmühl, Ses Commandment, Son Ministère: 1801–1815, avec Introduction et Notes par Charles de Mazade*, edited by Charles de Mazade, vol.. 4, pp. 570–71.

53. Byrne, *Memoirs*, vol. 2, pp. 233–34.

54. Byrne, *Memoirs*, vol. 2, pp. 234–35.

55. Byrne, *Memoirs*, vol. 2, pp. 235–36.

56. The Irish officers to Minister of War, signed by twenty-one officers, no date (presumed to be July 1815), Arch. Guerre, X^h 16a.

57. See the letter to Minister of War signed by the officers of the 3rd Foreign Regiment, dated 9 October 1815, Arch. Guerre, X^h 16a.

58. See Byrne, *Memoirs*, vol. 2, p. 239.

59. See Officers of the Irish Regiment to Minister of War, 9 October 1815, Arch. Guerre, X^h 16a.

60. See Officers of the Irish Regiment to Minister of War, 9 October 1815, Arch. Guerre, X^h 16a.

61. See Byrne, *Memoirs*, vol. 2, p. 237. Byrne refers to this unit as "the Legion of prince Hohenloe."

62. For a partial list of the towns approved by the government see the document signed by the members of the Council of Administration of the Regiment (Ware, Braun, Byrne, Captain Patrice d'Owitzky, and Gugelot) and dated 29 September 1815, Arch. Guerre, X^h 16a.

63. The author is unable to identify Gugelot, but his signature appears very legibly as a member of the Council of Administration at the bottom of the list of officers dated 1 September 1815, Arch. Guerre, X^h 16a.

64. See "Contrôle nominatif des Ms. les Officiers du Régiment au 1er Septembre, 1815," Arch. Guerre, X^h 16a.

65. See Byrne, *Memoirs*, vol. 2, p. 238.

66. "Rapport fait au Ministre," signed Chief of the Bureau of Infantry, September 1815, Arch. Guerre, X^h 16a. There is a second copy of this document in X^h 16a that is dated 21 November 1815.

67. "Rapport fait au Ministre," signed Chief of the Bureau of Infantry, September, 1815, Arch. Guerre, X^h 16a.

68. On Allen after his retirement see "Etat Nominatif de M. M. les officiers . . . à Tours," signature not legible, 28 January 1817, Arch. Guerre, X^h 16a; and Byrne *Memoirs*, vol. 2, pp. 189–90 and 239.

69. "Rapport fait au Ministre," signed Chief of the Bureau of Infantry, September 1815, Arch. Guerre, X^h 16a.

70. On Byrne's life after 1815 see his *Memoirs*, vol. 2, pp. 314–44.

71. "Rapport fait au Ministre," signed Chief of the Bureau of Infantry, September 1815, Arch. Guerre, X^h 16a.

72. "Rapport fait au Ministre," signed Chief of the Bureau of Infantry, September 1815, Arch. Guerre, X^h 16a.

73. See Byrne, *Memoirs*, vol. 3, pp. 97–99.

74. "Rapport fait au Ministre," signed Chief of the Bureau of Infantry, September 1815, Arch. Guerre, X^h 16a.

75. "Rapport fait au Ministre," Signed Chief of the Bureau of Infantry, September 1815, Arch. Guerre, X^h 16a; and Minister of War to M. de Caze, minister of Police, 12 December 1815, Arch. Guerre, X^h 16a.

76. Minister of War to M. de Caze, Minister of Police, 30 November 1815, Arch. Guerre, X^h 16a.

77. Arch. Guerre, X^h 16a.

78. Deboulard to Destabenrath, 14 December 1815, Arch. Guerre, X^h 16a.

79. Destabenrath to Minister of War, 16 December 1815, Arch. Guerre, X^h 16a.

80. Lawless and Jackson to Minister of War, 18 December, 1815, Arch. Guerre, X^h 16a.

Bibliography

Archival Sources

The principal source of information on the Irish Legion is the collection of documents at the Archives de la Guerre (Service Historique de l'Etat-Major de l'Armée) at the Château de Vincennes. The X^h series entitled "Bataillons et Régiments Etrangers" contains seven cartons of documents under the heading of "3e Régiment Étranger, Irlandais," which are numbered: 14, 15, 16a, 16b, 16c, 16d, and 17. On the formation and early years of the Legion the thirty-five cartons of the C^1 series, "Armée des Côtes de l'Océan (1804–1805)" were most helpful. Selective cartons from other series also contributed to this study: C^2 "Grande Armée; Armée du Rhin, Armées d'Allemagne, du Nord, etc. (1803–1814)"; C^7 "Armée de Portugal (1806–1814)"; and C^8 "Armée d'Espagne (1806–1814)." In Ireland the "Rebellion Paper" in the archives of Dublin Castle shed light on the lives of United Irishmen who joined the Legion. The rare books and manuscripts section of Trinity College Library was also helpful, as was the manuscript collection at the National Library in Dublin. The one single published volume that was indispensable was Miles Byrne's *Memoirs of Miles Byrne*. His personal experiences and his recollections, which on occasion required some corrections, contribute greatly to our knowledge of the Irish Legion.

Published Sources

Alger, J. G. *Napoleon's British Visitors and Captives, 1801–1815.* New York: J. Pott, 1904.

Arteche y Moro, José Gómez de. *Guerra de la independencia, Historia Militar de España de 1808–1814.* 14 vols. Madrid: Credito Commercial, 1868–1902.

Beckett, J. C. *The Making of Modern Ireland, 1603–1923.* New York: Knopf, 1969.

Bigger, F. J. "The Northern Star." *Ulster Journal of Archaeology*, 2nd. ser., vol. 1 (1895), pp. 33–35.

Bond, Gordon C. *The Grand Expedition: The British Invasion of Holland in 1809.* Athens: University of Georgia Press, 1979.

————. "The Siege of Flushing." *The Irish Sword*, vol. 11, no. 43 (Winter 1973), pp. 118–28.

Bourke, F. S. "The Rebellion of 1803. An Essay in Bibliography." *The Bibliographical Society of Ireland*, vol. 5 (1933).

Byrne, Miles. *Memoirs of Miles Byrne*. 3 vols. Shannon: Irish University Press, 1972.

Chandler, David. *The Campaigns of Napoleon*. New York: Macmillan Co., 1966.

Charles, P. "Le corps irlandais au service de la France sous le Consulat et l'Empire." *Révue historique des Armées*. vol. 2 (1976), pp. 25–54.

Clark, Brian, Tr. "Napoleon's Irish Legion, 1803–1815: The Historical Record." *The Irish Sword*, vol. 12, no. 48 (Summer 1976), pp. 164–72.

Correspondance du Maréchal Davout, Prince d'Eckmühl, Ses Commandment, Son Ministère: 1801–1815, avec Introduction et Notes par Charles de Mazade, Edited by Charles de Mazade. Paris: Librairie Plom, 1885.

Coughlin, R. *Napper Tandy*. Dublin: Anvil Books, 1977.

Curtin, Nancy J. "The Transformation of the Society of United Irishmen into a Mass-based Revolutionary Organization, 1794–6." *Irish Historical Studies*, vol. 24, no. 96 (November 1985), pp. 463–92.

Desbrière, Edouard. *Projets et tentatives de débarquement aux Iles Britanniques, 1793–1805*. 5 vols. Paris: R. Chapelot, 1900–1902.

Deschamps, Jules. *Les Iles Britanniques et la Révolution française, 1798–1803*. Brussels: Renaissance du livre, 1949.

Duval, Jules Celestin Xavier Auguste. *Napoléon, Bülow, et Bernadotte, 1813*. Paris: Charles-Lavauzelle, 1906.

Elliott, Marianne. *Partners in Revolution: The United Irishmen and France*. New Haven: Yale University Press, 1982.

Elting, John R. *Swords Around a Throne: Napoleon's Grande Armée*. New York: Free Press, 1988.

Emmet, Thomas Addis. *Memoir of Thomas Addis Emmet and Robert Emmet with Their Ancestors and Immediate Family*. 2 vols. New York: Putman's Sons, 1909.

Escande, Georges. *Hoche en Irlande, 1795–1798, d'après les documents inédits: lettres de Hoche, délibérations secrètes du Directoire, mémoires secretes de Wolf Tone*. Paris: F. Alcan, 1888.

Esposito, V. J., and J. R. Elting. *A Military History and Atlas of the Napoleonic Wars*. New York: Praeger, 1964.

Fieffé, E. *Historire des troupes étrangères au service de la France*. Paris, Dumaine, 1854.

Fortescue, J. W. *A History of the British Army*. Vols. 7 and 8. London: Macmillan and Co., 1912.

Fyers, Colonel William. "Journal of the Siege of Flushing, 1809." *Journal of the Society for Army Historical Research*, vol. 13 (1934), pp. 145–58.

Gallaher, John G. *The Iron Marshal: A Biography of Louis N. Davout*. Carbondale: Southern Illinois University Press, 1976.

Garros, Louis. *Quel roman que ma vie! Itinéraire de Napoléon Bonaparte (1769–1821)*. Paris: Les Editions de l'Encyclopédie Française, 1947.

Gilbert, John T. *Documents Relating to Ireland, 1795–1804*. Shannon: Irish University Press, 1970.

Glover, Michael. *The Peninsular War, 1807–1814: A Concise Military History*. Hamden: Archon Books, 1974.

Godechot, Jacques Léon. *France and the Atlantic Revolution of the Eighteenth Century, 1770–1799*. Tr. by Herbert Rowen. New York: Free Press, 1965.

Gribayedoff, V. *The French Invasion of Ireland in 1798*. New York: C. P. Somerby, 1890.

Guillon, Edouard Louis Maxime. *La France et l'Irlande pendant la Révolution, Hoche et Humbert, d'après les documents inédits des archives de France et d'Irlande*. Paris: Colin, 1888.

Hayes, Richard F. *Biographical Dictionary of Irishmen in France*. Dublin: M. H. Gill and Son, 1949.

———. *Ireland and Irishmen in the French Revolution*. London: E. Benn, 1932.

———. *The Last Invasion of Ireland*. Dublin: M. H. Gill and Son, 1937.

Hennessy, Maurice N. *The Wild Geese: The Irish Soldier in Exile*. London: Sidgwick and Jackson, 1973.

Horward, Donald D. *The Battle of Bussaco: Masséna Vs. Wellington*. Tallahassee: Florida State University Press, 1965.

———. *Napoleon and Iberia: The Twin Sieges of Cuidad Rodrigo and Almeida, 1810*. Tallahassee: Florida State University Press, 1984.

Jones, E. H. Stuart. *An Invasion That Failed: The French Expedition to Ireland, 1798*. Oxford: Basil Blackwell, 1950.

Kennedy, Brian A. "Light on a Revolting Duel Fought in 1804." *The Irish Sword*. vol. 4, pp. 136–38.

Las Cases, Marie Joseph Emmanuel, comte de. *Le Mémorial de Sainte-Hélène*. 2 vols. Paris: Flammarion, 1951.

Lawless, J. *The Belfast Politics, enlarged; being a compendium of the political history of Ireland for the last forty years*. Belfast: 1818.

Lecky, W. E. H. *A History of Ireland in the Eighteenth Century*. 5 vols., London, Longmans, Green and Co., 1892.

Lefebvre, Georges. *Napoleon: From 18 Brumaire to Tilsit 1799–1807*. New York: Columbia University Press, 1969.

Londonderry, Marquess of. *Narrative of the Peninsular War, from 1808 to 1813*. London: Henry Colburn, 1828.

MacDermot, Frank. "Arthur O'Connor," *Irish Historical Society*. vol. 15 (1966), pp. 48–69.

———. *Theodald Wolfe Tone and His Times*. 3rd ed. Tralee, 1969.

McDowell, R. B. *Ireland in the Age of Imperialism and Revolution, 1760–1801*. Oxford: Clarendon Press, 1979.

———. *Irish Public Opinion, 1750–1800*. London: Fabre and Fabre, 1952.

McLaughlin, Mark G. *The Wild Geese: The Irish Brigades of France and Spain*. London: Osprey, 1980.

MacNeven, William J. *Pieces of Irish History*. New York: William James MacNeven, 1807.

Madden, R. R. *The United Irishmen, Their Lives and Times*. 7 vols., London: J. M. Madden, 1842–46. Revised ed., 4 vols. London, 1857–60. Also 1 vol., Dublin: J. Duffy, 1857.

Maguire, W. A. "Arthur McMahon, United Irishman and French Soldier." *The Irish Sword*. vol. 9 (1970), pp. 207–15.

Marbot, Jean Baptiste Antoine Marcelin, Baron de. *The Memoirs of Baron de Marbot, Late Lieutenant-General in the French Army*. Trans. Arthur John Butler. 2 vols. London: Longmans, Green, and Co., 1913.

Martin, John. "Diary of Young Irelander John Martin." Unpublished MS at the Public Record Office of Northern Ireland, Belfast.

Masson, Frederic. *Le Département des Affaires Etrangères pendant la Révolution, 1787–1804*. Paris: Plon, 1877.

Maxwell, W. H. *History of the Irish Rebellion in 1798*. London: G. Bell, 1894.

Moody, T. W. "The Political ideas of the United Irishmen." *Ireland Today*, vol. 3 (1936), pp. 15–25.

Moore, T. *The Life and Death of Lord Edward Fitzgerald*. 2 vols. London, 1831.

———. *The Memoirs of Lord Edward Fitzgerald*. 2nd Ed. London, Downey, 1897.

Mullen Thomas J., Jr., "The Ranks of Death." Unpublished MS, Trinity College Library, MS 7108.

Murphy, W. S. "The Irish Brigade of France at the Siege of Savannah, 1779." *Georgia Historical Society*, vol. 38, pp. 307–21.

Murray, R. H. *Revolutionary Ireland and its Settlement*. London: Macmillan and Co., 1911.

Napoleon, I. *La Correspondance de Napoléon Ier*. 32 vols. Paris: Imprimerie Impériale, 1857–70.

A New History of Ireland. Vols. 4 and 5. Ed. by T. W. Moody, F. X. Martin, and F. J. Byrne. Oxford: Clarendon Press, 1972.

O'Broin, Leon. *The Unfortunate Mr. Robert Emmet*. Dublin and London: Clonmore and Reynolds, 1958.

O'Callaghan, John Cornelius. *History of the Irish Brigades in the Service of France*. Shannon: Irish University Press, 1969.

Oman, Sir Charles W. C. *A History of the Peninsular War*. 7 vols. Oxford: The Clarendon Press, 1902–30.

Pakenham, Thomas. *The Year of Liberty: The Story of the Great Irish Rebellion of 1798*. London: Hodder and Stoughton, 1969.

Pelet, Jean Jacques. *The French Campaign in Portugal, 1810–1811: An Account by Jean Jacque Pelet*. Ed. and Trans. by Donald D. Horward. Minneapolis: University of Minnesota Press, 1973.

Petre, Francis Loraine. *Napoleon's Last Campaign in Germany, 1813*. London and New York: J. Lane, 1912.

Postgate, R. W. *Robert Emmet*. London: M. Secker, 1931.

Reboul, Frederic. *Campagne de 1813: Les Préliminaires*. 2 vols. Paris: Chapelot, 1910–12.

Rodger, Alexander Bankier. *The War of the Second Coalition, 1798–1801: A Strategic Commentary*. Oxford: Clarendon Press, 1964.

Ross, Steven T. "The Military Strategy of the Directory: The Campaigns of 1799." *French Historical Studies*, vol. 5 (1967), pp. 170–87.

Rousset, Camille Félix Michel. *La Grande Armée de 1813*. Paris: Perrin, 1892.

Ryan, F. W. "A Projected Invasion of Ireland in 1811," *The Irish Sword*, vol. 1 (1962), pp. 136–41.

Short, John Tregerthen. *Prisoners of War in France from 1804 to 1814, Being the Adventures of John Tregerthen Short and Thomas Williams of St. Ives, Cornwall*. London: Duckworth, 1914.

Simms, J. G. *Jacobite Ireland, 1685–91*. London: Routledge and Kegan Paul, 1969.

———. *The Treaty of Limerick*. Dublin, 1961.

Teeling, Charles Hamilton. *History of the Irish Rebellion of 1798 and Sequel to the History of the Irish Rebellion of 1798*. Shannon: Irish University Press, 1972.

Thiébault, Paul Charles, Baron. *Mémoires du général baron Thiébault*. 5 vols. Paris: Plon-Nourrit, 1895–97.

Thiry, Jean. *L'Avenement de Napoléon*. Paris: Editions Berger-Levrault, 1959.

———. *Leipzig*. Paris: Editions Berger-Levrault, 1972.

———. *Lützen et Bautzen*. Paris: Edition Berger-Levrault, 1971.

Tone, Theobold Wolfe. *Life of Theobald Wolfe Tone, Written by Himself and Continued by His Son*. Ed. by W. T. Tone. 2 vols. Washington: Gales and Seaton, 1826.

Van Brock, F. W. "Captain MacSheehy's Mission." *The Irish Sword*, vol. 10 (1972), pp. 215–28.

———. "A Memoir of 1798." *The Irish Sword*, vol. 9 (1970), pp. 192–206.

———. "A Proposed Irish Regiment and Standard, 1796." *The Irish Sword*, vol. 11 (1972), pp. 225–33.

Wall, M. *The Penal Laws, 1690–1760*. Dublin: 1961.

Weller, Jack. *Wellington in the Peninsula: 1808–14*, New York: A. S. Barnes and Co., 1963.

Wellington, Arthur Wellesley, 1st Duke of. *Dispatches, Correspondence, and Memoranda of Field Marshal Arthur Duke of Wellington*. 11 vols. London: John Murray, 1867–80.

Widdess, J. D. H. *The Royal College of Surgeons in Ireland and its Medical School, 1784–1984*. 3rd ed. Dublin: Royal College of Surgeons, 1984.

Woods, C. J. "The Secret Mission to Ireland of Captain Bernard Mac-Sheehy, an Irishman in French Service, 1796." *Journal of the Cork Historical and Archaeological Society*. vol. 78 (1973), pp. 93–108.

Woodward, L. "Les projets de descente en Irlande et les réfugiés irlandais et anglais en France sous la Convention." *Annales historiques de la Révolution française*, vol. 8 (1931), pp. 1–30.

Wyld, James, ed. *Maps and Plans of the Principal Movements, Battles, and Sieges in which the British Army was engaged during the War from 1808 to 1814 in the Spanish Peninsula and the South of France*. London: James Wyld, 1841.

Index

Alexander I: Tilsit, 115; mentioned 120, 152, 186, 203

Allen, John: United Irishman, 12; in Spain, 120–29 passim; Peninsular Campaign, 1810–11, 133–34; POW, 142–143; campaign of 1813, 180, 189; *chef de bataillon*, 205; Restoration, 207–19 passim; mentioned, 74, 83, 90, 179, 194, 222

Almeida, siege of, 127

Amiens, Treaty of, 1, 17, 19, 23, 33, 36

Astorga, siege of, 128–29

Augereau, Pierre François Charles, Marshal: Army of Brest, 30–71 passim

Ballinamuck, battle of, 14

Bantry Bay, expedition to, 10–12

Barclay de Tolly, Michael, General: campaign of 1813, 182–83

Barker, William: wounded, 106; mentioned, 35, 90, 94, 96, 108, 157

Bayonne Affair, 16

Beauret, Colonel, 144

Beelart, Jacques, 112

Bernadotte, Jean Baptiste Jules, Marshal (Prince Charles John): campaign of 1813, 186–87

Berthier, Alexandre, Marshal: minister of war, 23–85 passim; mentioned, 132, 139

Bessières, Jean Baptiste, Marshal, 105

Blackwell, James Bartholomew, *Chef de Bataillon*: command of Irish battalion, 31–54 passim; removed from Legion, 48

Blackwell, Thomas, 15

Blücher, Gebhard Leberecht, General: campaign of 1813, 181, 183, 186–90, 193; Hundred Days, 212

Bonan, Captain, 210

Bonaparte, Joseph: king of Spain, 116–17

Bonaparte, Napoleon. *See* Napoleon I

Bond, Oliver, 12

Bourke, Hinderson: joined Regiment, 112; in Spain, 129

Bourke, Jean Raymond Charles, General: Restoration, 205, 207

Bouvet, François Joseph, Admiral: expedition to Bantry Bay, 10

Brangan, Patrick: in Spain, 120, 125, 129; mentioned, 90, 95, 107–9, 111

Braun, Anthony, 212, 215–16

Brennier, Antoine François, General: siege of Almeida, 148; in Spain, 149–50

Brevelet, Captain, 203

Brown, Thomas, 112

Bruce, Stewart, General: commanded Dutch on Walcheren, 98–100

Brune, Guillaume Marie Ann, Marshal, 153, 169

Buhlmann, 119

Bulow, Friedrich Wilhelm, General: campaign of 1813, 181

Burgess, John: discharged, 93; mentioned, 35, 37, 74, 88, 90

Burgh, John Richard: joined Legion, 67; requested discharge, 80

Bussaco, battle of, 136–37

Byrne, Miles: O'Connor/Emmet conflict, 26; formation of Legion, 28, 31–32, 35, 37, life in Paris, 31–32; on O'Connor, 39; life at Lesneven, 68; at Verdun, 78; on Clarke, 85; on the "fever," 88; in Spain, 120–49 passim; on defection of Fitzhenry, 145–47; campaign of 1813, 180, 185, 189, 191; wounded, 187; Restoration, 216–18

Byrne, Pat, executed, 13

Campbell, John; in Spain, 90, 93

Canton, Thomas: joined Legion, 112, mentioned, 129–30

Carnot, Lazare Nicolas, General: siege of

Antwerp, 197, 199, 200; Hundred
Days, 211
Carrandra: duel with Osmond, 69
Castlebar, battle of, 14
Castlereagh, Robert Stewart, Lord, 202,
215
Cauffield, George, 155
Chambers, John, 18, 29
Charles, archduke of Austria, 96
Charles IV, king of Spain, 116, 120
Charles John, Prince. *See* Bernadotte
Chatham, John Pitt, earl of: Walcheren
campaign, 100
Ciudad Rodrigo: siege of, 127–28
Clarke, Henri James, General, duc de Fel-
tre: minister of war, 89–201 passim;
Restoration, 206–21 passim
Clausel, Bertrand, General: in Spain, 126,
144, 148; siege of Astorga, 128; Penin-
sular Campaign of 1810–11, 135, 137,
140
Condorcet, Marie Jean Caritat, marquis
de, 75
Continental System, 115–16
Corbet, Thomas: formation of Legion, 26–
35 passim; Sweeny/Corbet affair, 42–52
passim, 63; duel with Sweeny, 50–52;
death of, 51–52
Corbet, William: formation of Legion, 31–
32, 35; Sweeny/Corbet affair, 43–51
passim; coronation of Napoleon I, 68;
question of seniority, 69–70; in Spain,
142; mentioned, 31, 54, 74, 75, 76
Cornwallis, Charles, General: battle of Ballinamuck, 14
Couasnon, Flixis, Major: duel with A.
O'Meally, 54–55
Cummins, John: discharged, 64; mentioned, 37
Curtis, Rev. Doctor: and Fitzhenry, 144–
45

Dalton, Alexander, Colonel: formation of
Legion, 23–37 passim
Dalton, William, 79
Darbon (d'Arbon), Gustav, 112
Darminac, General, 121
Davout, Louis N., Marshal: minister of
war, Hundred Days, 209–14 passim;
mentioned, 181, 197
De Cazes: minister of police, 219
Dejean, Jean François, General, 80
Delany, Lieutenant, 129

Delaroche, Jean Baptiste, General, 154
Delhora, Smalian: joined Legion, 83; men-
tioned, 84, 90
Demeyere, Jean Jacques, 130
Demonlague, Lieutenant, 129
Deral, Auther: wounded, 187
Derry, Valentin William, 32, 35, 37, 55,
63, 64
Desbureaux, Alexandre, Captain, 162
Desbureaux, Charles François, General,
157, 158, 160
Deschamps, General, 155, 158, 159, 164–
67, 196
Destabemath, Baron, General, 219
Devreux, Alexander: at Brest, 95; recruit-
ing, 110; in Spain, 129; mentioned, 90,
107, 108, 111
Dillon, Arthur, Colonel, 65
Dillon, Arthur, General, 2
Dillon, Auguste: in Spain, 150; men-
tioned, 177, 180, 194
Dillon, Henry, Colonel, 65–66
Dillon, Theobold, General, 150
Donzelot, François Xavier, General: chief
of staff to Augereau, 30; formation of
Legion, 35, 38; Sweeny/Corbet affair,
42–52 passim; organization of Legion,
58–63 passim; mentioned, 68
Dorsenne, Jean Marie, General, 150
Dowdall, William: wounded, 102; died of
wounds, 106; mentioned, 37, 43, 74,
90, 94, 108
Dowling, Jerome: in Spain, 93, 119, 125;
mentioned, 18, 90
Doxal, Lieutenant, 129
Doyer, Anthony: returned POW, 204
Doyle, 79
Dribinski, 95
Dupont de l'Etang, Pierre, General: battle
of Baylen, 116, minister of war, 201,
204, 208
Dupouget, Louis: Sweeny/Corbet affair,
43, death of, 93

Eagar, François: POW, 106; mentioned,
90, 107, 108
Eckardt, Christian: wounded, 187 mentioned, 199
Elliot, John: wounded, 187–88
Emmet, Robert: insurrection of 1803, 13,
28
Emmet, Thomas Addis: United Irishman,
8, 11–13; conflict with O'Connor, 17–

19; formation of Legion, 22–40 passim; sailed to New York, 30; mentioned, 45, 49, 53, 61, 142, 153
Esmonde, Laurent, 216, 218
Evens, Hampden, 29, 32
Evens, John: death of, 187

Fanconnet, General, 195
Fectze, Charles de, 212
Ferdinand VII: king of Spain, 116, 117, 120
Ferey, Claude François, General, 131
Ferguson, John: leaves Spain, 130, mentioned, 210
Fichaux, Sergeant, 114
Fitzgerald, Lord Edward: United Irishman, 8–9, 11–12, 17–18, 25
Fitzhenry, Jerome: in Spain, 117–40 passim; POW, 143; defection and court-martial of, 144–47
Fontenoy, battle of, 3
Foster, 79
Fouché, Joseph: Restoration, 201
Foy, Maximilien, General, 150
Fraser, General, 99
Frederick William III, King, 186

Gallagher, Patrick: formation of Legion, 23, 25, 32, 35; Sweeny/Corbet affair, 43–47; leaves the Legion, 54
Ganteaume, H. J. A., Admiral: expedition to Ireland, 61
Gassling, 199
Gauthier, *Chef de Bataillon*: Walcheren Campaign, 103
Geith, Captain, 205
Gérard, Maurice Etienne, General: campaign of 1813, 190
Gibbons, Augustin: resigned, 76
Gibbons, Edward, 43
Gibbons, John: unfit for service, 66; death of, 66, 93; mentioned, 35, 43, 90, 107
Gilmer, Joseph: Walcheren campaign, 102; POW, 106, mentioned, 73, 74, 90, 107, 108
Goldsmith, Lewis: publisher of the *Argus*, 32
Gordon, Robert, 210
Gougie, Charles A.: wounded, 128
Graham, General, 200
Gregoire, Victor, 90, 108
Grouchy, Emmanuel, Marshal: expedition to Bantry Bay, 10

Gugelot, 216
Gunning, M.: served in Prussian army, 79

Hamilton, Alexander, 112
Harispe, Jean Isidor, Colonel, 48
Harty, Oliver, General: expedition to Ireland in 1798, 15; formation of Legion, 25–28; commander at Landernau, 68; mentioned, 50, 55, 62, 67, 70, 85, 193
Hayne, William, *Chef de Bataillon*: command of 4th Battalion, 178; Restoration, 205; Hundred Days, 209, 211, 212; mentioned, 173
Hoche, Louis Lazare, General: meeting with Irish leaders, 9; expedition to Bantry Bay, 10; mentioned, 23, 25, 30
Hudson: prisoner at St. George, 18
Humbert, Jean Joseph, General: expedition to Ireland, 13–15, 76

Irish Brigade: disbanded, 2, 3, 5; mentioned, 21, 25, 35
Irish College, Paris, 21, 30, 35
Isembourg, Charles Frédéric L. M., Prince d', 120

Jackson, Thomas: in Spain, 129; Restoration, 216–19; mentioned, 111
James, Thomas, 66
James II: king of England, 2, 3
Junot, François Charles E., 204
Junot, Jean Andoche, General: Portugal (1807), 115, 121; siege of Astorga, 128–29; 8th Corps, Peninsular Campaign (1810–11), 132–50 passim; mentioned, 169

Keanlan, *Chef de Bataillon*, 198
Kearney, 66
Keller, William: commissioned, 120; mentioned, 194, 199
Kellermann, François Etienne, General (son of Marshal Kellermann): in Spain, 123
Kellermann, François Etienne Christophe, Marshal; 80, 82, 83, 112
Kelly, Patrick P.: returned POW, 170–71
Kerthen, Lieutenant, 203
Kilmainham, Treaty of, 13, 16–17
King, Rufus, U.S. minister in London: on Irish prisoners, 17
Klemps, Jean, 194, 199
Kosloski, Joseph: joined Legion, 82; Wal-

cheren campaign, 90, 94, 95, 108;
   POW, 106
Kutusov, Mikhail Golenischev, General,
   177, 181

Lacy, Louis: in Spanish army, 60; joined
   Legion, 73; marriage of, 75; in Spain,
   92, 116; defection of, 117, 119, 147
Lagrange, Jean Baptiste, General: in
   Spain, 127
Lagrange, Joseph, General: campaign of
   1813, 180, 183, 185
Lake, Gerard, General: battle of Cas-
   tlebar, 14
Lambert, Robert: discontented, 72–73; dis-
   charged, 75
Landy, Michael: discharged, 64
Landy, Richard: discharged, 64
Laroche, Antoine, General, 67
La Roche, Hercule, 213
Larrey, Dominique Jean, Baron: campaign
   of 1813, 188
Latour-Maugourg, Marie Victor, General:
   campaign of 1813, 189
Lauriston, Alexandre Jacque B., General:
   campaign of 1813, 180–90 passim
Lawless, Luke: mission to Ireland, 168,
   173; Restoration, 216–19
Lawless, William: formation of Legion, 29;
   life in Paris, 31; a troublemaker, 81–
   84; at Brest, 95; Walcheren campaign,
   102–6; wounded, 104; Legion of
   Honor, 105; on Fitzhenry's defection,
   146–47; named colonel of Regiment,
   169; campaign of 1813, 178–93 passim;
   wounded, 188–89; Restoration, 206;
   mentioned, 68–222 passim
Lebrun, Charles François, General, 196
Lecomte, Madame, 32
Legrave, Captain: ADC to Junot, siege of
   Astorga, 128
Le Meunier: ADC to Osten, 100
Lench, Patrick: wounded, 189
Leniennier: ADC to Osten, 98
Lewins, Edward, 11
Limerick, Treaty of, 3
Lipinski, Michael, 95
Loisen, Louis Henri, General: Peninsular
   Campaign of 1810–11, 135, 141
Louis XIV: king of France, 2, 3
Louis, XVIII (comte de Provence): king of
   France, restoration 200–216 passim

Lowry, Alexander: United Irishman, 8
Lynch, Patrick: returned POW, 204

MacCann, Patrick: wounded, 102; died of
   wounds, 106; mentioned, 90, 93–94,
   108
MacCarthy, James: joined Legion, 66;
   mentioned, 180
MacCarthy, John: leaves Regiment, 185
MacCarthy, Patrick: joined Legion, 112
McCormick, Richard: United Irishman, 8,
   12; formation of Legion, 29
MacDermotte, Bernard, 90
Macdonald, Jacques Alexandre, Marshal:
   campaign of 1813, 186, 188, 190 193
McDonnell, James Joseph, 29
MacEgan, James: commissioned, 120
MacGauley, William: wounded, 187
McGuire, John: formation of Legion, 25–
   28, 35; in Spain, 119, 127; mentioned,
   49, 90
MacKey, Thomas: Sweeny/Corbet affair,
   43; mentioned, 37
McMahon, Arthur: formation of Legion,
   29; POW, 106; escaped from England,
   107; mentioned, 29, 35, 108
MacMahon, Patrick, 35, 55, 90
MacNeven, William James: United Irishman, 8, 11–12; prisoner at St. George,
   17–18; Sweeny/Corbet affair, 42–45,
   51–52; resignation of, 54
MacSheehy, Bernard: named commander
   of Legion, 30; on men of the Legion,
   33–34; formation of Legion, 35–38;
   Sweeny/Corbet affair, 42–50; removed
   from Legion, 48–49; O'Meally/Couas-
   non duel, 54–55; reorganization of Legion, 58–59, 61; mentioned, 53, 56–57,
   59, 67, 81–84, 89, 93, 117, 122, 165,
   221
MacSheehy, Patrick: Sweeny/Corbet affair,
   42; Osmond/Carrandra duel, 69; on
   leave, 90, 93, 96
Magrath, Achille: ADC to General Casterole, 185; mentioned, 111, 157
Magrath, Patrick: Hundred Days, 213–14
Mahony, John F.: joined Regiment, 109;
   command of 3rd Battalion, in Spain,
   126–27, 129; relieved of command,
   132, 134; promotion of, 169; named colonel and command of Regiment, 198;
   Restoration, 203–8; Hundred Days,

209–10; mentioned, 111, 145, 166, 179, 193, 194, 196–97, 199, 202

Maison, Nicolas Joseph, General: campaign of 1813, 183–84; mentioned, 194, 196–97, 199

Marchand, Jean Gabriel, General: in Spain, 131

Markey, Thomas: dissatisfied, 65, 77; a troublemaker, 80–81, 83–84; in Brest, 95; recruiting, 110; purge of Regiment, 159, 160–61; mentioned, 40, 90, 107–9, 111, 162

Marmont, Auguste Frédéric, Marshal: expedition to Ireland, 61; in Spain, 142, 148–50; surrender of Paris (1814), 201

Martin, Christophe: wounded, 102; died of wounds, 106; mentioned, 37, 90, 108

Masséna, André, Marshal: command of Army of Portugal, 126; Peninsular Campaign of 1810–11, 127–43 passim; battle of Bussaco, 136–37; mentioned, 82

Masterson, Edward: recruited, 38; in British army, 60; marriage of, 75; mentioned, 90, 93

Maugourg, Marie Victor, General: campaign of 1813, 188

Menten, Joseph: commissioned, 111; in Spain, 129

Moke (Mokey), Doctor, 88, 105

Moncey, Bon Adrien J., Marshal, 117

Monnet de Lorbeau, Lows-Claude, General: commander of Walcheren, impressions of Irish Battalion, 87–91; Walcheren campaign, 98–106; mentioned, 89, 94–97

Montburn, General (brother of Louis Pierre), 181

Moore, John, General: death of, 121

Morfie, Sergeant, 155

Morisson, Fecorbert, 64

Morres, Hervey M., 15

Mortier, Adolphe Edouard, Marshal, 210

Mortine, Robert C., 155

Mougenot, Henri, 59

Mountcashel (Justin MacCarthy), Lord, 2, 3

Mullauny, Charles: in Spain, 120, 125; returned POW, 204

Mundt, Jean Frédéric, 204

Murat, Joachim, Marshal (King Joachim): governor of Paris, 68; in Spain, 92, 116

Murray, Paul: requested discharge, 80; in Brest, 95; in Spain, 129; Hundred Days, 212; mentioned, 37, 90, 107–9

Napoleon I, Emperor: expedition to Ireland, 22–23, 62; formation of Legion, 27, 29, 30–31, 36, 96; coronation, 68; campaign of 1805, 75; established 3rd Foreign Regiment (Irish), 96; Tilsit, 115, 152; Continental System, 116; and Spain, 117–49 passim; campaign of 1813, 181–200, passim; first abdication of, 199, 201; Hundred Days, 205–19 passim; second abdication of, 214; mentioned, 74, 78, 84–85, 90, 121, 157, 159–60, 163, 173, 175, 177

National Directory of United Irishmen, 9, 12

Neill, Daniel, 161–62

Neill, James, 161

Neilson, Sammuel: prisoner at St. George, 18

Nelson, Horatio, Admiral: battle of Trafalgar, 71

Ney, Michel, Marshal: command of 6th Corps in Spain, 126; siege of Ciudad Rodrigo, 127–28, 130; Peninsular Campaign of 1810–11, 134, 138–39, 141, 148; battle of Bussaco, 136, campaign of 1813, 182–83

O'Brien: served in Prussian army, 79

O'Brien, Daniel, Colonel, 2

O'Connell, Daniel, General, 5

O'Connor, Arthur, General: United Irishman, 8–9; arrested, 12; "Kilmainham Treaty," 13; prisoner at St. George, 17–19; arrived in Paris, 22; formation of Legion, 23–34 passim; named general of division, 39; marriage of, 75; mentioned, 53, 58, 61–62, 66–67, 70, 81, 142, 153, 217, 219, 221

O'Connor, Mrs. Arthur, 18

O'Herne, Eugene, 37, 60

O'Kelly, Patrick Paul: discipline, 57–58; duel with Thyroux, 58; removed from Legion, 63–64; mentioned, 35, 55, 60

O'Meally, Austin: duel with Couasnon, 54–55; in Spain, 120; mentioned, 37, 171

O'Meara, Daniel, Colonel: command of Irish Regiment, 96; command of Burgos, 121; in Spain, 122, 127, 153 removed from command, 130—34; mentioned, 108–9, 114, 123, 126, 129, 145, 155, 159, 162, 166, 169, 180

O'Meara, John (father of Daniel), 108

O'Meara, William: Sweeny/Corbet affair, 43; O'Meally/Couasnon duel, 54; with British army, 60; command of Magdeburg, 180; mentioned, 35, 108–9
O'Moran, James, General, 122
O'Morand, William Auguste: joined Legion, 66; mentioned, 35, 90
O'Neil, Charles, Captain, 122
O'Neil, John, General, 122
O'Reilly, Terence: Walcheren campaign, 102, 105; recruitment, 153, 158; campaign of 1813, 185, 189; Restoration, 216; mentioned, 55, 83, 90, 108, 125, 172, 178–79, 194, 198
Orr, Joseph: United Irishman, 8
Osmond, Augustin: in Spain, 120, 125, 153; campaign of 1813, 185; mentioned, 60, 156, 163, 180
Osten, Pierre Jacques, General: Walcheren campaign, 98–101
Oudinot, Nicholas Charles, Marshal: campaign of 1813, 186
Owidtzky, Patrice d', 216

Parrott, Joseph: discontent, 72; requests discharge, 80; in Spain, 119, 125, 130; returned to France, 140; campaign of 1813, 185; wounded, 187; Hundred Days, 211; mentioned, 172–73, 205
Pellet, General, 211
Peltier, Colonel, 211, 214
Perret, Joseph: Sweeny/Corbet affair, 42; mentioned, 90
Perry, Jacques: commissioned, 120; in Spain, 120, 130; Legion of Honor, 129
Petrezzoli, Antoine, Chef de Bataillon: named to command Legion, 47–48, 50; discipline, 57, 81–84; O'Kelly/Thyroux duel, 58; on L. Lacy, 73; on transfer requests, 74; ill with the "fever", 84; evaluation of Legion, 90; and MacCann, 93–94; Walcheren campaign, 100; named Monnet's chief of staff, 102; mentioned, 52–56, 66–67, 70, 76, 80, 83, 89, 93, 95–96, 108, 122, 123, 165, 171
Plunkett, Mr., 122
Powell, Patrick: Sweeny/Corbet affair, 42–45; conflict with Delhora, 83
Prevose, Louis, 93
Puthod, Jacques Pierre M., General: campaign of 1813, 182–83, 185, 187, 189–90

Read, Thomas: Sweeny/Corbet affair, 43; discharged, 64, mentioned, 55
Reiff, Lieutenant, 157
Reilly, John: in Brest, 95; recruiting, 110, 112; mentioned 90, 107–8, 111, 129
Reynier, Jean Louis, General: Peninsular Campaign of 1810–11, 126–27, 135, 138–39; battle of Bussaco, 136, 148
Reynoldt, Mathieu: discharged, 64
Rheno, General, 143
Rochambeau, Marie Joseph de Vimeur, General: campaign of 1813, 187
Romana, Marquis de, 123
Ross, George: joined Regiment, 112; mentioned, 157
Ruff, G., 194, 199
Russe, Andress, 155
Russel, Michael: commissioned, 120
Ryan, Charles: POW, 106; escaped from England, 107, 171; mentioned, 108

Saint Colomb, Maurice: Restoration, 205; Hundred Days, 211, 213–14
Saint Croix, Charles Marie E. de, General: in Spain, 131; battle of Bussaco, 136; Peninsular Campaign of 1810–11, 137
Saint George, Fort: state prisoners, 17–18
Saint Leger, Auguste: campaign of 1813, 188; mentioned, 112
Saint Leger, Edmond: Sweeny/Corbet affair, 42–47; in Spain, 120, 125; campaign of 1813, 180, 185, 188–89; mentioned, 37, 69, 90, 112, 130, 178–79, 194
Saint Leger, Patrick: ill with "fever", 88; death of, 93; mentioned, 35, 63, 69, 90
Sanchez, Don Julian, 142–43, 145
Sauland, Jean Baptiste, 203
Savannah, siege of (1779), 5
Saxe, Maurice de, Marshal: battle of Fontenoy, 3
Schroder, 199
Schwarzenberg, Karl Philipp von, Prince: campaign of 1813, 186, 188–89, 193
Scibie, General: campaign of 1813, 191
Sebastiani, Bastien Horace F., General: campaign of 1813, 190
Serier, Chef de Bataillon: Walcheren campaign, 103–4
Setting, Jacques: commissioned, 130
Sheare, Henry: executed, 12
Sheare, John: executed, 12

Shee, Henry, Colonel, 85
Shee (O'Shee), William, 84–85
Sheridan, Michael: in Spain, 120; mentioned, 55, 90
Simms, Robert: United Irishman, 8
Solignac, Jean, General: in Spain, 126, 145, 147–48; siege of Astorga, 128; siege of Almeida, 131–32; Peninsular Campaign of 1810–11, 135, 140, 142
Souham, J., General: campaign of 1813, 189–90
Soult, Nicolas Jean de Dieu, 149
Stuart, John, Colonel: commander of Fort St. George, 17, 19
Swanton, Robert: requested discharge, 75–76
Sweeny, John: formation of Legion, 29–54 passim; Sweeny/Corbet affair, 42–52, 62; duel with Corbet, 50–52

Tabarie, General, 164
Talleyrand-Périgord, Charles Maurice de, 11, 201
Tandy, James Napper: United Irishman, 6; expedition to Ireland, 15; mentioned, 28, 70
Teeling, Bartholomew, 8
Tennent, John: formation of Legion, 18, 31; Sweeny/Corbet affair, 43, 45; Napoleon's coronation, 68; confrontation with W. Corbet, 69, 70; promotion to *chef de bataillon*, 152; command of 1st Battalion, 174, 187; campaign of 1813, 178–79, 185; death of, 187–89; mentioned, 90, 96, 109, 111, 114, 153–54, 156–57, 163, 168, 206
Tennent, William, 152
Theridan, Second Lieutenant, 120
Therne, Eugene, 37
Thiébault, Paul Charles F., General: in Spain, 121
Thompson, Henry: recruited, 194; Hundred Days, 213
Thonières, Jean Guillaume, General: in Spain, 127, 131, 144
Thuillier, Jacques, 111

Thyroux, Denice: duel with O'Kelly, 58–59; discharged, 64; mentioned 90
Tobin, Colonel: Restoration, 209–11
Tone, Theobald Wolfe: United Irishman, 6, 9; expedition to Bantry Bay, 10; expedition to Donegal, 15; death of, 16; mentioned, 11, 23
Torres Vedras line, 138–39
Towne, William David, 216–17, 219
Trachenberg Plan, 186, 188–89
Trafalgar, battle of, 71
Trant, Nicholas, Colonel, 140
Tressan, de, Captain, 207
Tumoral, Lieutenant, 203
Tyrrel, Nicholas, 64–65

United Irishmen: formation of, 6; mentioned, 7, 8, 10–13, 15–22, 25, 27–28, 49, 57, 59, 62–63 65–67, 156, 220

Vacher, Captain, 114
Vacherau, General: campaign of 1813, 185, 187–89
Victor, Claude, Marshal, 142
Villeneuve, Pierre Charles de, Admiral: expedition to Ireland (1805), 71

Wall, Thomas, 157
Ware, Hugh: O'Meally/Couasnon duel, 54; in Spain, 93, 119, 131; campaign of 1813, 178–79, 185, 191, 193; wounded, 187, 189; mentioned, 35, 37, 51, 90, 156, 163, 194, 196, 198
Wellington, Arthur Wellesley, Duke of: Peninsular War, 127–50 passim; Hundred Days, 213
Wild Geese, ix, 222
William of Orange, 2, 3
Wittgenstein, Ludwig, General: campaign of 1813, 182–83

Yorch, H. D. L.: campaign of 1813, 182–83

Zelinski, John: wounded, 102; in Spain, 120; mentioned, 95, 108

John G. Gallaher was born in St. Louis, Missouri. After serving in the United States Marine Corps he received a B.A. from Washington University and an M.A. and Ph.D. from St. Louis University. He also studied at the Sorbonne and the University of Grenoble and spent a third year in France as a Fulbright scholar at the University of Poitiers. He is professor of history at Southern Illinois University at Edwardsville. He is the author of *The Iron Marshal: A Biography of Louis N. Davout* and *The Students of Paris and the Revolution of 1848*. He is at present writing a biography of General Alexandre Dumas.